SECOND EDITION

Comprehensive Behavior Management

SECOND EDITION

Comprehensive Behavior Management

Individualized, Classroom, and Schoolwide Approaches

Ronald C. Martella
Eastern Washington University

J. Ron Nelson
University of Nebraska, Lincoln

Nancy E. Marchand-Martella
Eastern Washington University

Mark O'Reilly
University of Texas at Austin

Los Angeles | London | New Delhi
Singapore | Washington DC

Los Angeles | London | New Delhi
Singapore | Washington DC

FOR INFORMATION:

SAGE Publications, Inc.
2455 Teller Road
Thousand Oaks, California 91320
E-mail: order@sagepub.com

SAGE Publications Ltd.
1 Oliver's Yard
55 City Road
London EC1Y 1SP
United Kingdom

SAGE Publications India Pvt. Ltd.
B 1/I 1 Mohan Cooperative Industrial Area
Mathura Road, New Delhi 110 044
India

SAGE Publications Asia-Pacific Pte. Ltd.
33 Pekin Street #02-01
Far East Square
Singapore 048763

Acquisitions Editor: Diane McDaniel
Editorial Assistant: Theresa Accomazzo
Production Editor: Belinda Thresher
Copy Editor: Karen E. Taylor
Typesetter: C&M Digitals (P) Ltd.
Proofreader: Scott Oney
Indexer: Kathleen Paparchontis
Cover Designer: Gail Buschman
Marketing Manager: Katharine Winter

Printed in the United States of America

Library of Congress Cataloging-in-Publication Data

Martella, Ronald C. Comprehensive behavior management: individualized, classroom, and schoolwide approaches / Ronald C. Martella, J. Ron Nelson, Nancy E. Marchand-Martella, Mark O'Reilly — 2nd ed.

p. cm.
Rev. ed. of: Managing disruptive behaviors in the schools : Boston : Allyn and Bacon, c2003.

Includes bibliographical references and index.

ISBN 978-1-4129-8827-8 (pbk.)

1. Classroom management. 2. Behavior modification. I. Nelson, J. Ron. II. Marchand-Martella, Nancy E. III. Martella, Ronald C. Managing disruptive behaviors in the schools. IV. Title.

LB3013.M35 2012
370.15′28—dc22
2010054556

This book is printed on acid-free paper.

11 12 13 14 15 16 10 9 8 7 6 5 4 3 2 1

Brief Contents

Detailed Contents

Preface

Purpose

One of the most critical issues facing teachers and related-services personnel today is behavior management. Behavior management consistently ranks as the most concerning issue in surveys completed by school personnel. Unfortunately, most do not feel well equipped to deal with the multitude of behavior problems they see every day in the schools. We wrote this textbook with these individuals in mind. It is critical for teachers and related personnel to receive high-quality training in behavior management; a solid textbook written by experts in the field that incorporates evidence-based best practices is an important foundational aspect of this training.

This textbook is designed differently from other management texts. We wrote this textbook to aid teachers and related-services personnel in the planning processes that must take place when preventing or responding to behavior management issues. We see this planning as occurring across three levels of support—individualized, classroom, and schoolwide. Other textbooks do not provide the balanced coverage of these levels of support as is done in this text. For example, many textbooks provide extensive coverage of classroom management supports but provide little, if any, coverage of schoolwide or individualized supports. Other texts provide extensive coverage of individualized supports but provide little, if any, coverage of schoolwide and classroom supports. Therefore, our goal is to provide extensive coverage of all three levels of support to help teachers and related-services personnel to plan for and respond to behavior management issues effectively.

This textbook can be used with undergraduate or graduate students in general education, special education, and educational and school psychology. Instructors teaching courses on behavior management, the principles of behavior, applied learning theory, and the classroom applications of educational psychology will find this textbook helpful.

Additionally, consultants and administrators can use this textbook as a foundational text for those receiving inservice training on individualized, classroom, and schoolwide support planning. Target audiences include teachers and related-services personnel (e.g., school psychologists, counselors, social workers, behavior specialists, and instructional assistants).

Major Features and Pedagogical Aides

There are several major features of this textbook.

First, important aspects of behavior management (i.e., *working with parents and families, ethics and the law, diversity, and data collection*) are infused in chapters throughout the book.

Second, every chapter includes *objectives* that provide a clear overview of what will be covered in the chapter.

Third, all chapters have a *vignette* at the beginning that highlights an important issue covered in the chapter. This vignette is revisited at the end, showing how the issue was addressed.

Fourth, chapter *headings are phrased as questions* to facilitate easier note taking and discussion.

Fifth, several *tables and figures* are evident in every chapter to aid in the understanding of key concepts.

Sixth, *discussion questions* are found at the end of each chapter to test student understanding of the content. Answers to these questions are provided in the instructor's manual.

Finally, an extensive *index* and *glossary* are included to aid in the location and definition of key terms.

Changes Made From the First Edition

We made several changes and additions to this second edition.

Changes Throughout the Book

First, we added a new author, Dr. Mark O'Reilly, from the University of Texas at Austin. Dr. O'Reilly brings specific expertise in individualized behavior management approaches including functional behavior assessments and behavior support plans. He also has a long and successful record in applied behavior analysis.

Second, we changed the title of the textbook to reflect the trend of addressing behavior management support as a comprehensive issue rather than an individual one. This comprehensive approach incorporates individual, classroom (including instructional), and schoolwide supports (including those for nonclassroom settings such as the cafeteria, playground, and hallways).

Third, the sequence of the chapters was changed to reflect how the material is most frequently taught in college classes. In the current edition, the chapter sequence in Part I remains the same. In Part II, individualized supports are described (this content was covered in Part IV of the first edition). Classroom supports continue to be addressed in Part III. Part IV contains information on schoolwide supports (this information was covered in Part II in the first edition). Finally, the term *supports* replaces *organizational systems* in the title of chapters to better reflect current terminology in the field.

Finally, all chapters were updated with current research, corresponding citations, additional tables and figures, and rewritten pedagogical features.

Chapter-Specific Changes

Significant changes were made to several chapters.

Chapter 1. New information was added to this chapter on the best practices in behavior management, and the section on ethics was expanded to include a statement on seclusion and restraint.

Chapter 5. Discussion of preference and choice, as well as of prompting strategies related to behavior issues, was added to this chapter.

Chapter 7. The material from the Think Time® chapter (Chapter 8) in the first edition was edited and integrated into this chapter.

Chapter 10. Information on the "school evaluation rubric" was removed and coverage of the *School-wide Evaluation Tool (SET)* and the *Benchmarks for Advanced Tiers (BAT)* was added to this chapter.

Chapter 11. This chapter was previously Chapter 5 in the first edition, and was rewritten to focus on what makes a program evidence based. It now includes coverage of the criteria for being defined as an evidence-based intervention and how schools assess the magnitude of the effects of an intervention.

Chapter 12. This new chapter provides coverage of the response to intervention (RTI) approach and how to integrate multitiered intervention models such as RTI with the schoolwide positive behavior intervention and support model (SWPBIS).

Ancillaries for Instructors

Additional ancillary materials further support and enhance the learning goals of the second edition of *Comprehensive Behavior Management: Individualized, Classroom, and Schoolwide.* These ancillary materials include the following:

Password Protected Instructor Teaching Site

This password-protected site (www.sagepub.com/martella) offers instructors a variety of resources that supplement the book material, including the following:

- **Test Bank (Word):** This Word test bank offers a diverse set of test questions and answers for each chapter of the book. Multiple-choice and short-answer/essay questions for every chapter help instructors assess students' progress and understanding.
- **PowerPoint Slides:** Chapter-specific slide presentations offer assistance with lecture and review preparation by highlighting essential content, features, and artwork from the book.
- **SAGE Journal Articles:** A "Learning From SAGE Journal Articles" feature provides access to recent, relevant full-text articles from SAGE's leading research journals.

Each article supports and expands on the concepts presented in the chapter. This feature also provides discussion questions to focus and guide student interpretation.

- **Web Resources:** These links to relevant websites direct instructors to additional resources for further research on important chapter topics.
- **Lecture Notes:** These lecture notes summarize key concepts on a chapter-by-chapter basis to help instructors prepare for lectures and class discussions.
- **Answers to In-Text Questions:** The site provides answers to the chapter discussion questions found at the end of each chapter.
- **Course Syllabi:** Sample syllabi—for semester, quarter, and online classes—provide suggested models for instructors to use when creating the syllabi for their courses.

We believe the changes and additions made to this second edition have significantly improved the quality of the textbook. We are confident the new information will be regarded as an important addition to the understanding of comprehensive and evidence-based behavior management supports.

SAGE would like to gratefully acknowledge the following peer reviewers for their editorial insight and guidance:

Robert L. Michels
Santa Clara University

Su-Je Cho
Fordham University
Graduate School of Education

Judith E. Terpstra
Southern Connecticut State University

DeAnn Lechtenberger
Texas Tech University

Suzanne McQuillan Jimenez
George Mason University

Karen Coughenour
Francis Marion University

Gholam Kibria
Delaware State University

Acknowledgments

We dedicate this book to our families. Further, to complete this textbook, several individuals were involved. We would like to thank all those at Sage for their continued support in the entirety of the project, especially Diane McDaniel, without whom this project would not have come to fruition. We would like to thank Karen E. Taylor for her excellent editorial work. To the students who helped with tasks associated with the production of this text—Crosby Wilson and Alana Neis—we extend our sincere thanks. And finally, we wish to thank the reviewers who provided invaluable feedback and suggestions to help us produce a better product.

Part I

Introduction to Behavior Management

1

Behavior Management Models

Chapter Objectives

After studying this chapter, you should be able to

- describe what is meant by discipline,
- explain how assertive discipline is implemented,
- define logical consequences,
- illustrate how to implement the reality therapy model,
- specify the approach of love and logic,
- describe the Ginott model,
- characterize the Kounin model,
- depict the Jones model,
- explain what character education is, and describe two character education programs,
- characterize the pros and cons of each of these models,
- list the five concrete recommendations to help teachers reduce common behavior problems,
- define the behavioral model and its characteristics,
- describe the misunderstandings of the behavioral model, and
- specify the right to effective behavioral treatment and the right to an effective education.

MS. JACKSON HAS A STUDENT in her seventh-grade classroom who is having difficulty due to his angry outbursts. Ms. Jackson has tried a variety of techniques to decrease José's outbursts, all without success. She has tried telling him how his actions affect others. She has also tried to help him manage his anger by counting to 10 before he speaks. As a last resort, Ms. Jackson has been sending José to the office, where he talks about his anger with a school counselor.

Ms. Jackson does not know what to do. She has discussed the problem with other teachers and has tried their suggestions. She has asked José's parents to help her by talking with José and by not allowing him to play video games after school if he has a difficult day.

Ms. Jackson recently learned José had been assessed two years previously for a suspected behavior disorder. The assessment team, however, determined he did not meet the criteria for such a disability. She has also learned José has had counseling services over the last few years but to no avail. Most teachers believe José is simply a student who has difficulty controlling his anger and that the best way to prevent his angry outbursts is to stay away from him and not to make any demands when he is in a bad mood.

Ms. Jackson, however, believes that not making demands on José to prevent outbursts is not a viable option. She believes doing so is not really helping her or José. She also believes her job is to teach José how to act appropriately while he is in her classroom. Therefore, Ms. Jackson decides to journey into the world of behavior management approaches to see what has been found to work in situations such as hers.

Overview

The topic of how to manage student **behavior** (i.e., a clearly defined and observable act) in schools has been around as long as there have been schools. Behavior management has been and still is the chief concern of educators across the country (Dunlap, Iovannone, Wilson, Kincaid, & Strain, 2010; Westling, 2010). When students misbehave, they learn less and keep their peers from learning. Classroom behavior problems take up teachers' time and disrupt the classroom and school. In fact, difficulty managing student behavior is cited as a factor associated with teacher burnout and dissatisfaction. For example, "50 percent of urban teachers leave the profession within the first five years of their career, citing behavior problems and management as factors influencing their decision to leave" (McKinney, Campbell-Whately, & Kea, 2005, p. 16). More should be done to create effective classroom environments through the use of better classroom management approaches (McKinney et al., 2005; Westling, 2010).

Every year, "new and improved" behavior management approaches hit the schools only to be thrown out by the end of the year. There are at least five possible causes for this cycle. First, preservice teachers may not be trained well in behavior management methods. Typically, a single classroom management class that provides a superficial view of behavior management is offered. Second, teachers may not be trained to analyze research on behavior management approaches. We tend to flock to the "flavor of the month" procedures without a great deal of regard for what has been shown to work. Third, there is no unified theory of behavior management. Because the causes of behavior problems are often not agreed on, teachers may become confused about the causes of student behavior. Fourth, schools often do not have a seamless and consistent approach to behavior management utilized across classrooms, teachers, and grade levels. Teachers tend to implement their own procedures causing confusion on the part of students. Finally, behavior management is often viewed as a reactive approach to behavior problems rather than as a proactive one.

We believe behavior management planning must occur at three levels. Figure 1.1 shows behavior management as three concentric circles. The smallest circle relates to the implementation of individualized behavior management supports for the most troubled students. Traditionally, behavior management training in special education has occurred at the individualized level. The middle circle is handled from a classroom perspective and includes effective instructional supports. Behavioral and academic programming are key aspects in the prevention of and reaction to problem behavior in the classroom. The largest circle represents schoolwide supports designed

Figure 1.1 Comprehensive Behavior Management Planning

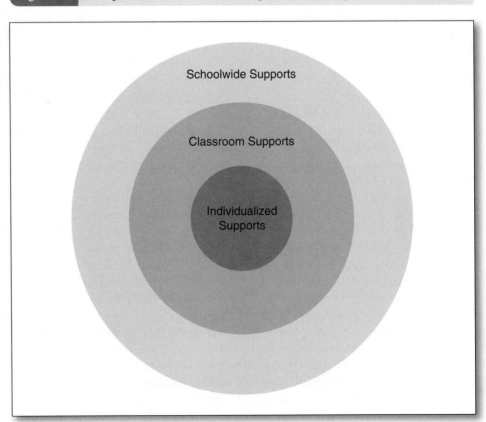

Teachers should discuss with students expected behavior in the classroom.

to prevent and respond to behavior difficulties at the school level. These concentric circles are dependent on one another and form a comprehensive approach to behavior management. This comprehensive approach is important given the recent shift by schools from a reactive approach to behavior management to a proactive one (Lane, Wehby, Robertson, & Rogers, 2007). Viewing behavior management in this way is also helpful in reducing the staggering drop-out rates in the United States (Dynarski et al., 2008).

This chapter describes what is meant by discipline and various models used in schools to deal with student behavior. An analysis of each of the models is provided including their positive aspects and weaknesses. Additionally, five concrete recommendations to help teachers reduce common behavior problems are described along with a description of the behavioral model. Given that the conceptual focus of this textbook is behavioral, we discuss the misunderstandings of the behavioral model. Finally, behavioral ethics are highlighted via position statements from the Association for Behavior Analysis. Essentially, these statements lay out the rights individuals have to effective behavioral treatments and to an effective education. If we use effective management methods derived from the research literature, we can make significant positive gains in the lives of teachers and students.

What Is Discipline?

Over the years, discipline has been equated with punishment, specifically, corporal punishment. Punishment and discipline, however, are not the same thing. Discipline involves teaching others right from wrong. Specifically, **discipline** includes methods to prevent or respond to behavior problems so they do not occur in the future (Slavin, 2009). The following are common definitions of the word *discipline* found in most dictionaries: training to act in accordance with rules, instruction, and exercise designed to train proper conduct or action; behavior in accordance with rules of conduct; and a set or system of rules and regulations. As seen in these definitions, discipline is about teaching students how to behave appropriately in different situations. It is not punishment, although punishment is one possible way of disciplining students.

What Are Some Popular Behavior Management Models Used in Schools?

With the changing attitudes toward the use of punishment-based disciplinary procedures, schools have looked for alternative models of student discipline. These models were and are aimed at developing and maintaining appropriate student behavior. The authors of these models try to describe why they work. Unfortunately, many of them have overlooked some important fundamentals; that is, they ignore the effects on students and fail to use scientific, functionally based definitions in their models. Following are brief descriptions of some of the various behavior management models used in schools. Table 1.1 provides a sample of the most commonly used models.

Table 1.1 Sample of Models Used in Schools

Model	Key Aspects
Assertive Discipline	Teachers have the right to determine the environmental structure, rules, and routines that will facilitate learning.
	Teachers have the right to insist that students conform to their standards.
	Teachers should prepare a discipline plan in advance, including statements of their expectations, rules, and routines and the type of discipline method to be used if and when students misbehave.
	Students do not have the right to interfere with others' learning.
	When students do not behave in a manner consistent with teacher expectations, teachers can respond in one of three ways: nonassertively by surrendering to their students, hostilely by showing anger, or assertively by calmly insisting and assuming that students will fulfill these expectations.
	Students choose to misbehave, and teachers should not accept their excuses for such misbehavior.
	Teachers should use positive and negative consequences to convince students that it is to their benefit to behave appropriately.
	Teachers should not feel bad if forced to use harshly negative consequences when necessary because students want teachers to help them control themselves.
	Teachers have the right to ask for help from parents and school administrators when handling student misbehavior.
Logical Consequences	Inappropriate behavior is motivated by unconscious needs, e.g., to gain attention, exercise power, exact revenge, or display inadequacy.
	If the motive for attention is satisfied, inappropriate behavior associated with other motives will not be manifested.
	Students can learn to understand their own motives and eliminate misbehavior by having teachers help them explore why they behave as they do.

Model	Key Aspects
	Presenting students with a choice offers a sufficient basis on which they can learn to be responsible.
	Students react to life based on their birth order.
	We learn through our interaction with our environment. Within this interaction, our behaviors are exposed to natural, arbitrary, and logical consequences.
	Natural consequences are usually the most effective form of negative consequences.
	If we cannot rely on natural consequences under all circumstances, we can use arbitrary or logical consequences.
	When teachers have the option of using arbitrary or logical consequences, logical consequences should be chosen because students behave more appropriately when they suffer the logical consequences for their misbehavior.
Reality Therapy	Students are self-regulating and can learn to manage their own behavior.
	Students learn responsible behavior by examining a full range of consequences for their behavior and by making value judgments about their behavior and its consequences.
	Student behavior consists of an effort to satisfy personal needs for survival, belonging and love, power, freedom, and fun.
	Students have a unique way of satisfying their own needs.
	Students cannot be forced to change what they believe about how best to satisfy their needs.
	There must be a warm, supportive classroom environment where students can complete quality work and feel good about themselves.
	Students should be asked to do only useful work, to do the best they can, and to evaluate their own work to improve upon it.
	Rules should be developed in the classroom.
	Teachers should establish a level of mutual respect with the students.
	Coercion should never be used in schools to control student behavior. If coercion is used, mistrust will prevail.
Love and Logic	Each student's self-concept is always a prime consideration.
	Students should always be left feeling as if they have some control.
	An equal balance of consequences and empathy should replace punishment whenever possible.
	Students should be required to do more thinking than the adults do.
	There are three types of teaching and parenting styles: helicopters, drill sergeants, and consultants.
	Teachers should focus on being consultants to their students.
	Adults should set firm limits in loving ways without anger, lectures, or threats.
	When students cause a problem, teachers should hand it back in loving ways.

(Continued)

Table 1.1	(Continued)

Model	Key Aspects
Ginott	Student behavior can be improved if teachers interact with students more effectively, treating them with understanding, kindness, and respect.
	Positive communication by teachers improves the self-concept of students, which produces better classroom discipline.
	Congruent communication should be used because students cannot think right if they do not feel right.
	Students can learn to be responsible and autonomous.
	Accepting and clarifying the feelings of students will improve their classroom behavior.
	The improper use of praise encourages student dependency on teachers.
	Punishment encourages student misconduct.
	Insulting students causes them to rebel.
	Promoting cooperation increases good discipline.
	Teachers can improve their relationships with students by ending their language of rejection and using a language of acceptance, inviting students to cooperate rather than demanding that a behavior occur, providing acceptance and acknowledgment for student behavior, conferring dignity upon the students, expressing anger with "I messages" versus "you messages," using succinct language rather than overtalking, and providing appreciative praise that describes student behavior rather than ability.
	Teachers need to model self-discipline to show their students how to deal with problems.
Kounin	Negative or positive moves by teachers toward students radiate out (the ripple effect) and influence others.
	Students need to be controlled by their teachers.
	Control can be improved by increasing the clarity and firmness of desists (i.e., remarks intended to stop misbehavior).
	Teachers can improve control by displaying "withitness" (i.e., being aware of what is going on around them).
	Teachers should use "momentum" by beginning lessons immediately after the start of class, keeping lessons moving with little downtime, bringing the lessons to a close, and making efficient transitions from one lesson to another.
	Teachers should achieve "smoothness" in a lesson by removing undue interference or changes that disrupt the students.
	Teachers can use group alerting by gaining students' attention to inform them of what is expected.
	Students should be made active learners by asking them to answer questions, to demonstrate concepts, or to explain how something is done.
	Teachers can control or have an influence over several activities at once by using "overlapping."
	Students are more successful when teachers make lessons interesting, avoiding "satiation" (i.e., when students are bored or frustrated, they tend to become less than interested in a topic). Lessons and seatwork should be enjoyable yet challenging.

Model	Key Aspects
	When students have been appropriately identified as problem students and when the teachers' moves are properly timed, greater control of student behavior is possible.
Jones	Children need to be controlled to behave properly.
	Teachers can achieve control through nonverbal cues and movements calculated to bring them physically closer and closer to the students.
	Parents and administrators can be used to gain control over student behaviors.
	Teachers should demonstrate skill clusters including body language and easy-to-implement group-based incentive systems that are tied to academic content using "Grandma's rule."
	Student seating should be organized so that students are easy to reach.
	Teachers should use graphic reminders that provide examples and instructions, quickly praise students for doing something correctly, and give straightforward suggestions that will get students going and leaving immediately.
	Teachers should utilize good classroom structure, limit setting, responsibility training, and backup systems.
Character Education	Character education promotes core ethical and performance values.
	Students learn to understand, care about, and act upon these core ethical and performance values.
	Programs should encompass all aspects of the school culture.
	Teachers should foster a caring school community.
	Students should be given opportunities for moral action.
	Character education supports academic achievement.
	Programs focus on the intrinsic motivation of students.
	Whole-staff involvement is key.
	Positive leadership of staff and students is essential.
	Parents and community members should be involved.
	Results are assessed and improvements are made.

Assertive Discipline

Canter and colleagues developed the assertive discipline model, originally based on nine major aspects (shown in Table 1.1). As seen in the table, discipline rests on how the teacher responds to misbehavior. It is up to the teacher to keep students in line during class. Canter and colleagues have modified assertive discipline over the years (Charles, 1996; Malmgren, Trezek, & Paul, 2005). Originally, Canter tried to get teachers to be strong leaders in the classroom. Therefore, his focus was on getting and keeping teachers in charge. In more recent times, however, Canter emphasizes the importance of focusing on student needs by talking with students more and teaching them how to behave appropriately. Therefore, Canter modified his model to make it more focused on positive discipline methods than on the use of force and coercion.

Canter and Canter (1992) describe the following five steps of assertive discipline. First, teachers must acknowledge that they can and do affect student behavior. Second, teachers must learn to display an assertive response style, which is the most effective style they can have. Third, teachers must make a discipline plan that contains good rules and clear, effective consequences. Fourth, teachers must provide student instruction on the discipline plan. Finally, teachers should instruct students on how to behave responsibly.

Malmgren et al. (2005) summarized the four main components of the model. First, teachers should develop a set of rules for the classroom. Second, teachers should determine a set of positive consequences for following the rules. Third, teachers should establish a set of negative consequences for not following the rules. Finally, teachers should implement the model with the students.

Even after being taught the discipline plan, however, some students will continue to misbehave. Three approaches are used to work with these difficult students. First, a one-on-one problem-solving conference is scheduled at which the student and the teacher try to gain insight into the student's behavior. The purpose is not to punish the student but to provide guidance. Second, a relationship is built from the use of positive support. The teacher should show the student that he or she cares about the student as a person and should make an attempt to get to know the student on a more personal basis. The student must feel that the teacher truly cares about him or her. Finally, an individualized behavior plan should be developed that is more specialized to the student's individual needs compared with the needs of the other students.

Analysis. Assertive discipline is based on the assumptions that teachers are the leaders of the classroom and that they should use punishment to bring control to the classroom, if needed. A major positive aspect of assertive discipline is the concept that student behavior in a classroom results from what teachers do in the classroom. Also, Canter has attempted to add more proactive methods of preventing management problems through teaching students about rules and expectations. Unfortunately, assertive discipline has several major weaknesses. An operational definition of punishment (see Chapter 2) is not used. Punishment is assumed to be in effect with Assertive Discipline. Second, there is inadequate research to suggest the approach works. Much of the reported data on assertive discipline includes teacher testimonials or perceptions (e.g., Wood, Hodges, & Aljunied, 1996) or poor research (Nicholls & Houghton, 1995; Swinson & Cording, 2002). Although testimonials are important to consider, other important data sources are missing, and many questions remain unanswered. Does assertive discipline result in a decrease in the level of student misbehavior in the classroom as measured by direct observation? Does assertive discipline result in a decrease in the level of office referrals? A third problem is the reliance on threats, warnings, and a discipline hierarchy. Research evidence suggests threats and warnings tend to escalate problem behaviors in the classroom (Nelson, 1996b). When teachers use threats and warnings, students are more likely to become aggressive than when threats and warnings are not used. Finally, Canter misuses the term *consequence* to suggest it refers only to punishment. A consequence is anything that occurs, such as a reinforcer or punisher, after a behavior occurs.

Assertive discipline seems to be a behavior reduction method that can work under certain circumstances. Unfortunately, if assertive discipline does work to suppress unwanted behavior, it does so in a manner that may well make the long-term problem of disruptive behavior worse. The use of threats and warnings along with a lack of reinforcement for appropriate behavior may seriously compromise the efficacy of this approach.

Logical Consequences

Dreikurs (1968) developed the logical consequences model, built on the belief that we learn through our interactions with the environment. Within this interaction, behaviors are exposed to three types of negative consequences: natural, arbitrary, and logical (Clarizio, 1986). Table 1.1 lists several major aspects of logical consequences. (See Dreikurs, Cassel, & Ferguson, 2004, for an expanded discussion of these concepts.) It is important to point out that teachers using logical consequences should attempt to prevent behavior issues by avoiding power struggles with students (Malmgren et al., 2005).

Natural consequences are those consequences that normally occur without any teacher intervention when we engage in some type of behavior. These are usually the most effective form of negative consequence for stopping unwanted behavior. A natural consequence of fighting is to get hurt. A natural consequence of lying is that no one believes the liar. A natural consequence of calling others names is to be ignored by peers. A problem with natural consequences is that they may be either too minor to have an effect, such as if a student breaks a toy when other toys are available, or they are not allowed to occur, such as when we prevent someone from being beaten up when a fight starts.

If we cannot rely on natural consequences under all circumstances, we have a choice as educators as to the type of consequences we can use; we can choose either arbitrary consequences or logical ones. **Arbitrary consequences** are those consequences that are not aligned with the offense. An arbitrary consequence for fighting is to send the student to the principal's office. An arbitrary consequence for a student who lies is that the student loses computer time. An arbitrary consequence for calling others names is to send the student to time out. For those behaviors that do not have natural consequences, arbitrary consequences can be applied, and these could involve sending a student to in-school suspension for a temper tantrum or taking away free time for drawing on a desk.

The second option is for teachers to use **logical consequences** rather than arbitrary consequences. Logical consequences are connected in some manner to the offense. A logical consequence for fighting during recess is to prevent the student from going to recess for a week. A logical consequence for a student who lies is for the teacher to tell the student he or she is not believable. For temper tantrums, a logical consequence is to remove the student from class until he or she calms down. When teachers have the option of using either arbitrary or logical consequences, logical consequences should be chosen.

Analysis. The basic assumption made in the logical consequences model might be correct: the motivation for classroom behavior might be to attract attention. Many students are motivated by gaining attention from teachers or peers. Whether this motivation is conscious or unconscious, however, is difficult to demonstrate. It seems adequate to determine if the motivation is or is not attention. Unfortunately, other motivational areas (e.g., exercising power, exacting revenge, or displaying inadequacy) are all inferences that cannot be substantiated through direct observation. In other words, to suggest that students are misbehaving in a classroom because they are attempting to exercise power is based on what the students are receiving in return for the behavior (e.g., to gain a tangible item). This return for the behavior is then inferred to be what motivated the behavior, and students are said to have a need for power. The major difficulty with this line of thought is that the focus is on the student as the cause of the behavior rather than on what the teachers do in response to student behavior.

The assumption that students behave more appropriately when they suffer logical consequences is also problematic. Although it is true that if logical consequences are effective the unwanted behavior will be less likely to continue, this does not mean that appropriate behavior will follow. What is needed, then, are logical consequences for appropriate behavior as well.

Another difficulty is that proponents of the logical consequences model equate arbitrary consequences with punishment. Logical consequences, however, can also function as punishment. In addition, what is an arbitrary consequence in one instance (e.g., sending the student to a part of the room away from peers for work refusal) may be a logical consequence in another context (e.g., sending the student away from peers for hitting another student). Therefore, what makes something an arbitrary or logical consequence is not the consequence in and of itself but the context in which it is presented. In other words, arbitrary and logical consequences can be the same things. Both types of consequences are provided to eliminate the behavior; thus, they are both meant to be punishers. Unfortunately, logical consequences may not be severe enough to overcome the reinforcement of the student's actions.

Two of the model's precepts are adequate: that students can learn to understand their own motives and that they should be provided with choices. Teaching students to determine why they emit certain behaviors is an important skill. Also, providing a choice of activities to students has been shown to increase the likelihood students will complete the chosen activity (Dunlap et al., 1994; Vaughn & Horner, 1997). Thus, allowing student choice should be part of a management program implemented in a classroom.

The logical consequences model can be an effective method of behavior management if implemented without the inferences of various motivations. The research base for this model, however, is limited (Grossman, 1995). Therefore, before the logical consequences model is used, we should make sure the approach has been determined to be effective through research.

Reality Therapy

Glasser (1965) developed control theory. Glasser's basic premise was that students are in control of their own behavior and choose whether to behave appropriately or not (Strahan, Cope, Hundley, & Faircloth, 2005). Classroom management should be designed to help students make better choices. Activities such as class meetings conducted weekly or more often can provide students feedback on how their behavior affects others. In addition, these meetings give students a variety of ideas about how to improve behavior in the future and provide support from peers to make behavior changes. Consequences for unwanted behaviors may or may not be used with students. The key to this approach is getting students to realize how their choices of behavior affect others. The term *control theory* was changed to *choice theory*. **Choice theory** is the underpinning foundation of reality therapy (Lawrence, 2004).

There are several key aspects that set the foundation for the **reality therapy** model, as shown in Table 1.1; essentially, students are motivated by five needs. First, students are motivated by the need for survival, which involves the need for food, shelter, and freedom from harm. Teachers can aid students in the satisfaction of this need by helping them feel safe in the classroom and by not using coercion to try to control behavior. Second, students have a need for belonging and love. Teachers can aid in fulfilling this need by creating a classroom environment in which students work together on meaningful activities, are included in class discussions, and receive attention from the teacher and others. Third, students have a need for freedom. Teachers should allow students to make choices regarding what they will study, how they will study it, and how they will demonstrate their execution. Fourth, students have a need for fun. Teachers should involve students in interesting activities and allow them to share their accomplishments with other students. Finally, students have a need for power. Teachers can help students meet their need for power by giving them responsibilities.

A key to reality therapy is the establishment of mutual respect between the teacher and student. This respect is achieved through the following positive teacher responses to students: supporting, encouraging, listening, accepting, trusting, respecting, and negotiating. Teachers should avoid interacting with students in the following ways: criticizing, blaming, complaining, nagging, threatening, punishing, and bribing. One way of improving the teacher-student relationship is for teachers to assist students in evaluating their feelings and behavior through nonjudgmental classroom meetings (Marandola & Imber, 1979).

Analysis. Glasser's reality therapy model has a number of positive attributes. For example, getting students involved in developing classroom procedures is positive. Also, who would not agree that making learning fun and exciting is an admirable goal? Glasser has also contributed to the overall change in behavior management perspectives that students' behaviors are affected by what teachers do in the classroom and that management methods should be positively based (e.g., encouraging, listening, respecting) rather than coercive (e.g., criticizing, threatening, punishing).

The basic premise that students are motivated by an effort to satisfy needs for love, power, freedom, and fun is difficult to substantiate, however. In other words, these things are inferences based on what we see students doing. For example, if a student is attempting to gain attention from the teacher, we may be tempted to infer the student is seeking love. Likewise, if a student refuses to follow a teacher's instructions, we may be tempted to infer the student is seeking power. These inferences, however, are based on what the student is doing and what the student receives in exchange for the behavior. Therefore, the inferences are not necessarily correct. We can simply stop at the point of saying the student receives attention for the behavior or the student is able to get out of a task when she refuses to complete a task. Also, assuming students choose their behavior in the way Glasser suggests puts the focus of responsibility on the students. Students do not have free choice in the classroom because the teacher sets up limits to behavior. Therefore, any choices students make are largely dependent on what the teachers do in the classroom. The focus, then, should be on what the teachers do that affects student behavior. Further, Glasser explains student motivation as coming from inside while also saying teachers can set up the environment to improve motivation by meeting the needs of the students. If teachers can help meet student needs, the control does not come from within the students but, ultimately, from what the teachers do, which is external. Therefore, Glasser's model is inconsistent with its basic premise of motivation and of what teachers can do to affect this motivation. A final problem with Glasser's model is the paucity of research documenting its effectiveness, which is especially troubling because a relationship between cause (i.e., satisfying needs) and effect (i.e., improved student behavior) cannot be demonstrated. This relationship cannot be shown because internal needs (a) are not directly observable and (b) cannot be directly controlled or manipulated.

Love and Logic

Fay (1981), at the Cline-Fay Institute, developed the love and logic model, which rests on several key aspects (see Table 1.1). Among these are the teaching and parenting styles the model outlines. According to Fay (1981), there are three types of teaching and parenting styles: helicopters, drill sergeants, and consultants. Helicopters tend to hover over students to rescue them from the hostile world. These teachers make excuses for students, take on the responsibilities of students, make decisions for students, and use guilt to get students to behave in a certain manner. Drill sergeants command students and direct their lives. These teachers tell students how they should feel and handle responsibility. They have many demands and provide absolutes. They also provide threats and orders and use punishment, including the infliction of pain and humiliation. Consultants provide guidance and consultant services for students. These individuals provide messages of self-worth and strength, share personal feelings about something, provide and help students explore alternatives, and then allow students to make their own decisions. These teachers aid students in experiencing natural consequences for their actions and in exploring solutions to problems. Clearly, teachers should focus on being consultants to their students.

When students are resistant to teacher guidance, several things should be attempted. For resistant behavior, teachers should catch students doing something good, interpret the resistant behavior, try to understand why the students are doing it, and provide qualified positive regard by telling students what the teachers liked. When students are disruptive, the teachers should ignore the behavior, catch it early before it escalates, talk it over with students, and, if needed, isolate misbehaving students from others. Praise should be used, but it should be specific, directed toward the task, and given sparingly.

The above consequences are frequently immediate and have problems in that teachers may provide these consequences when angry, use threats, have no time to plan the most appropriate consequence, and lack empathy. Alternatively, anticipatory consequences are more desirable. These consequences allow teachers time to determine the most appropriate response to an unwanted behavior. For example, if a student acts inappropriately, the teacher may tell the student that he or she will have to do something about the student's behavior but at a later time. The student is told to try not to worry about the future consequence. The words the teacher uses, such as "try not to worry about the consequence," will become conditioned as an anticipatory consequence itself.

Analysis. Being concerned with how students feel about themselves is an important role of teachers. Also, decreasing the use of punishment is an important goal for all educators. Leading students through a problem-solving process can be an effective means of changing student behavior, and providing choices to students can aid in their development as responsible individuals. The avoidance of threats and warnings and holding students accountable are positive aspects of the model as well. Also, catching the behavior early is an effective technique.

The model provides no systematic method of determining why students do what they do, though. It is not always true that, if students feel loved and are provided with choices, they will become more responsible. At times, catching students being good and ignoring unwanted behavior is not enough. Teachers need more guidelines to prevent and respond to unwanted behavior. Talking it over with students can be a positive technique, yet *when* the talking occurs is important. Talking it out immediately after the behavior occurs may make the problem worse over the long run (Sulzer-Azaroff & Mayer, 1991). In addition, isolating students for disruptions is a punishment technique and should be acknowledged as such.

Overall, the love and logic model has many positive features. Unfortunately, it provides many poorly defined procedures. Also, research demonstrating the overall effectiveness of the model is lacking, possibly due to the problem of not having precisely defined procedures and techniques.

Ginott

Ginott (1971) developed this model; Table 1.1 shows its key aspects. Ginott believes teachers are the essential element in classroom management and that effective alternatives to punishment should be found because students learn from how teachers respond to problems. Therefore, teachers who show self-discipline are able to show their students (even those who misbehave) how to deal with problem situations. According to Ginott, teachers with a lack of self-discipline lose their tempers, call students names, insult students, behave rudely, overreact, show cruelty, punish everyone for another's actions, threaten, give long lectures, back students into a corner, and make arbitrary rules without student input. Teachers who show self-discipline are those who recognize student feelings; describe the situation; invite cooperation; are brief; do not argue with students; model appropriate behavior; discourage physical violence; do not criticize, call names, or insult students; focus on solutions; allow face-saving exits for students; allow students to help set standards; are helpful; and de-escalate conflict.

Analysis. The use of cooperation is a positive aspect of this model; another is being concerned with how students feel themselves. Also, all teachers should adhere to avoiding the use of blame, shame, insults, and intimidation. Anything teachers can do to make the learning environment more pleasant should be done. Students function more favorably in a classroom where positive disciplinary methods, rather than punishment procedures, are used. Punishment procedures can, as Ginott observes, result in negative side effects, leaving students and the classroom worse off. Therefore, Ginott's stance on the use of positive procedures is important for teachers to follow.

The assumption that a better self-concept improves classroom behavior and performance by itself, however, has not been supported by past research (Scheirer & Kraut, 1979; Sulzer-Azaroff & Mayer, 1991). In fact, data obtained by Seligman (1995) indicate that many individuals with higher than normal levels of self-esteem have higher levels of disruptive behavior than those with lower levels of self-esteem. In addition, although Ginott does not preclude the use of praise in the classroom, his model tends to assume that praise can lead to student dependency. But praise is positive if that praise is used judiciously and made specific. Also, stating that punishment encourages misconduct is an indication that a technical definition of punishment (see Chapter 2) is not being used. Another problem is that, although many of the procedures used in this model are considered to be good practice (e.g., congruent messages, allowing choices), there is no mechanism built in for those students who continue to misbehave, nor is there any assessment to determine why students misbehave. Finally, there is a lack of research validating this approach.

Kounin

Kounin (1970) developed the Kounin model based on early intervention research of effective management skills (e.g., Kounin, Friesen, & Norton, 1966; Kounin & Gump, 1958; Kounin & Obradovic, 1968); this model has several key aspects shown in Table 1.1. To achieve meaningful behavior change, the Kounin model suggests using 10 concepts in the classroom: (a) the ripple effect, (b) withitness, (c) momentum, (d) smoothness, (e) group alerting, (f) student accountability, (g) overlapping, (h) the avoidance of satiation, (i) valence and challenge arousal, and (j) seatwork variety and challenge. The **ripple effect** is the tendency for primary-aged students to react to teachers' actions when those actions are aimed at other students. **Withitness** is being aware of what is going on in the classroom. **Momentum** is beginning lessons immediately after the start of class, keeping lessons moving ahead with little downtime, bringing lessons to a close, and making efficient transitions from one lesson to another. **Smoothness** is being able to conduct a lesson without undue interference or changes that disrupt the students. **Group alerting** involves making sure students are paying attention and then providing them with specific instruction on what they are supposed to do at any one time. **Student accountability** involves keeping students involved in the lesson. **Overlapping** means that the teacher can control or have an influence over several activities that overlap. **Satiation** can be defined as the feeling students get when they are too full—so stuffed and replete with instruction that they have no more interest or desire to learn. So teachers should avoid satiation by trying to make learning interesting and students successful rather than bored or frustrated. **Valence and challenge arousal** refers to teachers showing enthusiasm and using a variety of activities when teaching students, so learners have a positive reaction to the lesson. Finally, **seatwork variety and challenge** refers to the idea that teachers should strive to make seatwork interesting to students.

Analysis. As indicated in Table 1.1, the model recommends the use of clear and firm desists. The recommendation is practical; the use of effective desists can stop behavior problems from continuing. The use of the Kounin model can be effective for low-level misbehavior. All teachers should learn how to use desists and withitness to control student behavior. There is a rich research history demonstrating the effectiveness of this model and components of the model (e.g., Arlin, 1979; Borg, 1977; Borg, Langer, & Wilson, 1975). In fact, Kounin's influence is seen in much of Chapters 5 and 6. The problem with the model, however, is that it is not complete. It does not suggest what to do with those students who continue to misbehave even for effective teachers. A comprehensive management system might involve components of the Kounin model but would also need many more components to be effective for the most difficult-to-manage students.

Jones

Jones (1987) developed the Jones model, which rests on the key aspects shown in Table 1.1. Teachers must learn two major skill clusters. First, Jones indicates that 90% of effective discipline involves body language. Therefore, teachers should do the following: make eye contact, move close to the student (physical proximity), stand straight (body carriage), display appropriate facial expressions, and use gestures such as palm out to indicate to students to stop or thumbs up to indicate pleasure with their behavior. Second, teachers should use group-based "genuine incentive" systems such as watching films or having free time to pursue personal interests, and they should institute "Grandma's rule" (see Chapter 5)—the provision of incentives to finish assignments, so students earn something they want. These incentives should be easy to implement and be group based (see Chapter 7 for a description of group-oriented management programs). A key to this model is approaching student behavior in a calm and controlled fashion.

Teachers following the Jones model try to minimize teacher interventions by organizing the classroom, including seating arrangements and rules and routines (see Chapter 7) and using graphic reminders that provide students with examples and instructions, and they also leave students to their work by moving on quickly after praising a student for doing something correctly or giving straightforward suggestions that will get a student on task. Teachers can also use a **preferred activity time (PAT)** procedure that involves allowing students access to those things they enjoy but that are an extension of the academic content. For example, painting murals related to a unit on the *Mayflower* landing or developing plays based on historical events could be preferred activities. Teachers should predetermine a reward that can be given to the whole class. Students retain this preferred activity time with responsible behavior and earn it at the end of the predetermined time interval (e.g., at the end of the week). If a student misbehaves, teachers start a timer and subtract the length of time the student was off task from the total PAT.

Jones indicates that backup systems are needed when students continue to test the teacher. If all else fails, a teacher should use warnings, remembering to be relaxed and to maintain eye contact when talking. If warnings do not work, the teacher can "pull a card." Card pulling involves taking an index card out of a file box so that it is in plain view of the student. The card has the parent's phone number on it. If this method does not work, the teacher uses the "letter home on desk technique." This technique involves writing a letter home to the parents. The teacher then walks back to the student and tells her that the letter will be sent if she repeats the misbehavior within one week. The letter is taped to the student's or teacher's desk in plain view. The teacher allows the student to tear up the letter after the week is over if the misbehavior is not exhibited.

Analysis. The Jones model shows that preventive measures can be used in behavior management. Certainly, body language is important when attempting to communicate with students. In addition, approaching discipline in a calm manner is supported by research in behavior management. Also, the use of incentives as outlined by Jones is an effective method of reinforcing student behavior.

The PAT system, however, is an example of a punishment-based token economy system (see Chapter 5 for token systems). When teachers use an incentive system such as a token economy, the process should be one of earning the incentives rather than of working to avoid losing the incentives. The PAT system, however, is a response cost system (see Chapter 12), which is a punishment-based system. The PAT system functions by motivating students to behave appropriately to avoid the loss of time from the total time provided at the beginning. A more positive system is to motivate students to behave appropriately to earn the time: the better students are, the more time they earn.

Along these lines, the Jones model is limited in that it relies on threats and warnings when students continue to misbehave. The use of cards and letters is an attempt to get students to behave to avoid these things. Research has shown threats and warnings tend to make behavior problems escalate and get worse (Nelson, 1996b). It is in the best interests of teachers and students to avoid such aversive techniques. A final problem with the Jones model: it lacks research validation.

Character Education

Although character education is more of a philosophical approach to improving student behavior as opposed to a single model, we will discuss it here. (Key aspects of character education, taken from the Character Education Partnership [2010], are presented in Table 1.1.) Character education "is a fairly new and rapidly evolving topic for curriculum interventions. It is also broad, often overlapping with other program areas" (What Works Clearinghouse [WWC], 2007a, p. 1). **Character education** often includes focused work on teaching students respect, being fair and trustworthy, caring for others, being responsible, and being a better citizen.

WWC examined 93 studies of 41 programs in their 2007 review of character education programs. Of these 93 studies, only 18 met the WWC evidence standards. These 18 studies represented 13 programs. These programs included *Building Decision Skills, Caring School Community, Connect with Kids, Facing History and Ourselves, Heartwood Ethics Curriculum, Lessons in Character, Positive Action, Skills for Action, Skills for Adolescence, Too Good for Drugs, Too Good for Drugs and Violence, Too Good for Violence,* and *Voices Literature and Character Education.* Only two of these programs (i.e., *Positive Action* and *Caring School Community*) had enough evidence (i.e., more than one study, more than one school, and at least 350 students) to receive a rating of medium to large in the behavior category. Both of these character education programs will be discussed below.

Positive Action. WWC rated the *Positive Action* program as having positive effects on behavior. The program had the highest effectiveness rating of any program. The *Positive Action* program is a comprehensive program designed to prevent negative behavioral problems (e.g., substance abuse and office referrals) and develop positive behaviors (Beets et al., 2008). The focus of the program is on attributions (e.g., self-concept) and social relationships such as treating others with respect and kindness. "The program is based on the philosophy that you feel good about yourself when you think and do positive actions, and there is always a positive way to do everything" (WWC, 2007c, p. 1). It is a K–12 program designed to promote better school behavior and academic achievement. It includes six units with an additional seventh review unit (Flay & Allred, 2003; Flay, Allred, & Ordway, 2001; Ji et al., 2005).

Unit 1 focuses on self-concept. Unit 2 examines positive actions for body (physical) and mind (intellectual). In Unit 3, students learn positive social and emotional actions for managing themselves in a responsible manner. Unit 4 includes a focus on positive social and emotional actions for getting along with others. The focus in Unit 5 is on positive social and emotional actions for being honest about yourself and others. Finally, Unit 6 involves goal setting with a focus on social and emotional actions for improving oneself on a continual basis. These units are covered in an age-appropriate manner across three levels: K–6, middle school, and high school.

In addition to positive effects for behavior, *Positive Action* also received the highest rating (positive effect) by the WWC for academic achievement. There were no effects listed for knowledge, attitudes, and values.

Caring School Community. The *Caring School Community (CSC)* program (a modified version of the *Child Development Project*) was determined by WWC to have potentially positive effects for behavior. The overall goal of the program is to help schools become caring communities of learners (Battistich, Schaps, Watson, & Solomon, 1996; Solomon, Battistich, Watson, Schaps, & Lewis, 2000; Watson, Battistich, & Solomon, 1997) and to prevent problems at school (Battistich, Schaps, Watson, Solomon, & Lewis, 2000). It is a comprehensive school improvement program for elementary-age (K–6) students (Munoz & Vanderhaar, 2006). The program includes four parts: class-meeting lessons, cross-age "buddies" programs, "homeside" activities, and schoolwide community (WWC, 2007b). Class-meeting lessons involve focused instruction on core values such as fairness and personal responsibility. In class-meeting lessons, students get to know one another, talk about key issues, identify and solve problems collaboratively, and make important decisions. Cross-age "buddies" pair older and younger students to build caring relationships. The goal is to create trust among students through focused academic and recreational activities. Parents are involved in homeside activities during which students complete short conversations with their parents and then discuss them in the classroom. Finally, schoolwide community activities bring parents, students, and school staff together to build trust and a feeling of belongingness. Despite the potentially positive effects for behavior, no discernible effects for knowledge, attitudes, values, or academic achievement were noted by WWC.

Analysis. School reform models are emerging as an attempt to address the varied needs of students in Grades K–12. Character education appears to hold promise in the improvement of student behavior and academic achievement. A beneficial aspect of character education is the focus on learning to interact with others in a positive manner. The two programs described above are prevention based and are implemented across grade levels. Character education also focuses on behavior as well as on academic performance.

Unfortunately, much of the theory surrounding the programs is based on constructivist philosophy. Intrinsic motivation is emphasized along with self-esteem building. The scientific research on these approaches is limited at best. These programs also do not target those students who are the most difficult to manage and teach. Although character education is targeted to all students, a primary concern is with those students who cause the majority of our management problems. Additionally, when a model internalizes causal variables, as character education does, it is not possible to state the cause-and-effect relationship between program components and results. For example, if *Positive Action* leads to better self-concept and school behavior, it is not possible to state with confidence that the improved school behavior resulted from improvements in student self-concept. Just as possibly, "self-concept" improved as a result of better school behavior, or they simply both improved together without one affecting the other. We view "self-concept" as a set of behaviors (albeit internal ones), not as a *cause* of behaviors.

Finally, a significant issue with character education is the limited amount of research support it has garnered. Based on the 2007 WWC review, many programs are considered promising. Unfortunately, only two of the 41 programs (*Positive Action* and *Caring School Community*) had enough evidence to receive a rating of medium to large in the behavior category. Only one of the programs (*Positive Action*) was shown to have positive effects for behavior *and* academic achievement. Clearly, more research is needed before we can confidently say that character education as a whole is effective for improving the school climate.

Conclusion

The aforementioned models all have positive attributes. Some aspects of these models, such as getting students involved in behavior management programs and treating students with respect, can and should be used by teachers. Any model that aids students in becoming more self-sufficient should be strongly considered. For behavior management approaches to be successful, however, they must be well defined and able to be replicated. Also, teachers should be able to explain not only why a management method worked but also why it failed to determine what the next step should be in solving the management problem. This explanation requires a consistent manner of viewing and interpreting the outcomes of different approaches.

Unfortunately, many of the described models do not have a solid research base on which to make these explanations. In addition, an adequate behavior management model must have built-in assessment and evaluation techniques to determine what management procedures are most appropriate and whether the procedures are indeed working. Several of the aforementioned models do not include these systematic assessment and evaluation techniques.

These models do have one thing in common: they all rest on some form of consequence for misbehavior, although many argue against external control. Whenever we praise a positive behavior or use consequences for an unwanted behavior, the consequences come from the environment. To suggest that one model is superior to another because it does not use external control methods is simply incorrect. Along these lines, some professionals make a distinction between encouragement and praise (Dreikurs et al., 2004) in a "democratic classroom." However, the distinction between encouragement and praise is an artificial one and does not aid in the management of unwanted behavior. The issue is not one of encouragement versus praise but one of effective versus ineffective feedback. According to Hattie and Timperley (2007), feedback is an important variable that affects learning and achievement. However, Hattie and Timperley suggest feedback is more effective when it provides information on correct responses and improvement from previous attempts than when it provides information on incorrect responses. One form of feedback is praise. We will discuss the effective use of praise in Chapter 8. Once it is agreed that all management methods use some form of external control, it must be determined which method works the best. This analysis is what is missing from some of these models. Few of the models set out to determine systematically which external management method (a) works best for each student and (b) has the fewest negative side effects. The approach discussed in this book attempts to do just that—to determine which method works best for each student and the possible side effects of the methods.

Other problems with the aforementioned methods are the claims many of them make that students are free to choose their behavior and that the facilitation of this choice is critical in their development. Choices, however, are always limited. In fact, to affect their students' behaviors, teachers rely on a lack of *free* choice. If students had free choice, nothing teachers did would affect student behavior. Teachers are constantly attempting methods of directing the choice of students. Therefore, we must admit we are attempting to influence student behavior and thus take steps to do so in an appropriate manner. To suggest students should be allowed to take control over their behavior by having teachers allow them to choose their behavior and suffer or take responsibility for their actions is false and misleading.

Another area of concern with the aforementioned models is the paucity of scientific support each has. Ultimately, teachers must consider whether the model works. What should determine the form of disciplinary approach they use in the classroom is the research supporting the effectiveness of its procedures. Anyone can claim that his or her model or method is effective, and most do. It is far different to demonstrate over time that it actually leads to meaningful behavior change. Therefore, teachers must determine what has been shown in the research literature to work in the classroom. A major weakness of many of these approaches is that systematic observation and behavior-tracking methods are not built into the models. To implement a behavior management procedure effectively, we have not only to execute the procedure but also to establish formative measures to track its effectiveness.

Finally, many of the models assume that the causal variables of behavior change reside within the student. Unfortunately, there can be no direct demonstration of mental processes such as self-concept causing changes in overt behavior. Any claims to this effect are simply inferences made by the researcher. An adequate management model must demonstrate directly the causal variables in effect.

Although there are many issues with the aforementioned models, they are not all bad. They possess several positive attributes. Many of the positive attributes described in the models above will be expanded on in this textbook. The remainder of this chapter will describe approaches that the scientific research literature has shown to be effective in managing behavior.

What Are Best Practices in Behavior Management?

In a sense, the most important question we should ask regarding improving student behavior and academic performance is this: Does the model or procedure we implement actually work? Fortunately, there are large-scale evaluations on best practices for elementary-level and secondary-level students. Considering all the models available for behavior and instruction, the one that produces the largest gains with students with behavior and learning difficulties is the behavioral model (see Burns & Ysseldyke, 2009, for important details on evidence-based practices for working with students with behavior and learning issues).

Further, Epstein, Atkins, Cullinan, Kutash, and Weaver (2008) offer five concrete recommendations to help teachers reduce common behavior problems in the classroom. The WWC evidence standards were used to rate the quality of the evidence supporting these recommendations; ratings of moderate or strong were provided for each recommendation (see Table 1.2). First, teachers should identify the specifics of the problem behavior and the conditions that occur just prior to and after the behavior (rating = moderate evidence). Teachers should gather important information by observing students in the classroom. They should use the information they gather to develop effective and efficient intervention strategies tailored to individual student needs. Second, teachers should change the environment in such a way that problem behaviors decrease (rating = strong evidence). Environmental factors include academic expectations, behavioral expectations, the physical arrangement of the room, the class schedule, and learning activities. Third, teachers should actively teach social and behavioral skills to replace unwanted behaviors. While these skills are being acquired and afterward, teachers should reinforce these skills and maintain a positive classroom environment (rating = strong evidence). Fourth, teachers should include parents, other school personnel, and behavior specialists for support and guidance in the management of student behavior (rating = moderate evidence). Finally, teachers, along with other school personnel, should consider adopting a schoolwide approach to prevent and respond to student misbehavior and to increase positive social interactions among students and between students and school personnel (rating = moderate evidence). All these recommendations fit within a behavioral model (described below).

The Behavioral Model

The behavioral model used in this textbook is based on **applied behavior analysis (ABA)**. ABA is based on the understanding that the environment causes many of our behaviors to occur. Thus, the study of how the environment affects our behavior and how changing these environmental events will lead to behavior change is the focus of ABA. ABA has seven general characteristics (Cooper, Heron, & Heward, 2007). These seven characteristics include (a) applied (ABA is committed to improving people's lives by selecting behaviors that will lead to socially significant improvements); (b) behavioral (behavior to be changed is observable and measureable); (c) analytic (changes in observable and measureable behavior are demonstrated to be the result of changes in the environment); (d) technological (methods used to change behavior can be replicated by others); (e) conceptually systematic (procedures used for behavior change can be interpreted from the principles of behavior); (f) effective (behavior change must be shown to be socially significant); and (g) generalizable (behavior change should be shown to continue over time or in a new setting once the behavior program has been withdrawn).

To summarize, then, the behavioral model relies on an experimental analysis of environmental events to demonstrate a cause-and-effect relationship between environmental changes and behavior change. The behavior change should be seen by members of society as important and should occur in settings where the intervention did not occur (i.e., generalization) and over a period of time when the intervention is withdrawn (maintenance).

Table 1.2	Five Concrete Recommendations Noted by What Works Clearinghouse to Help Teachers Reduce Common Behavior Problems

1. **Identify the specifics of the problem behavior and the conditions that prompt and reinforce it.**

   Concretely describe the behavior problem and its effects on learning.

   Observe and record the frequency and context of the problem behavior.

   Identify what prompts and reinforces the problem behavior.

2. **Modify the classroom learning environment to decrease problem behavior.**

   Revisit, re-practice, and reinforce classroom behavioral expectations.

   Modify the classroom environment to encourage instructional momentum.

   Adapt or vary instructional strategies to increase opportunities for academic success and engagement.

3. **Teach and reinforce new skills to increase appropriate behavior and preserve a positive classroom climate.**

   Identify where the student needs explicit instruction for appropriate behavior.

   Teach skills by providing examples, practice, and feedback.

   Manage consequences so that reinforcers are provided for appropriate behavior and withheld for inappropriate behavior.

4. **Draw on relationships with professional colleagues and students' families for continued guidance and support.**

   Collaborate with other teachers for continued guidance and support.

   Build collaborative partnerships with school, district, and community behavior experts who can consult with teachers when problems are serious enough to warrant help from outside the classroom.

   Encourage parents and other family members to participate as active partners in teaching and reinforcing appropriate behavior.

5. **Assess whether schoolwide behavior problems warrant adopting schoolwide strategies or programs, and, if so, implement ones shown to reduce negative and foster positive interactions.**

   Address schoolwide behavior issues by involving a school improvement team.

   Collect information on the hot spots throughout the school—namely, the frequency of particular schoolwide behavior problems and when and where they occur.

   Monitor implementation and outcomes using an efficient method of data collection and allow ample time for the program to work.

   If warranted, adopt a packaged intervention program that fits well with identified behavior problems and the school context.

Misunderstandings of the Behavioral Model

Unfortunately, two major misconceptions prevent professionals from using some of the more effective behavior management procedures available today: intrinsic versus extrinsic rewards and the issue of control.

Extrinsic Versus Intrinsic Rewards. Several individuals have made statements indicating the use of extrinsic rewards or control procedures harms students. **Extrinsic rewards** are things given to a student such as praise, tokens, stickers, or candy. **Intrinsic rewards** are things that occur inside the individual such as pride, interest, and self-esteem. Interestingly, Deci and Ryan (1985) and Deci, Koestner, and Ryan (1999) have written that the use of extrinsic rewards tends to undermine intrinsic interest in subjects. In other words, when we reward students for reading, they may become less interested in reading for pleasure and will not read unless we give them something. Kohn (1993a, 1993b) has also discussed the negative effects of extrinsic rewards on the intrinsic motivation of children. There are, however, several difficulties with the conclusions of these authors. First, when Deci and colleagues and Kohn speak of rewards, they are not speaking of reinforcers. (The differences are discussed in Chapter 2.) Second, there is no agreed-on definition of an extrinsic reward. For example, is praise from a teacher extrinsic? What about discussing what a student has learned after that student has finished reading a book? Essentially, we can define virtually anything that goes on in the classroom environment as extrinsic. Third, the critics do not distinguish between behaviors that are reinforced on a continuous basis and those that are reinforced intermittently. In other words, if we see a behavior occur in the absence of an extrinsic reinforcer, is the behavior occurring due to intrinsic interest, or have we simply not seen the extrinsic reinforcer take place? (Schedules of reinforcement are discussed in Chapter 2.) Fourth, the critics have also forgotten that they are extrinsically reinforced for their views. It is probably a safe bet that the critics are paid for what they do and most likely would not continue to give workshops or teach for the sheer enjoyment of doing so. Thus, we are all extrinsically reinforced for what we do without the negative effects about which we have been warned.

Fifth, the critics have failed to make distinctions in regard to how the extrinsic rewards are provided. Chance (1992) wrote an interesting review of the research on the effects of extrinsic **reinforcers** (as opposed to rewards) on intrinsic motivation. According to Chance, extrinsic reinforcers can be task contingent, performance contingent, or success contingent. When we use **task contingent** reinforcers, we reinforce students for simply engaging in a task for some period of time. There is no requirement in regard to the quality of the task. The main goal is to get students to do something. According to Chance, task contingent reinforcers tend to decrease the likelihood that students will do the task in the future in the absence of any external contingencies. Thus, Chance indicated that this decrease in performing the task would support what the critics warned us about. Interestingly, the research cited by these critics has relied on task completion rewards. The second method of providing extrinsic reinforcers involves making them performance contingent. **Performance contingent** means that external reinforcers are provided if students have met a predetermined performance criterion. According to Chance, performance contingent reinforcers will increase intrinsic interest in a subject if students make the performance criterion. Those students who do not meet the performance criteria, however, will experience a decrease in their intrinsic interest in the subject. Finally, **success contingent** reinforcers reinforce students for meeting a predetermined criterion as in the performance contingent example, but students are also reinforced along the way. In other words, the task is broken into smaller subtasks, and students are reinforced for their progression to the final performance criterion. According to Chance, success contingent reinforcers tend to increase intrinsic interest in a subject. Therefore, it is not appropriate to make a general statement that extrinsic rewards should not be used with students. It is appropriate to state that we must make sure we are using reinforcers and not rewards and that we are using success contingent reinforcers rather than task completion reinforcers.

A final problem with the critics' assertion that we should not use external control procedures is their assumption that the reinforcers used in a management program are artificial (i.e., not natural). However, as explained by Cooper et al. (2007), there is no such thing as an artificial reinforcer. If a reinforcer is occurring in an environment, it is a **naturally occurring reinforcer** by definition. The distinction is between **contrived reinforcers** (i.e., those reinforcers not typically used in a particular setting, such as paying students for good behavior as part of a management program) and those that already exist in a given setting (e.g., praise or teacher attention). Rather than debating about intrinsic versus extrinsic reinforcers, it seems much more worthwhile to discuss effective versus ineffective consequences. "The extrinsic-intrinsic distinction between reinforcers may not even be valid" (Martin & Pear, 2007, p. 38).

It is hard to imagine a world devoid of external contingencies. Laws in society are tied to external contingencies; imagine a society without any laws. Thus, we must acknowledge that external reinforcers (and punishers) are always present. Once external reinforcers are acknowledged to exist, we can take steps to decrease the use of ineffective contingencies and increase our use of effective ones.

Issues of Control. Control is a concept often misunderstood by teachers. When the term *control* is used, people think of being manipulated and being made to do things against their will. Therefore, when we speak of controlling a behavior, we may become the objects of criticism. Control, however, is not always what it seems. In a sense, everything we do is under some form of control. We usually pay our taxes on time to avoid the penalty of not doing so. We typically slow down when going over the speed limit if we see a police officer. That you are reading this textbook is likely due to some form of "control" placed on you by a professor (who requires the textbook for a class) or because you are motivated to learn more about behavior management to make your professional or personal life better. If we think of control in this way, whatever we do with a child, adolescent, or adult will involve some sort of control. Telling a child to be quiet, giving an adolescent a curfew, or asking another adult to hand you the newspaper will involve consequences (either positive or negative). Having a student go through

Student hand raising is "controlled" by the teacher.

Glasser's problem-solving process is an attempt at control in that the teacher is trying to get the student to behave appropriately as a result of the problem-solving process. Making a school task more enjoyable and meaningful to students is an act of control because the teacher is attempting to increase the likelihood that students will be motivated to learn.

Therefore, when many professionals speak of control, they are not talking of using techniques similar to what may be used in a prisoner-of-war camp. What they are talking about are techniques that we all use every day of our lives; for example, tipping a waitress for good service may make the waitress more likely to continue to provide good service in the future.

Conclusion

There are misunderstandings about effective behavior management approaches. These misunderstandings can have a profound impact on whether we are successful or unsuccessful in managing students' classroom behaviors. If we are going to improve our behavior management skills and become more adept at the prevention of and the response to student misbehavior, we must use what has been shown to work in the short term as well as over time. Therefore, it is critical to have a knowledge base developed through scientific research (see Martella, Nelson, & Marchand-Martella, 1999, for an in-depth discussion of research methodology).

What Are Ethical Issues in Treating Behavior and Instructional Problems?

Before we leave this chapter, it is critical to get a foundation in ethics. ABA is a powerful technology and can be misused. Therefore, it is prudent for the reader to understand fully issues related to the appropriate use of behavior change methods. Ethics in behavior management refers to two primary questions: (a) Was the program the right thing to do under the circumstances, and (b) Did the management program result in behavior change that was socially significant and cost-effective? Several organizations have ethical codes. We will cover ethical statements from the Association for Behavior Analysis International (ABAI) in this chapter.

The Right to Effective Behavioral Treatment

ABAI outlines six rights individuals have when exposed to behavioral interventions (Van Houten et al., 1988). These rights (see Table 1.3) should be considered when a behavior program is designed and implemented. ABAI (2010) developed a set of guiding principles on the application of restrictive procedures that are consistent with the earlier statement on the right to effective and ethical treatment. These guiding principles are shown in Table 1.4, but they will be covered in more detail in Chapter 6.

Table 1.3	Association for Behavior Analysis International Statement on the Right to Effective Behavioral Treatment

Statement on the Right to Effective Behavioral Treatment, 1989

The Association for Behavior Analysis issues the following position statement on clients' right to effective behavioral treatment as a set of guiding principles to protect individuals from harm as a result of either the lack or the inappropriate use of behavioral treatment.

The Association for Behavior Analysis, through majority vote of its members, declares that individuals who receive behavioral treatment have a right to:

1. *A therapeutic physical and social environment:* Characteristics of such an environment include but are not limited to: an acceptable standard of living, opportunities for stimulation and training, therapeutic social interaction, and freedom from undue physical or social restriction.

2. *Services whose overriding goal is personal welfare:* The client participates, either directly or through authorized proxy, in the development and implementation of treatment programs. In cases where withholding or implementing treatment involves potential risk and the client does not have the capacity to provide consent, individual welfare is protected through two mechanisms: Peer Review Committees, imposing professional standards, determine the clinical propriety of treatment programs; Human Rights Committees, imposing community standards, determine the acceptability of treatment programs and the degree to which they may compromise an individual's rights.

3. *Treatment by a competent behavior analyst:* The behavior analyst's training reflects appropriate academic preparation, including knowledge of behavioral principles, methods of assessment and treatment, research methodology, and professional ethics; as well as practical experience. In cases where a problem or treatment is complex or may pose risk, direct involvement by a doctoral-level behavior analyst is necessary.

4. *Programs that teach functional skills:* Improvement in functioning requires the acquisition of adaptive behaviors that will increase independence, as well as the elimination of behaviors that are dangerous or that in some other way serve as barriers to independence.

5. *Behavioral assessment and ongoing evaluation:* Pretreatment assessment, including both interviews and measures of behavior, attempts to identify factors relevant to behavioral maintenance and treatment. The continued use of objective behavioral measurement documents response to treatment.

6. *The most effective treatment procedures available:* An individual is entitled to effective and scientifically validated treatment; in turn, the behavior analyst has an obligation to use only those procedures demonstrated by research to be effective. Decisions on the use of potentially restrictive treatment are based on consideration of its absolute and relative level of restrictiveness, the amount of time required to produce a clinically significant outcome, and the consequences that would result from delayed intervention.

This statement was developed by the Association for Behavior Analysis Task Force on the Right to Effective Behavioral Treatment [members: Ron Van Houten (Chair), Saul Axelrod, Jon S. Bailey, Judith E. Favell, Richard M. Foxx, Brian A. Iwata, and O. Ivar Lovaas]. This Position Statement was accepted by the ABA Executive Council in October 1987 and by the ABA membership in 1989.

SOURCE: Association for Behavior Analysis International (1989). Used with permission.

	Association for Behavior Analysis International Statement on Restraint and Seclusion

Statement on Restraint and Seclusion, 2010

The Association for Behavior Analysis International (ABAI) and its members strongly oppose the inappropriate and/or unnecessary use of seclusion, restraint, or other intrusive interventions. Although many persons with severe behavior problems can be effectively treated without the use of any restrictive interventions, restraint may be necessary on some rare occasions with meticulous clinical oversight and controls. In addition, a carefully planned and monitored use of timeout from reinforcement can be acceptable under restricted circumstances. Seclusion is sometimes necessary or needed, but behavior analysts would support only the most highly monitored and ethical practices associated with such use, to be detailed below.

This Position Statement on Restraint and Seclusion summarizes critical guiding principles. With a strong adherence to professional judgment and best practice, it also describes the conditions under which seclusion and restraint may be necessary and outlines proper strategy in order to implement these procedures appropriately and safely. This statement is consistent with ABAI's 1989 Position Statement on the Right to Effective Behavioral Treatment, which asserts numerous rights, including access to the most effective treatments available—while emphasizing extensive procedural safeguards.

I. **Guiding Principles:**

1. *The Welfare of the Individual Served is the Highest Priority* – Clinical decisions should be made based upon the professional judgment of a duly formed treatment team that demonstrates knowledge of the broad research base and best practice. Included in this process are the individuals being served and their legal guardians. The team should be informed by the research literature, and should determine that any procedure used is in that individual

(Continued)

Table 1.4 (Continued)

person's best interests. These interests must take precedence over the broader agendas of institutions or organizations that would prohibit certain procedures regardless of the individual's needs. A core value of ABAI with regard to behavioral treatment is that welfare of the individual being served is the absolute highest priority.

2. *Individuals (and Parents/Guardians) Have a Right to Choose* – ABAI supports the U.S. Supreme Court ruling that individuals have a right to treatment in certain contexts, and that many state and federal regulations and laws create such rights. Organizations and institutions should not limit the professional judgment or rights of those legally responsible for an individual to choose interventions that are necessary, safe, and effective. A regulation that prohibits treatment that includes the necessary use of restraint violates individuals' rights to effective treatment. The irresponsible use of certain procedures by unqualified or incompetent people should not result in policies that limit the rights of those duly qualified and responsible for an individual through the process of making informed choices.

3. *The Principle of Least Restrictiveness* – ABAI supports the position that treatment selection should be guided by the principle of the least restrictiveness. The least restrictive treatment is defined as that treatment that affords the most favorable risk to benefit ratio, with specific consideration of probability of treatment success, anticipated duration of treatment, distress caused by procedures, and distress caused by the behavior itself. One may conclude from this premise that a non-intrusive intervention that permits dangerous behavior to continue while limiting participation in learning activities and community life, or results in a more restrictive placement, may be considered more restrictive than a more intensive intervention that is effective and enhances quality of life.

II. Application:

1. *General Definitions*

   i. *Restraint* involves physically holding or securing the individual, either: a) for a brief period of time to interrupt and intervene with severe problem behavior, or b) for an extended period of time using mechanical devices to prevent otherwise uncontrollable problem behavior (e.g., self-injurious behavior) that has the potential to produce serious injury. When used in the context of a behavior intervention plan, restraint in some cases serves both a protective and a therapeutic function. These procedures can reduce risks of injury and can facilitate learning opportunities that support appropriate behavior.

   ii. *Seclusion* involves isolating an individual from others to interrupt and intervene with problem behavior that places the individual or others at risk of harm. When used in the context of a behavior intervention plan, seclusion in some cases serves both a protective and a therapeutic function. These procedures can reduce risks of injury and can facilitate learning opportunities that support appropriate behavior. ABAI is opposed to the use of seclusion when it is operationally defined as placing someone in a locked room, often combined with the use of mechanical restraint and/or sedation, and not part of a formal Behavior Intervention Plan to which the individual served and/or their Guardians have consented. We support the use of a planned time out treatment or safety intervention which conforms to evidence based research, is part of a comprehensive treatment or safety plan which meets the standards of informed consent by the individual served and/or legal guardian, and is evaluated on an ongoing basis via the use of contemporaneously collected objective data.

iii. *Time-out* from reinforcement is an evidence-based treatment intervention that involves reducing or limiting the amount of reinforcement that is available to an individual for a brief period of time. It can entail removing an individual from his or her environment, or it may entail changes to the existing environment itself. When time out involves removing an individual from the environment, it should only be used as part of an approved and planned Behavior Intervention Plan. Time out from reinforcement is not seclusion, but it may involve seclusion if it is not safe to have others in the room. In addition, some innocuous versions of timeout from reinforcement, such as having a child take a seat away from a play area, are not deemed to be intrusive. Such procedures are commonly used and are generally safe.

2. *Use of Restraint as part of a Behavior Intervention Plan*

i. The use of restraint in a planned Behavior Intervention Plan is done as part of an integrated effort to reduce the future probability of a specified target behavior and/or to reduce the episodic severity of that behavior. A Behavior Intervention Plan that incorporates contingent restraint must a) incorporate reinforcement based procedures, b) be based on a functional behavior assessment, c) be evaluated by objective outcome data, and d) be consistent with the scientific literature and current best practices.

ii. Procedures describing the use and monitoring of this type of procedure should be designed by a Board Certified Behavior Analyst, or a similarly trained and licensed professional who is trained and experienced in the treatment of challenging behavior.

3. *Use of Timeout (or in rare cases, seclusion) as part of a Behavior Intervention Plan*

i. Timeout may be used as part of an integrated Behavior Intervention Program designed to decrease the future probability of a pre-specified target behavior and/or to reduce the episodic severity of that behavior. The Behavior Intervention Plan that incorporates the use of time out must a) be derived from a behavioral assessment, b) incorporate reinforcement strategies for appropriate behavior, c) be of brief duration, d) be evaluated by objective outcome data, and e) be consistent with the scientific literature and current best practices.

4. *The Necessity for Using Emergency Restraint and Seclusion*

i. Emergency restraint involves physically holding or securing a person to protect that person or others from behavior that poses imminent risk of harm. These procedures should be considered only for dangerous or harmful behavior that occurs at unpredictable times that make the behavior not amenable to less restrictive behavioral treatment interventions and that place the individual and/or others at risk for injury, or that will result in significant loss of quality of life. The procedures should be considered only when less intrusive

(Continued)

Table 1.4	(Continued)

interventions have been attempted and failed or are otherwise determined to be insufficient given adequate empirical documentation to prove this point.

   ii. When applied for crisis management, restraint or seclusion should be implemented according to well-defined, predetermined criteria; include the use of de-escalation techniques designed to reduce the target behavior without the need for physical intervention; be applied only at the minimum level of physical restrictiveness necessary to safely contain the crisis behavior and prevent injury; and be withdrawn according to precise and mandatory release criteria.

  iii. Emergency restraint procedures should be limited to those included within a standardized program. Medical professionals should review restraint procedures to ensure their safety.

  iv. Consideration of emergency restraint should involve weighing the relative benefits and limitations of using these procedures against the risks associated with not using them. Associated risks of failure to use appropriate restraint when necessary include increased risk for injury, excessive use of medication, expulsion from school, placement in more restrictive, less normalized settings, and increased involvement of law enforcement.

   v. Crisis management procedures are not a replacement for behavioral treatment, and should not be used routinely in the absence of an individualized behavior intervention plan. The best way to eliminate restraint use is to eliminate behavior that invites restraint use via systematic behavioral treatment procedures. If crisis intervention procedures are used on a repeated basis, a formal written behavior plan should be developed, reviewed by both a Peer Review Committee and Human Rights Committee (when available), and consented to by the individuals served and their parents or legal guardians.

5. *Informed Consent*

   i. As members of the treatment team, the individual and/or parents/guardians must be allowed the opportunity to participate in the development of any behavior plan.

  ii. Interventions involving restraint or seclusion should only be used with full consent of those responsible for decision making. Such consent should meet the standards of "Information," "Capacity," and "Voluntary." The individual and his or her guardian must be informed of the methods, risks, and effects of possible intervention procedures, which include the options to both use and not use restraint.

6. *Oversights and Monitoring*

   i. Restraint or seclusion procedures (not including brief timeout procedures) for both treatment and emergency situations should be made available for professional review consistent with prevailing practices.

  ii. The behavior analyst is responsible to ensure that any plan involving restraint or seclusion conforms to the highest standards of effective and humane treatment, and the behavior analyst is responsible for continued oversight and quality assurance.

  iii. These procedures should be implemented only by staff who are fully trained in their use, regularly in-serviced, demonstrate competency using objective measures of performance, and are closely supervised by a Board Certified Behavior Analyst, or a similarly trained professional.

iv. The use of restraint or seclusion should be monitored on a continuous basis using reliable and valid data collection that permits objective evaluation of its effects.

v. Procedures involving restraint or seclusion should be continued only if they are demonstrated to be safe and effective; and their use should be reduced and eliminated when possible. Efficacy with respect to treatment programs refers to a reduction in the rate of the specified target behavior and/or reduction in the episodic severity of that behavior. With respect to emergency treatments, efficacy refers only to the time and risk associated with achieving calm.

A task force authorized by the Executive Council of the Association for Behavior Analysis International generated the above statement concerning the technique called Restraint and Seclusion. Members of the task force independently reviewed the scientific literature concerning Restraint and Seclusion and agreed unanimously to the content of the statement. The Executive Council has accepted the statement and it was subsequently approved by a two-thirds majority vote of the general membership. It now constitutes official ABAI policy.

SOURCE: Association for Behavior Analysis International (2010). Used with permission.

The Right to Effective Education

ABAI also outlines six rights students have when receiving educational services (Barrett et al., 1991). These rights should be considered when an educational program is designed and implemented. See Table 1.5.

Table 1.5	Association for Behavior Analysis International Statement on the Right to Effective Education

Statement on Students' Right to Effective Education, 1990

Based on the principles that have been demonstrated to improve student learning and performance, the following are recommended educational entitlements for all students:

1. **The student's overall educational context should include:**

   a. Social and physical school environments that encourage and maintain academic achievement and progress, and discourage behavior inconsistent with those goals;

   b. Schools that treat students with care and individual attention, comparable to that offered by a caring family;

   c. School programs that provide support and training for parents in parenting and teaching skills; and

   d. Consequences and attention at home that encourage and maintain success at school.

(Continued)

Table 1.5	(Continued)

2. **Curriculum and instructional objectives should:**

   a. Be based on empirically validated hierarchies or sequences of instructional objectives and measurable performance criteria that are demonstrated to promote cumulative mastery and that are of long-term value in the culture;

   b. Specify mastery criteria that include both the accuracy and the speed dimensions of fluent performance;

   c. Include objectives that specify both long-term and short-term personal and vocational success, and that, once mastered, will be maintained by natural consequences in everyday living; and

   d. Include long-term retention and maintenance of skills and knowledge as explicitly measured instructional objectives.

3. **Assessment and student placement should involve:**

   a. Assessment and reporting methods that are sufficiently criterion-referenced to promote useful decision making based on actual levels of skills and knowledge rather than on categorical labels such as "emotionally disturbed" or "learning disabled," and

   b. Placement based on correspondence between measured entering skills and skills required as prerequisites for a given level in a hierarchically sequenced curriculum.

4. **Instructional methods should:**

   a. Allow students to master instructional objectives at their own pace and to respond as rapidly and as frequently as they are able during at least some self-paced instructional session each day;

   b. Provide sufficient practice opportunities to enable students to master skills and knowledge at each step in the curriculum;

   c. Provide consequences designed to correct errors and/or to increase frequency of responding and that are adjusted to individual performance until they enable students to achieve desired outcomes;

   d. Be sensitive to and adjust in response to measures of individual learning and performance, including use of individualized instruction when group instruction fails to produce desired outcomes;

   e. Regularly employ the most advanced equipment to promote skill mastery via programs incorporating validated features described in this document; and

   f. Be delivered by teachers who receive performance-based training, administrative and supervisory support, and evaluation in the use of measurably effective, scientifically validated instructional procedures, programs, and materials.

5. **Measurement and summative evaluation should entail:**

   a. Decision making via objective curriculum-based measures of performance, and

   b. Reports of objectively measured individual achievement and progress rather than subjective ratings, norm-referenced comparisons, or letter grading.

6. **Responsibility for success should stipulate that:**

   a. Financial and operational consequences for school personnel depend on objective measures of student achievement;

   b. Teachers, administrators, and the general educational program assume responsibility for student success, and change programs until students achieve their highest performance levels; and

   c. Students and parents should be allowed and encouraged to change schools or school programs until their educational needs are met.

This statement was abstracted from a report by the Association for Behavior Analysis Task Force on the Right to Effective Education [members: B. H. Barret (chair), R. Beck, C. Binder, D. A. Cook, S. Engelmann, R. D. Greer, S. J. Kyrklund, K. R. Johnson, M. Maloney, N. McCorkle, J. S. Vargas, and C. L. Watkins]. The full report of the Task Force was accepted by the ABA Executive Council and was published in *The Behavior Analyst*, 1991, Volume 14(1). This abbreviated statement was subsequently approved by majority vote of the general membership. It now constitutes official ABA policy.

SOURCE: Association for Behavior Analysis International (1990). Used with permission.

VIGNETTE REVISITED — Controlling Angry Outbursts Through Evidence-Based Practices

Finding the past management attempts to be less than successful but also wishing to help José with his problem, Ms. Jackson reflected on the situation at hand. She thought that there surely must be other professionals with similar problems. There must be others who had found effective management procedures to use with students like José, but where could she find this information?

Ms. Jackson decided that she needed to find evidence-based practices. That is, she wanted to find management procedures that had been found to be successful with students like José. Ms. Jackson retrieved a long list of such evidence-based articles, and she discovered that the procedures found to be most effective are the ones built on behavioral principles. She also learned that one common theme among all management models is the need to provide guidelines for student behavior while simultaneously creating a positive learning environment. Finally, Ms. Jackson learned that much of what she had heard about the behavioral model was comprised of simplifications or misconceptions and that by implementing evidence-based procedures she could indeed improve José's behavior.

Now Ms. Jackson's goal is to learn more about these procedures and their underlying assumptions before designing a behavior management program. The information she learned is presented in the following chapters.

Summary

Student behavior is one of the most critical concerns in schools today. We are faced with misbehavior in our schools on a daily basis and need effective methods of preventing and responding to misbehavior. Several methods have been advocated over the years. It is important for teachers to be familiar with these models given their frequent use in schools. Unfortunately, few of these methods have demonstrated their effectiveness scientifically. We continue to use ineffective management methods even in the face of evidence that they do not work as claimed or that those claims have not been validated. Fortunately, we know what does and does not work.

Several of the positive aspects of the models covered were highlighted and are integrated throughout this textbook. However, there are several conceptual issues regarding the causes of the behavior change that results from the implementation of certain models or programs (e.g., self-concept). Character education holds some promise as a school reform model but needs a considerable amount of research showing the effects of each program.

Fortunately, Epstein et al. (2008) made five recommendations to help teachers deal with behavior management issues. These five recommendations are based on a review of the scientific research literature and should be considered by teachers. The recommendations made by Epstein et al. are consistent with the one model that has been shown over the years to be highly effective in dealing with behavior issues. The behavioral model is a scientifically based model that is grounded in applied behavior analysis (ABA) and has seven general characteristics that make it highly effective. It is critical that teachers become knowledgeable about ABA and skilled at implementing its principles if effective behavior management is going to take place in the schools.

Unfortunately, there are several misconceptions with regard to ABA. The intrinsic versus extrinsic reward debate is probably a waste of time, given there is no agreed-on definition of intrinsic reinforcement and there is a lack of evidence demonstrating its effects. Also, the issue of control is not a serious concern when one realizes that the form of control discussed in ABA is the same as the control exerted on an automobile driver using the highway (e.g., do not exceed the speed limit, keep to the right except to pass, wear a seatbelt). Contrary to critics' statements, control in ABA does not refer to "brainwashing" or involve a violation of one's personal rights.

Given that ABA is such a powerful technology, strict ethical behavior must be demonstrated when applying it. The Association for Behavior Analysis has position statements that should be followed. Our students have the right to effective behavioral treatment and a right to an effective education.

Key Terms

applied behavior analysis (ABA)   24

arbitrary consequences   11

assertive discipline   9

behavior   3

character education   19

choice theory   13

consequences   11

contrived   26

discipline   5

extrinsic rewards   25

Discussion Questions

1. What are the possible reasons for not using evidence-based management procedures?

2. What was your definition of discipline before reading this chapter? What is it now?

3. How are each of the models described in this chapter used?

4. What are the strengths of each of the models described in this chapter?

5. What are the weaknesses of each of the models described in this chapter?

6. What are the misunderstandings related to intrinsic versus extrinsic reinforcers?

7. What are the misunderstandings related to the issue of control?

8. How can we overcome these misunderstandings?

9. Why are scientifically validated management approaches important?

10. What does the right to effective behavioral treatment mean?

2

The Foundations of Behavior Management

Chapter Objectives

After studying this chapter, you should be able to

- illustrate the differences between cognitive and behavioral views of learning,
- note the A-B-Cs of learning,
- characterize the role of observational learning,
- explain the two categories of reinforcement,
- describe extinction,
- explain the two categories of punishment,
- distinguish between reinforcers and punishers,
- explain the conditioning of stimuli to be reinforcers or punishers,
- specify the concepts of deprivation and satiation and explain how they affect the reinforcing value of something,
- describe the process of stimulus control,
- explain how shaping takes place,
- illustrate the different methods of chaining, and
- specify the schedules of reinforcement and how these schedules affect student performance.

VIGNETTE	**Learning More About the Foundations of Behavior Management**

MR. HUANG IS A FIRST-GRADE TEACHER in an inner-city school. He has several students who refuse to follow his directions. Two boys in particular cause the majority of the problems in the classroom. Mr. Huang has met with each boy's parents to explain his concern about their behavior and how their behavior affects other students. The parents of the two boys seemed annoyed at Mr. Huang's suggestion that their children could even cause such problems. They appeared to be angry with the boys as well.

Mr. Huang believes the boys may be having some emotional problems. The boys told Mr. Huang they were afraid their parents would get angry and yell. They did not, however, provide any other information. Mr. Huang believes their problem behaviors may be caused by their emotional instability. He discusses this possibility with the school counselor, who also sees the emotional aspects of the boys' home lives as being the cause of their problem behaviors.

Not knowing what to do about the behavior of these boys, Mr. Huang approaches the school's behavior specialist. He provides the same information to this specialist and is surprised to hear what this specialist has to say about the two boys. The specialist says the boys' emotions are not causing the problem behaviors. She says emotions do not cause behaviors to occur but are, in themselves, behaviors. Therefore, Mr. Huang should find out what is the cause of the boys' behaviors in the classroom. The specialist believes the behavior problems have resulted from their reinforcement in the classroom, from appropriate behavior being punished, or from some combination of these two circumstances. Mr. Huang reports he does not use punishment with his students, and he certainly would not reward unwanted behavior. The behavior specialist encourages Mr. Huang to learn more about the foundations of behavior management because the manner in which he is using the terms *reinforcement* and *punishment* may not be accurate. She also suggests he find out about how unwanted behaviors can be shaped in the classroom environment.

Having the motivation to solve these behavior problems, Mr. Huang sets out to learn more about the foundations of behavior management.

Overview

Perhaps the most important aspect of behavior management is learning the foundations upon which management methods are based. One mistake is to think of behavior management as a set of procedures that can be used to solve problems. Thinking of behavior management as a set of "tricks we pull from a bag" is a mistake because it does not allow for problem solving to occur if we fail in our attempts to solve the behavior problem. Imagine for a moment that a teacher uses a certain intervention to reduce students' problem behaviors in the classroom and that the intervention has the intended effects. The reasons for this success are not likely to be a major concern for the teacher because the goal of reducing the problem behaviors has been achieved. The teacher may not have the time to reflect on the reasons for this success and will probably move on to address other issues in the classroom. Suppose, however, the intervention is not successful; no change is evident in the behaviors. What then? What typically occurs is the teacher tries another intervention and another intervention until she finds an effective one. Unfortunately, for a few students, the teacher may run out of "tricks in her bag." Even if she does find an effective intervention, a great deal of time will have been lost through an almost hit-or-miss approach to behavior management.

Now suppose the teacher considers why the intervention she used failed. If the reasons for this failure can be determined, she will most likely identify the next step to solving the problem. To figure out why a particular intervention has failed, we must understand the conceptual and technical aspects of the interventions or procedures used. Techniques work or fail for reasons, and these reasons are critical to understand, especially if we fail in our attempts to solve a problem behavior.

Determining why an intervention works or does not work requires a conceptual system. We can use a conceptual system to interpret successes or failures from a cognitive, behavioral, humanistic, constructivist, psychoanalytic, or other perspective. The perspective we use to interpret the reasons for successes or failures will be critical in determining future successes. This book approaches behavior management from a behavioral model perspective. We use this perspective to understand why our interventions work or fail. The **behavioral model** assumes that human behavior is determined by a person's interaction with his or her environment, which includes the physical setting such as the home, school, and classroom and the social surroundings such as peers, teachers, and parents. This perspective is a firmly grounded scientific approach.

This chapter will discuss how behavior is learned and will include a discussion of the differences and similarities between behavioral and cognitive views of learning. The role of observational learning along with definitions of the important terms *reinforcement* and *punishment* will be highlighted. A discussion of how reinforcers and punishers are conditioned will be provided. Finally, terms and concepts involved in stimulus control, shaping, chaining, and schedules of reinforcement will be defined and explained.

How Is Human Behavior Learned?

There are several theories of learning. Many of these theories seem solid conceptually, but there are some critical differences between and among them.

The Difference Between Cognitive and Behavioral Theories

Cognitive Theory. If we compare the two general theories of learning—cognitive and behavioral—we see there are major similarities and few differences. These differences, however, could have a large effect on how we view student behavior and how we respond to the behavior. As shown in Figure 2.1a, the basic cognitive model has four critical areas related to learning: environmental antecedents, cognitive processes, behavioral output, and environmental consequences. Antecedents are those things that occur just before the behavior, whereas consequences are those things that occur just

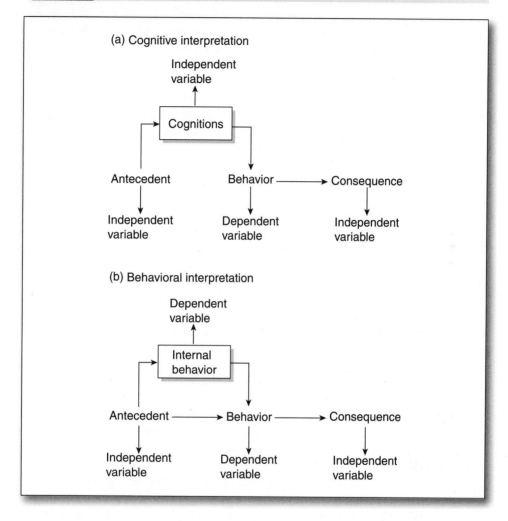

Figure 2.1 Models for Cognitive and Behavioral Interpretations of Behavior Causes

after the behavior. In between the antecedent and the behavior are cognitive processes. These processes can be shown through several cognitive theories. Consider the following cognitive theory as an example. Suppose we have a particular antecedent, such as telling a student to sit in his seat. This antecedent enters into the student's head and into his sensory registers. Note that there are almost limitless antecedent stimuli entering the sensory registers—such as other classroom sounds, lighting, and movement and tactile and kinesthetic stimuli, such as the feel of the chair and the position of the student's body. Thus, all these stimuli may enter the sensory registers. A student's attention to a particular antecedent stimulus will allow the stimulus to enter into the working or short-term memory. This memory system is what you're using when you read this book. The processes that are occurring in working memory have an impact on whether or not a student follows directions. For example, the way the student perceives your instruction to sit down is dependent on his past and present experiences and his future expectations. If you have had a good relationship with the student, you'll be more likely to have the student sit down. On the other hand, if the student sees you as being manipulative and not respectful of his needs, he may refuse to sit down.

Assume the student follows directions and sits down. You praise him for sitting down. How the student views the praise will affect whether he follows rules in the future. Your praise and the student's reaction to it will likely be placed in the student's long-term memory until a later time when you provide another instruction to the student. Therefore, a student's behavior is dependent not only on your instructions (environmental antecedent) and how you respond to the student's compliant or noncompliant behavior (environmental consequence) but also on how the student processes these antecedents, interprets past consequences, and has expectations for future consequences. As shown in Figure 2.1a, three things, called independent variables, affect a student's behavior. **Independent variables** are things under teacher control that are being manipulated in order to change a behavior. These variables have an effect on the student's behavior. A student's behavior can be called a dependent variable because its occurrence is dependent on the independent variables. **Dependent variables** are the behaviors that are changed when the independent variables are manipulated.

The environmental antecedents and consequences are labeled as "secondary" independent variables (signified here as lower case *i,* little *v*) because they are important but are not the main focus. Of course, how you provide an instruction and what you do after the student responds are important, but how the student perceives the instruction and consequence are critical here. Therefore, the cognitive processes of the student versus the environmental antecedents and consequences are the "primary" Independent Variables (signified as upper case *I,* capital *V*). So, where would an intervention be focused based on this theory? An intervention would focus not only on the antecedents and consequences of a behavior but also on how a student perceives or processes the information received from the antecedents and consequences.

If we had a student who was aggressive after she was provided an independent work assignment, we might focus the assignment. What type of assignment was it? Was it too hard? Was the student given adequate feedback in the past on her performance? In addition, we would try to "fix" the inner difficulty. That is, we would try to change how the student goes through the cognitive process leading to the aggressive episodes. To do so, we might provide the student with some other way to process the information. We could teach her to control her anger by talking to herself to calm down. We could also have her visualize something soothing such as walking through a park. We teach her how to deal with the anger she is feeling because it is this anger that causes her aggressive acts.

Behavioral Theory. As shown in Figure 2.1b, the behavioral model is similar to the cognitive one in that there are three environmental events: antecedents, behaviors, and consequences. (This model, like the cognitive one, is simplified for illustrative purposes.) The antecedents and consequences, however, are considered to be "primary"

*I*ndependent *V*ariables, whereas the cognitive position is that the antecedents and consequences are "secondary" *i*ndependent *v*ariables. The behavior in the behavioral model is the dependent variable, as it is in the cognitive model. The major difference occurs when we consider the role of inner cognitions or behaviors. From the behavioral perspective, inner behaviors are behaviors. They are dependent variables, not independent variables. What goes on inside the head is affected by what is occurring in the world around us. These inner behaviors are not causes of outward behavior independent of environmental events, but they are behaviors too.

So, what would we do differently from a behavioral perspective as opposed to a cognitive one? We would take the inner behaviors, such as feelings and thoughts, into consideration, but we would assume these inner behaviors were caused by what is occurring in the student's world. For example, consider again a student who becomes aggressive when he is given independent work to do. The anger he feels is important information for us to consider. He is angry and becomes aggressive. The anger and aggressiveness are assumed to come from the same source: assigned independent work. The cause of the student's aggressive behavior comes from the work, not from his anger. From a behavioral perspective, we would not focus specifically on the student's anger; we would instead focus on the antecedents (e.g., providing the work) and the consequences (e.g., the type of feedback the student gets when doing and finally completing the work). We might find the work is too hard or the student does not have the prerequisite skills to complete it adequately. We might find the student is tired and does not know he can ask for help. We might find there is little praise for his efforts, and only negative comments for errors. If we can learn what is causing the aggressive acts to occur, we can also determine what is causing the anger.

Interestingly, we might also want to provide other skills that would interfere with anger or prevent it from occurring in the first place, such as thinking about something that is soothing, going for a walk in the park, counting to 10 before acting, or practicing relaxation techniques. The difference between the cognitive and behavioral perspectives, then, is how we interpret the interventions and not necessarily which interventions are considered effective. Effective interventions are effective no matter if they are designed and used by cognitivists, humanists, constructivists, or behaviorists. The various interpretations of why these things work or do not work is what makes the perspectives of these theorists different, which explains why having a conceptual system is so critical. The conceptual system will allow us to interpret what we see. From a behavioral perspective, everything we do to change the cognitive processes is an environmental manipulation. Therefore, how we respond to what a student does can be viewed as an attempt to change the environment in some manner to lead to changes in the person's outward (overt) as well as inner behavior.

A person's overt behavior will tell us, to a certain extent, what is going on inside the individual. These overt behaviors often come in the form of "body language"; for example, when we're depressed, we may slump over. Facial expressions such as smiling when we're happy, physical acts such as punching others when we're angry, and verbal behavior such as saying we feel sad are other examples. All these adjectives—happy, angry, and sad—are labels of inferences we see or hear coming from others.

These labels do not cause behavior to occur but are behaviors that tell us something about particular individuals' environmental history.

The unifying aspect of any behavior management system should be determining if what is done actually works. If we rely on the student's behavior to tell us if what we're doing is working or not and we take this information into consideration in the future, we all should end up in the same place, no matter what model we follow. It is our position that the behavioral model will lead to this place of success sooner. As we'll see later, assessments required by law for students with disabilities when unwanted behaviors are demonstrated (called functional behavior assessments) are dependent on the assumptions of the behavioral model. Therefore, the behavioral model is used throughout this book to interpret why certain behaviors (positive as well as negative) are occurring.

The A-B-Cs of Learning

The simplest model to explain behavior is the **three-term contingency**, which is made up of the antecedent, behavior, and consequence (Cooper, Heron, & Heward, 2007; Malott & Trojan Suarez, 2008; Miltenberger, 2007; Skinner, 1953). These three aspects of behavior work together to determine if a behavior will be performed now and at a later time. For example, suppose a student, when called a name, hits another student. The name-calling would be the antecedent, and the hitting would be the behavior. Once the act is committed, there will be a consequence of some sort. The person who was hit might cry. The consequence, if it is a reinforcer (defined later), will make it more likely that the behavior will be repeated in the future under similar circumstances, with similar antecedents. Thus, the three aspects of behavior work in unison. Consequently, to understand why people behave as they do, we must understand what the antecedents, behaviors, and consequences are.

Although this model is simple at first glance, it is actually quite complex when we consider all the possible antecedents, behaviors, and consequences we are exposed to every day. In addition, the three-term contingency can be expanded to four, five, or more terms. Once we get past four terms, though, we need computer models to track the possibilities.

Consider what could happen when we move to a **four-term contingency**. The first term in the four-term contingency can be called a *setting event* (also termed a *contextual stimulus*). The **setting event** is something in the environment that sets the occasion for certain behaviors and changes the dynamics of the other three parts: antecedent (A), behavior (B), and consequence (C). For example, consider Figure 2.2. As shown in Figure 2.2a, we have a student who is given an assignment (antecedent). We see a refusal to complete the work (behavior) and the teacher reprimanding the student (consequence). If we move to a four-term contingency as shown in Figure 2.2b, we see a setting event (contextual stimulus), which could be the teacher who gives the assignment. In the first case, Teacher A gives the assignment. When Teacher A does this, the student refuses to complete the work and is reprimanded. When Teacher B gives the assignment, the student complies and the teacher praises her. Setting events change

Figure 2.2	Example of a Teaching Interaction With and Without Considering a Contextual Stimulus

(a)		Antecedent	Behavior	Consequence
		Teacher gives student assignment	Student refuses to work	Teacher provides reprimand
(b)	**Contextual Stimulus**	**Antecedent**	**Behavior**	**Consequence**
	Teacher A	Teacher gives student assignment	Student refuses to work	Teacher provides reprimand
	Teacher B	Teacher gives student assignment	Student completes work	Teacher provides praise

the dynamics of the other three terms. Therefore, to understand the causes of a student's behavior, we might have to consider more than the relationship among the three aspects of behavior; we might have to consider a fourth aspect—the context of the antecedent, behavior, and consequence.

What Is the Role of Observational Learning?

Modeling

Modeling is an important concept in the understanding of human behavior. **Modeling** is a demonstration of a behavior. According to Cooper et al. (2007), models can be planned or unplanned. A planned model might involve showing a student how to ask for help and then asking the student to imitate you. A teacher may show a video in class of students playing cooperatively with one another and then point out what is going on in the video that should be practiced in the classroom. The students are then told to imitate the model.

An unplanned model might involve a student watching another student who is working hard on his assignment and beginning her own work in a similar fashion. Unfortunately, unplanned models can occasion inappropriate behavior. If a student sees another student getting out of work by swearing at the teacher, he might also swear in order to get out of work. Both types of modeling are very powerful procedures in the classroom; the trick is to have students imitate appropriate models rather than inappropriate ones.

Modeling, then, is a possible reason for the display of many behaviors we see in school (Alberto & Troutman, 2009; Zirpoli, 2008). Students are faced with a multitude of models, both good and bad. Once a student imitates a model, however, it must be reinforced in some manner for the behavior—either wanted or unwanted—to continue. Therefore, it is important to know what reinforcement is and how to use it to strengthen the kinds of behaviors we want.

What Is Reinforcement?

Teachers should model appropriate behavior and request that students do the same, for example, by raising a hand to ask for help.

Over the years, there has been a great misunderstanding concerning what reinforcement is and what it is not. We hope to clear up this misunderstanding so that terminology will be used appropriately. **Reinforcement** is the presentation or removal of something as a consequence for behavior that increases the future likelihood of the behavior.

Reinforcement can be placed into two categories: positive and negative.

Positive Reinforcement

When we think of positive reinforcement, we might think of something that is given to a student. The "something" given to a student, however, is a **reward**. Rewards and reinforcers are not the same things. We give rewards, but they may not have an effect on behavior. On the other hand, positive reinforcers do have an effect on behavior. The definition of **positive reinforcement** has three components (Skinner, 1953). First, positive reinforcement requires something to be added to the environment. This something can be virtually anything. Praise, reprimands, spankings, good grades, or a surprised look: any of these can result in positive reinforcement. Second, positive reinforcement requires presenting this something contingent on behavior. The behavior must occur for something to be presented. When we behave, we change our environments in some manner. This change could be the presentation of something into our environments. As indicated by this second component of the definition of positive reinforcement, we do not reinforce people; instead, we reinforce behaviors. Third, positive reinforcement requires an increase in the future likelihood of the behavior. This statement does not mean the behavior has to increase in the future, only that the behavior is more likely to be repeated due to something being presented.

Thus, a reinforcer is different from a reward. Rewards do not require the increased likelihood of the behavior. If a reward is provided to a student and the behavior is more likely to occur again in the future, the reward becomes a reinforcer. The two are not the same. Therefore, if a teacher says she gave a student a reinforcer but, over time, nothing happened, she most likely gave a reward. Reinforcers, by definition, must increase the likelihood of the behavior.

Another frequent mistake is indicating that a student behaves in a certain manner to get a reinforcer. The correct way to look at this scenario is that a student behaves in a certain way because his behavior was reinforced under similar circumstances in the past. Remember reinforcers require an increase in the *future* likelihood of the behavior. Thus, positive reinforcers are defined by what was presented in the past and what occurs in the future (Cooper et al., 2007). The reason this point is so important is that, if a student is displaying a behavior (either wanted or unwanted), it can be assumed the behavior is occurring due to reinforcers presented in the past under similar circumstances. If we can determine what those past circumstances were, how they are similar to present circumstances, and what occurred after the behavior, we have gone a long way to finding the cause of this behavior. Once a likely cause is determined, we can design an effective management system. Assessments designed to find these causes are functional behavior assessments and are discussed in Chapter 4.

Note that positive reinforcers increase not only desirable behaviors but also undesirable ones. One mistake we make is to reinforce unwanted behavior inadvertently by doing something, such as providing attention for misbehavior. If we do provide attention for misbehavior and the attention serves to reinforce this student's unwanted behavior, the misbehavior will increase.

Negative Reinforcement

Negative reinforcement is frequently mistaken for punishment. They are not the same. Negative reinforcement actually makes a behavior more likely to occur. The definition of **negative reinforcement** has three components (Skinner, 1953). First, negative reinforcement requires the removal of something **aversive**, which is anything that results in an escape or **avoidance response** (i.e., a response that allows for the removal or delay of something aversive). Anything a student attempts to avoid or escape, such as a test, is probably aversive. Second, the removal of something aversive must be contingent on the behavior. That is, for an aversive to be removed, the behavior must occur. Third, there must be an increase in the future likelihood of the behavior.

At first, it seems difficult to provide examples of negative reinforcement. If we look around, though, we will see them everywhere. For example, what do we normally do when we see a police officer on the highway and are driving above the speed limit? We probably slow down. There is an ongoing aversive in this example. It is the threat or possibility of a ticket if we continue to speed. Slowing down is an attempt to avoid a ticket. Therefore, when we do not get stopped, our slowing down behavior is probably reinforced. We will be more likely to slow down again when we see a police officer. The police officer represents the ongoing aversive. Slowing down removes the threat of a ticket. The removal of the threat of a ticket is the negative reinforcer. Another example of a negative reinforcer is an alarm clock. When it goes off in the morning, we probably get out of bed to turn it off. To increase alarm effectiveness, we use the most obnoxious sound we can and place the clock as far away from the bed as possible. Paying our rent or mortgage on time is another example. We probably would incur a penalty for any bill we pay late. The avoidance of late charges is a potential negative reinforcer. Paying our taxes on time is another behavior that most of us do to avoid fines. Finally, some cars are equipped with buzzers that terminate only when seat belts are worn. The escape or avoidance of the buzzer is designed to serve as a negative reinforcer to get us to put on our seat belts.

Many times we attempt to get others around us to do things they may not want to do by using negative reinforcement. If we nag another person to take out the trash, that person may take out the trash to stop our nagging. The removal of the nagging, then, is functioning as a negative reinforcer. In the classroom, we frequently use negative reinforcement to get students to do things. We might warn students that, if they do not study, they will fail their test. Students would then study so as to avoid failing. We might warn students that, if they continue to misbehave, they will lose recess. Again, the students could behave well to avoid missing recess. The removal of threats and warnings based on specific behavior are negative reinforcers.

Although negative reinforcement can be effective in getting students to act as we would like, there are several problems with its use (Sulzer-Azaroff & Mayer, 1991; Zirpoli, 2008). First, negative reinforcement requires something aversive. Aversives are those things we try to escape or avoid. Therefore, the threat of a bad grade unless we study may be an aversive if it is something we attempt to avoid by actually studying. Second, negative reinforcement may occasion negative side effects. These side effects, including those listed in Table 2.1, occur due to the presence of an aversive. Finally, negative reinforcement may make it more difficult to learn. According to Catania (1998), it may take longer to learn a skill if negative reinforcement is used as the motivational technique. Catania discusses research with lower animals such as rats because human experimentation would be considered unethical, but examples can be seen every day in our lives. The model adapted from Catania to explain why learning is more difficult with negative reinforcement is shown in Figures 2.3 and 2.4. Figure 2.3 shows an instance of a behavior. The vertical line indicates a behavioral event. In this example, the behavioral event may be answering a question correctly. The flat line *before* the behavior indicates no behavior. The box represents an instance of positive reinforcement (in this case, verbal praise from the teacher). Notice the positive reinforcer comes *after* the student answers a question correctly.

Figure 2.4 shows an instance of negative reinforcement. The box shows an ongoing aversive for the student—the threat of a bad grade. The behavior in this example—answering a question correctly—is the same as that shown in Figure 2.3. As in the positive reinforcement example, the flat line in the negative reinforcement example (Figure 2.4) indicates no behavior. Notice, however, that negative reinforcement requires an ongoing aversive that comes *before* the behavior, which has the potential to bring about other behaviors that may interfere with answering a question correctly.

Table 2.1	Negative Side Effects of the Use of Aversives

The *possible* negative side effects include

- Making students avoid person providing aversives
- Making students fearful of person providing aversives
- Stopping other student behavior or provoking withdrawal
- Modeling the use of aversives
- Promoting negative self-esteem
- Promoting aggression toward the person providing aversives
- Negatively reinforcing the behavior of the person providing aversives
- Overusing aversives

Figure 2.3	Example of Learning Through a Positive Reinforcement Paradigm (Adapted From Catania, 1998)

Positive Reinforcement

Answers a question
correctly

Receives praise

Figure 2.4	Example of Learning Through a Negative Reinforcement Paradigm (Adapted From Catania, 1998)

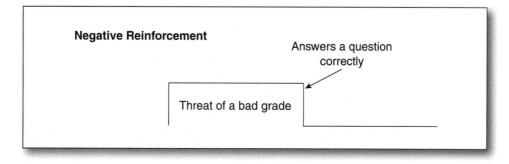

Negative Reinforcement

Answers a question
correctly

Threat of a bad grade

These behaviors could include getting nervous, thinking negatively (e.g., "I'm going to fail"), worrying that a wrong answer will affect one's grade, and so on. These behaviors slow learning. Everyday examples of the effects of ongoing aversives, such as when students display test anxiety, react with aggression to an assignment, or get emotional when an assignment is given, can be seen in the classroom. When these interfering behaviors occur, negative reinforcement may be present.

How does negative reinforcement affect classroom management? Teachers and other professionals may use negative reinforcement more often than other behavior management procedures. Unfortunately, they may be unaware they are using negative reinforcement to get the students to work. Behavior management systems that require warnings and threats are examples. If these threats and warnings are aversive to students, they will occasion behaviors that may interfere with learning. Examples include telling students their test will be extremely difficult, so, if they do not study, they will fail; explaining that, if students do not come to class on time, they will be sent to the principal's office; and warning that, if students continue to misbehave, their parents will be called or they will be sent to time-out.

Sidman (1989) warned of the use of negative reinforcers:

> Negative reinforcement is the first of two major categories of control that I define as coercive. (The second category . . . is punishment.) Both positive and negative reinforcers control our behavior, but I do not call positive reinforcement coercion. When we produce things or events that we usually consider useful, informative, or enjoyable for their own sake, we are under the control of positive consequences. But when we get rid of, diminish, escape, or avoid annoying, harmful, or threatening events, negative reinforcers are in control; with that kind of control, I speak of coercion. The distinction is not arbitrary. . . . Negative reinforcement . . . engenders side effects, often unintended, that poison our everyday social and institutional relationships. . . .
>
> A person who is largely sustained by positive reinforcement, frequently producing "good things," will feel quite differently about life than will a person who comes into contact most often with negative reinforcement, frequently having to escape from or prevent "bad things." (pp. 36–37)

The alternative to the use of negative reinforcement seems obvious: use positive reinforcement whenever possible. Instead of using threats and warnings, tell students what good things will come from studying for a test, coming to class on time, or displaying positive behavior in the classroom. This change is a difficult one to make because we are all exposed to negative reinforcement every day of our lives (pay rent on time or pay a penalty, pay taxes on time or pay a fine, go the speed limit or get a ticket). We are experts in the use of negative reinforcement; it is engrained in our society. Yet it is not the most effective manner of behavior management in the long run. Ultimately, we want our students to behave well because of the good things that come from doing so rather than the bad things that come from not doing so. We want our students to come to learn because of the positively reinforcing aspects that result rather than the negative things that occur when they do not act in a certain manner.

Now, the reply that frequently comes about is this: "Students should not always expect to get things in return." In addition, statements such as "motivation to learn comes from within the student" are common. When we make these statements, we are probably using negative reinforcement to get students to act the right way. Simply expecting a behavior to occur usually means that, if it does not occur, negative consequences will result. Therefore, effective behavior management requires us to think about human behavior differently than we have before. It requires us to be more effective in our planning and implementation of behavior management programs. It requires us to be teachers rather than taskmasters.

What Is Extinction?

To implement effective behavior management systems, we must learn about an important concept—extinction. We know if a behavior is reinforced (positively or negatively), it will continue in the future (Cooper et al., 2007). We also know if a behavior is not reinforced, it will cease to exist. According to Cooper et al. (2007), extinction is the process in which a behavior gradually decreases to its prereinforcement level or ceases to exist altogether. **Extinction** is the permanent removal of the source of reinforcement for a behavior. Consider our own behavior. If we were no longer paid to work, work behavior would probably stop, for that particular job at least. If our friend stopped talking to us, we probably would not have that friend for very long. If pushing on the gas pedal of our car no longer made it go forward, we probably would stop driving that car. In all these examples, when reinforcement is removed, we stop engaging in the behavior for that particular job, with that particular friend, or in that particular car. Student behavior is the same as ours. If a student does not receive good grades for hard work, hard work will stop, if good grades are functioning as reinforcers for working hard. If a student no longer receives our attention for asking a question properly, asking questions properly will decrease if our attention functioned as the reinforcer for this behavior. In addition, if we no longer show anger when a student misbehaves, the student might stop misbehaving if our anger served as the reinforcer for the misbehavior.

Extinction is critical in that it can be used to decrease behaviors we do not want. Extinction has four problems, however. First, extinction requires us to know what is reinforcing a behavior. If the source of reinforcement cannot be determined, extinction cannot be used. Determining the source of reinforcement is covered in Chapter 4. Teachers sometimes report that extinction does not work, saying, "I ignored the student's misbehavior, and it continued to occur." Unfortunately, in these cases, extinction was not being used. By definition, extinction works. Therefore, the teachers in this example are mistaken in assuming that teacher attention was functioning as a reinforcer. Likely, the reinforcement is coming from another source, such as other students.

The second problem with extinction is that it is frequently accompanied by an increase in some aspect of the behavior (Cooper et al., 2007). This increase is called an **extinction burst**, a rapid increase in the frequency, duration, or intensity of the behavior (see Figure 2.5). These bursts, which we have all experienced, are often difficult to

Figure 2.5	Example of an Extinction Burst and Spontaneous Recovery for Tantrum Behavior

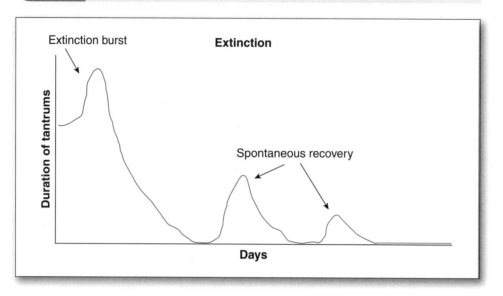

live through. Take a baby who will not sleep through the night. Once the baby is fed, changed, and warm, we may choose to ignore the crying, so she will learn to sleep through the night. We keep track of the behavior and are likely to see an increase in the loudness and duration of the crying. This behavior is an extinction burst. What happens to our behavior when a friend or partner ignores us? We will probably see a burst in our own behavior. We may get louder when trying to talk to our friend or partner, we may speak faster, or we may tap the person on the shoulder and say, "Please listen to me!" When an extinction burst occurs, it is safe to assume we have removed the source of reinforcement. Removing the source of reinforcement is aversive to the individual; doing so may bring about the negative side effects of aversives (see Table 2.1). The burst does, however, tell us we are on the right track and to continue on if, and only if, the burst is not dangerous to the person or to others and we can live through the burst of behavior. If we see the burst as causing more harm than good, extinction should stop. Similarly, if we do not think we can live through the extinction burst, we should not attempt extinction in the first place. The problem with beginning extinction and then stopping its use because we cannot tolerate the burst is that it will most likely reinforce the individual's outburst. Thus, nontechnically speaking, what we do by stopping an extinction program because we cannot live through the burst is to teach the individual this lesson: When people try to change my behavior by doing something that I don't like, all I have to do is increase the frequency, duration, or intensity of that behavior to get them to stop. Therefore, although extinction can be a very important tool to use to decrease a behavior problem, side effects accompany its use. If we cannot deal with the side effects of extinction, we should not use it.

Third, even when the behavior seems to be eliminated, it can come back at various times. This phenomenon is called **spontaneous recovery** (Cooper et al., 2007). There are several theories concerning why spontaneous recovery takes place, but a discussion of these theories is beyond the purpose of this book. The important things to know about spontaneous recovery are that it can happen and it can be stopped. When a behavior spontaneously reoccurs, the extinction program must remain in place. If the behavior is inadvertently reinforced, it will strengthen and become a problem again. Thus, spontaneous recovery describes a situation in which we believe the behavior is gone, but it comes back and surprises us—it catches us off guard. We usually describe spontaneous recovery in lay terms by saying the student is testing us. If we are able to keep the extinction program in place, the behavior will again be eliminated. The next time there is spontaneous recovery, it should be at a lower level than before and take less time to eliminate. Figure 2.5 shows a model of spontaneous recovery for tantrum behavior. It is important to remember to refrain from inadvertently reinforcing this recovery of behavior.

A fourth problem with extinction is that it does not teach a desirable behavior; instead, it only eliminates an unwanted one. Therefore, if we use extinction, we should always incorporate a positive reinforcement program for a behavior we want to take the place of the behavior we don't want. This point is discussed in more depth in Chapter 6.

What Is Punishment?

Although professionals differ at times in terms of defining punishment (see Catania, 1998; Michael, 1993; Sidman, 1989; Skinner, 1953), we define **punishment** using the more commonly accepted definition—presentation or removal of something as a consequence for behavior that reduces the future likelihood of the behavior. Similar to reinforcement, punishment can be placed into two categories: positive and negative.

Positive Punishment

The definition of **positive punishment** has three components (Miltenberger, 2007). First, positive punishment requires that something be added to the environment. In this case, we add something aversive. Second, positive punishment requires presenting the aversive contingent on the behavior. Finally, positive punishment requires a decrease in the future likelihood of the behavior. If there is no decrease in the likelihood of the behavior being repeated in the future, there is no punishment. Therefore, punishment is essentially the opposite of reinforcement. Remember, reinforcement results in an increase in the future likelihood of the behavior, whereas punishment requires a decrease.

This definition calls for us to view what happens to the behavior once something is presented. Assuming a spanking functions as a punisher is a mistake. A spanking may function as a reinforcer (we describe why later). Punishers, like reinforcers, cannot be defined beforehand. Again, this view is foreign to the way we have been taught. We are taught that punishers are what we do not like, whereas reinforcers are what we like. What is likeable or not likeable, however, is not always the same for all people. Just because we would not like to be reprimanded by a teacher but would like to achieve good grades does not make the same true for others.

Although punishment does decrease the likelihood of a behavior being repeated in the future, there are several problems with its use. In fact, many professionals in the field discourage the use of punishment techniques (see Sidman, 1989, for a discussion on the use of coercion). Some professionals say punishment does not work. We must ask, however, "Work for what?" Punishment does work in reducing the likelihood of the behavior. On the other hand, punishment may not result in long-term changes. Once punishment is that withdrawn, the changes that have come about may not last. The same is true of reinforcement, however. Another, and perhaps most critical, disadvantage of positive punishment is that it requires the presentation of something aversive. The same negative side effects of negative reinforcement come into play here. The problems associated with the use of aversives, as shown in Table 2.1, are true of positive punishment procedures. Therefore, we should attempt to avoid the use of positive punishment and use it only as a last resort.

Negative Punishment

Negative punishment also decreases the likelihood of a behavior being repeated in the future. Unlike positive punishment, which requires the presentation of something aversive, **negative punishment** requires the removal of something reinforcing contingent on a behavior (Miltenberger, 2007). For example, terminating computer time for a day for sidestepping filters and accessing inappropriate websites may be a negative punisher if the student stops accessing inappropriate websites in the future. Negative punishment works based on extinction principles. Once a source of reinforcement is removed from a behavior, the behavior will extinguish. With negative punishment, if the source of reinforcement is removed from the behavior for even a short period, the behavior will be less likely to occur in the future.

As with negative reinforcement and positive punishment, negative punishment has unwanted side effects. The removal of a reinforcer can be said to be aversive. Therefore, several of the side effects of the use of aversives are present when one uses negative punishment (see Table 2.1). The main advantage negative punishment has over positive punishment and negative reinforcement is that negative punishment is not an *active* presentation of an aversive. Thus, negative punishment can be seen as a more desirable method of behavior management than the other two (positive punishment or negative reinforcement), but positive reinforcement is the most desirable of the four (positive reinforcement, negative reinforcement, positive punishment, and negative punishment).

How Do We Distinguish Between Reinforcers and Punishers?

As shown in Figure 2.6, we can determine what type of reinforcer or punisher is in effect for a particular behavior. If something is ever presented, we have a "positive" something. If something is removed, we have a "negative" something. Notice that "positive" does not mean "something good" and "negative" does not mean "something bad." In addition, if the likelihood of the behavior increases in the future, we have a reinforcer, and if the likelihood of the behavior decreases in the future, we have a punisher.

| Figure 2.6 | Reinforcement and Punishment Grid |

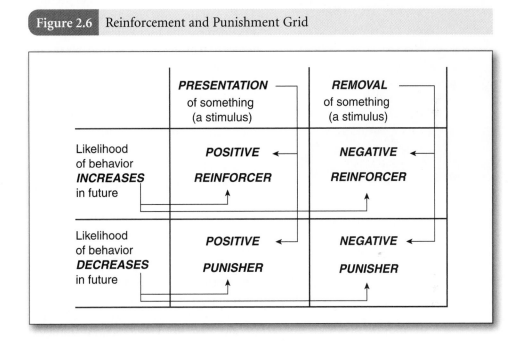

How Are Reinforcers and Punishers Learned?

Typically, we do not think of how something becomes reinforcing or aversive to us. Our reinforcers and punishers likely change throughout our lives. Reinforcers and punishers can be categorized into two areas: primary or secondary.

Primary and Secondary Positive Reinforcers

Primary Positive Reinforcers. **Primary positive reinforcers**, also called *unconditioned reinforcers*, are those things that are biologically important (Miltenberger, 2007). They are inborn. These reinforcers are those things that allow for the survival of the species. Primary reinforcers include food, water, warmth, and sex. For example, when we're hungry and it has been a long time since we've eaten, food will function as a strong

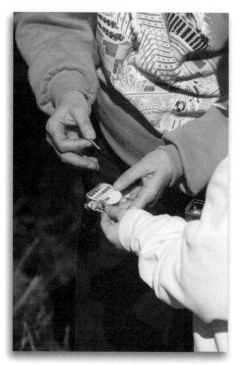

Teachers can reinforce positive student behavior with a secondary reinforcer (e.g., a token).

reinforcer. Consequently, we will behave in some manner because this behavior has resulted in our getting food in the past under similar circumstances.

Secondary Positive Reinforcers. Secondary positive reinforcers, also called *conditioned reinforcers,* are those things that are learned as we interact with our environment (Miltenberger, 2007). If we look around, we will see unlimited numbers of secondary reinforcers; the clothes we wear, the cars we drive, and the cell phones we use are all examples of secondary reinforcers. Two of the most common secondary reinforcers (if they increase the future likelihood of a behavior) are money and praise. Praise is probably the most common secondary reinforcer in schools. Money is probably the most common reinforcer at work. Other examples of secondary reinforcers are grades, points, and awards.

Secondary reinforcers are learned. We are not born with an appreciation for money or praise. Many students in school still do not have an appreciation for good grades. Still others react to praise as if we are ridiculing them. Why do these stimuli function as reinforcers for some and as punishers for others? The reason is an individual's conditioning history.

Conditioning of Secondary Positive Reinforcers. At birth, an individual will respond to a limited number of reinforcers, and these are only primary reinforcers. When parents, for example, provide a primary reinforcer such as food to a baby, however, they are also providing other things such as attention, the sound of their voices, the look of their faces, and the way they hold the baby, and these provisions may have no effect on the child; that is, they are "neutral." These "neutral" things (i.e., stimuli) are paired with the primary reinforcer (e.g., food). Through this pairing, these neutral things will take on reinforcing properties. In this model, shown in Figure 2.7, the pairing is critical in the conditioning of praise as a secondary reinforcer. Figure 2.8 also shows conditioning taking place, but this conditioning is slightly different from that shown in Figure 2.7. In this example, the good grades (neutral stimulus) are paired with a previously conditioned one (praise). Therefore, the conditioning of secondary reinforcers can grow exponentially. One potential problem with secondary reinforcers is that they will lose their reinforcing properties unless they are occasionally paired with the same or different reinforcers.

At some point in time, we will begin to pair secondary reinforcers with reinforcers different from those that were initially paired. When we have the type of multiple pairings as shown in Figure 2.9, we have what is called a **generalized reinforcer**—a reinforcer paired with several other reinforcers (both primary and secondary). Thus, a generalized reinforcer is not dependent on the same reinforcer

Figure 2.7	Conditioning of New Secondary Reinforcer via Pairing With a Primary Reinforcer

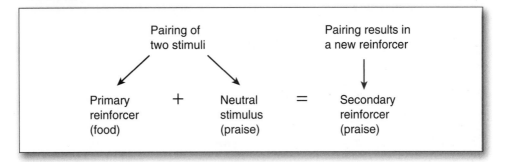

Figure 2.8	Conditioning of New Secondary Reinforcer via Pairing With an Established Secondary Reinforcer

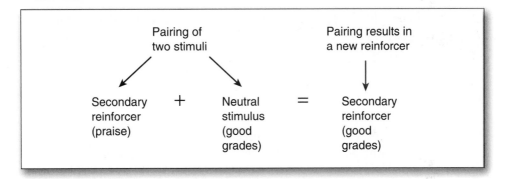

used for conditioning, such as that shown in Figure 2.7 or 2.8. Figure 2.9 shows the pairing of good grades with several other reinforcers, such as hugs, privileges, and special prizes, making good grades a generalized reinforcer. The best example of a generalized reinforcer is money. Money can buy not only food but also other primary reinforcers, such as shelter, and secondary reinforcers, such as expensive cars or designer jeans. The advantage of a generalized reinforcer is that, when one of the reinforcers with which it is paired is removed, it will still be a reinforcer. Therefore, if money could no longer buy food, money would still be reinforcing because it could buy shelter and other reinforcers.

To see this conditioning occur in an explicit manner, watch a teacher work with a student with severe or profound intellectual disabilities. A student's response might be reinforced with food such as candy because food is a primary reinforcer. The teacher could provide the candy and see what the student does. The teacher will also provide praise when the candy is being provided. What the teacher is doing is not only teaching a particular response but also teaching (conditioning) praise as a reinforcer.

| Figure 2.9 | Generalized Conditioning of a Secondary Reinforcer via Pairing With Several Reinforcers |

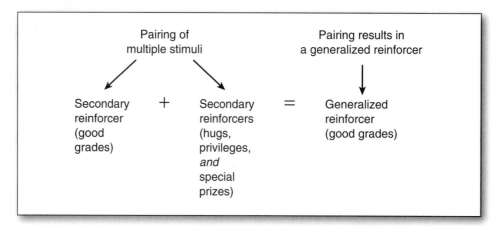

Eventually, the provision of candy will gradually be faded out but praise will continue to be used as a reinforcer.

Typically, we do not condition reinforcers in such an explicit manner. The conditioning process occurs naturally. Here is what makes us all different from one another in terms of motivators. We all have different learning histories or life experiences, and these teach us that some things are reinforcers and others are not. The reason grades are reinforcing for some and not for others has to do with past experiences with grades. Students who are reinforced for good grades likely have parents who pair good grades with other reinforcers such as praise, or these students have had their good grades paired with reinforcers in some other manner in the past. Another possibility is that bad grades have been paired with punishers; therefore, the students avoid the bad grades by getting good ones. In this case, bad grades have undergone conditioning of another sort, described below.

Primary and Secondary Aversives

There are two major categories of aversives—primary and secondary.

Primary Aversives. Similar to primary reinforcers are primary aversives. **Primary aversives** are things that are not learned but that result in an escape or avoidance response (Cooper et al., 2007; Kazdin, 2001). These things are aversive to humans from the time we are born. Examples are electric shock, nauseating smells and tastes, and pain.

Secondary Aversives. **Secondary aversives** are those things that are learned that result in an escape or avoidance response (Cooper et al., 2007; Kazdin, 2001). These things are not aversive from the time we are born. Examples are reprimands, praise, grades, and some people. These things were originally neutral to us but took on conditioned aversive properties because of our experiences. For example, we are not born trying to escape reprimands. Poor grades are not something we consider to be bad unless we learn they are not good. How does this learning or conditioning take place?

Conditioning of Secondary Aversives. The conditioning process of secondary aversives is the same as that for secondary positive reinforcers. Initially, a primary aversive such as pain is paired with something that is neutral, such as the word *no*. The word *no* will take on conditioned aversive properties through time (Dorsey, Iwata, Ong, & McSween, 1980; Miltenberger, 2007). In fact, the word *no* probably becomes a generalized conditioned aversive because it is usually paired with a variety of other primary and secondary aversives over time. For example, if a small child approaches a hot stove and we shout "no" just before she touches the stove and gets burned, the word *no* is likely to take on aversive properties. Similarly, if reprimands are paired with spankings, reprimands are likely to take on aversive properties. Therefore, if we watch a student try to avoid something or someone, it is highly probable this something or person has been paired with an aversive. In the same manner as with secondary positive reinforcers, secondary aversives can result from something neutral being paired with a previously conditioned secondary aversive. For example, we could pair bad grades (neutral) with a reprimand (previously conditioned secondary aversive) and condition bad grades to be aversive.

Advantage and Disadvantage of Conditioning of Positive Reinforcers and Aversives. The major advantage associated with all this conditioning is that it enables us to function much more successfully in a culture or society. Most of us ultimately learn the boundaries by which we must live in our culture through this conditioning. If we think of a classroom as a culture, we can see how critical it is for our students to learn what the accepted reinforcers and punishers are and respond accordingly. Therefore, we learn that good grades are reinforcing and that misbehavior in the classroom will result in a reprimand (an aversive).

Unfortunately, conditioning can go the other way as well. Conditioning is not subjective but objective. We do not only condition "desirable" things to be positive reinforcers and "undesirable" things to be aversive. We can inadvertently do just the opposite. Consider a student who has learned that attention is a reinforcer. This student will behave in some manner because doing so has resulted in attention in the past under similar circumstances. Now suppose the only time this student gets attention (a conditioned positive reinforcer) is when he misbehaves. When the student misbehaves, he is reprimanded. Reprimands are always paired with attention. Therefore, reprimands can take on reinforcing properties (Martin & Pear, 2007). Essentially, if the attention the student gets is negative attention, he will continue to misbehave.

Not only can we condition social interaction to be reinforcing, but we can condition what should be primary aversives such as spankings, as secondary positive reinforcers (Martin & Pear, 2007). Say a father wants to know why his three-year-old daughter hits her baby brother. When she hits her brother, the father spanks her. He is confused about why she would continue to hit her brother when he is punishing her. The first thing we should consider is whether or not the spankings are functioning as a punisher. Because she continues to hit her brother, the spankings may actually be functioning as a reinforcer. Perhaps she does not get as much attention as she used to before her brother was born. The father says he is preoccupied with the baby and does not give her as much attention as he used to. If we consider the conditioning of reinforcers, we can develop a hypothesis about what is going on. First, we know the spankings were probably a primary aversive because they usually brought about pain. Second, we can assume attention for the daughter is a reinforcer. Before her baby brother was born, she received her father's full attention. Third, we can assume spankings were paired with attention from the father. Therefore, we can see a scenario in which a primary aversive (spanking) is paired with a secondary positive reinforcer (attention), and this pairing conditions the aversive as a secondary positive reinforcer. In this case, the spankings were actually functioning as a positive reinforcer.

This example shows how something we would probably deem to be a punisher actually functions as a reinforcer. Although this fact seems counterintuitive, it occurs frequently. Therefore, the critical thing we can learn from these instances is not to define a reinforcer or punisher beforehand but to determine if something is a reinforcer or punisher after viewing what happens to the behavior when the consequence is provided.

Deprivation and Satiation States

The effectiveness of anything as a reinforcer depends on motivating operations (Cooper et al., 2007; Michael, 2004). **Motivating operations** are environmental variables that change the reinforcing value of something. Motivating operations take two forms. First, if a person has been deprived of something, such as food, the value of the food increases as a reinforcer. Imagine it has been a long time since you have eaten a good home-cooked meal. You say you're "starving" and go home for a holiday. If, once you arrive, your mother asks you to set the table so the family can eat, the likelihood that you will set the table quickly increases because you are hungry and have been deprived of a good home-cooked meal. You have been in a state of deprivation. **Deprivation** can be defined as an increase in the reinforcing value of something due to a lack of it. When the reinforcing value of something increases, it is called an establishing operation. An **establishing operation** is defined as an environmental event that increases the value of something as a reinforcer.

Second, if a person has had ample access to something, such as food, the value of food may decrease as a reinforcer (at least until the person becomes hungry again). Suppose you arrive home from college for a holiday and your mother gives you a rather large meal. After the meal, she tells you that, if you clear the table, she will give you more to eat. The likelihood that more food will motivate you to clear the table is probably low. You might clear the table for other reasons, but not for more food. In this case, you have been satiated by the food. Therefore, **satiation** is a decrease in reinforcer effectiveness due to receiving "a lot" of that reinforcer, usually in a short period. When the reinforcing value of something decreases, it is called an abolishing operation. An **abolishing operation** is defined as an environmental event that decreases the reinforcing value of something.

The critical point here is that what is reinforcing for a student can change throughout the week, day, or hour depending on motivating operations. Teachers should continuously monitor the effects of reinforcers and vary the types of reinforcers they use.

What Is Stimulus Control?

Stimulus control refers to a situation in which a behavior is changed because of the provision or removal of an antecedent stimulus (Cooper et al., 2007). This antecedent stimulus is something present, given, or taken away just prior to the occurrence of a behavior. Consider a student's behavior, such as taking her seat. A teacher has stimulus control over the student's in-seat behavior if he tells the student to sit down (antecedent stimulus), and she sits down (behavior). If the teacher does not have stimulus control, the student would not consistently sit in her seat when told to do so.

Stimulus control is all around us. When we come to a stop sign (antecedent stimulus), we usually stop (behavior). This antecedent stimulus, called a discriminative stimulus, is symbolized by S^D. Thus, a stop sign is an S^D for stopping. In the presence of a stop sign (antecedent stimulus), we are more likely to stop (behavior). A green light is an S^D for going through an intersection. A **discriminative stimulus** is essentially a signal indicating a response in its presence was reinforced in the past and will likely result in a reinforcer in the future. In the classroom, teachers who flick the lights as an indication it is time to get to work are using stimulus control if the students comply. We hope the flickering light is an S^D for getting into one's seat and working. Classroom rules are set up to be S^D's for appropriate behaviors. If these rules are S^D's, students will follow the rules.

We can further this concept by showing two categories of discriminative stimuli. The first involves S^{D+} and S^{D-}. An S^{D+} indicates a behavior occurring in its presence was positively reinforced in the past. For example, if we provide a good citizen award to a student who followed directions (S^{D+}), we will make it more likely the behavior will occur again under similar circumstances (assuming that good citizen awards are reinforcers). An S^{D-} is an indication that a behavior (escape or avoidance) that occurred in the presence of this stimulus was negatively reinforced in the past. Another way to look at the S^{D-} is as a punishment if an escape or avoidance response is not made. For example, Mr. Yuk labels on medicine bottles are attempts at gaining stimulus control over not consuming bottle contents. The labels can be interpreted as indications that consuming the contents will result in sickness or not consuming the contents (avoiding them) will result in staying well (not getting sick). Similarly, if one is speeding, seeing a police officer on the highway is an S^{D-} for slowing down to avoid a ticket. The second category of discriminative stimulus is an **S-delta** or S^Δ. The S^Δ is an indication that a behavior in its presence will not be reinforced. Faculty members who put up "do not disturb" signs on their doors are attempting to control behavior by indicating that the probability of reinforcement for knocking (i.e., getting the door to open) is very low or nonexistent.

The way we gain stimulus control over a behavior is to reinforce this behavior in the presence of something but not in the presence of something else (Cooper et al., 2007). Red stoplights generally gain control over stopping behavior because going through the red light may result in negative consequences, whereas stopping at the red light generally allows you to avoid these negative consequences. Going through a green light generally is reinforcing because it allows us to avoid getting yelled at from those behind us if we were to stop and enables us to get to our destination more quickly. Telling students to line up at the door will gain stimulus control if we reinforce this behavior when students line up at the door appropriately but do not reinforce it when they do not. Reinforcing in the presence of something (the S^D) while not reinforcing in the presence of something else (S^Δ) is called **differential reinforcement.** (Differential reinforcement is used in another manner described below.)

What Is Shaping?

Shaping is the reinforcement of successive approximations of behavior (Cooper et al., 2007; Skinner, 1953). We reinforce when the behavior gets closer to the goal behavior. Think of behavior as a lump of clay. Our goal is to mold this clay into a bowl. At the start, the clay looks nothing like a bowl. As we gradually mold the clay, it begins to look more and more like a bowl until it becomes a bowl. Human behavior is much the same, especially in schools. When we begin to teach a student to write a paper, rarely is the paper perfect. There are usually spelling errors, grammatical errors, and content errors. If we were to grade student essays based on our ideal of a well-written paper from the beginning, most students would fail. What we can do is gradually change the students' paper-writing skills over time until, after many drafts, their papers begin to meet our ideal. We do so by having steps along the way. Because our criterion is set at a lower level for the first draft, the initial paper may look nothing like the final version. Each successive version should become cleaner and cleaner until the final product is acceptable.

Therefore, much of our teaching is shaping the skills of our students. Although the first instance of the behavior is acceptable now, it will not be later. A poor paper that was acceptable earlier is not reinforced now. The criteria change and become more stringent when the individual student can meet them successfully. We also see the process of shaping with children when they begin to talk. A mother gets excited when she hears her young child say "mmm." She hugs the child and makes a big deal about it. After a while of hearing "mmm," she begins to lose interest until the child says "mmmo." She again gets excited until the child says "mmmooom." Notice how the new sounds are reinforced while the former ones are ignored. Essentially, the child saying "mommy" is being shaped. This shaping, then, is achieved through differential reinforcement. One behavior is not reinforced while another one is.

Shaping may or may not be planned. We typically do not systematically implement a "say *mommy*" program. Shaping, however, occurs naturally as we interact with our environment. Thus, inappropriate or unwanted behaviors as well as positive or appropriate ones can be shaped in this interaction. Unfortunately, we shape the unwanted behaviors of our children too often. Take, for example, the case of a child not sleeping through the night. Many people will tell you to let the child cry himself to sleep as long as he is dry, fed, and warm, but that is very difficult for parents to do. With good intentions, parents may start by trying to ignore the crying child. At some point, the crying will get to the parents, and one or both parents will go to the child's room, pick him up, and comfort him. The next time the parents attempt to ignore the crying, they may wait for a longer period of time. At some point, though, they might break down and go the child's room. This cycle will continue, thereby shaping the duration and intensity of the child's crying. In the classroom, a similar phenomenon occurs. A teacher might ignore minor inappropriate behavior until the behavior reaches a point at which it cannot be ignored. When attention is then provided, if attention is a reinforcer, the more serious behavior will occur more rapidly and last until attention is gained. Therefore, we can shape unwanted behaviors into serious obstacles to learning.

While this shaping is going on, parents and teachers are often unaware of what is happening. They might not even notice the increasing duration, frequency, or magnitude of the behavior. This situation is similar to one in which parents know their children are growing physically but cannot notice this growth from day to day. Thus, it is crucial to understand that unwanted behavior can be unknowingly shaped by teachers inadvertently reinforcing increased levels of the behavior.

What Is Chaining?

Chaining is a concept that describes the process wherein individual behaviors are put together to form a more complex behavior (Skinner, 1953). These individual behaviors are called links. Each link serves a dual purpose, called a *dual stimulus function* (Cooper et al., 2007). Each link serves as an S^D for the next link and as a conditioned reinforcer for the previous link. This dual function of all the steps except the first and last links is called a **dual stimulus function**. Therefore, chaining requires the identification of a **task analysis**—breaking a task into several links or steps. Figure 2.10 shows such a task analysis for the completion of a research paper. (The links are rather large and could be further broken down into sub-behaviors.) As shown in the figure, the first link in a chain acts as an S^D for the next link. The completion of the first link sets the occasion for the second. The second link serves as a conditioned reinforcer for the first link because being able to begin the second link can occur only after the first link is completed. The completion of the second link is also an S^D for the next link, and so on. The final link is a conditioned reinforcer for the previous link only. Of course, the completion of the final link is reinforced by the end product. As shown, the grade for the paper is the reinforcer (hopefully) for turning it in.

If you think about it, virtually everything we do, we do in a chain. For example, driving a car requires behaviors that must be put together, such as getting into the car, putting on the seat belt, putting the key into the ignition, and so on. Putting together a child's toy on her birthday also requires a chain of behavior. In fact, if we think about the instructions, they show what the chain of behaviors is to put the toy together. There are three

| Figure 2.10 | Task Analysis for Writing a Research Paper |

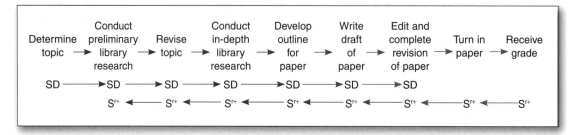

NOTE: Figure shows the dual stimulus function of each behavior. SD = discriminative stimulus and S^{r+} = secondary positive reinforcing stimulus.

ways to teach through the use of chaining: total task or whole task chaining, forward chaining, and backward chaining. Because this book is oriented toward preventing or responding to behavior difficulties, only a brief discussion of each of the chaining methods is presented; these methods are the ones related to teaching behaviors, either academic or adaptive. The concept of chaining can also be used to decrease the probability of a behavior occurring. This approach to chaining is covered in Chapter 6.

Total or Whole Task Chaining

Total or **whole task chaining** (Cooper et al., 2007) involves teaching the chain of behaviors all at once. Thus, the steps to completing a research paper would be taught together. Most of us learn a chain of behaviors through this approach.

Forward Chaining

Forward chaining involves teaching the first step first until the student masters it (Cooper et al., 2007). Once the student can complete the first step independently, the first and second steps are taught together. Once the student can complete the first two steps independently, the first three steps are taught together, and so on, until all the steps have been taught and are mastered.

Backward Chaining

Backward chaining is an approach that involves teaching the student to complete the final step of the chain until it is mastered (Cooper et al., 2007). For example, if we were teaching a student how to make a sandwich, we would make the sandwich up to the point of putting the two slices of bread together. The student would be taught first how to put the slices together. Once the last step has been mastered, the next-to-last step and the last step are taught until mastered, such as putting the mustard on one slice and then putting the slices together, and so on. In this way, the teacher teaches the task by beginning instruction with the last behavior or link and working back though the chain until the first behavior is reached, such as taking out the bread from the cupboard. One advantage of backward chaining is the conditioning of each step as a reinforcer. Then, the next-to-last step is paired with the final step, which conditions the next-to-last step to be a conditioned reinforcer, and so on.

What Are Schedules of Reinforcement?

What reinforcement is and what it is not have already been discussed. Reinforcement occurs every day, yet reinforcement for each and every behavior does not necessarily occur. How often a behavior is reinforced will partially determine how difficult it will be to extinguish the behavior. Therefore, to work successfully with behavior problems, we must know the basic schedules of reinforcement (Ferster & Skinner, 1957). **Schedules of reinforcement** are the points at which reinforcers are delivered for the purpose of increasing or maintaining behavior (see Table 2.2).

Table 2.2	Definitions of the Four Basic Schedules of Reinforcement (Fixed Interval, Variable Interval, Fixed Ratio, and Variable Ratio)

- *Fixed interval (FI):* Reinforcement is delivered for the *first* appropriate response occurring after a specified period of time.
- *Variable interval (VI):* Reinforcement is delivered for the *first* appropriate response occurring after an average period of time.
- *Fixed ratio (FR):* Reinforcement is delivered after a specified number of correct responses.
- *Variable ratio (VR):* Reinforcement is delivered after an average number of correct responses.

Continuous Reinforcement Schedule

A **continuous reinforcement schedule** (also called fixed-ratio one or FR-1) is a schedule in which each time a student displays a particular behavior it is reinforced. For example, if a student talks out three times in class and is given attention each of those three times, she is on a continuous reinforcement schedule (assuming attention is a reinforcer for her). Because a continuous reinforcement schedule strengthens a behavior, continuous reinforcement schedules should be used when we are attempting to teach a behavior (Cooper et al., 2007). Unfortunately, continuous reinforcement schedules strengthen not only positive behaviors but also unwanted ones.

In terms of unwanted behaviors, continuous reinforcement schedules have one positive attribute: behaviors that are reinforced on continuous reinforcement schedules tend to extinguish rather quickly. An extinction burst may still occur, but generally it takes a short amount of time for the behavior to stop compared with behaviors that are on intermittent reinforcement schedules.

Intermittent Reinforcement Schedules

When an individual's behavior is reinforced, the reinforcement may not occur after each occasion of the behavior; this situation describes an **intermittent reinforcement schedule**. There are four basic intermittent schedules of reinforcement: fixed interval, variable interval, fixed ratio, and variable ratio.

Fixed-Interval Schedule. A **fixed-interval schedule of reinforcement** is defined as reinforcement of the first response after a set time has elapsed. The definition does not say reinforcement occurs after a set amount of time has elapsed; a response is critical to the definition. For example, suppose your mail came at an exact time of the day, say 2:00 PM (signified FI-2:00 PM). Also suppose you are expecting some important mail to come, but you do not know which day. It is unlikely that you would go to the mailbox during the early part of the day; the likelihood of your going to the mailbox increases as it approaches 2:00 PM. As 2:00 PM approaches, the rate of your response looks similar to that shown in Figure 2.11a. This response pattern will be repeated on successive days. This pattern is called a fixed-interval scallop. The first response after the mail comes is reinforced. It does not matter how many times you go to the mailbox during the day; only one response will be reinforced, and that is the response that occurs after the mail has come. Therefore, a fixed-interval schedule of reinforcement produces a lower rate of response, because only one response is required for reinforcement and a noncontinuous response rate (i.e., the rate is low and then increases as the time gets nearer).

Another example of a fixed-interval schedule of reinforcement is telling students the computer they want to use is not available for half an hour; they cannot access the computer for 30 minutes but can immediately start a computer game after that time (FI-30 minutes). Their "going to the computer" behavior will not be reinforced until the 30 minutes has elapsed.

Variable-Interval Schedule. A **variable-interval schedule of reinforcement** involves reinforcement of the first response after an average amount of time has elapsed. For example, suppose the mail in the above example does not come at 2:00 PM every day, but, on average, it comes at 2:00 PM (signified as VI-2:00 PM). Sometimes the mail comes at 10:00 AM, sometimes at 4:00 PM, and sometimes at 2:00 PM, but you never know when the mail will come. Therefore, your response rate may look more like

| **Figure 2.11** | Response Rates With Fixed-Interval, Variable-Interval, Fixed-Ratio, and Variable-Ratio Schedules of Reinforcement |

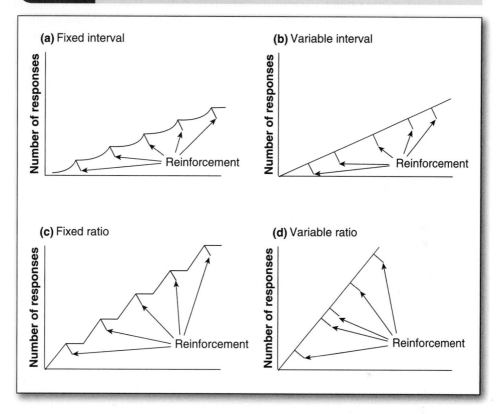

that in Figure 2.11b. You cannot anticipate when the reinforcement (i.e., mail) will come. Therefore, you continue to go to the mailbox throughout the day to check for mail.

Another example is making a phone call. Imagine you call someone and get a busy signal. Now suppose you know exactly when the other person will get off the phone, that the person you are trying to call will spend some length of time on the phone (say 30 minutes, signified as FI-30 minutes). Your calling behavior will probably look more like the response pattern depicted in Figure 2.11a. Usually, however, you do not have this information. So you would probably hit the redial button several times quickly until your rate of response decreased and you spaced out your calling. After a while, your rate would become similar to that shown in Figure 2.11b (VI-30 minutes). The rate will be low to moderate (because the number of calls does not increase the probability of someone getting off the phone, but how long one waits until placing the next call does), and the responses will be continuous (because one never knows whether the next call will be answered).

A final example similar to a variable-interval schedule of reinforcement is providing pop quizzes. We're trying to get students to study consistently throughout the week. We don't want the students to cram only before a big test. Therefore, we provide unannounced quizzes, on average, every two days (VI-2 days). A quiz could come tomorrow, the next day, or four days from now, though. Because the students do not know when a quiz will come, they are more likely to study on a more consistent basis.

Fixed-Ratio Schedule. A **fixed-ratio schedule of reinforcement** is reinforcement of a certain number of responses. Technically, what is reinforced is the last response in a series of responses. For example, if we required students to complete 20 math problems each day before they could go out for recess, we would have a fixed ratio of reinforcement (signified as FR-20). The 20th response is reinforced each day. It does not matter how long it takes the students to complete the 20 responses, only that they complete them. The response pattern seen with a fixed-ratio schedule is found in Figure 2.11c. As shown, the response rate will be high in that students will try to get their work done quickly to go outside (if going outside is a reinforcer). Also notice the response rate is noncontinuous because, once the 20th problem is completed, the students will wait awhile before beginning a new set of 20 problems. This delay is called a **postreinforcement pause.**

Variable-Ratio Schedule. A **variable-ratio schedule of reinforcement** is one in which an average number of responses will result in reinforcement (again, technically, the last response in an average number of responses is reinforced). The variable-ratio schedule of reinforcement may be the most frequently used schedule of reinforcement in today's classrooms. Teachers rarely plan to reinforce a particular student behavior at a set time, but they will reinforce behaviors on an almost random schedule. For example, when students are working on a problem, a teacher might go over and praise the students after they complete one or two problems and then again after they complete eight problems. The average number of problems the students would have to complete before receiving praise might be something like four (signified as VR-4). However, the number of problems to be completed for reinforcement to take place is not the same each time.

Misbehavior is frequently on a variable-ratio schedule of reinforcement. Teachers usually do not attend to each and every misbehavior but will attend to misbehavior at various points in time, say after 2 misbehaviors, or 10, or 20. On average, some number of misbehaviors will be reinforced. The response pattern seen with a variable-ratio schedule of reinforcement is shown in Figure 2.11d. As shown, the response rate is high (because reinforcement depends on the number of responses) and steady (because the individual cannot predict whether the next response will be reinforced).

Extinction

As with response rates, extinction is affected by the type of schedule of reinforcement in place. Essentially, extinction takes less time when one uses a continuous reinforcement schedule rather than an intermittent one (Cooper et al., 2007). Consider the reason for this difference. If we received a reinforcer for every instance of a behavior and then that reinforcement was suddenly removed, we would probably detect this difference. Thus, we would likely stop responding soon thereafter. On the other hand, if we received a reinforcer every so often and then the reinforcer was suddenly removed from the behavior, it would be more difficult to detect this change. We would continue to respond for some period because the next response might be reinforced.

When we examine differences in the extinction of behaviors under the various intermittent schedules, we find that variable schedules are more resistant to extinction (Cooper et al., 2007). It takes longer for a behavior to extinguish when one uses a variable reinforcement schedule rather than a fixed one, which makes sense. Imagine you are getting reinforced for every fifth response and then the reinforcer is removed. You would soon know that a behavior was not being reinforced when it should have been. Therefore, you would be more likely to stop that behavior. If, on the other hand, a reinforcer were to be removed that you expected to receive after an average of five responses, you would have a more difficult time determining that the reinforcer had been withdrawn. You would continue to respond for some time because the next response might be reinforced; you just would not know. As the variable schedule is thinned out (say from a VR-4 to a VR-10), the behavior becomes more and more difficult to extinguish. A person who is "addicted" to slot machines might be on a VR-1000. How long would it take for this person's behavior to extinguish? It would take a very long time.

When working with students who have a long history of misbehavior, we can be fairly confident the misbehavior is on some form of a variable schedule of reinforcement. Knowing this should lead us to understand that it might take a great deal of time to extinguish the behavior.

VIGNETTE REVISITED — Learning More About the Foundations of Behavior Management

After studying the causes of behavior problems, Mr. Huang concludes it is better to look at what is going on in his classroom to explain why the students are behaving as they are than to assume the misbehavior is due to some other variable beyond his control. Mr. Huang begins to understand that even students who come from difficult home environments can learn to behave acceptably. What is needed is an effective reinforcement system that strengthens their positive behavior and ignores their unwanted behavior.

Mr. Huang has also learned that what he thought was punishment—removing the students from the classroom—could actually be working as a reinforcer. Mr. Huang's response to the students' unwanted behaviors might be having an effect opposite to the one he had expected. He has also learned that, on the many occasions when he tried to ignore the students' minor misbehaviors but ended up attending to them when they reached an unacceptable level, he was making these problem behaviors worse by shaping them to a more disruptive level. Mr. Huang is interested in learning more about how to use this information to prevent future behavior problems.

Summary

Understanding the role our environments have in shaping our behaviors is critical in understanding why we behave as we do. It is not adequate to blame students for their unwanted behavior. The blame never gets us anywhere. When students display unwanted behavior, an opportunity arises. This opportunity is an educational one because unwanted behavior is an indication that a student has learned an unwanted behavior and must learn a more appropriate one. Therefore, the educator's job is to determine what learning must take place to reduce the unwanted behavior.

If we are to place blame for unwanted behavior, we must place it where we can have the most control. We cannot control a student's home life; we cannot control a student's physiology. We can, however, control or change a student's school and classroom environments to bring about changes in behavior. Although the school and classroom environments are not the whole story behind the student's unwanted behavior, they are the only sources of behavior on which we can have an effect.

The remaining chapters in this book discuss ways to determine what in the school or classroom is affecting student behavior (both wanted and unwanted). In addition, ways to make changes in the student's immediate environment are discussed.

Key Terms

abolishing operations   60

aversive   47

avoidance response   47

backward chaining   64

behavioral model   40

chaining   63

continuous reinforcement schedule   65

dependent variables   42

deprivation   60

differential reinforcement   62

discriminative stimulus   61

dual stimulus function   63

establishing operations   60

extinction   51

extinction burst   51

fixed-interval schedule of reinforcement (FI)   66

fixed-ratio schedule of reinforcement (FR)   68

forward chaining   64

four-term contingency   44

generalized reinforcers   56

independent variables   42

intermittent reinforcement schedule   66

modeling   45

motivating operations   60

negative punishment   54

negative reinforcement   47

positive punishment   53

positive reinforcement   46

postreinforcement pause   68

primary aversive   58

primary positive reinforcers   55

punishment   53

reinforcement   46

reinforcers   55

reward   46

Discussion Questions

1. When one designs a program from a behavioral standpoint, what is the first thing that should be addressed?

2. Compare and contrast the behavioral and cognitive perspectives on behavior management.

3. Explain why Sidman (1989) classifies negative reinforcement as coercive but does not see positive reinforcement as coercive.

4. Why is it important to understand what is reinforcing the student's behavior?

5. What is extinction and spontaneous recovery?

6. Explain how something becomes a generalized reinforcer.

7. Discuss the differences between primary and secondary aversives.

8. What is stimulus control?

9. What is chaining, and how is it different from shaping?

10. Compare and contrast the basic schedules of reinforcement.

Part II

Individualized Supports

3

Pinpointing and Tracking a Behavior Problem

Chapter Objectives

After studying this chapter, you should be able to

- characterize the considerations to be made before deciding to develop a behavior support plan,

- explain why writing goals and objectives for behavior problems is important, and describe the four components that should be present in objectives,

- illustrate how to write behavioral definitions,

- depict different recording methods,

- illustrate how to develop recording instruments to track behavior,

- explain the purpose of conducting interobserver agreement checks, and describe the calculation methods,

- describe the factors that influence interobserver agreement, and

- depict different single-case experimental designs.

| **VIGNETTE** | **Conducting a Functional Behavior Assessment** |

MRS. LOPEZ WAS INFORMED she was going to have a new student, Karl, in her tenth-grade class. The student was from an alternative school that educated students who had behavior problems. Mrs. Lopez was concerned Karl was going to be disruptive to her classroom. The teachers at the alternative school, however, assured her Karl was much better behaved now.

The time came for Karl to enter Mrs. Lopez's room. He was pleasant in the beginning. He followed the rules and was polite. He seemed to try hard on his assigned work. Then, Mrs. Lopez noticed that Karl was beginning to swear more and say negative things about her and his classmates when he was frustrated. He also began to finish fewer and fewer assignments. Mrs. Lopez phoned Karl's former teacher at the alternative school and asked what she should do. The teacher told Mrs. Lopez she should first consider if there was indeed a problem. The teacher's concern was that Karl's reputation was affecting how Mrs. Lopez viewed his behavior. In other words, the teacher asked Mrs. Lopez whether she thought Karl's behavior could be consistent with that of her other students but that she considered him more disruptive due to her knowledge of his past behavior problems. Mrs. Lopez indicated that she did not think her knowledge of Karl's past problems was affecting her view of him and his behaviors but would consider this a possibility.

Mrs. Lopez asked other teachers whether they had noticed a change in Karl's behavior and they found his school behavior to be problematic. Mrs. Lopez also compared Karl's performance with that of the rest of the class and found that he was acting much differently than the other students. She also had evidence that his problem behaviors were getting worse.

Overview

All teachers attempt to prevent or correct student behavior problems. These attempts are generally successful for many students. For some students, however, typical classroom strategies do not work. Teachers might have to individualize their supports for these students, the ones who do not respond positively to attempts to prevent or correct behavior problems. At the individualized level, teachers will develop systematic and comprehensive support plans for each of these students.

When implementing these support plans, teachers are often concerned about issues of fairness, especially about how other students in the class will perceive differentiated teacher responses to behavior. An individualized behavior support plan, by its very nature, means treating some students differently from others. Every effort should be made to prevent having to design individualized behavior support plans. Some students simply need a more prescribed system. It is no different than with instruction. Therefore, designing an individualized behavior support plan should not be an obstacle. The one major consideration teachers should make is what to tell the other students. In most cases, it will not be necessary to tell them anything. In some cases, it may be worthwhile to tell the students that it is sometimes necessary to have supports for students who need extra help with their behavior.

This explanation can and should be made without specifically naming the student or students involved.

We all know who these students are. These students stand out from the others. Nelson (1996b) called them "target" students, ones who always test the system. They seem to defy attempts to correct their behavior difficulties.

When students continue to misbehave despite attempts to improve their behaviors, several decisions need to be made. First, the need for individualized intervention is discussed. Second, a method of measuring the behavior must be determined. Measuring the behavior tells how severe the behavior is and then helps determine if the individualzer behavior management procedure was effective. Finally, the data collected must be represented in some fashion. Graphing is one of the most helpful methods of representing the data. In addition, the attempt to solve the behavior difficulty can be subjected to an experimental design that will help determine if the management program was successful and responsible for the observed changes in the student behavior.

It is important to realize that the information contained in the next four chapters (3, 4, 5, and 6) is not mutually exclusive. In fact, the division of knowledge across these chapters is somewhat arbitrary. For example, in this current chapter we talk about operationalizing behavior and developing measurement and evaluation systems. Chapter 3 content is inextricably related to the development and use of functional behavior assessments described in detail in Chapter 4. Additionally, most behavior support plans will include interventions to increase (Chapter 5) and decrease (Chapter 6) behavior.

This chapter will discuss the considerations that must be made prior to implementing an individualized behavior support plan. These considerations include defining a behavior and developing goals and objectives, recording behaviors, developing recording instruments, and obtaining the level of **interobserver agreement**—interobserver agreement is the measurement of the agreement between two independent observers. In addition, the factors influencing interobserver agreement will be discussed. Finally, because it is important to determine if a program is working, single-case designs will be discussed.

What Are the Considerations We Must Make Prior to Implementing an Individualized Behavior Support Plan?

Developing an individualized behavior support plan can be a complicated task often involving the cooperation of school administrators, the family, classroom aides, and other teachers. It also involves additional day-to-day tasks for the teacher, such as modifying curricula, implementing consequence-based strategies, and collecting ongoing data on student behavior. An individualized behavior support plan can also have negative consequences, such as the stigmatization of the student in question. Therefore, individualized behavior support plans should not be entered into lightly. Before any intervention takes place, teachers must ask whether or not an intervention *should* take place. To answer this question, they should consider several factors (see Table 3.1) (Sulzer-Azaroff & Mayer, 1991). Not every item in this list of considerations

Table 3.1	Considerations Before a Behavior Management System Is Developed

- Do we have a realistic identification of the problems and goals?
- Are there several independent requests for assistance with the same student?
- Is the student functioning differently from members of a comparison group?
- Are there dramatic changes in the student's behavior as seen by multiple sources?
- Is the behavior related to a physical or medical problem?
- Is this system for our benefit or for the student's?
- Are there logistical problems, such as the physical surroundings, staff responsibilities, and types of demands?
- Is the student willing to change?
- Are the procedures in use demonstrated to be effective?
- Is this an emergency or a critical event?
- Do we have public or supervisory support?
- Do we have control of the goals, including the antecedents and consequences?

will be directly relevant in all cases. The following discussion of several of these considerations will help to illustrate. A teacher should consider whether the behavior of the student in question is dramatically different from that of the class peer group. This consideration may help the teacher evaluate whether individualized supports should be developed or classroom supports (see Chapters 7 and 8) might be modified or implemented. If concern about an individual student's behavior is raised by multiple sources, such as other students and other teachers, then this is often a strong indicator that some form of individualized intervention is needed. Sometimes, the problem does not lie with the student. It might be an issue of changing teacher behavior. For example, there could be a cultural disconnect between the teacher and student. A teacher could see as disruptive what are actually typical behavior patterns within a particular cultural group. This disconnect might be addressed through learning more about a student's culture and modifying teacher behavior accordingly.

How Do We Define Behavior and Develop Goals and Objectives?

Once a probable need for an individualized behavior support plan is established, a series of steps need to be taken. The first step is to clarify the problem behavior. This step entails providing a clear definition of the student's problem behavior so that it is observable and measurable. A clear picture of the problem behavior is critical to enable measurement of the success of the support plan. A clear definition of the problem behavior also facilitates communication among all concerned (i.e., student, teacher, family, and behavioral support specialist) during the process. Next, goals should be established along with specific behavioral objectives that allow for an evaluation of whether or not the goals of the support plan have been achieved.

Defining Behavior

The first step to be completed before an intervention is implemented to decrease unwanted behavior or increase wanted behavior is to determine the current level of these unwanted and wanted behaviors. Before a behavior can be recorded, it must be defined in such a manner that it can be measured (Cooper, Heron, & Heward, 2007; Martella, Nelson, & Marchand-Martella, 1999). This requirement means that a behavior must be defined so minimal inferences are used. For example, recall the magic carpet in the Disney movie *Aladdin*. When the carpet slumped over and walked slowly, most people said that the carpet was "sad" or "depressed." Sadness or depression in this case is clearly an example of an inference. Sadness or depression is not observable. The behaviors we see that allow us to make the inference are the behaviors on which we should focus. Therefore, if teachers are concerned with a student being sad or depressed, they must work with the behaviors they see that allow them to make that inference. Another example is the term *anger*. Anger is an initial behavior. Observable behaviors such as getting red in the face, clenching one's teeth, or swearing are examples of behaviors that can be labeled as angry. Table 3.2 lists a series of words that are not observable behaviors and a list of words that are indicative of observable behaviors. As shown on the left side of the list, many terms used to refer to behaviors are really inferences of behaviors. Therefore, to write a good behavioral definition, a teacher must determine what exactly the behavior of concern is. The label of the behavior is not critical; the definition of the behavior to which the label refers is.

Table 3.2 Examples of Observable and Unobservable Behaviors

Observable Behaviors	Unobservable Behaviors
Speaks	Appreciates
Kicks	Discovers
Verbalizes	Comprehends
Hands in	Initiates
Hits	Perceives
Arrives	Respects
Sits	Believes
Swears	Intends
Asks	Knows
Gives	Commits
Waits	Recognizes
Touches	Realizes

According to Hawkins and Dobes (1977), behavioral definitions must contain three characteristics:

1. The definition should be objective, referring only to observable characteristics of the behavior (and environment, if needed) or translating any inferential terms (such as "expressing hostile feelings," "intended to help," or "showing interest in") into more objective terms.

2. The definition should be clear in that it should be readable and unambiguous so that experienced observers could read it and readily paraphrase it accurately.

3. The definition should be complete, delineating the "boundaries" of what is to be included as an instance of the response and what is to be excluded, thereby directing the observers in all situations that are likely to occur and leaving little to their judgment. (p. 169)

Cooper et al. (2007) provide two requirements for a good behavioral definition. First, a good behavioral definition must be operational. That is, the definition must provide complete information on when the behavior occurs and when it does not occur. Second, a good behavioral definition must be accurate, so program decisions can be guided by the occurrence or nonoccurrence of the behavior. In addition, the behavioral definition must be believable to those invested in the effectiveness of a behavior management program.

Table 3.3 lists examples of definitions. As seen in the table, the definitions meet the three criteria described above. Writing behavioral definitions takes practice. The best way to think of behavioral definitions is to ask, "What exactly do I see the student doing?" Describe the behavior so that you can see it and immediately recognize it from your

---

Table 3.3 Examples of Behavioral Definitions

Positive Statements

Positive words or statements separated by a break in speech directed toward self, others, objects, or tasks (e.g., "I can do this," "You look nice today," "That is a nice shirt," "I like to read")

Negative Statements

Derogatory single words or statements separated by a break in speech directed toward self, others, objects, or tasks (e.g., "I'm so stupid," "I'm going to kill you," "I hate this f_____ calculator," "Math sucks")

On Task

In seat (buttocks on the seat of the chair unless otherwise permitted [feet do not have to be on the floor]), remaining quiet during the task (no verbalizations unless permitted), working on the assigned task, and engaging in bodily movements related to the assigned task, such as using a pencil

---

(Continued)

> **Table 3.3** (Continued)

Off Task

Not in seat (buttocks not on the seat of chair unless permitted [feet do not have to be on the floor]), talking with others (talking, whispering, or mouthing to others without permission), interrupting others (passing a note, touching another student's body or possessions), not working on the assigned task (such as scribbling or doodling instead of writing or reading a magazine instead of the text), and engaging in bodily movements unrelated to or interfering with the assigned task (such as playing with a pencil or ripping paper)

Compliance

Responding either motorically or verbally to an instruction (including instructional stimuli or cues such as "Tell me this word") within 5 seconds

Aggression

Any pushing, shoving, hitting, or pinching that could result in damage (does not include behaviors that occur when playing, such as when wrestling)

Destruction

Any throwing, kicking, punching, tearing, or biting objects that could result in damage

description. When you write a behavioral definition, pretend to be explaining the behavior to a friend. Another positive practice is to provide examples of the behavior within the definition. These examples should cover as many as possible of the behaviors the student might display. Finally, think of what the student might do that would be an example of the behavior but does not meet the definition. For example, suppose noncompliance is defined as not following directions once an instruction is provided. What if the student follows through with the instruction but does so one hour after it was delivered? Most people would still consider this behavior to be noncompliance; the latency to compliance is too long. The behavior of the student does not meet the definition of noncompliance, however, because the student followed the instruction, albeit late. Therefore, some time element, such as "responding to the instruction within five seconds," should be added.

Goals

A **goal** is a broad statement about outcomes that teachers expect to occur within a specified time (Alberto & Troutman, 2009; Lignugaris/Kraft, Marchand-Martella, & Martella, 2001). If we were having difficulty keeping a student on task for an instructional period, our goal might state the following: "Given reading materials and a 30-minute reading period, Bobby will remain on task for the entire period for five consecutive days." Other examples of goals are the following: "During a 20-minute free play period, Latoya will interact with other students in an appropriate manner for the entire period"; or "During transition time from lunch, Jorge will enter the social studies class before the class bell rings every school day." Once the goal is identified, behavioral objectives are determined.

Behavioral Objectives

One of the more important skills a teacher can have is the skill of writing behavioral objectives. **Behavioral objectives** are specific statements about student performance, and they typically include information about the conditions under which a student will perform the behavior, the behavior (in observable terms), and criteria under which the student will display the behavior. As stated by Alberto and Troutman (2009), objectives should be written "to clarify the goals of a student's behavior-change program and thus to facilitate communication among people involved in the program" (p. 24). They continue:

> Because it is a written statement targeting a specific change in behavior, the objective serves as an agreement among school personnel, parents, and students about the academic or social learning for which school personnel are taking responsibility.
>
> A second reason for writing behavioral objectives is that a clearly stated target for instruction facilitates effective programming by the teacher and ancillary personnel. A clearly stated instructional target provides a basis for selecting appropriate materials and instructional strategies. (pp. 24–25)

A good format for writing behavioral objectives is based on the model proposed by Mager (1962) and Lignugaris/Kraft et al. (2001). This format proposes the following parts to an adequate behavioral objective: condition, student's name, behavior, and criterion. Objectives are short-term statements that are designed to lead to the goal. These short-term statements usually are based on what can be accomplished in 12 to 16 weeks.

Identify the Condition. The **condition** is a description of the context under which the target behavior is measured. For example, "When provided a worksheet and told to complete it" is the context under which "Bobby will work on the sheet quietly." The condition should be stated in such a manner that another person reading the objective could replicate the context for the behavior. Examples of conditions include "Given a written list of . . . ," "When verbally requested to . . . ," "When provided with a verbal directive by the teacher . . . ," and "Given a second-grade level basal reader and told to read a passage. . . ."

Identify the Student. Writing behavioral objectives individualizes the behavior management system. Thus, statements such as "Bobby will . . . ," "Susan will . . . ," and "Jacob will . . . " are part of the objective.

Identify the Behavior. The behavior or behaviors of interest are included at this point of the behavioral objective. Again, these are the observable behaviors that are in need of change and that have been discussed earlier in the chapter.

Identify the Criterion. Behavioral objectives should include the **criterion** or the minimum level required for acceptable performance. The teacher sets this level with feedback from others, such as parents, administrators, school counselors, and school psychologists. The criterion tells teachers when the student has acquired the appropriate behavior. The criterion level should be specific, so someone naive to the program could determine how well the student is expected to perform the skill. This criterion level should be ambitious yet attainable. It is not unreasonable to expect all students to be well behaved in class. Examples of criterion levels include the following: "80% correct for three consecutive days," "100% of the time for five consecutive sessions," and "at least 70% of the intervals for eight out of ten consecutive days." The criterion that is set is essentially arbitrary, but teachers can use some standard by which to set these criteria, such as the behavior of well-behaved students. If other students are on task 70% of the time, a realistic level of on-task behavior is 70%. If successful students turn in their homework 80% of the time, a criterion of 100% of the time for the target student would not be realistic. Thus, look at what "model" students do, and use this as a possible criterion level. Methods of recording behaviors to determine if the student has met the criterion level are described later in the chapter.

Common Problems in Writing Objectives. As shown in Table 3.4, several possible problems can result when one writes behavioral objectives (Lignugaris/Kraft et al., 2001). These problems often involve missing or ambiguous parts.

Table 3.4   Common Problems in Behavioral Objectives

Poor Objective	Problem	Improved Objective
Upon entering the classroom, Ben will sit in his seat, ready to work.	Criterion is missing. Behavior is not well specified.	Ben will sit in his seat with materials on his desk within 15 seconds upon entering the classroom for 3 consecutive days.
When given independent seatwork, Sarah will improve her on-task performance to 70% of the time.	Behavior is not appropriate. Criterion is incomplete.	When given independent seatwork, Sarah will remain on task 70% of the instructional time for 5 consecutive days.
Jerry will engage in no negative verbalizations.	Condition is not specified. Criterion is incomplete. Objective is negatively worded.	When provided an academic task, Jerry will interact positively with others for 4 consecutive days.
When engaged in free play activities with other students, Jackie will respect the rights of others 100% of the time for 3 consecutive days.	Behavior is not observable.	When engaged in free play with other students, Jackie will engage in appropriate play behavior 100% of the time for 3 consecutive days.
When given instructions, Barry will follow them 80% of the time for 3 consecutive days.	Criterion is not complete.	When given at least 10 instructions, Barry will follow 80% of them within 5 seconds across 3 consecutive days.
Terry will turn in her homework completed 100% of the time for 5 consecutive days.	Condition is not specified. Criterion is not complete.	Within 30 seconds of entering the classroom at the beginning of each school day, Terry will turn in her completed homework for 5 consecutive days.

How Do We Record Behaviors?

Teachers should take direct observation data if a behavior is of concern.

Once behavioral goals and objectives are clearly identified, a method of measuring the student's behavior on an ongoing basis must be selected. Ongoing measurement of the student's behavior is necessary to determine the effectiveness of the behavior support plan. Measuring behavior can take various forms, from standardized tests to direct observations. For the purposes of this book, direct observation methods are covered because teachers use them most often. Information on other measurement methods, such as standardized tests, rating scales, and checklists, can be found in most assessment textbooks (e.g., Cohen & Spenciner, 2011; Matson, 2007; McLoughlin & Lewis, 2008; Salvia, Ysseldyke, & Bolt, 2010).

Several direct observation methods, including permanent product, event or frequency, duration, latency, and time sampling recordings, are available (Alberto & Troutman, 2009; Martella et al., 1999). Table 3.5 provides a brief description of each recording method as well as information on when each is appropriate to use. It is important to note that certain behaviors are more amenable to certain recording protocols. Teachers should also take into account the amount of effort needed to use each of these protocols accurately.

Table 3.5	Direct Observation Recording Methods		
Measure	**Definition**	**Example**	**Use When**
Permanent products	Observation of the student's behavior	Number of windows or chairs broken	Behavior leaves an enduring product
Event recording	Record each behavior as a frequency	Number of times tardy, number of times student uses profanity	Behavior is discrete, equal in duration, and transitory
Duration recording	Record the length of time a behavior occurs	Length of a tantrum, length of time engaged in an academic task	Behavior is discrete and transitory

(Continued)

| Table 3.5 | (Continued) |

Measure	Definition	Example	Use When
Latency recording	Record length of time between onset of antecedent and behavior	Length of time it takes from instruction to compliance	Behavior is discrete and transitory
Interval recording	Record the presence or absence of a behavior within a specified time frame	On-task behavior, in-seat behavior	Behavior does not have a clear beginning and end, is continuous, or occurs at a high rate
Whole interval	Record behavior if it occurred for the entire interval	On-task behavior, in-seat behavior	Behavior is to be increased
Partial interval	Record behavior if it occurred at least once during the interval	Off-task behavior, out-of-seat behavior	Behavior is to be decreased
Momentary time sample	Record if behavior is occurring at the end of the interval	Off-task behavior, out-of-seat behavior	There is not enough available time to observe the entire interval

Permanent Products

Perhaps the most frequently used method of recording by teachers to assess the effects of instruction is permanent product recording (e.g., completed worksheets or puzzles, written examinations, written spelling words). **Permanent product recording** involves the teacher observing the enduring product or outcome of a student's behavior. The actual behavior itself is not observed. For example, a teacher might use the number of windows or chairs broken during an aggressive episode. Permanent product recording is used whenever a behavior leaves an endurable product. In other words, whenever something left over from a behavior is observed or counted at a later time, permanent product recording is being conducted. This recording method is a relatively easy measurement procedure for teachers to use.

Event or Frequency Recording

Teachers may simply tally the number of times a response (e.g., talk outs) occurs within a defined period of time to assess the effects of an intervention. **Event recording** (also called frequency recording) establishes the numerical dimension of behavior. This observation procedure is used in cases in which there is a discrete behavior with a clear beginning and end and each episode of the behavior is roughly equivalent in duration. Examples of behaviors that are amenable to event recording include a tally of the number of times a student is tardy or absent, the number of times a student uses profanity, and the number of aggressive episodes a student exhibits, such as hitting someone. Examples of behaviors without a clear beginning and end include off-task behavior, being out of one's seat, and poor social engagement. Event recording is not good to use with high-frequency behaviors (e.g., motor movement of a student with attention deficit disorder) because the observer becomes overwhelmed and may lose count when trying to tally the behaviors. Again this recording procedure is relatively easy for teachers to use.

Duration and Latency Recording

Duration recording measures the time a response or behavior lasts. Duration recording, like event recording, is used in cases in which there is a discrete behavior with a clear beginning and end; in contrast with event recording, however, the behaviors exhibited are not typically equivalent in time. For example, say that tantrums occur often for a young student but vary in length (e.g., one lasts 10 minutes, and the next lasts 15 minutes). Simply counting these behaviors loses large amounts of information. What is worse, one tantrum or two? The answer is not really known without duration recording; one tantrum could have lasted 45 minutes, but the two other tantrums combined could have lasted a total of 10 minutes. Duration recording can also be used to measure appropriate behavior such as the amount of time a student appropriately interacts with others on the playground.

Latency recording involves recording the time from a specified event to the start of the targeted behavior or completion of the response. Latency recording is also used in cases in which there is a discrete behavior with a clear beginning and end, and the behaviors exhibited are not typically equivalent in time. For example, latency recording could be used to measure the time between a request from a teacher to begin work on an assignment to the actual completion of the assignment by the student. Latency recording is especially appropriate when conducting compliance training (i.e., teaching a student to follow directions in the classroom). As noted above, event recording establishes the numerical dimension of behavior (how many times the behavior occurs); duration and latency recording provide the temporal dimension (how long the behavior lasts or takes).

The difference between the duration and latency recording methods is that duration recording simply involves measuring the length of time a response lasts, whereas latency recording involves the length of time between a stimulus (e.g., instruction) and the occurrence of the target behavior. Both latency and duration recording require teachers to pay undivided attention in order to provide accurate measures. So, if a tantrum lasts for 45 minutes, it may be very difficult for the teacher to do anything else efficiently other than record the duration of the tantrum. In other words, these measures may be difficult to implement in a classroom setting without additional staff support.

Interval Recording

Teachers can use interval recording to provide an estimate of the number of occurrences and the duration of behaviors. **Interval recording** provides an estimate of the percentage of intervals in which a behavior occurred. This recording method involves dividing observational periods into units of time. Interval recording is useful for nondiscrete behaviors that do not have a clear beginning and end, that occur over different lengths of time, and that occur relatively frequently. There are three basic types of interval recording procedures: whole-interval recording, partial-interval recording, and momentary time sampling.

Whole-Interval Recording. **Whole-interval recording** is a procedure used to record behaviors only if they have occurred throughout the entire specified time interval. This procedure provides a conservative estimate (i.e., underestimates the occurrence) of an observed behavior because it does not count a behavior unless it occurs for the entire interval. For example, Figure 3.1 shows that a particular behavior occurred in the middle of interval 2 and progressed to the middle of interval 4. The tally of when the behavior occurred, however, includes only the occurrence in interval 3 because that is the only interval during which the behavior occurred the entire time. We would conclude that the behavior occurred 20% of the time. Notice that the behavior actually occurred 40% of the time. Therefore, we have a conservative estimate of the incidence and duration of the behavior, which is an underestimation of the behavior's occurrence. This method can also be a difficult procedure for teachers to implement, as it requires undivided attention.

Partial-Interval Recording. With **partial-interval recording**, a behavior is recorded if it occurs at any point during the specified time interval. This recording system contrasts with whole-interval recording, in which the behavior has to occur for the entire interval for it to be scored as occurring; consequently, the partial-interval recording method should be used for behaviors we want to decrease. Figure 3.2 shows that the behavior occurred one time in interval 2 and five times in interval 5, but the occurrence of the behaviors is counted the same in both intervals. The partial-interval method can be somewhat easier for teachers to implement than whole-interval recording. However, it is still a time- and attention-consuming method of data collection and can be difficult to implement accurately unless the teacher has additional staff support in the classroom.

Momentary Time Sampling. The **momentary time sampling** procedure involves observing the student at the end of each interval and recording whether the student is

---

Figure 3.1 Example of Whole-Interval Recording

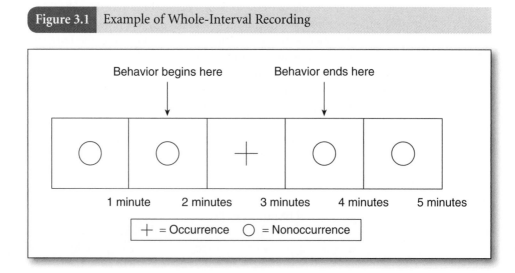

| Figure 3.2 | Example of Partial-Interval Recording |

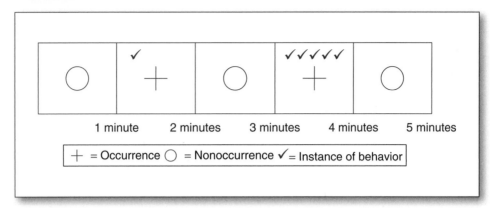

1 minute   2 minutes   3 minutes   4 minutes   5 minutes

$+$ = Occurrence $\bigcirc$ = Nonoccurrence $\checkmark$ = Instance of behavior

engaged in the targeted behaviors. If the student is engaging in the target behaviors, then the teacher scores the behavior as occurring during that interval. This recording procedure is a robust assessment method and is the easiest of the interval procedures for the teacher to use. The teacher does not need to engage in an ongoing observation of the student throughout the intervals, leaving him or her free to engage in other classroom duties. An obvious concern with momentary time sampling is whether the behavior at the end of the interval represents the behavior during the entire interval.

How Do We Develop Recording Instruments?

Once the method used to record the data has been determined, a data sheet must be developed. The most frequently used method of recording is simply to use paper and pencil (Miltenberger, 2007). All teachers use a recording instrument of some form; a grade book is one example. Obviously, the main reason to use a data-recording instrument is that it aids teachers in being efficient and organized. For the recording instrument to help in this way, however, a data sheet must be developed before data are taken.

To create a data sheet, teachers must determine what information is to be recorded. For example, the student's name or identification number, location, teacher's name, date, length of observation, and definition of the target behavior should be placed on the data sheet. Another consideration is how much data should go on each data sheet. Should there be one page of data per day or several days of data on one sheet? Also, the data sheet should be clear and easy to use. Many data sheets are simply too involved and take a great deal of training to implement. Therefore, the simpler the data sheet, the better. The best way to create a data sheet is to develop a rough one and then modify it after it has been tried several times. Gradually refine the data sheet until it meets your needs. Figures 3.3 through 3.6 show different data sheets. Figure 3.3 shows a sample data sheet for event recording, Figure 3.4 shows a sample data sheet for duration recording, Figure 3.5 shows a sample data sheet for latency recording, and Figure 3.6 shows a sample data sheet for interval recording.

Figure 3.3	Event Recording Data Sheet

Student _____   Observer _____

Teacher _____   Classroom/School _____

Behavioral definition(s):

Date: _____

Start time: ___ : ___

End time: ___ : ___

_____ (Total number of behaviors)

÷ _____ (Total number of minutes)

_____ = Rate

> Note: Place mark for each behavior seen.

Date: _____

Start time: ___ : ___

End time: ___ : ___

_____ (Total number of behaviors)

÷ _____ (Total number of minutes)

_____ = Rate

> Note: Place mark for each behavior seen.

Date: _____

Start time: ___ : ___

End time: ___ : ___

_____ (Total number of behaviors)

÷ _____ (Total number of minutes)

_____ = Rate

> Note: Place mark for each behavior seen.

| **Figure 3.4** | Duration Recording Data Sheet |

Student _____   Observer _____

Teacher _____   Classroom/School _____

Behavioral definition(s):

Date: _____

Start time: ___ : ___

End time: ___ : ___

_____ (Total duration)

÷ _____ (Total number of behaviors)

_____ = Average duration per behavior

_____ (Total duration)

÷ _____ (Total session length)

_____ = Percentage of total session time

> Note: Record duration of each behavior seen.

Date: _____

Start time: ___ : ___

End time: ___ : ___

_____ (Total duration)

÷ _____ (Total number of behaviors)

_____ = Average duration per behavior

_____ (Total duration)

÷ _____ (Total session length)

_____ = Percentage of total session time

> Note: Record duration of each behavior seen.

Figure 3.5	Latency Recording Data Sheet

Student _____   Observer _____

Teacher _____   Classroom/School _____

Behavioral definition(s):

Date: _____

Start time: ___ : ___

End time: ___ : ___

_____ (Total number of latency minutes)

÷ _____ (Total number of antecedent events)

_____ = Average latency per event

Note: Record each latency here.

Date: _____

Start time: ___ : ___

End time: ___ : ___

_____ (Total number of latency minutes)

÷ _____ (Total number of antecedent events)

_____ = Average latency per event

Note: Record each latency here.

Figure 3.6	Interval Recording Data Sheet

Student _____   Observer _____

Teacher _____   Classroom/School _____

Behavioral definition(s):

Date: _____   _____ (Total number of "+" intervals)

Start time: ___ : ___   ÷ _____ (Total number of intervals)

End time: ___ : ___   _____ = Percentage of occurrence

Interval length _____

Note "+" = occurrence; "–" = nonoccurrence

1	2	3	4	5	6
7	8	9	10	11	12

Date: _____   _____ (Total number of "+" intervals)

Start time: ___ : ___   ÷ _____ (Total number of intervals)

End time: ___ : ___   _____ = Percentage of occurrence

Interval length _____

Note "+" = occurrence; "–" = nonoccurrence

1	2	3	4	5	6
7	8	9	10	11	12

A couple of suggestions can be made with regard to the use of a data-recording system. First, the recording sheet must be practical. It must not cause much disruption to ongoing class activities, such as requiring the teacher to stop instruction to make a recording. The data sheet should not draw attention to the teacher. The instrument should not cause reactivity on the part of the student who is being observed. Second, the data should be recorded immediately or as soon as possible. The longer the wait to record data, the more likely there are to be inaccuracies in the data (Miltenberger, 2007).

What Is Interobserver Agreement?

A critical aspect of observation is determining if the manner in which the data are gathered is consistent. For example, we could change the way we define a behavior. A negative verbalization one day might not be viewed as inappropriate at another time. It is critical, however, that we remain consistent in the collection of the data so that each observation day can be compared with a previous or future one. To make the determination of how consistently we are observing and recording the instances of behavior, we can conduct interobserver agreement assessments. **Interobserver agreement** requires a second observer to collect the data at the same time the teacher does, and then a comparison of the data collected is made. The two observers should record the data independently (not checking each other's results during the observation process). Agreement between observers should be high, about 80%. Through these assessments, we will be able to determine if we are consistent in our collection of the data. Below is a description of each of the types of interobserver agreement methods used in the classroom environment. These are not strategies that will be used on an ongoing basis by teachers in classrooms. However, they can be helpful strategies within the classroom, especially when implemented with the assistance of behavioral consultants. For example, a behavioral consultant or school psychologist who checks in on a student to assess progress in the behavior support plan could conduct an interobserver agreement session with the teacher to examine for consistency of data collection. Above and beyond the practical use of interobserver agreement methods, these are important concepts for practitioners to understand. Interobserver agreement is reported in published research on behavior management strategies in schools. To be an educated consumer of this research, both practitioners and consultants should understand the nature of interobserver agreement. Also, many readers of this book will, it is hoped, go on to do research in this area of education and will therefore routinely use the formulae described below.

Permanent Products

The following formula is used to establish the percentage of agreement between independent observers measuring permanent products. The percentage of agreement equals the number of agreements between observers divided by the total number of agreements and disagreements multiplied by 100%:

$$\text{Percentage of agreement} = \frac{\text{Agreements}}{\text{Agreements} + \text{Disagreements}} \times 100\%$$

Inspection of the above formula reveals that, as the number of disagreements goes up, the percentage of agreement becomes lower. For example, say that interobserver agreement was achieved on three of four damaged desks. In this scenario, disagreement between observers occurred on one desk. Substituting these numbers into the above formula, the percentage of interobserver agreement is 75% (i.e., 3 agreements/[3 agreements + 1 disagreement], with a result of .75 multiplied by 100%).

Event or Frequency Recording

The following formula is used to establish the percentage of agreement between independent observers measuring events. The percentage of agreement equals the smaller total divided by the larger total multiplied by 100%. As the discrepancy between the smaller total and larger total becomes greater, the level of interobserver agreement decreases.

$$\text{Percentage of agreement} = \frac{\text{Smaller total}}{\text{Larger total}} \times 100\%$$

The percentage of agreement with event recording should be interpreted cautiously because it does not provide any assurance that the two observers were recording the same event. For example, imagine that one observer records that a student said 20 swear words during a 60-minute observation period, and a second observer records 25 swear words during the same period. The first observer, however, recorded 15 occurrences during the first 30 minutes of the observation period and 5 occurrences during the last 30 minutes, whereas the second observer recorded only 5 occurrences during the first 30 minutes of the observation period and 20 occurrences during the last 30 minutes. The calculation for this observation is the smaller total of 20 divided by the larger total of 25, resulting in .80, which is then multiplied by 100% for a percentage agreement of 80%. Thus, the percentage of agreement would have been inflated and would not accurately reflect the observers' actual level of agreement. A solution to this problem is to shorten the time interval within which interobserver agreement is computed. The 60-minute observation period used in the above example could be broken down into six 10-minute intervals. The percentage of agreement could then be calculated for each interval. Therefore, it is important to look at the length of interval used to compute the percentage of agreement in the case of event recording.

Duration and Latency Recording

The following formula is used to establish the percentage of agreement between independent observers measuring the duration or latency of behavior.

$$\text{Percentage of agreement} = \frac{\text{Shorter duration or latency}}{\text{Longer duration or latency}} \times 100\%$$

An example of using this formula to calculate interobserver agreement is as follows. Say one observer recorded 10 minutes of a student's off-task behavior and the other observer recorded 12 minutes of off-task behavior. The interobserver agreement percentage is 10 (short duration) divided by 12 (longer duration), which equals .83. This value is then multiplied by 100% for a percentage of agreement of 83%.

Two problems are experienced by observers when interpreting interobserver agreement using latency and duration recording. First, the procedures for ensuring that both of the observers begin the observation period at the same time must be established. Small variations in start time between observers can distort the percentage of agreement. Second, as with event recording, high agreements do not necessarily ensure that the observers reported the same latencies or durations for the same occurrences of behavior. These issues should be examined whenever the results of a behavior support plan are assessed.

Interval Recording

The following formula is used to establish the percentage of agreement between independent observers for each of the interval recording procedures. The percentage of agreement equals the number of agreement intervals divided by the total number of agreement and disagreement intervals multiplied by 100%.

$$\text{Percentage of agreement} = \frac{\text{Agreement intervals}}{\text{Agreement intervals} + \text{Disagreement intervals}} \times 100\%$$

The basic method for establishing interobserver agreement with interval recording involves computing the level of agreement for all the intervals (total agreement). To provide a more conservative estimate of interobserver agreement, both the scored interval (i.e., occurrence agreement) and unscored interval (i.e., nonoccurrence agreement) methods for establishing interobserver agreement should be used (Cooper et al., 2007; Hawkins & Dotson, 1975). Both methods use the above formula (agreement intervals [scored or unscored] divided by the total agreement and disagreement intervals [scored or unscored] multiplied by 100%). An example of total, scored, and unscored interval interobserver agreement is provided in the following paragraph.

Look at the example of the scored intervals provided in Figure 3.7. One minute's worth of 10-second intervals will be compared. Agreement was noted for intervals 1, 2, 4, 5, and 6. Therefore, the number of agreements (5) is divided by the number of agreements (5) plus disagreements (1) and then multiplied by 100% for a total agreement percentage of 83%. Now look at occurrence interobserver agreement. There is agreement on intervals that were scored (i.e., behavior occurred recorded as a check) for intervals 1, 2, and 5. There was disagreement on whether the behavior occurred in interval 3. Therefore, the number of agreements of when the behavior was scored as occurring (3) is divided by the number of agreements (3) plus disagreements (1) and then multiplied by 100% for an agreement percentage of 75% for scored intervals. Finally, look at nonoccurrence interobserver agreement. There is agreement on intervals that were unscored (i.e., agreement that the behavior did not occur, recorded as a zero) for intervals 4 and 6, but disagreement on whether the behavior occurred in interval 3. Therefore, the number of agreements of when the behavior was scored as not occurring (2) is divided by the number of agreements (2) plus disagreements (1) and then multiplied by 100% for an agreement percentage of 67% for unscored intervals. Analyzing the data in this way gives the important information on how often the observers agreed on what they saw and what they did not see.

Figure 3.7   Example of Interobserver Agreement With Interval Recording

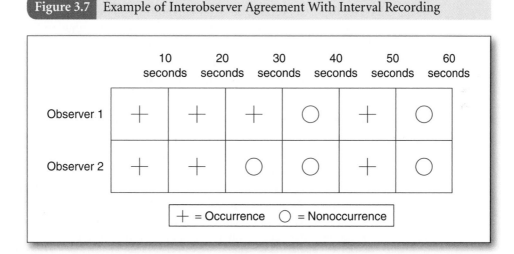

What Factors Influence Interobserver Agreement?

A number of environmental conditions can affect observers and can influence the quality of data collected. These environmental conditions include reactivity, observer drift, complexity of the measurement system, and observer expectations (Martella et al., 1999;

Miltenberger, 2007). These factors should always be considered when conducting inter-observer agreement. It is very important to try to minimize negative influences so as to ensure that observations accurately reflect the student's behavior.

Reactivity

Reactivity refers to differences in interobserver agreement that result from observers being aware that their observations will be checked. Reactivity typically results in higher levels of interobserver agreement and accuracy of observations. It can be accomplished by providing random interobserver checks, audio- or videotaping the observations and randomly selecting those that will be scored, or conducting interobserver agreement checks 100% of the time.

Observer Drift

Observer drift occurs when observers change the way they employ the definition of behavior over the course of the behavior support plan. In contrast to what we may think, observer drift does not necessarily result in lower levels of interobserver agreement. Observers can develop a similar drift if they work closely together and communicate about how they record the observed behavior. This drift will affect the consistency of the data over time. Conversely, observer agreement will decrease over the course of the behavior support plan if observers do not work closely together and do not communicate about how they record the observed behavior. Observer drift can be prevented or at least diminished through booster training on the definitions of the behaviors and by having data collected by individuals experienced in conducting observation sessions.

Complexity of the Measurement System

The complexity of the measurement system is influenced by the number of individuals observed, the number of behaviors recorded, the duration of the observations, the duration of the time intervals in interval recording, and the complexity of the data-recording instrument. Generally, the greater the complexity, the lower the levels of interobserver agreement. Thus, researchers or practitioners must balance the complexity of the measurement system with the need to obtain reasonable levels of interobserver agreement. Achieving this balance can involve observing fewer individuals, recording fewer behaviors, making the duration of the interval smaller, or simplifying the recording instrument.

Observer Expectations

Observer expectations can influence observations. **Observer expectations** could be in effect if observers expect the support plan to have a specific effect and are more likely to record this expected change in a behavior, even when this behavioral change is not present. In other words, the observers' observations and recordings may not accurately reflect what is actually going on with the behavior. Observers' expectations appear to be most problematic when someone provides them feedback about how the behavior support plan is progressing, what the intervention is, and how the individuals are responding. The effect of observer expectations can be decreased by keeping the observers "blind" as to the specifics of the program (e.g., the program condition, purpose of the program) and by using individuals experienced in conducting observations.

What Are Single-Case Experimental Designs?

The reason teachers collect data on student behavior is to make some form of determination as to whether or not the behavior support plan is having the intended effect (e.g., decreasing unwanted and increasing prosocial behaviors or improving academic performance). The simplest way to do this is to collect data on the target behaviors before, during, and following the implementation of the plan. If the program is effective, the teacher should expect changes to follow a logical sequence: evident problem behavior prior to intervention, decreases in problem behavior during the support plan until the behavior is at acceptable levels, and maintenance of behavior change following the removal or fading of the behavior support plan. There are a number of systematic ways in which the teacher can introduce and evaluate the effects of a treatment. Taken as a whole, these strategies are called single-case experimental designs. The purpose of a **single-case design** is to use the student as his or her own control so a relationship can be shown between the management program (independent variable) and the student's response to the program (dependent variable). Routinely, teachers will use the simplest form of this type of design (i.e., the A-B design described below). Other more complicated designs are often used in behavioral support research. It is therefore important for teachers, who should be consumers of this research, as well as researchers themselves to be familiar with these types of single-case experimental designs. Below are descriptions of these single-case experimental designs. (For additional information on these designs, see Barlow, Nock, & Hersen, 2009; Kennedy, 2005; Martella et al., 1999; O'Neill, McDonnell, Billingsley, & Jenson, 2011.)

Teachers may review graphic displays of data of student performance.

A-B Design

To understand single-case designs, one must know the meanings of the symbols used in them. In single-case designs, "A" refers to baseline.

A **baseline** is the repeated measurement of a behavior under natural conditions. The baseline indicates the level at which the student performs a behavior without the intervention. It is of critical importance when considering single-case designs because it is the best estimate of what would have occurred had the intervention not been applied. The baseline, then, provides a comparison to the intervention condition, or "B." The **intervention condition** is the period when the behavior support plan is in effect. Typically, the "B" condition is used in isolation. In other words, a skill is usually taught and measured over a period of time. A "B" design, however, is especially problematic because it is not possible to indicate where the student was before the intervention. Unfortunately, the "B" design is how many teachers attempt to determine the effects of a behavior support plan. Assessment of the behaviors to be targeted by the support plans should be conducted prior to the intervention. Therefore, the **A-B design**, which combines the baseline or pre-intervention measurements ("A") with a "B" condition to determine the effectiveness of the behavior support plan, should be the minimum level of data analysis a teacher uses before and during the implementation of a plan.

Figure 3.8 shows an A-B design. As can be seen, several assessments occur before the intervention, and several more occur during the intervention. In Figure 3.8, the intervention seems to be effective. This type of A-B analysis would be sufficiently

Figure 3.8	The Frequency of Fights Across Baseline and Self-Management Conditions: A-B Design

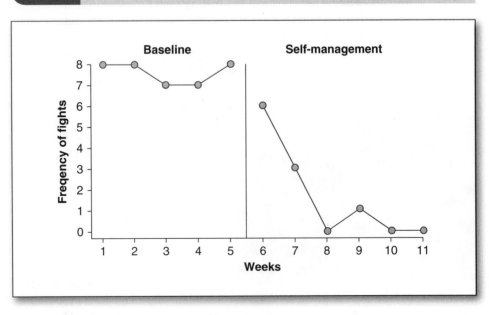

rigorous during routine positive behavior support (PBS) programs implemented by teachers. But, from a research point of view, there is a major problem with A-B designs: they fail to demonstrate convincingly that a management program caused a change in a student's behavior. To solve this problem, the A-B design can be extended into an A-B-A or withdrawal design.

Withdrawal Design

The **withdrawal** or **A-B-A design** involves a subsequent removal of the intervention or a return to the baseline (A) following some period of intervention. If behavior returns to its pre-intervention level (as in the original "A" or baseline condition), then a clear demonstration of the relationship between the behavior support plan and changes in the target behavior has been accomplished. At this stage, the intervention can be re-introduced, providing the teacher or researcher with a further confirmation of the effectiveness of the intervention (i.e., **A-B-A-B design**). In this way, a functional (or causal) relationship between the intervention and the behavior can be shown. Figure 3.9 provides data indicating a functional relationship using a withdrawal design.

Figure 3.9	The Frequency of Fights Across Baseline and Self-Management Conditions: A-B-A Design

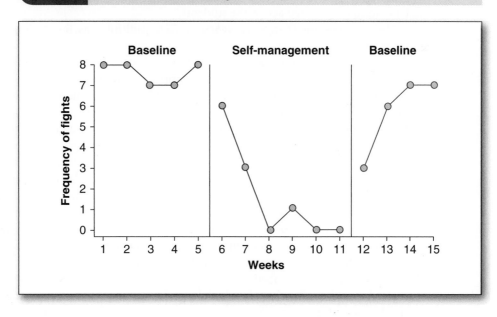

Multiple-Baseline Designs

One alternative to the withdrawal design is the multiple-baseline design. **Multiple-baseline designs** can be thought of as a series of staggered A-B designs. In this way, multiple-baseline designs have several advantages over withdrawal designs. For example, in a multiple-baseline design, there is no requirement to remove or withdraw the intervention. There is not a need to return to baseline levels in the future. Thus, multiple-baseline designs are appropriate for investigations related to skill acquisition, motivational problems, and the reduction of unwanted behaviors. In many ways, multiple-baseline designs are more versatile than withdrawal designs. In addition, multiple-baseline designs allow for the replication of intervention effects across behaviors, students, and settings.

Multiple-Baseline Design Across Behaviors. The **multiple-baseline design across behaviors** requires at least two separate behaviors, which are independent of one another. In other words, if a teacher applies an intervention to one behavior, there should not be a corresponding change in the other behavior. Once these behaviors are targeted and a measurement system is put into place, baseline data should be collected for each behavior. Figure 3.10 shows the results of a behavior management program across two different behaviors.

Multiple-Baseline Design Across Students. The **multiple-baseline design across students** is similar to the multiple-baseline design across behaviors in that two or more baselines are required. There is, however, a need for two or more students. The teacher then takes frequent measures of the targeted behavior for each student during and after baseline. Figure 3.11 shows a multiple-baseline design across students. As can be seen, the graphs indicate who the students are. Also notice how the teacher kept the second and third students in baseline while the first student received the program. The intervention is staggered across the students.

Multiple-Baseline Design Across Settings. The **multiple-baseline design across settings** is similar to the previous two designs except that the teacher selects two or more settings in which to implement the intervention. This design is especially useful in determining the generalizability of a behavior support plan to other classrooms or other settings, such as the lunchroom, playground, or physical education class. The teacher measures the student's behavior in each of these settings. The teacher takes baseline measures in each setting and then introduces the behavior support plan in only the first setting. The student's behavior in the second setting is not exposed to the program until later. Figure 3.12 displays data for a multiple-baseline design across settings. The figure indicates that there are two settings (science and language arts) included in the assessment.

Multiple-Probe Design. One potential problem with multiple-baseline designs is the need for repeated measurements (i.e., repeatedly collecting data on behavior prior to and during interventions). At times, repeated measurements can be impractical as they can interfere with teaching duties or student performance. An alternative to frequent or repeated measurements is to use a **multiple-probe design** in which the behavior is assessed or "probed" every so often (e.g., once every couple of days). Probes can also be used in situations in which behaviors are not the target of intervention, as in the case of assessing the generalization, transfer, or maintenance of behavior

Figure 3.10 Multiple-Baseline Behavior Management Across Behaviors

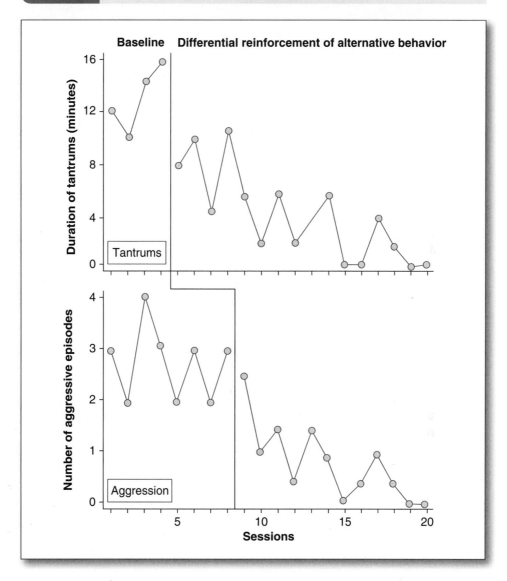

support plans. For example, if a teacher were to determine the extent to which improved classroom performance translated into improved behavior at home, he or she could have the parents probe behavior at home (see Figure 3.13 for home probes). In this case, a combination of multiple-baseline and multiple-probe designs could be used, with frequent (multiple-baseline) measurements applied to behaviors that are targeted for change and probes conducted to assess generalization or transfer.

Figure 3.11

Percentage of Intervals of Off-Task Behavior Across Baseline and Self-Monitoring Conditions for Paul, Susan, and Amy

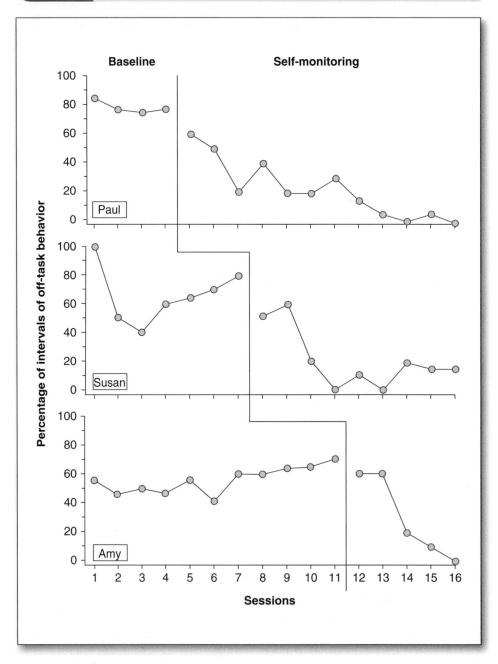

| Figure 3.12 | Multiple-Baseline Behavior Management Across Settings |

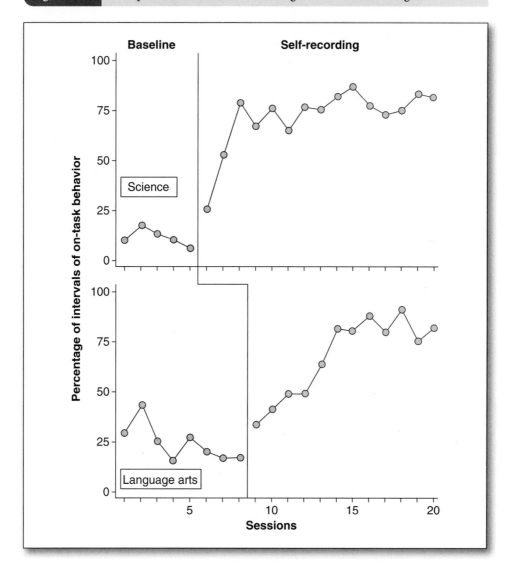

Changing-Criterion Design

The **changing-criterion design** is a single-case research design that is used to examine a gradual or incremental change in student behavior. Figure 3.14 shows a changing-criterion design. As seen in the figure, a baseline condition is conducted, followed by the behavior support plan (teacher-student contracting). Essentially, without the "phase" lines (i.e., changes within the intervention condition), the design looks the same as an A-B design. The difference between a changing-criterion design and an A-B design is the use of a

| Figure 3.13 | Multiple-Baseline Assessment Across Behaviors With Home Probes |

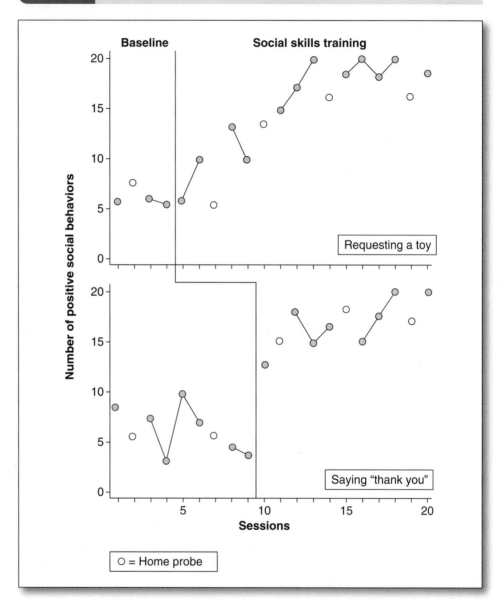

criterion within each phase. As shown in the figure, the horizontal lines between each set of phase lines depict the criteria. Think of a changing-criterion design as an attempt to reduce or increase some behavior in a stepwise manner. In fact, that is what the design is intended to do: increase or decrease a dependent variable gradually, step by step.

The method of implementing a changing-criterion design is a combination of planning and good (educated) guessing. In other words, teachers should plan the

Figure 3.14	Minutes of Continuous On-Task Behavior Across Baseline and Teacher-Student Contracting Conditions

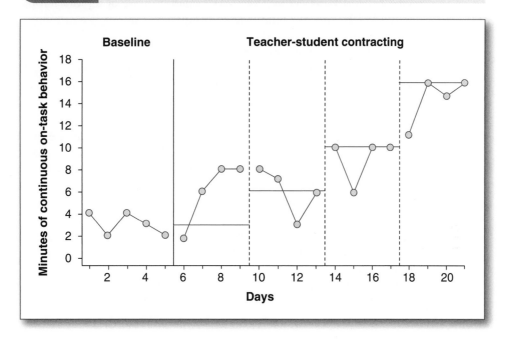

implementation of a behavior support plan as they would any other program. The plan and target behaviors must be well defined, the method of data collection must be determined, and the students must be prepared to become involved in the program. Teachers need to rely on good guessing because they must determine the level of criterion changes throughout the program, ensuring that the changes are not too small (student may become bored) or too large (student may not be able to achieve the desired changes). To implement a changing-criterion design, teachers or researchers must do the following. First, they must collect baseline data. Second, the first criterion level should be set around the average of the baseline. Third, once the student meets some predetermined criterion level, such as three data points at the criterion, the criterion should be changed to a new level.

Alternating Treatments Design

Suppose we wished to implement a behavior support plan with a student who exhibited unwanted behaviors. We could have a choice of one or two behavior support strategies. For example, we could use a time-out or a response cost system (described in detail in Chapter 6). How would we decide which method would be the most effective in reducing the unwanted behavior, other than a "best guess"? One way to determine which method would work best for a particular student is to use an alternating treatments design (Barlow et al., 2009). The main purpose of an **alternating treatments design (ATD)** is to make simultaneous comparisons among two or more conditions or behavior support methods, such as baseline and a behavior support plan or multiple behavior support programs. The other single-case designs discussed thus far are planned only to determine if a behavior support plan works over already existing classroom strategies (baseline). On the other hand, an ATD attempts to demonstrate the superiority of one support procedure over the other.

Essentially, an ATD splits the student into equal parts and provides different methods to each part. For example, suppose that we wished to compare two methods of classroom support, such as in-class time-out and reprimands. We alternate the support procedures to see the relative effects of each on the classroom behavior of the student. The manner in which we alternate the procedures can vary. For example, we could split the day in half and run one procedure in the morning and the other in the afternoon. We could also run one on Monday, Wednesday, and Friday during the first week and Tuesday and Thursday during the second week and then repeat the sequence. We would then run the other procedure on the other days. We must randomly determine when each procedure is in effect.

Figure 3.15 shows an example of an ATD. In the figure, interventions are alternated daily. Conclusions can be drawn based on the data in the figure. It seems as

| Figure 3.15 | The Daily Duration of Tantrums Across Time-Out and Reprimand Conditions |

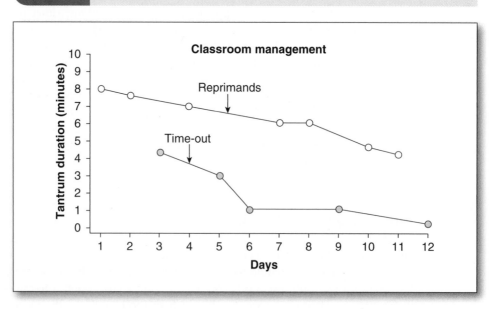

though the time-out was more effective than the reprimands. Notice there is no baseline in Figure 3.15. The teacher only sought to determine which support strategy was most effective. A baseline condition was not needed.

| VIGNETTE REVISITED | Conducting a Functional Behavior Assessment |

After careful deliberation, Mrs. Lopez found Karl's behaviors were indeed problematic. Therefore, she conducted a functional behavior assessment (described in Chapter 4). She also defined as best she could what she believed to be Karl's problem behaviors. She knew her definitions must be observable for her to track Karl's behavior. For example, she defined negative statements as "any derogatory statements or words that contain commonly considered four-letter swear words directed at self or others without a break in speech." Mrs. Lopez also considered the goals for Karl's behavior. She thought about what she could reasonably expect from him by the end of the year. For instance, for appropriate classroom behavior statements, Mrs. Lopez's goal was as follows: "Karl will work quietly in the classroom." She then worked backward from where she would like Karl to be by year's end to where he is now. She planned three steps toward her goal. Mrs. Lopez wrote three short-term objectives she thought Karl could reach on his way to improved behavior. For example, the first objective, which would help him reach the goal of working quietly, was as follows: "When in the classroom during independent seatwork, Karl will work quietly for three consecutive school days." (Another goal that Mrs. Lopez developed to go along with working quietly was to improve Karl's social skills.)

Next, Mrs. Lopez designed a method of tracking Karl's behaviors. She marked down every instance of swearing she heard. She also documented the percentage of time Karl was on task. She kept detailed information on Karl's seatwork completion and performance levels.

Finally, Mrs. Lopez set up a graph to provide a visual description of Karl's behavior. She plans to use this graph to track where Karl is now and how he progresses once she develops an individualized behavior plan for him. Using this graph, Mrs. Lopez will be able to determine if her efforts are successful or not.

Summary

An interesting aspect of teacher preparation is that preservice teachers are trained to engage in detailed planning for instruction. Instructional goals are laid out, and methods of instruction are decided on. A frequently missed area of planning, however, is behavioral support, despite the high numbers of students in need of such interventions. Behavioral support should be looked at no differently than any other instructional planning process. In other words, goals and objectives should be developed for classroom behavior as well as for student learning. It is critical that these behavioral goals and objectives be developed in a manner that allows for the assessment and measurement of the target behavior.

Assessment and measurement of classroom behavior first involve defining the behavior in such a way that it can be observed and measured. Once behaviors have been defined, they must be recorded in some manner. Teachers should develop data-recording instruments to track the levels of behaviors. Developing these instruments is no different from setting up a recording system to assess the levels of various academic skills. Some form of interobserver agreement check should be used when the data are recorded. In addition, if teachers wish to determine whether the behavior support plan was responsible for a change in student behavior, they should use some measure of behavior before, during, and after the behavior support plan's implementation.

A common argument made against developing a comprehensive behavior support plan for students is that such a system is too difficult, too time-consuming, or a waste of effort. Behavior support plans are difficult in some cases, and they are time-consuming, but they are never a waste of time. As with instruction, behavioral support will be more likely to yield success the more planning and effort teachers invest in it. Teachers who are good at managing student behavior take the time to do it correctly.

Key Terms

A-B design   98

A-B-A-B design   99

across behaviors   100

across settings   100

across students   100

alternating treatments
   design (ATD)   106

baseline   97

behavioral objectives   81

changing-criterion design   103

conditions   81

criteria; criterion   81

designs   97

duration recording   85

event (frequency) recording   84

goals   80

interobserver agreement   92

interval recording   85

intervention condition   98

latency recording   85

momentary time sampling   86

multiple-baseline designs   100

multiple-probe designs   100

observer drift   96

observer expectations   96

partial-interval recording   86

permanent product recording   84

reactivity   96

recording   84

single-case designs   97

whole-interval recording   86

withdrawal design (A-B-A design)   99

Discussion Questions

1. What are the potential negative consequences of developing individual support plans? How can these be avoided?

2. Why is it critical to provide a clear definition of a student's problem behavior? According to Hawkins and Dobes (1977), what are the three characteristics of behavioral definitions that will aid in this process?

3. What is the relationship between behavioral goals and objectives? What is a good format for writing a behavioral objective?

4. Under what conditions would you use each of the recording methods?

5. How can factors that influence interobserver agreement be overcome? Why is it important to minimize these factors to the greatest extent possible?

6. Describe a situation in which you would utilize an A-B design. Make sure to include which type of recording you would use as well as how you would measure interobserver agreement.

7. Describe a situation in which you would utilize a withdrawal design. Make sure to include which type of recording you would use as well as how you would measure interobserver reliability.

8. Describe a situation in which you would utilize one form of multiple-baseline design. Make sure to include which type of recording you would use as well as how you would measure interobserver agreement.

9. Describe a situation in which you would utilize a changing-criterion design. Make sure to include which type of recording you would use as well as how you would measure interobserver agreement.

10. Describe a situation in which you would utilize an alternating treatments design. Make sure to include which type of recording you would use as well as how you would measure interobserver agreement.

4

Functional Behavior Assessments and Behavior Support Plans

Chapter Objectives

After studying this chapter, you should be able to

- explain what it means to say that behavior is contextual,

- illustrate the different functions of behaviors,

- explain why functional behavior assessments are important,

- describe the types of indirect assessments,

- characterize the types of descriptive analyses,

- describe the characteristics of a functional analysis,

- describe the advantages and disadvantages of each type of functional behavior assessment,

- depict when each type of assessment should be conducted, and

- characterize how to develop an individualized intervention based on assessment data.

VIGNETTE	Developing a Behavior Support Plan

MR. MALONE WAS A SIXTH-GRADE TEACHER. He seemed to have good management methods in his classroom, and the students were generally well behaved. Mr. Malone set good rules and routines, and the students followed them for the most part. Mr. Malone also provided effective instruction. The students' academic performance was good on the whole.

Unfortunately, Mr. Malone had a female student named Katrina who seemed to have difficulties following rules. She was frequently out of her seat, rarely raised her hand to answer a question, and tended to blurt out answers, disturbing the other students. Mr. Malone tried warnings and time-outs for Katrina when she broke a rule or caused disruptions. These techniques worked at first but quickly lost their effectiveness. Mr. Malone was at the end of his rope. He had tried every management technique he could think of, even going as far as asking Katrina's parents for suggestions. Katrina seemed to know what she was doing. When asked to explain what she had done, Katrina would correctly describe her behavior. She could also describe why her behavior was inappropriate. Katrina indicated, however, that she could not help her behavior. She could not tell Mr. Malone why she was misbehaving; she would only say that she was sorry and would not do it again. Then, at a later time, she would repeat the unwanted behavior.

Mr. Malone was not sure what to do. He generally liked Katrina. She could be pleasant to be around when she was behaving appropriately. He knew something had to be done, though, because her unwanted behavior was becoming more frequent. Mr. Malone was also concerned about improving Katrina's behavior soon because he was beginning to suspect that an emotional disturbance was causing her to act this way.

Overview

Typically, there are three explanations for a student's behavior. First, it can be said that a student is behaving in a certain manner due to some physiological reason. She was born with a particular temperament, which is why she acts as she does. Second, a student may act a certain way because she comes from a particular social context or background. Finally, a student may behave a certain way because of a variety of immediate happenings in the school context. Figure 4.1 shows these three main explanations for behavior: physiological predispositions, cultural reasons, and the past or immediate environment. Thus, physiology, culture, and the learning environment account for why we, as teachers and students, do what we do.

Suppose we take each of the three possibilities to describe why a behavior occurs (i.e., physiology, culture, and environment). First, physiology is a critical aspect of a behavior. We are all physiological beings, and our physiologies interact with the environment. However, are physiologies sufficient in explaining why we do something? The answer is no. Physiologies interact with the environment and are, to a large extent, dependent on the environment. This being said, mental health problems, many of which are physiological in origin (e.g., schizophrenia), can have an enormous impact

| Figure 4.1 | Causes of Behavior |

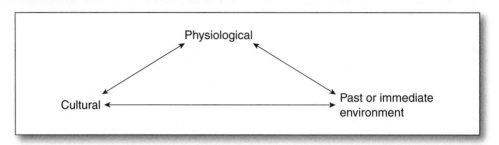

on student behavior in school. Culture comprises our broader learning history including family, social group, and nationality. Culture, like physiology, will have an enormous impact on the behavior of students within a school context. Such dynamics as peer group affiliations can be influenced by the broader cultural context, as will interactions between teachers and students, especially if cultural differences make it difficult for these two groups to communicate and interpret one another's behavior. The school environment (e.g., school and teacher responses to behavioral support needs, bullying by peers, instructional strategies used, nature and content of curriculum) is critical in explaining behavior, but, again, by itself, it does not tell us the influence physiology and culture can have over behavior. Thus, to understand why we do what we do, we must consider these three aspects of human behavior.

It is critical that teachers take into account physiological and cultural influences on student behavior and how they will impact behavior support plans. A **behavior support plan** (also called a **behavior intervention plan [BIP]**) is comprised of written documents describing the environmental changes that will need to take place to bring about changes in a wanted or an unwanted behavior. Ultimately behavior support plans will impact the nature of instruction, curriculum, and other aspects of the school routine for students. Teachers can change the way they teach, the way they interact, and the way they respond to a student. Therefore, when discussing why students do what they do, teachers must look for clues in the immediate classroom environment. That is not to argue that the classroom environment explains everything; instead, the classroom environment and its corresponding effect on behavior are what teachers should focus on when it comes to building behavior support plans because these are the aspects of behavior over which teachers have some control.

This chapter describes environmental reasons why students behave as they do. The purposes of this chapter are to provide explanations for student behavior and describe how assessments aimed at finding these explanations are conducted. Additionally, an explanation will be provided on how to use findings from these assessments to develop effective individualized behavior support plans.

The content of the current chapter and the previous one are inextricably related. Both of these chapters deal primarily with the assessment of behavior. In Chapter 3, we discussed the process of identifying behavior and tracking behavior change. In the current chapter, we describe methods of understanding the context that may influence challenging behavior. The information in this chapter is essential in terms of selecting interventions to be used as part of an effective behavior support plan.

What Are the Assumptions of Behavior Support?

Before developing a behavior support plan, a **functional behavior assessment (FBA)** should be conducted; an FBA is an assessment that is used to determine the environmental functions of wanted and unwanted behaviors. Certain assumptions must be made during the FBA for it to be successful. These assumptions come from a particular conceptual position of why we behave the way we do. There are several such conceptual systems including psychoanalytic, constructivist, cognitive, humanistic, and behavioral systems. The conceptual system used throughout this book comes from a behavioral model. A behavioral model assumes all behavior is caused and that the cause is ultimately external and physical. So our assessments and our support plans focus on finding external or environmental factors that contribute to challenging behaviors (when we assess) and that support adaptive behavior (when we build behavior support plans).

Contextual Behavior

Human behavior is contextual; it should be interpreted based on environmental factors. So assessment of behavior and support plans will focus on the student's environment (e.g., school, physiological, home). Assessment and intervention will steer away from internal or mentalistic reasons that students behave the way they do. Mentalistic explanations produce circular definitions of behavior and have not proven successful in terms of developing empirically validated, successful support plans for students with challenging behavior. So to understand behavior, we must have a clear picture of what the behavior is (see Chapter 3), and then we must get a clear picture of the context in which it occurs. This context may include culture, physiology, and school context. Other professionals, such as a medical practitioner or psychiatrist, can provide us with insight regarding physiological variables (e.g., mental health problems, illnesses) that influence a student's behavior. Interviews with the student's family or the student can provide us with insight into cultural influences on the student's behavior. Both physiological and cultural influences need to be taken into account as part of assessment and intervention within a behavioral framework. Finally, the school context, both broadly (school rules, peer relationships) and specifically (curriculum and instruction), needs to be examined with regard to its influence on behavior.

Functions of Behavior

What happens following a behavior influences the probability of the behavior. If a behavior increases in probability under certain environmental conditions and following

Behavior in the classroom is affected by what it receives in return.

certain consequences, then those consequences are called reinforcers. If a behavior decreases following consequences, then those consequences are called punishers. What we try to do with our assessments is to identify the relationship between the behavior of interest and various consequences. We try to find the consequences that maintain a behavior or reduce the likelihood of a behavior. This interaction between behavior and consequences is called a **functional relationship**. These contextual events will reliably occur either just before the behavior or just after the behavior. A functional relationship is similar to what others talk about as a cause-and-effect relationship (e.g., my behavior support plan caused an improvement in student behavior).

Now consider the information required if we are to know the function of a behavior. Say we know that, when a teacher provides an instruction to begin work (antecedent), there is a high likelihood a tantrum (behavior) will result or that, when a student has a tantrum (behavior), the teacher will send the student away from the group (consequence). Therefore, the probability of a particular behavior occurring is higher when a particular instruction is provided or when the teacher responds to the behavior in a certain way. What could this information provide to the teacher? Once the function of a behavior is known, it may become possible to change the instruction to avoid the unwanted behavior or to react to the unwanted behavior in another way. Thus, determining the function of a behavior can be critical in developing an adequate behavior support plan for the student.

Essentially, functions can be divided into two categories. As shown in Figure 4.2, the categories involve positive reinforcement and negative reinforcement. Under positive and negative reinforcement there are several subcategories: sensory (internal stimuli), social (attention), and tangible (objects or activities). Under both positive and negative reinforcement categories, behaviors increase as a function of consequences. A student may engage in behaviors because, in the past, doing so allowed the student to gain access to consequences, such as teacher attention or certain activities. The student can also engage in behaviors because doing so once allowed the student to escape attention or avoid activities. Increases in behavior that resulted in the removal or avoidance of consequences are termed negatively reinforced. Increases in behavior to gain access to items or activities are termed positively reinforced. The processes of positive and negative reinforcement describe increases in behaviors. Distinguishing between these two categories of reinforcement is critical in terms of developing effective support plans for students.

Also, notice the sensory feedback category. Sometimes, consequences maintaining behavior may be internal or physiological. In the positive reinforcement category, we see that students can behave to obtain some type of feedback from one or more of the senses, such as visual stimulation, rhythmic rocking, or an endorphin release. Students with

| Figure 4.2 | Potential Functions of Behavior |

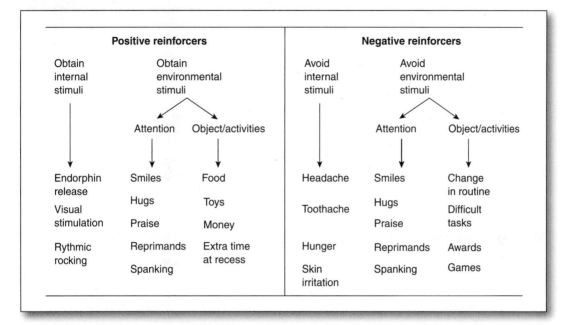

autism spectrum conditions often engage in such behavior patterns (O'Reilly et al., 2010). Likewise, at times we attempt to escape or avoid sensory stimulation by emitting a behavior to do so. For example, if a student is sleep deprived, he could engage in negatively reinforced challenging behavior that will result in his avoidance of academic work tasks (Sigafoos, Arthur, & O'Reilly, 2003).

Broader influences, above and beyond the consequences that maintain certain behavioral responses, can also affect behavior. We have discussed these broader influences in terms of physiological and cultural variables earlier in the chapter. However, these additional broader influences should be understood in terms of this functional description of behavior as well. Such broader contextual influences can act as setting events or establishing operations, conditions that influence the power of reinforcing consequences (Sigafoos et al., 2003). For example, sleep deprivation and hunger, both physiological variables, may increase student aversion toward academic tasks and thereby increase the probability of tantrums to escape and avoid such activities. A white teacher from a privileged middle-class background may study the culture and language of immigrant Hispanic students in her class and adapt her curriculum and instruction accordingly, thereby increasing academic engagement and decreasing acting out from these students. These examples are potential setting events or establishing operations, and they explain why it is important to consider such broader variables when examining the function of challenging behavior and developing behavior support plans.

Other Assumptions

Two other assumptions should be considered when one conducts an FBA. First is the assumption that an FBA will lead to an intervention. We do assume that, if we can find out what the function of a behavior is, we will be much more likely to be successful when we develop a behavior support plan. Second is the assumption that, when we remove the function or source of reinforcement from a behavior, the behavior will end. This assumption is basic to any behavioral interpretation of human behavior. This interpretation flows from the **Law of Effect** proposed by E. L. Thorndike (1905), which says that, when a behavior is reinforced, the behavior will be more likely to occur in the future, whereas, when a behavior is punished, the behavior will be less likely to occur in the future. The process of the behavior becoming less likely to occur in the future is called extinction. Therefore, we assume that, if we can find the source of reinforcement and remove it, the behavior will decrease in probability in the future.

Why Is It Important to Know About Functional Behavior Assessments?

There are two major reasons it is important for teachers to understand and be able to implement FBAs. First, interventions derived from FBAs are more effective and less intrusive than interventions that are not derived from FBAs (Carr et al., 1999). Therefore, an FBA is an evidence-based best practice. Second, teachers are required by law to use FBAs to develop behavior support plans. These issues are discussed in detail below.

FBAs examine the circumstances surrounding the occurrence and nonoccurrence of challenging behavior. The goal of these assessments is to identify events that are reliably or consistently present when the challenging behavior occurs and does not occur. FBAs are considered important for two reasons. First, an FBA is believed to improve the quality and potential success of a behavioral intervention. In other words, the more that is known about the behavior, the better the intervention that can be designed to fit the needs of the particular situation. Second, FBAs are believed to lead to less aversive behavioral interventions. Interventions designed following FBAs are considered less aversive because they involve determining the likely reinforcers for a behavior, which allows the removal of the source of reinforcement for challenging behavior and the use of this form of reinforcement to increase appropriate skills, an overall process that decreases the need to use punishment or negative reinforcement (e.g., warnings). Behavior support plans derived from an FBA focus on educational interventions to replace challenging behavior rather than on interventions designed to reduce challenging behavior.

Under certain circumstances, FBAs are required by federal law (Individuals with Disabilities Education Improvement Act [IDEA], 2004). An FBA and behavior support plan (also called a behavior intervention plan [BIP]) are considered to be a matter of best practice and may be required in some states (Zirkel, 2009). Under IDEA regulations, they are sometimes "a required IEP team consideration":

> In such cases, depending on the frequency and severity of the learning–interfering behaviors, an FBA and/or BIP may be appropriate, but neither is required as a general matter.

The only situation in which IDEA specifically requires an FBA and BIP is for a disciplinary change in placement for behavior that is a manifestation of the child's disability (§ 300.530[f][a]). Less strongly, the IDEA regulations require an FBA "as appropriate" and "behavior intervention services and modifications" designed to prevent reliance upon (a) a disciplinary change in placement for behavior that is not a manifestation of the child's disability, or (b) the district's permissible (i.e., for weapons, drugs, or serious bodily injury) removal of the child to a 45-day interim alternate educational setting (§ 300.530[d][ii]). (Zirkel, 2009, p. 74)

Therefore, all educators should have at least a working knowledge of FBAs. In addition, although FBAs are required to be used in the development of a behavior support plan for individuals with identified disabilities, these assessments should also be used for all students for whom such a support plan is needed, irrespective of disability.

What Are the Types of Functional Behavior Assessments?

Before a description of FBAs is provided, it should be pointed out that the federal law does not define the key features of an FBA and has provided little guidance on how they should be completed (Scott, Anderson, & Spaulding, 2008). As a result, the effectiveness with which schools implement FBAs has been questioned (Blood & Neel, 2007; Couvillon, Bullock, & Gable, 2009). With this in mind, we will provide a description of what is considered best practice—that is, how FBAs *should* be conducted. There are three types of FBAs that teachers can use to identify environmental factors that may be maintaining challenging behavior: indirect assessments, descriptive analyses, and functional analyses (Sigafoos et al., 2003). The strengths and weaknesses of each category of assessment are included in Table 4.1 and are discussed in detail below. These assessments are described in an order moving from the least extensive assessment (indirect assessment) to the most extensive assessment (functional analysis).

Table 4.1	Types of Functional Behavior Assessments

Indirect Assessments: Subjective verbal reports of behavior under naturalistic conditions	
Examples:	Interviews, checklists, rating scales
Advantages:	Efficient, easy to use, good starting point
Disadvantages:	Reliability and validity questionable, starting point not endpoint

(Continued)

Table 4.1	(Continued)

Descriptive Analyses: Quantitative direct observation of behavior under naturalistic conditions

Examples:	A-B-C analyses, observation forms, scatter plots
Advantages:	Objective, conducted in actual setting, see behavior firsthand, may be endpoint
Disadvantages:	Complexity, inability to identify subtle or intermittent variables, time-consuming, potential masking by irrelevant events, may not be endpoint

Functional Analyses: Quantitative direct observation of behavior under preselected and controlled conditions

Examples:	Alternating treatments designs, other designs
Advantages:	Objective, high degree of control over behavior, high reliability and validity, endpoint
Disadvantages:	Complexity, potential insensitivity to high idiosyncratic events, prompting unwanted behavior to occur, potential risk of establishing new behavioral function

Indirect Assessments

Indirect assessments involve gaining information from sources other than a first-hand analysis of the environmental events. These assessments can involve interviewing those who work directly with the student. They are usually "subjective verbal reports of the behavior under naturalistic conditions," in other words, reports concerning when the behavior occurs and what the antecedents and consequences of the behavior are (Iwata, Vollmer, & Zarcone, 1990, p. 305). Examples of methods used to gain this information are interviews, checklists, and rating scales. These assessments have advantages over other forms of assessments in that they are efficient, are easy to use, and provide a good starting point. The difficulties with indirect assessments are that their reliability and validity are questionable. If possible, it is advisable to supplement indirect assessment with other forms of assessment prior to developing a behavior support plan. Following is a description of the types of indirect assessments.

Interviews. Interview assessments are perhaps the most widely used form of FBAs. **Interview assessments** seek to determine the source of reinforcement for a behavior by asking people in the student's life what they think the likely function of the challenging behavior is. There are several types of interview assessments. Table 4.2 summarizes the information found in many interview assessments. This information can be separated into five categories: behaviors, setting events, antecedents, consequences, and interventions (O'Neill et al., 1997).

Table 4.2	Information Contained in Many Functional Behavior Assessment Interviews

Behaviors

1. Topography, frequency, duration, intensity
2. Response chains: behaviors that occur together

Setting Events

3. Medications, medical or physical conditions, sleep patterns, eating routines
4. Schedule of activities: predictability, choices, staffing patterns, other students or people present, noise levels

Antecedents

5. Day of the week, time, setting, people present, activity, instructions

Consequences

6. Positive and negative reinforcers

Interventions

7. Efficiency of the behavior: effort, reinforcement schedule, immediacy of the reinforcer
8. Functional alternatives and methods of communication in student's repertoire (motoric, verbal responses, expressive or receptive language skills)
9. Methods currently used to avoid problem behaviors
10. Potential reinforcers for a person's behavior: tangible, social, activity, edible
11. Past attempts to control student behavior: targeted behaviors, past programs, length of programs, effects of programs

Caregivers such as teachers, parents, and instructional aides are not the only individuals who can be interviewed. The students themselves can be interviewed, although they are often left out of the assessment process. Nevertheless, many times, students can provide information that is valuable in leading to a hypothesis concerning the function of their challenging behavior. O'Neill et al. (1997) developed a student-guided interview form. The information contained in such an interview is shown in Table 4.3. A critical part of the student-guided interview is targeting the behavior that got the student into trouble. Having students explain exactly what they did that resulted in the teacher's response is critical. Second, setting events should be considered with the students. Questions such as these could be asked: "How did you feel before you did that?" or "Were you in a bad mood at the time and why?" In addition, the immediate antecedents to the challenging behavior should be considered; the interviewer could ask questions such as "What

Table 4.3	Information to Be Included in a Student-Guided Functional Behavior Assessment Interview

Behaviors

1. The behaviors that got him or her into trouble at school and how intensely the behaviors occur (rated on an intensity scale)

Setting Events

2. Important events, places, or activities that are associated with the behavior (e.g., lack of sleep, illness, physical pain, hunger, trouble at home, noise or distractions, class or activities)

Antecedents

3. His or her subjects and activities and his or her teachers each class period

4. The class periods or times of day when the behaviors occur

5. Each situation that makes the behavior occur (e.g., class demands that are too hard, boring, unclear, long; teacher reprimands; peer teaching; or encouragement)

Consequences

6. Staff and student reactions when he or she misbehaves

Interventions

7. What he or she thinks would improve the situation

occurred just before you did the unwanted behavior?" or "What subject were you working on?" or "Who was around you at the time?" The consequences should also be probed through asking, "What happened when you did the unwanted behavior?" or "How did the teacher or other students react to what you did?" Finally, getting students' opinions on what they think could improve the situation can be important. For example, if the students indicate they did not think that the teacher respected them, additional probing into what the teacher did to result in that opinion could be done. Teachers many times do what they have always done in the classroom with students; students, however, may misinterpret an instruction presented in some manner as an indication of a lack of respect, for example. Simple changes in the manner in which instructions are presented could help improve students' behavior in the classroom. Gaining information on their views can be important. In addition, interviewing the students can also show them their input is valued, which could result in the students being more likely to "buy into" the resulting behavior management program.

Nelson, Roberts, and Smith (1998) developed the user-friendly interview or self-report form shown in Figure 4.3. As can be seen, the information requested on the form attempts to determine the setting events, antecedents, behaviors, and consequences associated with the challenging behavior.

Figure 4.3	Interview or Self-Report Form

INTERVIEW/SELF-REPORT FORM

Student <u>Ellen</u>   Respondent <u>Ms. Brown (teacher)</u>   Date <u>11/18/__</u>

I. Problem Definition

1. Describe the student's target behavior(s)—primary problem behavior(s)—in objective terms.
<u>Ellen Shouts profanities.</u>

II. Events and Situations Related to the Occurrence and Nonoccurrence of the Target Behavior(s)

2. In what situations does/do the target behavior(s) occur?

Location	*Time*	*Person(s)*	*Instructional Context*
☑ In Class	○ Arrival to school	☑ Teacher(s)	○ Entire group
○ Hallways	☑ Morning	○ Specialist(s)	○ Small group
○ Cafeteria	○ Lunch	○ Support staff	☑ Individual
○ Special classes	☑ Afternoon	○ Bus driver	○ Transition
○ Bus	○ Recess/break	○ Peer(s)	○ Other
○ Other _____	○ Other _____	○ Other _____	○ Other _____

Comments: <u>Occurs in class when given an assignment to work on independently.</u>

3. In what situations are the student's behaviors most appropriate?

Location	*Time*	*Person(s)*	*Instructional Context*
○ In class	☑ Arrival to school	○ Teacher(s)	☑ Entire group
☑ Hallways	○ Morning	☑ Specialist(s)	☑ Small group
☑ Cafeteria	☑ Lunch	☑ Support staff	○ Individual
☑ Special classes	○ Afternoon	☑ Bus driver	☑ Transition
☑ Bus	☑ Recess/break	☑ Peer(s)	○ Other _____
○ Other _____	○ Other _____	○ Other _____	

Comments: <u>Does not occur during group instruction or nonacademic activities.</u>

4. Are there any other internal and external events that influence the target behavior(s)?

Internal Events	*External Events*
○ Medication_____	○ Conflict at home_____
○ Physical health_____	○ Illegal drug use_____
☑ Academic skills <u>Occurs more in math class</u>	○ Negative peer influence (gangs, etc.)_____
○ Other _____	☑ Other <u>When asked to work on an assignment.</u>

Comments: _____

III. Events That Occur Prior to (Antecedents) and After (Consequences) the Target Behavior(s)

5. What typically happens prior to the student exhibiting the target behavior(s)?

○ Low levels of adult attention	☑ Presentation of activity or task	○ Under varied conditions
○ Low levels of peer attention	○ Social interaction with adult	○ Other_____
○ Unavailability of object/activity	○ Social interaction with peers	

Comments: <u>I ask her to work on an assignment independently.</u>

6. What typically happens after the student exhibits the target behavior(s)?

○ Start-up request	○ Reprimand	○ Ultimatum	○ Time out
○ Ignore	○ Response cost	○ Office referral	☑ Other <u>Redirect</u>

Comments: <u>I redirect her and/or work with her on the assignment.</u>

Checklists. Checklists can also be used in an indirect assessment. In **checklists**, caregivers such as parents or teachers check off possible antecedents and consequences that the students might be exposed to when specific behaviors occur. Several checklists are available, including one described by Rolider and Van Houten (1993). This checklist was developed for parents or other mediators to determine the precursors of problem behaviors of individuals with developmental disabilities. Checklists should contain as many antecedents and consequences as possible. Antecedents could include whether demands or requests were made of the students and whether students were sitting alone, interacting with others, engaging in academic tasks, or interacting with adults. Consequences could include removing students from class, providing students with attention, ignoring students, and administering possibly aversive stimuli such as reprimands.

Rating Scales. **Rating scales** are similar to checklists except that teachers or parents can provide a level of likelihood that an antecedent or consequence would occur before or after the target behavior. As with checklists, several rating scales are available. Perhaps one of the better-known rating scales is the **Motivation Assessment Scale (MAS)** by Durand and Crimmins (1987). This 16-item rating scale requires a specific description of the challenging behaviors and a description of the settings in which they occur. The questions are separated into four categories of function: sensory, escape, attention, and tangible. Examples of questions in each category include the following: "Would the behavior occur continuously, over and over, if this person were left alone for long periods of time, such as several hours?" (sensory); "Does the behavior occur when any request is made of this person?" (escape); "Does the behavior occur whenever you stop attending to this person?" (attention); and "Does this behavior stop occurring shortly after you give this person the toy, food, or activity he or she has requested?" (tangible). The likelihood of occurrence of each of these situations is rated on a Likert-type scale from 0 (*never*) to 6 (*always*). The average rating per category is calculated, and a relative ranking is determined based on each average score.

The **Problem Behavior Questionnaire** (Lewis, Scott, & Sugai, 1994) is a 15-item rating scale in which the frequency with which an event is likely to be seen is rated. The range of the rating scale is "never" to "90% of the time." Examples of functions of behavior and correlated items include the following: "When the problem behavior occurs, do peers verbally respond to or laugh at the student?" (access to peer attention); "Does the problem behavior occur to get your attention?" (access to teacher attention); "If the student engages in the problem behavior, do peers stop interacting with the student?" (escape/avoidance of peer attention); "Will the student stop the problem behavior if you stop making requests or end an academic activity?" (escape/avoidance of teacher attention); and "Is the problem behavior more likely to occur following unscheduled events or disruptions in classroom routines?" (setting events).

The **Functional Analysis Screening Tool (FAST)** is an 18-item rating scale (Iwata & DeLeon, 1996). It is recommended that FAST be administered to several individuals who interact with the student frequently. An indication of "yes" or "no" is used to determine if an item statement accurately describes the student's unwanted behavior. Examples of the maintaining variables and correlated items include the following: "When the behavior occurs, do you usually try to calm the person down or distract the person with preferred activities such as leisure items or snacks?" (social reinforcement); "When the behavior occurs, do you usually give the person a 'break' from ongoing tasks?" (negative reinforcement); "Does the behavior occur at high rates regardless of what is going on around the person?" (automatic reinforcement, sensory stimulation); and "Does the behavior occur more often when the person is sick?" (automatic reinforcement, pain attenuation).

Summarizing Data. Once an indirect assessment has been conducted, the data must be summarized in some form. It is important to look for patterns in the data. Teachers should ask, "Was a particular antecedent (e.g., academic instruction) usually present when the behavior (e.g., swearing) occurred, usually resulting in a particular consequence (e.g., being removed from the group)?" Setting events should also be considered. For example, whenever the student comes to school sleepy, does he usually display a higher instance of the unwanted behavior? Also, teachers should look to see if different types of contexts produce similar responses from the student. For example, providing the student an instruction to begin her math assignment may occasion the same response from the student as requiring her to clean up a work area. Although these two events (i.e., academic requirement and cleanliness requirement) are seemingly unrelated, they nonetheless result in the same unwanted behavior. Additionally, behaviors that seem unrelated (e.g., aggression to peers, noncompliance with teacher instructions) may produce similar consequences (e.g., attention from peers). So contexts and behaviors that may seem unrelated may be functionally equivalent (i.e., produce the same consequences for the student). This information will be critical in terms of developing effective behavior support plans.

Once antecedents, behaviors, and consequences have been identified, summary statements can be made. Figure 4.4 shows such a summary statement. Essentially, the information is placed into a four-term or three-term contingency arrangement. As shown in the figure, the setting event is corrective feedback on an assignment, which results in a high probability of hitting or swearing (behavior) when the teacher provides instruction to begin work on an academic task (antecedent). The hitting or swearing (behavior) then results in being removed from the room (consequence). Now there is a possible sequence of events. This possible sequence gives information on the possible functions of the challenging behavior. The setting event (corrective feedback)

Figure 4.4 Summary Statement for a Behavioral Episode

Setting event	Antecedent	Behavior	Consequence
John receives corrective feedback.	When John is given an instruction to begin work	he will hit or swear,	which results in his removal from the classroom.

increases the probability of challenging behavior during instruction (when he is told to begin work), and this produces a negatively reinforcing consequence (removal from the class). In the example just provided, the function of the behavior may be escape or avoidance of an academic task. This information is then used in the next step in the assessment process—descriptive analyses.

Descriptive Analyses

Descriptive analyses involve the direct observation of the student in the natural environment where the challenging behavior is most likely to occur. Descriptive analyses can take several forms, such as A-B-C analyses, observation forms, and scatter plots.

Teachers may need to take observational data of student behavior to determine why a behavior is occurring and what to do about it.

The main advantage of descriptive analyses is they are more objective than indirect assessments because they involve a direct assessment or observation of the unwanted and wanted behaviors (Sigafoos et al., 2003).

A-B-C Analysis. Figure 4.5 shows an A-B-C form. At first glance, an A-B-C analysis seems to be simple. A-B-C analyses, however, can be quite complex to conduct. Essentially, an **A-B-C analysis** involves an observer (e.g., teacher, student teacher, parent, behavior specialist, school psychologist) observing the student during typical activities. The observations should occur during school activities when the behavior is most likely to happen. The length of the observations depends on several factors, such as the frequency of the target behaviors seen and the amount of resources the school has to conduct the observations. Such observations should be conducted on two or three occasions to get a comprehensive picture of the student's behavior.

When conducting the observations, a teacher should write a narrative of events occurring just prior to (antecedents) and just after (consequences) the targeted behaviors. A-B-C analyses are similar to conducting an observation study in qualitative research. Their purpose is to aid in the development of hypothesis statements about the possible functions of the unwanted behavior. The narrative should include episodes not only of the targeted, unwanted behaviors but also of the wanted behaviors. Essentially, all interactions with the student should be documented. For this narrative, the observer should develop a system of abbreviations and summaries to keep pace with the behavioral events. Narrative recordings take experience and practice so that all necessary events can be reported. These narrative events should occur over a minimum period of three days. We recommend the observations occur over a period of five to seven school days.

| Figure 4.5 | A-B-C Analysis Form |

Antecedent	Behavior	Consequence

Antecedent: What conditions are present just before the behavior occurs.

Behavior: The student's response (what he or she does).

Consequence: What occurs immediately after the student's behavior.

Once the observations are completed, the narrative should be reviewed. The critical aspect of any functional assessment, as noted earlier, is finding patterns in the data. Therefore, similar antecedents present before unwanted as well as wanted behaviors should be identified. For example, most of the time when the teacher asks the student to perform an academic task, the student swears. When the teacher requests that the student do a nonacademic task, such as line up at the door, however, the student complies. Similar consequences should also be categorized together. For instance, most of the time when the student is on task, the teacher does not attend to her. But when she misbehaves the teacher attends to her (giving attention in the form of reprimands). So misbehavior may function to get attention from the teacher.

Nelson, Roberts, and Smith (1998) present an alternative observation form. As shown in Figure 4.6, the form is a modification of the one in Figure 4.5. This modified form prompts for summary statements to be made based on information gathered from the form, which helps teachers to summarize the information of a descriptive assessment.

Observation Forms. There are a variety of observation forms available for conducting descriptive analyses. **Observation forms** structure the observations into a checklist format with operational definitions of each of the target behaviors similar to the narrative recording method. One of the more popular observation forms was developed by O'Neill et al. (1997). Figure 4.7 shows an example of such a form. As shown in the figure, the behaviors of concern are written in the provided columns. There should be an operational definition of each behavior so that the person conducting the observations is sure of what to examine. The predictors are provided. In addition, information on setting events and other antecedents, such as the particular people working with the student or the individuals with whom the student is interacting, can be written in the provided columns. Next, the perceived functions of the behaviors are provided. Notice that there are two major categories provided: get/obtain (positive reinforcement) and escape/avoid (negative reinforcement). Within the get/obtain category are attention, desired item/activity, and self-stimulation. Within the escape/avoidance category are demand/request, activity, and person. The actual consequences delivered based on the behaviors should be provided as well. Finally, the time of observation should be written on the left side of the form. O'Neill et al. (1997) recommend that the observations be taken for a minimum of three days. As with A-B-C analysis, observations should be scheduled when the unwanted behavior is most likely to occur; the observations should be long enough to get a valid representation of the student's interaction with his or her environment.

Figure 4.8 shows a form filled out for John. There were two behaviors of concern—hitting and swearing. There were 11 episodes of these behaviors on the day of the observation. The behaviors were not allocated to one particular teacher or time period. The behaviors occurred either during times when something was asked of John (a demand or request) or during difficult tasks. The consequence was usually a time-out. The perceived function was to escape or avoid demands or activities. Thus, time-out seemed to be functioning as a negative reinforcer. The summary statement for John is that when something is demanded or requested of him or when he is given activities to complete, he will hit or swear or do both to escape the task or activity by being sent to time-out.

Figure 4.6	Observation and Analysis Form

OBSERVATION AND ANALYSIS FORM

Student <u>Ellen</u>   Observer <u>Ms. Brown (teacher)</u>   Date <u>11/18/</u>___

Target behavior(s) observed <u>Profanities</u>

I. Direct Observations

Start: 9:30	**Setting:**	**Activity:**
End: 10:30	Classroom	Math
Antecedent:	**Behavior:**	**Consequence:**
Get Started	Profanity	Redirected
Comments:		

Start: 9:30	**Setting:**	**Activity:**
End: 10:30	Classroom	Math
Antecedent:	**Behavior:**	**Consequence:**
Get to work	Profanity	Sat with her
Comments:		

Start: 9:30	**Setting:**	**Activity:**
End: 10:30	Classroom	Math
Antecedent:	**Behavior:**	**Consequence:**
Work on your math	Profanity	Redirected helped with math
Comments:		

II. Summary

1. Identify the settings, activities, and consequences that appear to be related to the occurrence and nonoccurrence of the target behavior(s).
   <u>Ellen shouts profanities when I give her a direction to start her math assignment.</u>

2. Identify the events that occur prior to and after the target behavior(s).
   <u>A direction occurs prior to the behavior at which time I redirect her and/or help her with her assignment.</u>

3. Are they consistent with other information collected?   ☑ Consistent   ○ Inconsistent

   Comments: _____

SOURCE: From J. R. Nelson, M. L. Roberts, and D. J. Smith, *Conducting Functional Behavioral Assessments in School Settings.* Copyright © 1998 by Sopris West. Reprinted with permission from Sopris West Educational Services, Longmont, CO. 800-547-6747. (Packs of forms are available for purchase from Sopris West.)

Figure 4.7	Functional Assessment Observation Form

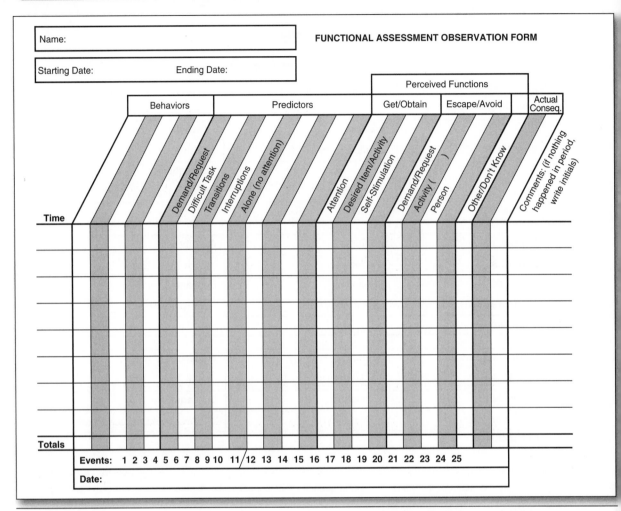

SOURCE: From O'Neill/Horner/Albin/Sprague/Storey/Newton. *Functional Assessment and Program Development for Problem Behavior*, 2E. © 1997 Wadsworth, a part of Cengage Learning, Inc. Reproduced by permission. www.cengage.com/permissions

Scatter Plots. Another form of assessment is the scatter plot devised by Touchette, MacDonald, and Langer (1985). The **scatter plot** enables observers to monitor targeted behaviors over an extended period of time. Figure 4.9 shows a scatter plot. As seen in the figure, the time of day is provided on the vertical axis and successive days are listed on the horizontal axis. The time of day can be divided into hour, half-hour, quarter-hour, or smaller increments, depending on what the observer wants to represent. The coding system involves three possibilities. An open box refers to a lack of target behavior. A slash through the box represents a low level of the behavior. A filled-in box represents a high level of the behavior. Whether a behavior is at a minor level or a major level is set somewhat arbitrarily. For example, a slash could represent the behavior occurring fewer than five times during the interval. The filled-in box could represent the behavior

Figure 4.8	Functional Assessment Observation Form With Data

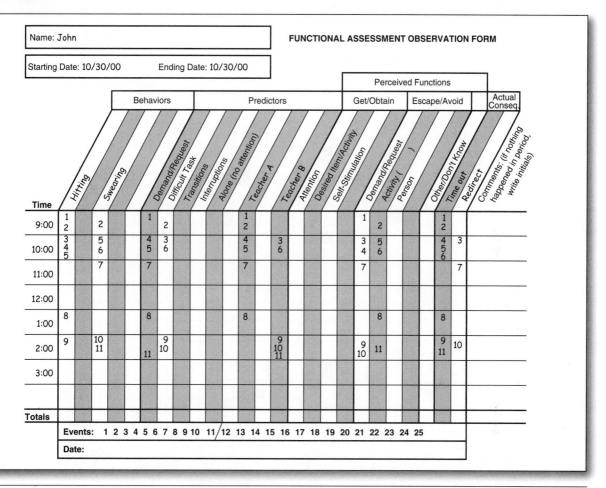

occurring five or more times. The grouping of the slashed or filled-in boxes is an indication of when the behaviors are emitted throughout some time span. (Numbers can be placed in the boxes to give a more accurate representation of the frequency of the unwanted behaviors at various points in time.) A difficulty with the scatter plot is that environmental conditions that are related to behaviors on a time-cyclical basis cannot be determined (Axelrod, 1987b). Also, the scatter plot does not determine the potential functional relationships of the unwanted behaviors, but it does lead the teacher to narrow down when an unwanted behavior is likely to occur so that a finer analysis, such as an A-B-C analysis, can be conducted at those times. Additionally, these results could also be used to supplement the results from interviews or other checklists.

Figure 4.9 Scatter Plot With Data

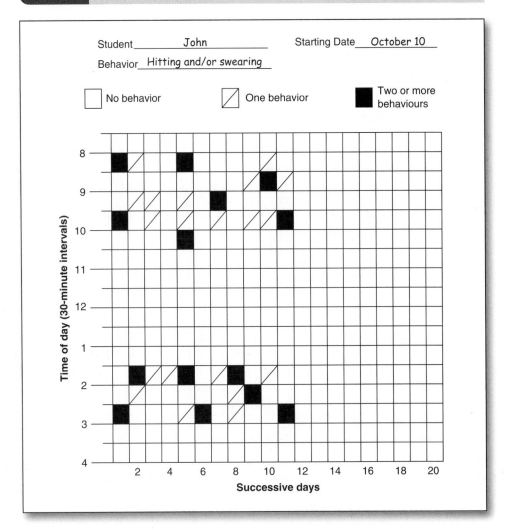

For the example presented in Figure 4.9, it can be seen that the behavior tends to occur in the morning and afternoon. There is little problem behavior after 10:30 AM and before 1:30 PM. Therefore, a teacher would want to determine what is occurring, who is with John, and the types of interactions going on during those times. For example, it is possible that academic tasks that are more aversive to John occur during the times of the outbursts. It is possible a particular person, such as an instructional aide, is working with John during those times. Another possibility is that John is engaged in individualized seatwork at those times when the behavior is likely to occur and in cooperative learning groups when the behavior is least likely to occur. The time could also be a factor in and of itself. The outbursts tend to occur shortly after the beginning of school and about 1 to 1.5 hours before the end of school. Some setting events could be present that make John more likely to misbehave, such as getting into fights before and after school. Therefore, the scatter plot can function to help the teacher narrow down the possibilities, and it also allows the teacher to focus on a more defined range of times during which the unwanted behavior occurs so that a more fine-grained analysis can be conducted then. An A-B-C analysis could be conducted before 10:30 AM and after 1:30 PM to get an idea of the function of the unwanted behaviors John is exhibiting.

Summarizing Data. Once the descriptive analyses have been conducted, the data will need to be summarized again. This summarization is similar in form to the one completed for the indirect assessment. The summary of descriptive analysis results should be compared with indirect assessment results to determine if the two are consistent. Frequently, they will be. At times, however, the two summaries will differ in some manner. The summary presented in Figure 4.4 indicates the setting event was receiving corrective feedback. Direct observation, however, found corrective feedback was not a reliable predictor of the problem behavior; rather, the manner in which feedback was provided to the student was a critical setting event. During the indirect assessment, the teacher may have identified feedback as being a setting event, but the teacher did not take into consideration that the form of that feedback may have had an effect on the behavior. Suppose during the observation it was shown that, when the teacher provided feedback by first discussing what the student did correctly (e.g., "I see that you put a lot of effort into this assignment") and then provided an effective error correction sequence (e.g., "You were on the right track in figuring out the math problems until you had to borrow. Watch how I borrow in this math problem. Let's try the next problem together. Great. Now try this one on your own"), the student was not likely to misbehave. However, when an ineffective error correction sequence was used (e.g., "You did not borrow the correct way. You knew this yesterday. Let's try again"), the behavior was much more likely to be seen when a new instruction was presented. Thus, a revised summary statement based on the descriptive analysis is presented in Figure 4.10.

Nelson et al. (1998) provide two forms that will help in the development of summary statements and, ultimately, in the development of behavior support plans (see Figure 4.11 and Figure 4.12).

Figure 4.10	Summary Statement for a Behavioral Episode After Descriptive Information Is Gathered

Setting event	Antecedent	Behavior	Consequence
John receives corrective feedback in a negative fashion. →	When John is given an instruction to begin work →	he will hit or swear, →	which results in his removal from the classroom.
John receives corrective feedback via a positive error correction procedure. →	When John is given an instruction to begin work →	he will work, →	which results in praise from the teacher.

Figure 4.11 Temporal Analysis and Ranking Form

TEMPORAL ANALYSIS AND RANKING FORM

Student _Ellen_____ Rater _Ms. Brown (teacher)_____ Week of _11/18/___

Dimension being rated: ☑ Frequency ○ Duration ○ Intensity ○ Other_____

Target behavior(s) observed _Profanities_____

Directions: Rank the student's target behavior(s) for the designated time period.

All scales rated from 1(low) to 10 (high)

DAY		TIME (Increments should align with distinct changes in settings/activities.)

DAY	8:30	9:30	10:30	11:30	12:30	1:30	2:30	3:30			
Mon		|||								
Tues		|||								
Wed		||||								
Thur		|||									
Fri		||									

1. In what situation(s) are the rankings of the target behavior(s) highest?

Location	**Time**	**Person(s)**	**Instructional Context**
☑ In class	○ Arrival to school	☑ Teacher(s)	○ Entire group
○ Hallways	☑ Morning	○ Specialist(s)	○ Small group
○ Cafeteria	○ Lunch	○ Support staff	☑ Individual
○ Special classes	○ Afternoon	○ Bus driver	○ Transition
○ Bus	○ Recess/break	○ Peer(s)	○ Other
○ Other	○ Other	○ Other	

Comments: _Profanities occur during math class and are directed toward me._

2. In what situations are the rankings of the target behaviors lowest?

Location	**Time**	**Person(s)**	**Instructional Context**
☑ In class	☑ Arrival to school	○ Teacher(s)	☑ Entire group
☑ Hallways	○ Morning	☑ Specialist(s)	○ Small group
☑ Cafeteria	☑ Lunch	☑ Support staff	☑ Individual
☑ Special classes	○ Afternoon	☑ Bus driver	☑ Transition
☑ Bus	☑ Recess/break	☑ Peer(s)	○ Other
○ Other	○ Other	○ Other	

Comments: _Behavior doesn't occur during group instruction/nonacademic tasks or with others._

3. Are they consistent with other information collected? ☑ Consistent ○ Inconsistent
   Comments: _____

SOURCE: From J. R. Nelson, M. L. Roberts, and D. J. Smith, *Conducting Functional Behavioral Assessments: A Practical Guide.* Copyright © 1998 by Sopris West. Reprinted with permission from Cambium Learning Group-Sopris West Educational Services, Longmont, CO. 800-547-6747. (Packs of forms are available for purchase from Sopris West.)

Figure 4.12	Summary Analysis Form

SUMMARY ANALYSIS FORM

Student _Ellen_   Date _11/25/__

Staff Present _Ms. Brown (teacher)_   _____

            _____   _____

            _____   _____

I. Data Collection Procedures

  1. Procedures used to collect information for the functional behavioral assessment.
      ☑ Interview/Self-Report   ☑ Observation   ☑ Temporal Analysis/Ranking   ☑ Other _reviewed_
                                                                 math performance

II. Events and Situations Related to the Occurrence and Nonoccurrence of the Target Behavior(s)

  2. What key events appear to be related to the occurrence of the target behavior(s)?
      Direction to complete her math assignments independently

  3. What key events appear to be related to the nonoccurrence of the target behavior(s)?
      Not giving a direction to work on her math assignment
      Other academic tasks or instruction aside from math
      Nonacademic tasks

  4. Are there any other internal and external events that influence the target behavior(s)?
      A direction—external
      Poor math skills—internal

III. Events That Occur Prior to and After the Target Behavior(s)

  5. What typically happens prior to the student exhibiting the target behavior(s)?
      A direction

  6. What typically happens after the student exhibiting the target behavior(s)?
      Redirected and/or I work with her on the assignment.

IV. Potential Function of Target Behavior(s)

  7. What is the potential function of the target behavior(s)?

○ *Access*	☑ *Escape Avoidance*	○ *Autonomic Reinf.*	○ *Multiple*
○ Object/activity	☑ Activity	○ Comment:	○ Access
○ Adult attention	○ Adult engagement		○ Escape/avoidance
○ Peer attention	○ Peer engagement		○ Autonomic reinf.

      Comments: _Uses profanity to get attention._

Functional Analyses

Functional analyses are another type of FBA. Functional analyses allow for an experimental demonstration of the function of a target behavior. **Functional analyses** are defined as "quantitative direct observations of behavior under preselected and controlled conditions" (Iwata et al., 1990, p. 305). In essence, the student is assessed in a number of predetermined contexts (e.g., academic demands, low attention). If challenging behavior occurs more often in one context than in others, teachers can infer that the consequences in that context are maintaining behavior.

These types of assessments provide a high degree of control over the behavior and are considered to have high **reliability** (i.e., consistency of results over time) and **internal validity** (i.e., the degree to which the independent variable made the difference rather than a change being due to something else). Consequently, they can provide the necessary information required to determine the function of a behavior. However, the **external validity** (i.e., the generalizability) of these assessments is questionable. While there is a large body of research on these functional analysis techniques, there is limited research demonstrating the social validity and veracity of classroom-based behavior support plans derived from such assessments. Of course, this concern could be expressed for most FBA techniques discussed in this chapter.

It can be helpful to run brief functional analyses in situations where other FBAs have not produced a clear picture of what is maintaining a student's challenging behavior. A functional analysis can be conducted by repeatedly presenting a variety of social contexts. Teachers could use a research design such as the alternating treatments design or an A-B-A-B design (discussed in Chapter 3) to control for the systematic presentation and removal of the different social contexts. For example, the teacher might present 10 minutes of a demanding academic activity. This demand could be followed by 10 minutes in which no demands are placed on the student and he receives no attention from the teacher. These social conditions could be repeated over a number of days. If challenging behavior occurs in the demand condition, then we can infer that the student engages in this behavior to escape from academic activities. If behavior occurs in the social attention condition, then we can say that the behavior probably occurs to get attention from others.

These functional analyses have typically been conducted in clinical settings with individuals who have developmental disabilities and very severe challenging behaviors. So the ultimate value of functional analysis protocols in school contexts and with students who do not have developmental disabilities is still up for debate. If a functional analysis is suggested for a student, then it should be conducted or, at the very least, supervised by a professional who has been trained to run such a protocol. This person will probably be a behavior specialist or school psychologist.

When to Use Each Type of Assessment

There are several types of FBAs. The type used depends to a large extent on the form of assessment recommended or required within various school districts or learned in behavior management classes or inservice workshops. No matter what type of FBA is used, the type of data needed to create a behavior support plan must be considered. Table 4.4 shows a general decision-making process for conducting FBAs that lead to effective behavior support plans. As shown in the table, the collection of information through an indirect assessment method is the first activity. The first step is to identify and define the target behavior. The second step involves identifying the events or circumstances associated with the problem behavior. The final step involves the determination of the possible functions of the problem behavior.

Once the indirect assessment is finished, a descriptive method should be conducted. It is not recommended that a behavior support plan be developed based solely on the information obtained through an indirect method of assessment. The general recommendation for conducting a descriptive method of assessment is to observe for at least three days (O'Neill et al., 1997). The target behavior observed should be compared with the definition of the behavior obtained during the indirect assessment. For example, aggressive behavior may have been defined as any hitting, scratching, or kicking of another individual. In some cases, the behavior observed will match the definition developed earlier (e.g., aggressive episodes will involve the behaviors described in the original definition). At other times, the definition may need to be revised to reflect the behavior observed (e.g., spitting was also observed and added to the definition). Finally, new behaviors not identified in the indirect assessment may need to be defined and considered (e.g., oppositional behavior also occurred throughout the day). The descriptive analysis should either verify the events that were thought to be associated with the

Table 4.4	Decision-Making Process for Conducting Functional Behavior Assessments

1. Collect information through an indirect method.
   - Identify and define the target behavior.
   - Identify events and circumstances associated with the problem.
   - Determine the possible functions of the problem behavior.

2. Collect information through a descriptive method for at least two to three days.
   - Identify and define the target behavior.
   - Identify events and circumstances associated with the problem behavior.
   - Determine the possible functions of the problem behavior.
   - Compare results with information obtained through an indirect method.

3. If behavior's function or functions are apparent, go to step 5. If functions are not apparent, collect additional descriptive information for three to five days.

4. If behavior's function or functions are apparent, go to step 5. If functions are not apparent, conduct a functional analysis.

5. Develop hypothesis statements about the behavior.
   - Determine the events and circumstances associated with the problem behavior.
   - Determine the likely function or functions of the behavior.

problem behavior (e.g., as the teacher reported, the behavior would usually occur when a demand was placed on the student) or result in a new event or circumstance being associated with the problem behavior (e.g., how the task was demanded was associated with the unwanted behavior or the student was more likely to misbehave when left alone than when asked to complete a task). The function of the problem behavior also needs to be verified. For example, the teacher may have indicated that the likely function was escaping a task. The function, however, might be shown to be different than the function hypothesized from the indirect assessment. Perhaps receiving attention rather than escaping a task is the function. The teacher could have indicated that there were no obvious consequences after the unwanted behavior occurred because she ignored the student, whereas the descriptive analysis could indicate that the other students were providing attention to the student after the unwanted behavior.

In many cases, the function of the behavior will be apparent after the descriptive analysis. If so, hypothesis statements about the behavior can be developed. These statements describe the events or circumstances associated with the problem behavior. Once these events or circumstances are determined, the likely function of the behavior can be stated.

If the function of the behavior is not apparent as a consequence of the descriptive analysis, this analysis should be extended for another three to five days. If the function of the behavior becomes apparent, hypothesis statements can be made. If the results of the descriptive analysis are inconclusive, however, a functional analysis should be conducted by a person qualified to conduct such analyses.

Some professionals in the field may feel that a functional analysis should be conducted even if a descriptive analysis provides enough information to develop a hypothesis statement. They may indicate that a functional analysis should be conducted to further validate the information received from the descriptive analysis. Another way to validate the information obtained through a descriptive analysis is to implement an intervention based on that information. Both approaches have merit. The difficulty with functional analyses, however, is that they require specialized training to implement. Teachers or other school personnel should not conduct functional analyses unless they have received training and supervision from a competent behavior analyst who has specific training in such analyses.

How Do We Develop a Behavior Support Plan?

Once the data from an FBA are gathered, a behavior support plan can be developed. If the behavior support plan does not flow from the FBA, however, the FBA was essentially a waste of time and resources. Thus, if developing a behavior support plan, school personnel must be committed to conducting an FBA and to using the data gathered appropriately.

When one builds a behavior support plan, several considerations must be made (O'Neill et al., 1997). First, the plan must indicate how those involved in the student's environment will change, not just how the student will change. If it is assumed that the environment influences unwanted behavior, others must be considered as part of the environment. Therefore, teachers should not only consider how the student must make different "choices"; they must look to themselves and determine how they can change to bring about a student's positive behavior.

Second, the plan should be based on the data gathered from the FBA. Recall that an FBA assumes that behaviors serve a function for the student. In other words, there is something reinforcing the behavior. The purpose of an FBA is to determine the function of the behavior. If the function is determined, this information can be used to make meaningful changes in the student's environment, which, in turn, will result in improved behavior.

Third, the plan should be technically sound. In other words, the plan should be based on the principles and laws of human behavior (covered in Chapter 2). Also, the plan should include intervention procedures that have been shown to be effective in the research literature (covered in Chapters 5 and 6). There are three main areas of focus for a behavior support plan. First, we must teach the individual skills that will lessen the need to exhibit the unwanted behavior. For example, a child may, at first, grab an item from another person, and find that this grabbing is successful. Thus, the grabbing behavior becomes relevant to the child. If, however, the child learns to obtain the item by asking for it, grabbing the item becomes irrelevant. Second, we must make the problem behaviors inefficient. Many unwanted behaviors receive reinforcement fairly immediately and continuously. To make the behavior inefficient, we need to stop reinforcing it. In addition, many unwanted behaviors, such as tantrums, require a great deal of effort on the part of the student. If we are able to provide an alternative behavior that receives reinforcement more immediately and consistently and that takes less effort, the individual will display the wanted behavior instead of the unwanted behavior because the unwanted behavior becomes inefficient, especially in comparison to the alternative behavior. Third, we need to make the problem behaviors ineffective. We know that a behavior will continue to be exhibited if it is reinforced. We also know that if a behavior is not reinforced, it will cease to exist. Thus, our goal is to remove the source of reinforcement for a behavior so as to make the behavior ineffective in gaining reinforcement.

Finally, the behavior support plan should be a good fit with the values and skills of the people responsible for implementation. Behavior support plans can be difficult to implement correctly. If one is designed and the people responsible for its implementation do not agree with the plan or do not have the skills to implement it, it will fail. Therefore, before a behavior management plan is implemented, staff members or those responsible for the implementation of the plan should be encouraged to provide their input. If there are any concerns before the plan is implemented, it should be revised. It is far better to make changes before a plan is implemented than to attempt to overcome difficulties after a plan has been implemented.

Building the Behavior Support Plan

Our summary statement of the FBA for John in Figure 4.10 provides a description of the antecedents and consequences that are maintaining his challenging behavior. This summary statement is now elaborated in Figure 4.13 to aid in the development of a

| Figure 4.13 | Diagram to Be Used in Behavior Support Plans |

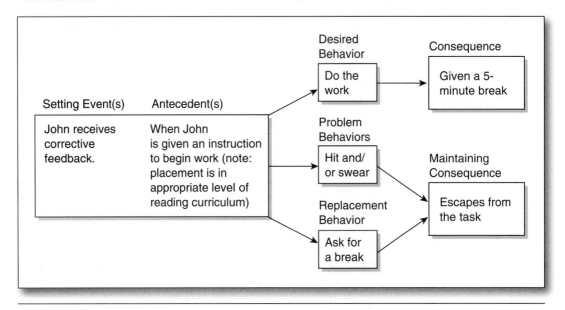

SOURCE: Adapted from R. E. O'Neill, R. H. Horner, R. W. Albin, J. R. Sprague, K. Storey, and J. S. Newton, *Functional Assessment and Program Development for Problem Behavior: A Practical Handbook.* Copyright © 1997 by Brooks/Cole. Used with permission.

behavior support plan for John. The diagram in Figure 4.13 highlights seven issues that should be considered when building a behavior support plan. First, the setting event (if any) needs to be documented. As stated before, the setting event can be anything that changes the way an individual is predisposed to respond at any given point in time, such as being tired, getting into a fight, or being punished at home.

Second, what happens immediately prior to challenging behavior, or what is commonly known as *the antecedent,* must be documented. In John's case, a variety of instructions associated with beginning work serve as antecedents to challenging behavior, such as instructions to "sit down," "sit," "park it," or "relax." Similarly, several possible instructions to begin work on a variety of academic tasks can act as antecedents to challenging behavior: "Get out your workbook. Let's turn to page X." There is a general class of antecedents that prompt challenging behavior, and these can be called "instructions to begin work."

Once the antecedents have been determined, three behaviors or responses to them must be determined: desired behavior, problem behavior, and replacement behavior (the third, fourth, and fifth issues to be included in the behavior support plan). The desired behavior is what the teacher wants to see. It is the behavior that well-behaved students exhibit. In the example, the desired behavior is the performance of the task. The problem behavior is the behavior that needs to be curtailed. A single behavior may not be the problem, but several behaviors may be. If several behaviors are a problem and they receive the same consequence or have the same function, the functional class should be documented by stating the behaviors in the class. In the example, there are two behaviors that seem to occur together or for the same reason: hitting and swearing. The replacement behavior, or the behavior that can be taught to replace the unwanted behavior, should also be determined. The replacement behavior in the example is asking for a break.

The sixth and seventh issues are concerned with how the teacher responds to the student's behaviors. It is important that the teacher not provide reinforcement for the challenging behavior. Equally, it is important that the teacher provide immediate reinforcement for the appropriate replacement behavior. So, if the student begins to act out, the teacher continues with the task. Once the student asks appropriately for a break, then a break is given immediately. In this situation, the appropriate behavior receives reinforcement (asking appropriately to escape the academic task) while the challenging behavior (acting out to escape from the task) is placed on extinction. Initially, the replacement behavior must be reinforced immediately and on a continuous reinforcement schedule (every time it occurs). We can see from Figure 4.13 that the new behavior achieves the same outcome as the unwanted behavior (i.e., the same reinforcer). Therefore, the appropriate behavior and the unwanted behavior are functionally equivalent (achieve the same outcome). During the intervention, the teacher may initially prompt the student to use the new behavior ("If you need a break, don't forget to ask for one."). Once all of these issues are addressed, a behavior support plan can be written.

Writing the Behavior Support Plan

Once the diagram has been developed, the behavior support plan can be written. As shown in Figure 4.14, the operational definitions of the target behaviors are provided. Next, the summary statements are documented with a diagram of the three possible behavior categories (i.e., desired behavior, target behavior, replacement behavior). The diagram in Figure 4.14 shows that asking for a break is the replacement behavior for swearing.

The general approach to solving the behavior problem is presented next. A strategy for changing the setting events (if any) to prevent the problem behavior is stated. If a negative method of correction makes the student more likely to hit or swear, change the way correction is provided. If the behavior occurs when the student seems tired, speaking with his or parents about getting him or her to bed earlier may be a strategy. The predictor strategies are stated and involve methods of preventing the unwanted behavior by changing the antecedents to the task. For example, a teacher may change the way instructions are given, from a question (e.g., "Could you begin your work?") to a statement (e.g., "Please begin your work"). Another critical aspect of predictor strategies is to diagnose why a task is aversive to a student in the case of an escape or avoidance-motivated behavior. The task may be too difficult or require the student to concentrate or to sit still for too long. If the task is too difficult, then modifying the curriculum to add instructional supports might be appropriate. If the task requires too much on-task time of the student, the appropriate solution could be to break the task into smaller units of time. If the problem is with attention seeking, the solution might be to provide more attention for appropriate behavior. Instructional strategies can also involve teaching the student alternative behaviors to access

Figure 4.14	Behavior Support Plan for John

Problem Behavior

1. Hitting: Any contact with the hand to another person or object with the intent to harm.
2. Swearing: Stating verbally words commonly considered to be swear words (i.e., four-letter words).

Functional Assessment Summary Statement

When given instructions to begin working on a task after corrective feedback has been given, John will hit and/or swear. These behaviors are maintained by removing the task and sending John to time-out. Time-out allows John to escape or delay the task.

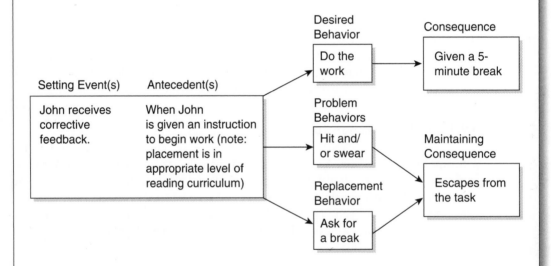

General Approach

Setting event strategies: When providing feedback, an effective error correction procedure will be used. This procedure will involve praising John for his effort, modeling the correct answer (e.g., "that word is father"), guiding him to the correct answer (e.g., "let's say the word together"), and having him provide the answer independently after a prompt (e.g., "What word is this?").

Predictor strategies: (a) Instruct John to complete his work versus asking him to do so.

(b) Although there is no indication that the work is too difficult for John, make sure to provide assignments that John can do independently (i.e., at his instructional level).

Teaching strategies: Conduct a 15-minute training session with John on how to request a break when he is feeling agitated (i.e., raise hand and ask for a break when called upon).

Consequence strategies: (a) When John begins to work on the assignment, the teacher will praise him for getting started. When John completes the work, he will be praised for the completed work and given a 5-minute break. (b) If John begins to become agitated, the teacher will remind him to ask for a break if he thinks he needs one. Minor behaviors will be ignored. If John's behavior (e.g., aggression) requires his removal, the teacher will provide a short booster training session on how to ask for a break immediately after John reenters the classroom. After the booster session, John will be instructed to complete the work he attempted to avoid.

Routines

Praise John when he begins working on his assignment and when he turns it in completed. Allow John to have a short 2-minute break when he asks for one in the prescribed fashion.

If John becomes agitated, prompt him to ask for a break. For more serious incidents such as aggression, send John to time-out and have him practice appropriate "asking for a break" behavior upon his reentry to the classroom. Make sure John returns to the work that he attempted to avoid.

Monitoring and Evaluation

The observation form will be used to monitor the frequency of John's hitting and swearing behaviors. The teacher will review the data each morning prior to the start of class and at the end of the week to determine if changes in the plan are needed. The plan will formally be reviewed with John and his parents at the end of 1 month after its implementation.

SOURCE: Adapted from R. E. O'Neill, R. H. Horner, R. W. Albin, J. R. Sprague, K. Storey, and J. S. Newton, *Functional Assessment and Program Development for Problem Behavior: A Practical Handbook.* Copyright © 1997 by Brooks/Cole. Used with permission.

the reinforcing consequences. For example, if a behavior is attention maintained, then the student should be prompted to gain attention using appropriate behaviors. The student could be prompted to use appropriate requests to escape from tasks, for example. Table 4.5 provides a guide for interventions based on the function of the behavior.

The routines are also presented in Figure 4.14. The routines should indicate the manner in which the work will be provided. For example, if the student is having difficulty completing an assignment, the method of breaking the assignment into smaller units should be specified. That could involve drawing a line one-third and two-thirds of the way through the assignment and informing the student that, when she reaches each line, a break may be taken. Also, if an unwanted behavior occurs, some appropriate response should be made by the classroom staff. The response may be simply ignoring the unwanted behavior or calling for assistance from the office. Whatever the routines are, they should be stated in specific terms so that all staff members understand what is to be done and when.

Finally, the effects of the behavior support plan on the targeted student behavior should be monitored. This monitoring should be completed as described in detail in Chapter 3. It is important to get a clear evaluation as to the effectiveness of the support plan. If the plan is not working, then aspects of the plan may need to be changed or the FBA may need to be conducted again.

| Table 4.5 | Guiding Principles for Functions for Target Behaviors |

Function	Guiding Principle
Access • Object/activity • Attention (adult/peer)	• Reinforce and support the student when he or she is actively engaged with desirable objects or activities • Provide the student attention (reinforce) when he or she is exhibiting appropriate behaviors
Escape/avoidance • Activity • Social (adult/peer)	• Reinforce and support the student to meet the performance expectation • Reinforce and support the student when he or she is engaging in desirable and important social situations
Autonomic reinforcement	• Minimize or eliminate the effects of the intrinsic factor and reinforce the student when he or she exhibits appropriate behaviors
Multiple functions	• Use the guiding principles related to the particular functions in operation

Assessing the Fidelity of the Behavior Support Plan

It is critical to utilize procedures such as those described in this text when developing an effective behavior support plan. Further, educators should ensure that these plans are implemented accurately and consistently to facilitate treatment fidelity. Cook et al. (2010) described an analysis conducted by Etscheidt (2006) in which "52 published court decisions indicated that the first thing hearing officers look for when making a decision is whether the BIP was implemented as planned (i.e., treatment integrity)" (p. 11).

The *Behavior Support Plan–Quality Evaluation Scoring Guide (BSP-QE)* (Browning-Wright, Saren, & Mayer, 2003) can be used to evaluate and rate the quality of content in the behavior support plan. It is considered to be a technically adequate tool and is based on six key, evidence-based concepts including (a) behavior function, (b) situational specificity, (c) behavior change including environmental alteration and teaching strategies, (d) reinforcement, (e) reactive strategies, and (f) team coordination and communication (Cook et al., 2010). Twelve items are included and are rated on a 3-point Likert-like scale from 0 to 2, with a maximum score of 24 (Cook et al., 2010). This instrument was used in a survey of professionals evaluating the relationship among evidence-based quality behavior support plans, treatment integrity, and student outcomes:

> The findings from this research suggest that school staff should strive to develop BIPs that include critical evidence-based components. . . . [D]eveloping a BIP that is consistent with the research base should be viewed as a necessary but not sufficient condition to effective positive behavior change. Rather, school staff must diligently monitor and

ensure the integrity of its implementation. Ensuring the integrity of implementation is paramount because it represents the mechanism by which key evidence-based concepts are translated into actual practice. . . . [I]t also has merit in terms of providing the context for making valid and legally defensible decisions to modify, intensify, maintain, or discontinue a BIP. (Cook et al., 2010, p. 10)

VIGNETTE REVISITED   Developing a Behavior Support Plan

Mr. Malone approached the district's behavior specialist and asked for suggestions. First, the behavior specialist made sure there was indeed a problem. Once he was convinced there was a problem (see Chapter 3), he told Mr. Malone there were several steps to take to solve this problem, and he suggested that Mr. Malone was going to have to change some assumptions about Katrina and her behavior. The behavior specialist indicated that labels such as "emotional disturbance" do not cause a behavior to occur or not occur. He told Mr. Malone there is a reason to be found in the classroom for Katrina's difficulties. The behavior specialist told Mr. Malone Katrina's unwanted behavior was being positively reinforced by something such as attention from Mr. Malone or the other students or negatively reinforced by something such as the removal of the requirement that she complete classroom work.

The specialist told Mr. Malone he should conduct an FBA to be sure of the likely cause of her behavior. He gave Mr. Malone some forms to complete. Also, he told Mr. Malone that, once the "function" of the behavior was known, he should develop a behavior support plan. Mr. Malone was told to make sure the behavior support plan had a summary statement that included possible setting events, antecedents, behaviors, and consequences. This summary statement should show what the likely function of the behavior is. The behavior support plan should also describe how teachers will attempt to teach Katrina other ways of gaining access to the reinforcer. For example, if Katrina tries to gain attention inappropriately, Mr. Malone was told, he should ignore the unwanted behavior and teach Katrina to get attention in a more appropriate way. Finally, the specialist told Mr. Malone he should also consider how he was going to monitor the plan to see whether it was effective.

Summary

FBAs are a critical aspect of developing behavior support plans. FBAs have their theoretical origins in a behavioral understanding of why we do what we do. Hence, an understanding of context and of function underpins FBAs. Our behavior is primarily influenced by our context, including our physiological makeup, our broader cultural influences, and the immediate environment. An FBA targets an understanding of how these contexts influence a student's behavior. FBAs examine the setting events, antecedents, and consequences that maintain behavior. Setting events are those broader contexts that predispose a person to behave in certain ways. Antecedents are those immediate events that tend to trigger the occurrence of challenging behavior. Consequences describe that which happens in the environment following a behavior and increases the probability of that behavior in the future. An FBA must address all of these contextual elements. There are a number of different types of FBAs including interviews, checklists, observations, and functional analyses. It is typical to conduct a couple of these assessments when implementing an FBA. Correspondence between two or more assessments with regard to what may be causing and maintaining challenging behavior can produce more confident conclusions and suggestions for a behavior support plan. The behavior support plan is derived from the results of the FBA. These plans should address setting events, antecedent influences, and maintaining consequences (Killu, 2008). Behavioral supports are generally educational in nature, as they typically teach the student alternative appropriate behaviors to replace the unwanted behavior. Behavior support plans also focus on arranging setting events and antecedents in a manner that enhances appropriate behavior and preempts unwanted behavior. The effectiveness of the support plan is ultimately determined by positive changes in the student's behavior. If positive change is not achieved, then the assessment and intervention development process may need to be revisited.

Figure 4.15 summarizes the process of conducting FBAs and developing behavior support plans (also termed BIPs) (Nelson et al., 1998). If teachers follow this process, their effectiveness as behavior managers should increase.

Figure 4.15	Stages in Conducting Functional Behavior Assessments and Developing Behavior Support Plans

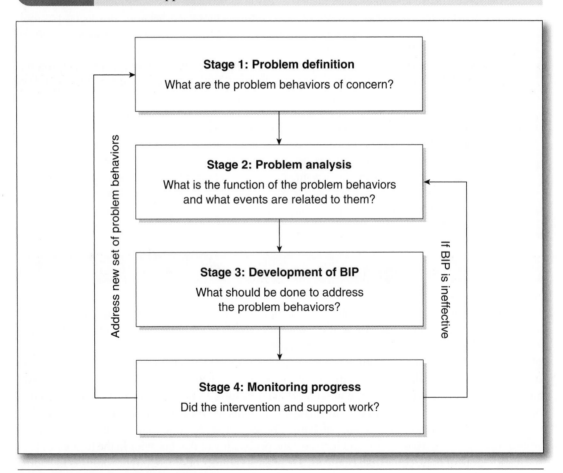

NOTE: BIP = Behavior intervention [or support] plan

SOURCE: From J. R. Nelson, M. L. Roberts, and D. J. Smith, *Conducting Functional Behavioral Assessments: A Practical Guide.* Copyright © 1998 by Sopris West. Reprinted with permission from Cambium Learning Group-Sopris West Educational Services, Longmont, CO. 800-547-6747. (Packs of forms are available for purchase from Sopris West.)

Key Terms

Discussion Questions

1. What do we mean by context?

2. What do we mean by function?

3. Why would you want to complete a functional behavioral assessment before you develop and implement a behavior support plan?

4. Of the three categories of functional behavioral assessments, which one or ones do you see as being most usable by classroom personnel? Why?

5. Why is it important to conduct and document the results of a functional behavioral assessment?

6. Why are indirect assessments used so much by school personnel?

7. Describe the major characteristics of the A-B-C analysis.

8. Describe the major characteristics of the scatter plot assessment.

9. What are the possible limitations of conducting a functional analysis?

10. How should the FBA impact the development of a behavior support plan?

5

Increasing Desirable Behaviors

Chapter Objectives

After studying this chapter, you should be able to

- explain why teachers should target behaviors to increase rather than simply attempting to decrease behaviors,

- illustrate how different prompting strategies can increase wanted behaviors,

- depict the process of shaping,

- characterize the Premack principle and the response deprivation hypothesis,

- explain the concept of behavioral momentum,

- describe self-management,

- illustrate correspondence training,

- explain behavioral contracts and how they are developed,

- depict token economy systems and how they are developed,

- describe procedures for promoting the generalization of behavior change, and

- explain procedures for promoting the maintenance of behavior change.

MS. ARMSTRONG WAS BECOMING more and more frustrated with Juan. Juan was in Ms. Armstrong's ninth-grade social studies class and was failing due to his unwillingness to participate in class activities. Juan tended to sit in the corner of the room, and he did not interact with any of the other students. When Ms. Armstrong asked Juan to work in a group, he would simply refuse verbally or ignore her request altogether.

Exacerbating the problem was that Ms. Armstrong could not find anything to coax Juan to interact in the groups or with other students. She offered Juan points, candy, sodas, and extra time on the computer if he would just become involved in the class. None of these rewards worked. She then tried warnings such as telling him she would send notes home to his parents, send him to the principal, or send him to time-out if he refused to become involved. These techniques failed to get him to participate in any academic activity.

Ms. Armstrong was becoming increasingly concerned because Juan was at the point of no return. If Juan did not begin to put forth the required effort now, he was not going to pass the class. Therefore, Ms. Armstrong decided to bring her concerns to the building assistance team.

The building assistance team was a group of teachers who met twice per month to discuss students' academic and behavioral difficulties and develop plans to remedy these. Ms. Armstrong had heard that the team had helped other teachers with students, so she was eager to talk to them about Juan.

Overview

A primary assumption used in this book with regard to effective behavior support is that students' behavior is exhibited due to things going on around them rather than or in addition to things going on inside them (see Chapter 4). With this assumption made, we must examine the classroom environment to explain how and why a particular behavior occurs. Knowing that environment affects behavior, however, is not enough to solve the problem. We must determine what steps are necessary to decrease the likelihood of the unwanted behavior and to increase the likelihood that a wanted behavior will occur in its place. Whether to change the antecedents of challenging behavior (such as changing the way instruction is provided) or to change the consequences of the behavior or to modify some combination of both must be established. Some procedures used to increase the likelihood that desirable behaviors will be exhibited are examined in this chapter.

This chapter will discuss how we can reduce challenging behavior by increasing appropriate behavior. These proactive methods include prompting strategies, shaping, the Premack principle and the response deprivation hypothesis, and behavioral momentum. Self-management, an important skill for students to learn, will also be described. Additionally, the use of preference and choice and token economy systems will be highlighted. Finally, methods of generalization and maintenance programming will be explained.

How Can Challenging Behavior Be Decreased by Increasing Appropriate Behavior?

A very important aspect of behavior change is not only to decrease the behavior that is unwanted but also to increase a wanted behavior. Increasing a wanted behavior to take the place of the unwanted one is called the *fair-pair rule* (White & Haring, 1980; Zirpoli, 2008). The **fair-pair rule** simply indicates that, whenever there is a behavior we want to decrease, a wanted behavior should be taught to take its place (Wolery, Bailey, & Sugai, 1988). This tenet is basic to developing the behavioral support that is a central precept of this book. Prior to the advent of behavioral support, behavior management programs focused on decreasing unwanted behavior. Fortunately, today's aim is to treat an unwanted behavior as an opportunity to teach something else. Unwanted behavior can be treated as a teaching opportunity.

Educators are in the business of educating students. This education moves beyond teaching the three R's. Students must also be taught how to behave appropriately. Therefore, the occurrence of unwanted behavior is an opportunity to determine what needs to be taught. Unwanted behavior should be seen as an indication that the students have skills missing from their repertoires; these missing skills are appropriate behaviors. This approach parallels what good teachers do when students show deficits in academic areas. Good teachers teach not only academic skills but also behavior skills. To do so, a teacher must be adept at using prompting and fading procedures.

How Can Prompting Strategies Be Used to Increase Desirable Behaviors?

Prompting strategies may be thought of as methods of teaching academic-related behaviors (see Chapter 8); these strategies, however, can be useful in promoting the occurrence of wanted behaviors. There are several prompting and fading strategies, such as antecedent prompt and test, most to least, antecedent prompt and fade, least to most, graduated guidance, and time delay (Cooper, Heron, & Heward, 2007; Miltenberger, 2007; Wolery et al., 1988).

Teacher prompting can be used to get students on a task.

Antecedent Prompt and Test Procedure

The **antecedent prompt and test** procedure involves prompting students and then providing them with practice or test trials after removing all prompts. This procedure involves the following: "I do" (model), "we do" (guided practice), and "you do" (independent practice). This procedure has also been called modeling (Cooper et al., 2007), the model-test, model-lead-test, and prompt-practice strategy (Wolery et al., 1988). It involves having the teacher present a prompt such as a model (e.g., "This is how you ask for a break: 'May I have a break?'"). Next, the teacher performs the skill or task with the student or presents a test or practice trial. This test or practice trial can occur immediately after the initial prompt or sometime later (e.g., "When you want a break, you say, 'May I have a break?' Now you show me how you would ask for a break when you want one"). Correct independent responses are reinforced (e.g., "How do you ask for a break?" Student responds correctly. "That's the way to ask for a break"). Incorrect responses are corrected and feedback is provided (e.g., "This is how you ask for a break. 'May I have a break?' How do you ask for a break?" Student responds correctly. "Exactly. That is how you ask for a break").

Most-to-Least Prompting

Most-to-least prompting involves decreasing assistance to a student in a progressive fashion (Cooper et al., 2007; Wolery et al., 1988) and creating a prompt hierarchy. A most-to-least prompting hierarchy involves a number of prompts listed in order of intrusiveness (i.e., the amount of control exerted over the student's response). For example, a physical prompt (e.g., hand-over-hand prompting) is much more intrusive than a verbal prompt (e.g., telling a student what to do). With this approach, the teacher begins with the most intrusive prompt (e.g., guiding the student to his or her seat). Once the student is able to meet a predetermined criterion for this prompt (freely moves to seat with no resistance for three consecutive trials), the next intrusive prompt of the hierarchy is provided (e.g., placing teacher's hand on student's shoulder to guide the student to his or her seat). This prompting continues until the student can perform the behavior independently, with the least intrusive level of prompting (e.g., telling the student to go to his or her seat).

Antecedent Prompt and Fade Procedure

The **antecedent prompt and fade** procedure involves providing a more intrusive prompt on initial instructional trials and then removing the prompt in a systematic manner (Cooper et al., 2007; Wolery et al., 1988). The fading of prompts can involve presenting the controlling prompt less frequently (e.g., teacher placing index finger to his or her mouth and saying "shhh" fewer times) or fading the intensity of the prompt (e.g., teacher moving from a loud voice to a soft voice). For example, the teacher may wish to get students on task as soon as she asks for the students to begin. Therefore, the teacher flicks the lights on and off several times while saying "everybody needs to quiet down and get to work." Once the students seem to be quieting down faster and getting on task, the teacher flicks the lights on and off twice while saying the same verbal prompt. Again, once the students are able to get on task even faster, the teacher may flick the lights on and off once while providing the same verbal prompt. If students take longer to get on task, the teacher provides an error correction (e.g., "You need to quiet down when I ask you to"). The decision of when to move from one level of prompt to another is not typically defined (Wolery et al., 1988). Therefore, this decision is based on teacher judgment. A critical aspect of this strategy is to assess whether students continue to get on task immediately as prompts are faded. If not, the more intrusive prompt may need to be re-implemented.

Least-to-Most Prompting

Least-to-most prompting involves increasing assistance when a student does not perform a behavior (Cooper et al., 2007; Wolery et al., 1988); thus, a prompt is necessary to get the behavior to occur. Similar to the most-to-least procedure, least-to-most prompting orders prompts according to their level of intrusiveness. The difference between this procedure and the most-to-least procedure is that the beginning prompt in the least-to-most procedure is the least intrusive prompt. In addition, all levels of the prompts may be used in a single trial. For example, a teacher could define a list of prompts from verbal (least) to full physical (most) prompts. The teacher may provide an instruction to a student to clean up a work area. The teacher waits for a predetermined time (response interval) to see if the student begins to clean up the area. If the student does not begin cleaning the area, the teacher moves to the next level of prompt, such as a verbal and gestural prompt (e.g., verbalizing to the student to clean up the work area while pointing to the area). If the student continues to be noncompliant, the teacher moves to the next level of prompt, such as a verbal, gestural, or light physical prompt (e.g., touching the student on the shoulder while telling the student to clean up the area, which the teacher points toward). If the student begins to clean the area when the initial instruction is provided, the student is reinforced. In essence, the student's behavior determines the level of prompt that will be provided.

Graduated Guidance

Graduated guidance is similar to the most-to-least prompting procedure except that it involves more of a fluid movement from the highest level of prompt to the lowest level. In other words, prompts are removed immediately, as soon as they are no longer needed by students (Cooper et al., 2007; Miltenberger, 2007; Wolery et al., 1988). A good way to picture graduated guidance is to imagine teaching a child to ride a bike without training wheels. First, you grasp the bike firmly while the child is riding, but you gradually lessen the amount of assistance you provide until the child is riding independently. The difference between this method and most-to-least prompting is that the latter involves a series of steps that the child would need to accomplish and repeat with some consistency while riding successfully with an adult holding on, and then the child would repeat the procedure while riding successfully with an adult lightly touching the bike, and so on. With graduated guidance the teacher's prompts are adjusted moment to moment and gradually faded out. For example, if a noncompliant student is instructed to hang up her coat, the teacher provides a hand-over-hand physical prompt at first while the student is hanging up the coat. As the student begins to hang up the coat independently, the teacher immediately removes the level of prompt. The level of prompt provided is dependent on the student's level of need. The teacher provides as much of the prompt as is needed to get the behavior going and then backs off as the student engages in the behavior.

Time Delay

Time delay involves presenting at the same time an initial prompt and the prompt to which you ultimately want the students to respond. This process occurs for several trials (Wolery et al., 1988). Then, a time delay is introduced. The delay may be a set amount of time provided between the two prompts (**constant time delay**), or the time delay between the two prompts may be gradually increased (**progressive time delay**) on subsequent learning trials (Cooper et al., 2007; Wolery et al.). With a constant time delay, a delay interval is decided on based on the normal time it takes students to respond to an instruction (e.g., five seconds). If a student responds within the time delay, the student is reinforced. When that occurs, there is a transfer in stimulus control from the initial prompt (e.g., instruction) to the prompt to which you ultimately want the students to respond. The point when this transfer begins to occur is called the **moment of transfer** (Sulzer-Azaroff & Mayer, 1991). If there is no response, the teacher prompts for the behavior.

For example, suppose a student will not begin the morning's initial start-up activity from the board unless the teacher specifically requests the student to begin to work on the problems written on the board. In a constant time delay procedure, the teacher immediately tells the student to begin the start-up activity as soon as the student enters the room at the beginning of the day. This prompt may occur over five days. After these beginning trials, the teacher watches the student take his or her seat. If the student begins working on the start-up activity before the verbal prompt is given (after waiting five seconds after the student is seated), the student is reinforced. If the student does not begin working on the start-up activity within five seconds of being seated, the teacher provides the verbal prompt (e.g., "You need to begin working on the problems from the board"). If the student begins to work after this prompt, the student is reinforced. If the student still does not respond to the delayed prompt, whatever was used as a consequence for the correct responses should be reviewed. With the progressive time delay procedure, the same procedure is used except the time delay is gradually and systematically expanded. For example, the teacher provides the prompt (e.g., "You need to begin working on the problems from the board") at 0 seconds initially over five days, then at 1 second for three days, then 2 seconds for the next three days, and so on. The hope is that the student will engage in the behavior before the verbal prompt, as soon as he or she sees the problems on the board.

What Is Shaping?

Shaping, a strategy discussed in Chapter 2, can also be used to increase appropriate behavior. Teachers require some form of sustained activity or attention from students during the learning process, and when students cannot for whatever reason maintain this activity or attention level for the required time, difficulties often ensue. Therefore, some way to increase the on-task time of the student may need to be devised. Shaping is a method that can be beneficial to the goal of increasing on-task time. To use shaping, teachers set the initial on-task time requirement to the student's current level, such as 30 seconds. When the student is on task for 30 seconds, the student is reinforced in some manner. Once the student is able to maintain on-task behavior for 30 seconds consistently, the time is increased to 45 seconds, for example. When the student is on task for 45 seconds, the student is reinforced. Again, once the student is able to maintain on-task behavior for 45 seconds consistently, the time is again increased. Thus, the length of time the student is on task is gradually increased through the process of shaping. In this situation, shaping adds just a little bit of extra structure, and, by making the criteria for reinforcement obtainable, the teacher may help students overcome psychological barriers (such as the feeling that they will never succeed). Again, the criteria for reinforcement can be gradually increased as a student succeeds.

The critical point to understand with shaping is that the process can be used to "catch" the appropriate behavior and to ensure that it is reinforced; then, teachers can gradually move to higher response expectations. This method is preferable to setting the initial requirement for the student so high that she or he fails to reach the criterion. Therefore, think of behavior development as a progression from where the student is now to where you would ultimately like to see the behavior.

What Are the Premack Principle and the Response Deprivation Hypothesis?

It is critical to get students to display appropriate behaviors in the classroom. To get appropriate behavior to occur, teachers may need to provide some incentive to students. A time-tested method of providing students incentives is to give them access to something that is reinforcing to them. This method can be interpreted in two ways—through the Premack principle or with the response deprivation hypothesis.

Premack Principle

The Premack principle is a concept that has been around for many years. More commonly called **"Grandma's rule"** (Cipani, 2008), the **Premack principle** simply says that to get a less preferred behavior to occur, reinforce it with a more preferred one. Examples include "If you eat your vegetables, you will get dessert" and "If you finish your homework, you can go out to play." Technically, the Premack principle indicates that a high-probability behavior can reinforce a low-probability behavior (Premack, 1959). The relative probabilities of the behaviors are critical. Thus, if it is more likely that a child would eat vegetables than dessert, the dessert cannot be used as a reinforcer for vegetables. If doing homework is more likely than going out to play, going out to play cannot be a reinforcer for completing homework. Therefore, to use the Premack principle, one must know which behavior is more or less likely to occur than the other.

The Premack principle has been shown to be very effective in encouraging behavior to occur (Martin & Pear, 2007; Sulzer-Azaroff & Mayer, 1991). Most people over the years have known it works; it is used all the time not only with children but also with adults. Because it has been established as conventional wisdom, it is called Grandma's rule: Grandma knows that it works. According to some people, however, the Premack principle is a bribe, but calling it a bribe takes away from this effective method. The Premack principle and all reinforcement procedures would be considered bribes if the purpose of offering the reinforcer were to achieve an advantage for the person or persons providing it and if the offer involved an illegal activity (Malott & Trojan Suarez, 2008; Sulzer-Azaroff & Mayer, 1991). Fortunately, ethical professionals implement legal reinforcement-based systems not for their own good but for the good of students. Another difference between bribery and reinforcement is that bribery aims to promote immoral or dishonest behavior that corrupts those involved. It would be difficult to find instances in schools in which a teacher's use of reinforcement was aimed at corrupting students. A final difference between bribery and reinforcement is that reinforcement, by definition, comes after the behavior; bribery often comes before the act. Therefore, the ethical use of reinforcement is not bribery.

Response Deprivation Hypothesis

A question arises with the Premack principle: Can a low-probability behavior be used to reinforce a high-probability behavior? In other words, can a behavior that is less likely to occur, such as eating vegetables, be used to reinforce a more likely behavior, such as eating dessert? Theoretically, the answer to these questions may be yes. The response deprivation hypothesis builds off the Premack principle. One takes a high-probability behavior and increases the likelihood of a low-probability behavior by reinforcing the low-probability behavior with the high one. The reason for the effectiveness of the procedure, however, may not be what was originally thought. According to the response deprivation hypothesis, the relative probabilities are not important (Cooper et al., 2007; Sulzer-Azaroff & Mayer, 1991). It is not true that less likely behaviors can only be reinforced with high-probability ones. In reality, more likely behaviors can be reinforced with less likely ones. The **response deprivation hypothesis** indicates that any behavior that is reduced below its baseline level can function as a reinforcer (Cooper et al., 2007; Timberlake & Allison, 1974). In other words, the behavior reduced below baseline levels can function as a reinforcer for another behavior. Children usually eat some vegetables once in a while, for example. If this level of vegetable eating is decreased below its normal level, vegetable eating will become a reinforcer.

Take a more likely classroom scenario. Suppose there is a student who sits in the corner of the room and does not interact with anyone. The goal is to get this student to be part of the student group. Nothing works, not offering extra recess time, not prompting the student back to group, not threatening a poor grade if he does not join the group. Perhaps this student does not have any reinforcers because nothing gets the wanted behavior (sitting with the group) to occur. The Premack principle suggests finding a more likely behavior to get the student to sit with his peers, but the teacher cannot think of anything the student finds reinforcing. The response deprivation hypothesis can help lead the way. Under this hypothesis, essentially any behavior can serve as a reinforcer as long as the student is doing the behavior at some level. Thus, the first step is to see what the student does. In this case, the student sits in a corner of the room. This behavior, then, is the potential reinforcer. The technique to try is to tell the student that if he sits with the group for some short time, such as two minutes, he can go back and sit alone for the rest of the period. If the student refuses to go with the group, the teacher sits next to the student. Thus, the only way the student can be left alone is by interacting with the group for a short period of time. Once the student sits with the group for two minutes for some criterion level (e.g., three consecutive days), the requirement could be increased to, say, four minutes. The beauty of this technique is that, if the teacher is able to decrease sitting alone to a level below that which normally occurs, it will function as a reinforcer. If it functions as a reinforcer, the behavior it reinforces will increase in probability. Thus, interacting with the group will become more likely if sitting alone is a reinforcer. As interacting with the group becomes more and more likely, sitting alone becomes less and less likely, which in turn puts sitting alone in a more deprived state and increases its reinforcing properties. Ultimately, the hope is that reinforcing things going on in the group will reinforce being with the group, thereby overriding the reinforcement received for sitting alone. A transfer from one reinforcer (e.g., sitting alone) to another reinforcer (e.g., interacting with others) could ultimately be seen.

The response deprivation hypothesis takes away the claim that nothing reinforces this student, or "I can't find anything that reinforces this student." Yet, there is a potential problem about which teachers must be cautious: creating a deprivation state can be aversive. Therefore, decreasing a behavior such as sitting alone below its normal occurrence level could result in negative side effects. It is important for the teacher not to take on a confrontational role in such circumstances. So, for example, changing seating arrangements may be an indirect way of reducing opportunities for sitting alone. Remember, the focus of such interventions is to educate, to increase appropriate behavior, not to create aversive situations for the student, class, or teacher.

What Is Behavioral Momentum?

Behavioral momentum can be an important aspect of a behavioral support procedure. **Behavioral momentum** (also termed *interspersed requests, pretask requests,* and, most frequently, *high-probability request sequences*) is based on the idea that desired behaviors are more likely to occur if preceded by reinforcement for other behaviors (Cooper et al., 2007). The fact that the student has been reinforced for other behaviors increases the probability that she or he will engage in a low-probability behavior. Say we have a student who is oppositional. When we provide the student an instruction to complete cleaning the work area, he or she usually refuses. Other directions, however, the student is likely to follow, such as coming when called, helping another student, or running an errand to the office. If we precede the instruction to clean up the work area with a number of instructions that the student will comply with, then there is a higher probability that she or he will clean up the work area. Behavioral momentum has been empirically demonstrated to be effective with a variety of learners in many applied settings (Mace & Belfiore, 1990; Mace et al., 1998; Oliver & Skinner, 2002; Singer, Singer, & Homer, 1987).

What Are Self-Management Procedures?

One of the more important skills students with behavior issues can learn is how to manage or control themselves (Heward, 2009). Self-management is also called self-control or self-regulation. **Self-management** is defined as "the personal application of behavior change tactics that produce a desired change in behavior" (Cooper et al., 2007, p. 578). We self-manage by engaging in a behavior (target behavior) to control the occurrence of another behavior (Miltenberger, 2007). This definition of self-management is different from the traditional one. We typically assume that self-management or self-control lies within the individual. Statements such as "He does not have the willpower to lose weight" or "She must show some self-control and begin studying more" are not unusual. Where, however, does this self-control come from? Does it come from within the individual or from somewhere else? If it comes from within or is not learned, there is not much anyone can do to aid people in their self-control. If, however, self-control is a learned set of behaviors, much can be done to improve the situation.

As Cooper et al. (2007) indicate, self-management or self-control comes from how we respond to the situations around us. We do not manage our own behavior independently from our learning environments but as part of these environments. Self-management or self-control comes from behaving in such a way that we change our environment. This change in the environment facilitates the behavior we want to occur. Thus, self-management or self-control is a way of behaving. It is a skill we exhibit at specified times. It is a skill that we can teach. If that is true, we can begin to understand why we may not display self-control in certain situations and how we can teach self-controlled behavior for these situations.

Reasons for a Lack of Self-Control

Typically, there are two behavior categories of concern when we look at student behavior: behavioral deficiencies and behavioral excesses. **Behavioral deficiencies** include behaviors that do not occur enough, such as completing homework or getting to school on time, whereas **behavioral excesses** involve behaviors that occur too often, such as talking too much or swearing. Malott and Trojan Suarez (2008) have determined that there are two main reasons behavioral deficiencies and excesses are present. First, the long-term outcomes (e.g., good grades) of a behavior (e.g., studying) are small though often cumulative. Second, the long-term outcomes of a behavior may be too improbable (e.g., the overall probability of getting caught when one indulges in stealing behavior may be low). Therefore, Malott and Trojan Suarez indicate that for self-control to be demonstrated (such as getting good grades and not stealing), the longer-term consequences of desired behavior must be large or significant and must have a high probability of occurring (educational and vocational success).

Translating that conclusion into classroom practice, teachers must show students the benefits of behaving appropriately and must reinforce appropriate behavior when it occurs. For example, complying with rules is critical in the classroom. Complying with rules, however, often does not result in positive consequences, only in decreasing the probability of receiving negative consequences. In effect, teachers should arrange the curriculum so that it produces short- and long-term positive consequences for the students. In this way, students begin to learn that appropriate behavior today produces positive consequences not only today but also tomorrow and in the longer term—they learn self-control.

Reasons for Teaching Self-Management

Why should educators improve student self-control? Table 5.1 shows several reasons. First, acting independently is valued and expected by society. The goal for teachers is to get students to be independent, not dependent. Second, teachers may not be able to continue to implement behavioral support strategies successfully at all times. Often, teachers simply cannot be available for a student; they must attend to other students as well. Third, when students demonstrate self-managed behavior, teachers can spend more time actually teaching. If students could manage their own behaviors, our instructional time

Table 5.1	Reasons for Teaching Self-Management

- Acting independently is valued and expected by society.
- A teacher may not be able to implement external control successfully.
- When students control their own behavior, teachers can spend more time teaching important skills.
- Students learn to behave appropriately when adult supervision is not available.
- Self-management may lead to more durable changes because students are learning a strategy.
- Self-management can result in generalized responding.

would increase, and less time would be spent trying to solve management issues. Fourth, when teachers are not present, students will continue to behave appropriately, which is important especially in instances when substitute teachers or others have to take over the instruction of the class. Fifth, students who are taught self-management skills may be more likely to display these skills over a longer period. Self-management skills are strategies that students can use in the future. Finally, students who display self-managed behavior may be more likely to display such behavior in other settings, such as on the playground, on the bus, during assemblies, or in other classes. Overall, self-management strategies enhance independence, positive behavioral repertoires, and self-determination for students. Self-management strategies should therefore be routinely taught.

Types of Self-Management Skills

Several self-management skills can be taught to students. These skills include goal setting, self-recording, self-monitoring, self-charting, self-evaluation, self-instruction, self-reinforcement and self-punishment, and problem solving (Martella, Marchand-Martella, & Cleanthous, 2001). These skills are described in isolation, but they are usually used in combination with one other.

Goal Setting. **Goal setting** involves the establishment of performance criteria and the identification and use of solutions to meet an established goal (Alberto & Troutman, 2009). The hope of goal setting is that, if students have a hand in setting their own goals, they will be more likely to try to reach these goals. Therefore, goal setting initially involves the students and teachers sitting down and determining what goals would be appropriate for students. These goals are determined mutually through discussion. In the discussion, teachers should provide rationales for the importance of setting goals and reaching them. Teachers should provide examples of goals as part of the discussion process. Goals such as completing work on time, turning in homework, getting high marks on assignments, and graduating from school are examples. Teachers can also provide examples of goals that would not be appropriate, such as being the toughest student in the school, being initiated into a gang, or not attending school. Teachers can provide examples of goals that are currently attainable and those that are not. For example, for someone who is failing in every subject, a goal of straight A's is probably not attainable immediately. Getting straight A's may be obtainable later on; a more realistic goal is passing every class with at least a B or C. The student should also be taught about long-term and short-term goals. In addition, students should be taught how long-term goals can and should be broken into several short-term goals. For example, a goal of graduating from college might be divided into passing all high school classes, then getting A's or B's, followed by then applying to a college, and so on. Getting good grades may also need to be broken into even shorter-term goals, such as the completion of each assignment (see Table 5.2).

Students should also be able to provide to their teachers examples of appropriate goals and inappropriate goals. Once the students have demonstrated an understanding of goals and of ways to attain these goals, the goals must be set. These goals should be

Table 5.2	Examples of Goal Setting for School Activities

Assignment	What Do I Have to Do?	Did I Do It?
Reading	Read pages 19 and 20 Identify the main character and the setting	___Yes ___No
Math	Problems 1–10 on page 20	___Yes ___No
Music	Follow the teacher's instructions	___Yes ___No
Lunch	Follow the five BIG RAM rules	___Yes ___No
Science	Measure and record the length of four objects	___Yes ___No

Four or five completed assignments = go home on time (3:00).
Fewer than four completed assignments = stay after school for 10 minutes (3:10).

documented, so students can refer back to them. Teachers and students should monitor each goal to make sure continuously that progress has been made.

Self-Recording. Self-recording (also called self-monitoring by many researchers and practitioners) involves observing and recording one's own behavior (Cooper et al., 2007). However, Martella, Leonard, Marchand-Martella, and Agran (1993) make a distinction between self-recording and self-monitoring. **Self-recording** involves observing and recording one's own behavior *when prompted to do so.* This prompt can be anything that evokes the recording behavior. For example, a student who has negative verbalizations (e.g., swears and makes derogatory statements) may be told by teachers to record whenever the student makes a negative verbalization. Students who are frequently off task can be taught how to record whether they are on or off task whenever a bell sounds. Self-monitoring does not require such a prompt (see the following description of self-monitoring).

Due to its reactivity, self-recording has been shown to be effective in decreasing unwanted behavior. In other words, when we are prompted to record what we do or do not do, this recording usually affects our behavior in some manner. Say you are biting your fingernails and record each time you begin to bite your nails. It is likely that your nail biting will decrease. The same thing happens with students who engage in unwanted behavior. The self-recording of the behavior tends to have a reactivity effect. As with all data-collection procedures (see Chapter 3), self-recording requires the development of a data-collection form similar to that used by the teacher. Any data-collection form, however, must be simple enough for students to use. Figure 5.1 shows an example of a self-recording form, with positive and negative interactions and positive and negative comments (Sprick, 1981). Students mark each time they say something nice or something derogatory. For younger students, instead of typewritten words on a page, pictures can be used, with a behavior resulting in the opportunity to color in a circle (see Figure 5.2).

| Figure 5.1 | Self-Recording Form |

Figure 5.2	Self-Recording Form for Younger Students

Use the frog chart by filling in or by having a student fill in a circle whenever
he or she works hard or engages in a specific positive behavior.

To teach self-recording, teachers must complete several steps (Martella, Leonard, et al., 1993). The first step is called preteaching. In this step, teachers provide a rationale for self-recording. The second step involves demonstrating how the self-recording form is used. This form will then be used throughout each of the remaining steps. The third step involves providing students with several examples (e.g., 10 examples) of the unwanted and wanted behaviors. Before each example is provided, the teacher names the type of example, saying, "This is an unwanted behavior." The fourth step involves providing students with the examples again but having them indicate which behaviors are wanted and which are unwanted. The final step involves having the students generate a list of unwanted and wanted behaviors while labeling each behavior at the same time. The students are finished with this preteaching when they accurately record which statement is a wanted behavior and which is an unwanted one.

Once preteaching is finished, the teachers must determine what the prompt to record will be, such as telling students to record a behavior when it occurs or using some signaling device such as a wristwatch with a chronograph function. Finally, teachers must monitor students' self-recording to make sure it is occurring.

Self-Monitoring. **Self-monitoring** is a procedure in which a student observes and records his or her own behavior (Cooper et al., 2007) Self-monitoring is similar to self-recording except that it occurs without the external prompt (Dalton, Martella, & Marchand-Martella, 1999). (Note: Many researchers and practitioners do not make a distinction between self-recording and self-monitoring and lump both under the category of self-monitoring.) Because it relies on students to remember to track their own behavior and involves a finer discrimination of when a particular behavior occurs or does not occur, self-monitoring is much more difficult for students to perform. For example, Dalton et al. (1999) taught two middle school students with learning disabilities how to use a self-monitoring form to track their on-task performance in three general education classes (see Figure 5.3). Thus, the students monitored their behavior rather than simply recording when a behavior occurred. The preteaching was conducted in the same way as for the introduction of self-recording.

Self-Charting. **Self-charting** involves teaching students how to graph their own behavior (Martella et al., 2001). These charts can be a great motivational technique in areas such as reading instruction. If teachers are conducting timed reading passages, the students can graph their reading rates and accuracy levels. Students can then see the progression of their reading performance over time. Goal setting can easily be combined with self-charting, with students and teachers setting a goal in reading speed and placing a data point on the graph. Students can then see and chart the progression toward their goals.

Self-charting can also be used for unwanted behaviors (Martella, Leonard, et al., 1993). For example, students can take the data from a period of self-monitoring and plot the level of positive statements on a graph (as shown in Figure 5.4). Again, students get visual feedback on the level of their behavior from the graph.

Self-Evaluation. **Self-evaluation** involves teaching students how to measure their own behavior against some specified standard (Martella et al., 2001). Students who stop trying in class may have a weakness in this skill of self-evaluation. These students may see their performance as weak in comparison to others. On the other hand,

Figure 5.3 Self-Monitoring Form

Are you working and staying on task? (Circle yes or no.)

Monday

11:00	11:05	11:10	11:15
Yes No	Yes No	Yes No	Yes No
11:20	11:25	11:30	11:35
Yes No	Yes No	Yes No	Yes No
11:40	11:45		
Yes No	Yes No		

Tuesday

11:00	11:05	11:10	11:15
Yes No	Yes No	Yes No	Yes No
11:20	11:25	11:30	11:35
Yes No	Yes No	Yes No	Yes No
11:40	11:45		
Yes No	Yes No		

Wednesday

11:00	11:05	11:10	11:15
Yes No	Yes No	Yes No	Yes No
11:20	11:25	11:30	11:35
Yes No	Yes No	Yes No	Yes No
11:40	11:45		
Yes No	Yes No		

Thursday

11:00	11:05	11:10	11:15
Yes No	Yes No	Yes No	Yes No
11:20	11:25	11:30	11:35
Yes No	Yes No	Yes No	Yes No
11:40	11:45		
Yes No	Yes No		

Friday

11:00	11:05	11:10	11:15
Yes No	Yes No	Yes No	Yes No
11:20	11:25	11:30	11:35
Yes No	Yes No	Yes No	Yes No
11:40	11:45		
Yes No	Yes No		

| Figure 5.4 | Example of a Self-Charting Graph |

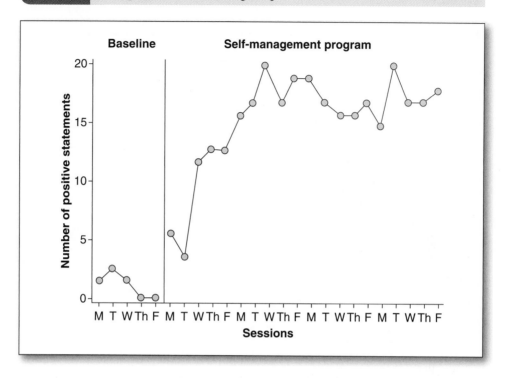

Seligman (1995) indicates that students who think too much of their work tend to be more aggressive when provided with feedback on their weak performance. Seligman indicates that students must receive accurate feedback on their performance. Students can be taught to make these evaluations themselves if teachers provide them with accurate feedback on their performance and with examples of good and poor performance. For example, after discussing samples of common writing problems, high school students could be given an example of a well-written paper, and their papers could be evaluated against this standard. Their evaluations would then be matched with the teacher's evaluations. Therefore, self-evaluation is taught through providing students with accurate and honest feedback on their performance and by providing examples of performances that meet and do not meet a particular standard. The pre-teaching process used in self-recording and self-monitoring is an appropriate and effective way to teach self-evaluation skills.

Table 5.3 shows a self-evaluation form used by Dalton et al. (1999). As shown, students were instructed to circle "yes" or "no" to questions referring to behaviors to be exhibited before, during, and after class. In addition, each student was instructed to rate his or her overall behavior. This rating was compared with a rating provided by the teacher. Teacher ratings were operationally defined so that consistency of ratings could be ensured (see Table 5.4).

Table 5.3	Self-Evaluation Form

Dates	Mon.		Tues.		Wed.		Thurs.		Fri.	
Before Class										
1. Do I have my homework completed?	Yes	No	Yes	No	Yes	No	Yes	No	Yes	No
2. Did I bring my materials (pencil, assignment log, and composition book)?	Yes	No	Yes	No	Yes	No	Yes	No	Yes	No
3. Did I find out what I will be doing in class (listen to the teacher, look for the assignment, ask if I don't know)?	Yes	No	Yes	No	Yes	No	Yes	No	Yes	No
4. Did I write the assignment/ activity in my assignment log?	Yes	No	Yes	No	Yes	No	Yes	No	Yes	No
5. Did I get started on time within 60 seconds?	Yes	No	Yes	No	Yes	No	Yes	No	Yes	No
After Class										
6. Did I ask myself during the period, "Am I working?"	Yes	No	Yes	No	Yes	No	Yes	No	Yes	No
7. Did I follow the teacher's directions?	Yes	No	Yes	No	Yes	No	Yes	No	Yes	No
8. Did I work on the assignment during the entire time I was given?	Yes	No	Yes	No	Yes	No	Yes	No	Yes	No
9. Do I have homework tonight? If yes, write in my assignment log.	Yes	No	Yes	No	Yes	No	Yes	No	Yes	No
10. Rate my behavior: (Circle the number) 1 = poor 2 = needs improvement 3 = okay 4 = good 5 = great	1 2 3 4 5		1 2 3 4 5		1 2 3 4 5		1 2 3 4 5		1 2 3 4 5	
For the Teacher										
11. Please rate the student's behavior: 1 = poor 2 = needs improvement 3 = okay 4 = good 5 = great	1 2 3 4 5		1 2 3 4 5		1 2 3 4 5		1 2 3 4 5		1 2 3 4 5	

Table 5.4	Criteria for Teacher Ratings

1 = student was off task for most of the period (more than 40 minutes), did not follow classroom rules, was reprimanded regarding behavior more than two times, was removed from the classroom.

2 = student worked on the assigned task, followed classroom rules for less than half the period (30 minutes or less), or was reprimanded regarding behavior two times.

3 = student worked on the assigned task, followed classroom rules for over half of the period (30 minutes or more), or was reprimanded regarding behavior two times.

4 = student worked on the assigned task, followed classroom rules, or had only one minor incident, such as speaking without permission.

5 = student worked on the assigned task, followed classroom rules, or had no warnings or reprimands.

Self-Instruction. **Self-instruction** training involves teaching individuals how to "talk themselves" through a particular set of behaviors (Martella et al., 2001) or how to provide themselves with rules (Taylor & O'Reilly, 1997). Meichenbaum and Goodman (1971) originally described self-instruction training and recommended a five-step sequence: (a) teachers perform a task, instructing aloud while students observe; (b) students perform the task while teachers instruct aloud; (c) students perform the task while self-instructing aloud; (d) students perform the task while whispering; and (e) students perform the task while self-instructing covertly.

Research on self-instruction training shows that it can be an effective way of improving appropriate behavior (Alberto & Troutman, 2009; Miltenberger, 2007). Researchers, however, are not in agreement on the causal effects of self-instruction (see Agran & Martella, 1991; Martella, 1994; and Taylor & O'Reilly, 1997, for a discussion of the causal effects of self-instruction). Self-instruction may prompt or cue a behavior to occur (e.g., telling ourselves that we need to get on task may get us on task), but it may simply be a parallel behavior to the overt behavior we want to see (e.g., telling ourselves we need to get on task may be a second behavior independent of getting on task). Unfortunately, researchers have not determined conclusively which view is correct.

Self-Reinforcement and Self-Punishment. **Self-reinforcement** and **self-punishment** involve teaching students how to provide consequences for their own behavior. Self-reinforcement could be in the form of praise (e.g., I did a good job), of a tangible item (e.g., a new outfit), or of an activity (e.g., going to a movie) if a behavior is exhibited (Martella et al., 2001). Self-punishment usually involves self-reprimands, but it can also involve the removal of a potential reinforcer (e.g., removing the possibility of going to a movie). The teaching of self-reinforcement involves having students say good things about themselves when they enact a positive behavior. For example, when students respond favorably to instruction, teachers could have the students tell themselves that what they did was a good thing. Teachers could also allow students to go buy themselves drinks after a positive response to instruction. Self-punishment works in a similar manner except that the students would be told to say to themselves that not following directions is not a good thing to do.

Self-reinforcement and self-punishment are methods that can be effective in getting wanted behaviors to occur and unwanted behaviors to stop (Alberto & Troutman, 2009). Technically, however, self-reinforcement and self-punishment are not accurate terms. Such procedures involve establishing a positive consequence or an aversive consequence if a behavior goal has or has not been met. It is probably the self-recording or self-evaluation part of this process (described above) that truly affects behavior change. As with self-instruction, the active ingredient of the intervention is once again unclear.

Problem Solving. **Problem solving** involves teaching students how to reach a successful conclusion to a problem situation (Martella, Agran, & Marchand-Martella, 1992). A problem occurs when there is no specific response to a situation and a response must be generated in some manner. Problem-solving training typically involves a four- to five-step procedure (Foxx, Martella, & Marchand-Martella, 1989). D'Zurilla and Goldfried (1971) outline one such five-step sequence. The first step involves the identification of the problem (e.g., I am getting angry). Teaching individuals to discriminate a problem situation from one that is not a problem must be achieved in this step. The second step involves defining what the problem is (e.g., another student is teasing me). This step is critical in that knowing exactly what the problem is will aid in developing a method to overcome the problem. The third step involves the generation of alternative actions. This step can be achieved through brainstorming or generating as many alternatives as possible without regard to their consequences (e.g., I can hit the student, I can walk away from her, I can tell the teacher, I can leave class, I can tell her to leave me alone). The key to this step is to steer clear of judgmental statements about the student's alternatives. The fourth step, decision making, involves considering the possible consequences—both positive and negative—of each solution (e.g., If I hit the student, she probably would leave me alone but I would get into trouble; If I tell the teacher, he will tell her to stop but I could be labeled a tattletale; If I walk away, I might avoid a confrontation but I could be seen as being afraid; If I told her to leave me alone, she might comply but she could also become more obnoxious). Once the pros and cons have been laid out, students must decide which alternative is likely to have the best outcome (e.g., I will tell her to leave me alone, and, if that does not work, I will tell the teacher). The final step involves verification. In other words, the students must be able to determine if the alternative works. If it does work, the students should be prepared to use it again. If it does not, another solution should be attempted.

The Need for Consequences

A particularly important aspect of any self-management program is arranging for consequences for the self-management skills we want to develop and maintain (Martella et al., 2001). For example, there must be some positive consequence for self-recording or self-instruction for such behaviors to continue. These consequences may initially come from the teacher. Dalton et al. (1999) used a daily report card to reinforce appropriate classroom behavior (see Figure 5.5). Later, if self-management

Figure 5.5 Daily Report Card

Daily Report Card

*Remember:

8 out of 10 "Yes" responses = 5 points

A "3" to "5" behavior rating = 5 points

If your points = 10 for the day, you get 10 minutes of free time in your study class.

You get 2 extra credit points EACH TIME you get a "5" for behavior from your teacher.

A total of 10 points for 4 consecutive days = A tangible reward of your choice, and the points will go toward your overall grade.

For the teacher:

Record points here--

Dates	Mon.	Tues.	Wed.	Thurs.	Fri.

training has been done correctly, the maintaining consequences will come from more naturally occurring sources, such as other students. Therefore, simply teaching students to problem solve, self-instruct, self-reinforce, self-monitor, self-evaluate, self-record, or self-chart is not enough. Teachers must set up some system to maintain these behaviors or skills until students receive naturally maintaining contingencies from elsewhere in their environments.

What Is Preference and Choice?

Teachers should also be cognizant of student preferences and of including opportunities for students to make choices during the school day. Teachers should become aware of preferred curricular activities (e.g., math or social studies) and preferred learning contexts (e.g., working alone in relative silence versus small group activities). The curriculum should be flexible to accommodate a mix of preferred academic demands. Adapting instructional methods (e.g., using additional visual prompts or reducing the number of tasks to complete within an academic period) may accommodate different students and reduce challenging behavior. Working on a task alone versus engaging in group activities may allow the student to focus more and may reduce peer pressure to act out. Long periods of non-preferred academic activity may predispose the student to challenging behavior. Interspersing preferred with non-preferred academic activities can act as a powerful antecedent intervention to increase academic engagement and reduce the probability of challenging behavior (Luiselli, 2006). Incorporating student choice within the daily curriculum can also function to reduce challenging behavior. Teachers should think actively about incorporating choices within all aspects of the curriculum. Apparently, the act of making a choice, even between two non-preferred academic activities, can pre-empt challenging behavior. So offering choices between different academic assignments or between methods of completing different academic assignments can increase academic success and also act to reduce the probability of challenging behavior (Luiselli, 2006).

What Is Correspondence Training?

Correspondence training is similar to self-management training. Self-management training, however, involves teaching individuals how to change the environment to facilitate future behavior, whereas **correspondence training** involves teaching students how to report accurately on what they have done or will do (Lloyd, 2002; Risley & Hart, 1968). When individuals report what they will do in the future, one hopes they will be more likely to do it. Thus, reporting what we have done or will do in the future is an aspect of self-management. Several possible relations in correspondence are important for students to learn: (a) doing what we say we will do (e.g., "I will study" and I do study), (b) accurately reporting what we have done (e.g., "I hit her" when I have hit another student), (c) not doing what we say we will not do (e.g., "I will not write on the desk again" and I do not write on the desk), and (d) accurately reporting what we have not done (e.g., "I did not steal" when I did not steal).

Clearly, correspondence in children is a critical aspect of responsible behavior, but it may need to be explicitly taught. This teaching is accomplished by training children to recognize when there is a correspondence between saying and doing and by reinforcing this correspondence. For example, when students say that they will complete an assignment and do so, teachers should reinforce the correspondence between what the students say and actually do. Likewise, if the students cheat on a test but accurately report that they cheated, teachers should reinforce the correspondence. Note that the behavior of cheating may still receive a negative consequence by, say, giving a failing grade for the test, but the accurate reporting of the event may be reinforced by allowing the students to take an alternative form of the test with 25% of the points taken off the top.

The critical aspect of correspondence training is to note when students are telling the truth. This aspect is critical for behavioral support; working with students who do not exhibit correspondence (e.g., do not accurately report what they have done) is much more difficult because the information obtained from them is always suspect.

What Are Behavioral Contracts?

Behavioral contracts (also called *contingency contracts*) are popular methods of increasing appropriate behavior (Cooper et al., 2007; Zirpoli, 2008). A behavioral contract is similar to any other contract. It spells out what each party to the contract must do to satisfy the agreement. The behavioral contract involves three main components: the task, the consequence, and the task record (Cooper et al.). Figure 5.6 shows an example of a behavioral contract.

The task must be stated in observable terms. In other words, teachers must be able to see when the behavior occurs (e.g., coming to class). The task must also be accomplished in some time period (e.g., coming to class before the bell rings). Also, how much of the task is required must be documented (e.g., each day of the week).

The consequence for performing the task must be equally explicit. First, it must be very clearly stated what exactly the students will earn if they meet the expectations. Asking the students what they would like to earn for completing the task can generate possible consequences. The consequences selected for performing the task must motivate the student to complete the task. In other words, the consequences must have some reinforcing properties. Second, when the consequence will be delivered must be included in the contract (e.g., Friday afternoon at 2:00 PM). Third, the contract must specify how often the consequence will be provided (e.g., every 15 minutes). Teachers must be sure that the delivery of the consequence occurs after the task expectations have been met.

Finally, a record-keeping system must be in effect. A task record could be attached to the contract, and teachers can record on it. Another system, however, is to integrate self-recording or self-monitoring into the task record. Thus, the teachers or the

Figure 5.6 Example of a Behavioral Contract

CONTRACT

Who: Sandy	Who: Ms. Brown
What: Complete all work assigned	What: Verify that work is completed; place a "+" for each day for each subject
When: Every school day	When: Every school day
How well: Sandy will complete 15 of 20 work assignments over the week and will earn one of the following: (a) lunch with Tammy on Monday. (b) 10 extra minutes of computer time before the end of school on Friday. (c) 10 extra minutes in the gym in the afternoon on Friday. (d) 10 minutes of free time before the end of school on Friday. BONUS: If Sandy completes 20 out of 20 assignments, she will receive an "Excellent Student" note sent home to her parents.	How much: Ms. Brown will provide one of the rewards listed. A bonus "Excellent student" note will be sent home for completion of all 20 assignments.

Sign here: _____

Date: _____

Sign here: _____

Date: _____

	Mon.	Tues.	Wed.	Thurs.	Fri.
Math					
Science					
Reading					
Social studies					

---

students mark whether or not the students have met the behavioral expectations each day. Self-recording or self-monitoring can enhance the effectiveness of the contract. There must be an area of the contract that the teachers and students sign. Gaining the students' signature aids in getting their commitment to become involved in the contract, increasing the probability that the contract will lead to more instances of wanted behaviors.

What Are Token Economy Systems?

Token economy systems, described in detail by Ayllon and Azrin (1968), are effective in bringing about positive behaviors. **Token economy systems** are procedures wherein tokens are provided if a behavior occurs; these tokens can be turned in for

backup reinforcers. Therefore, tokens serve as secondary reinforcers. We all exist within token systems. If you have ever used money, you have used a token system. Money is a token. A dollar by itself holds no value. The value of a dollar comes from what we can purchase with it. The things we can purchase with money are likely primary reinforcers, such as food and shelter, and secondary reinforcers, such as nice clothes, fancy cars, and movies. Tokens, then, are conditioned or secondary reinforcers because they get their reinforcing value from being paired with an established reinforcer (see Chapter 2). Money is also considered to be a generalized reinforcer because you can use it to buy many

Teachers and students can together develop and agree on a behavioral contract.

pleasant items and activities, as previously described. Tokens, including money, are things that are provided contingent on some behavior, and they can be turned in for (or used to purchase) backup reinforcers.

Setting up a token system is like developing a banking system. Table 5.5 shows the steps involved (Cooper et al., 2007). Token systems are difficult to administer effectively because they take a great deal of planning and monitoring. They also require a great deal of consistency. These systems work because the token becomes a secondary reinforcer. Teachers can use the tokens to reinforce a wanted behavior immediately. Token systems also bridge the time gap between the behavior and the established reinforcer. Therefore, tokens are excellent tools for providing immediate consequences for appropriate behavior without interfering with ongoing educational activities.

The problem with token systems in the classroom is that they are not typically present in most educational situations (Cooper et al., 2007; Sulzer-Azaroff & Mayer, 1991). They are effective, but once they are used in one class, there may be a lack of generalization of appropriate behavior if students transition to another class where token systems are not used (Cooper et al.). Therefore, tokens should be used more as a last resort to gain control over unwanted behaviors, or some plan must be made to fade out the system. Fading out token systems is important in planning for the maintenance of a behavior change.

Fading out token systems can be achieved in several ways (Cooper et al., 2007; Sulzer-Azaroff & Mayer, 1991). First, delay the provision of the token after the behavior has been emitted. Second, provide the token on an intermittent basis. Third, decrease the number of tokens earned for each behavior. Fourth, increase the number of behaviors

Table 5.5	Steps in Establishing a Token System

1. Design a record system.
2. Select tokens.
3. Design a method of delivering the tokens immediately.
4. Set the number of tokens per behavior (specify conditions for token delivery).
5. Select backup reinforcers (things that can be purchased).
6. Set backup reinforcer prices.
7. Train staff.
8. Design the system to maintain consistency of the program.
9. Pair token delivery with positive social feedback (i.e., praise).
10. Build in a response cost system (Chapter 6).
11. Maintain a positive balance of tokens.
12. Provide access to the backup reinforcer.
13. Fade out the system.

required for each token. Fifth, increase the delay between the token deliveries and the availability of the established reinforcers. Sixth, increase the prices of the established reinforcers. Finally, provide the established reinforcers on an intermittent basis.

How Do We Produce Generalization of Behavior Change?

Generalization is a critical aspect of any behavior change program. If generalization is not realized, the veracity of the behavior support plan must be questioned. Therefore, teachers and other individuals designing and implementing a behavior support plan must consider it an important goal. Below are two forms of generalization (response and stimulus generalization). The methods that teachers and others can use to plan for generalization were originally described by Stokes and Baer (1977) and Stokes and Osnes (1989) and are also described in this chapter.

Response Generalization

Response generalization refers to a behavior being more likely to occur in the presence of something as a result of another behavior having been reinforced and strengthened in its presence (Cooper et al., 2007; Kazdin, 2001). Children who call their mothers "mom" after having been reinforced for calling them "mommy" are exhibiting response generalization. Another example occurs when students who have been reinforced for saying "thank you" when they are provided with something are more likely to say "thanks." Therefore, response generalization can provide an instructional advantage in that, as a result of one behavior being taught, other behaviors come about. This advantage is seen in problem-solving training as well. For example, a problem situation may call for a certain response, such as when students are challenged to a fight by others. One student may have been taught to walk away and report the incident to a teacher. If teachers are not present or if this student is prevented from walking away, however, another response would need to be generated and response generalization could come into play. In this case, the student might attempt to engage in conflict resolution by talking it out with the other students because, in most problem-solving training programs, students are taught to generate several possible solutions to a problem situation. When students have been taught problem solving as a response, the probability that a solution can be reached is increased. There are two general methods of programming for response generalization when increasing desirable behaviors: train sufficient response exemplars and vary the acceptable responses during training.

Train Sufficient Response Exemplars. **Training sufficient response exemplars** involves teaching students several appropriate responses to a given situation. For example, students who get frustrated when provided with difficult tasks and become verbally aggressive can request a break instead by saying, "May I take a break?" or "I need help" or "I need a rest." Problem-solving teaching methods frequently teach a number of possible solutions to a problem and have been shown to promote novel appropriate responses (Foxx et al., 1989; Martella et al., 1992).

Vary the Acceptable Responses During Training. A similar procedure, **varying the acceptable responses during training**, is to require students to give different responses during behavioral instruction. For example, requiring students to wait for five minutes to take a break, requiring them to clean off their desks before going on a break, or requiring them to finish one more question before taking a break are methods of teaching a variety of responses for taking a break. This technique was used by Goetz and Baer (1973) to increase the creativity of the block building of nursery school children.

Stimulus Generalization

Although response generalization is an important concept, stimulus generalization is usually of more concern to educators. In the context of this discussion, **stimulus generalization** (also termed *setting* or *situation generalization*) essentially involves a student using new and appropriate behaviors in school contexts other than where they have been taught (Cooper et al., 2007; Kazdin, 2001). Examples of stimulus generalization abound in the real world. Young children calling all men "daddy" is an example of stimulus generalization. Sometimes, this form of generalization can be comical. One of the authors has a lack of scalp hair. One morning, his one-year-old daughter was in the living room watching a cartoon on television, and he was in the kitchen. He heard his daughter yell "daddy" and his wife say, "Good girl, that's daddy." As it turns out, his daughter was pointing excitedly at the television, thinking she was seeing daddy.

She was not seeing daddy, however, but Elmer Fudd. There are several methods of teaching this type of generalization: one can program common stimulus, train sufficient stimulus exemplars, train loosely, and use the sequential modification of the training situation (see Stokes & Baer, 1977, and Stokes & Osnes, 1989).

Program Common Stimuli. **Programming common stimuli** essentially means providing instruction or support under conditions that are broadly available in different classrooms and other environments within the school. This instruction enhances the probability that the behavior learned in one context will be generalized to other contexts. For example, the consequences for appropriate behavior or challenging behavior should be the same across resource and regular classrooms. This technique was used by Walker and Buckley (1972) when they employed the same academic materials in a general education classroom and in the resource room where social and academic classroom behaviors were taught.

Train Sufficient Stimulus Exemplars. **Training sufficient stimulus exemplars** simply means using multiple examples of the targeted skills during teaching. For example, when teaching how to respond appropriately to criticism, a teacher could use examples of corrective feedback from several teachers, classroom peers, parents, and other sources. Using this process teaches the students to respond to a variety of different but related situations. Additionally, the student is taught to modify his or her responding to the different situations. Because the student is taught across a variety of exemplars, there is a higher likelihood that he or she will generalize appropriate responses to novel situations (e.g., when receiving corrective feedback from a police officer). Problem-solving approaches frequently use this technique by providing as many different problem situations as possible. For example, Martella, Marchand-Martella, and Agran (1993) used a problem-solving format with several stimulus exemplars to improve the adaptability (independence) of high school students with mild disabilities.

Train Loosely. Training loosely has also been called *incidental teaching, naturalistic teaching, nonintensive teaching,* and *minimal intervention* (Alberto & Troutman, 2009). **Training loosely** involves varying the situation under which the behavior support plan is introduced. For example, have several teachers or adults in the classroom implement the program rather than one adult, vary the way instructions are provided, vary the tone of voice, or teach in noisy and quiet areas. Training loosely then aids in the generalization to other situations that may be different in some way from the one provided.

Modify the Training Situation Sequentially. **Sequential modification of the training situation** involves successfully implementing the management program in one setting and then changing the management system in another setting to match that of the first setting. For example, if teachers have students who display unwanted behaviors in the classroom who are going to transition to another classroom, they may train the other teachers in the new setting to implement the management system in their classroom. Essentially, they are replicating the effects of the management program in future environments. This modification was accomplished by Dalton et al. (1999) when the self-management program they employed was sequentially applied to each of three general education classrooms.

How Is Consequence-Imposed Behavior Change Maintained?

Another important consideration among those implementing behavioral support is how to ensure the maintenance of a behavior change. **Maintenance** is defined as the endurance of a behavior after a portion or all of the intervention has been removed (Cooper et al., 2007; Kazdin, 2001). Formal individualized behavior support plans should not be thought of as permanent procedures. Rather, they should be thought of as temporary attempts to get behavior under control. Once an unwanted behavior is reduced or eliminated or a wanted behavior is increased sufficiently, the behavioral support procedure should be faded out. Therefore, whether the improved behavior continues in the future without the behavior management program in place must be determined. There are several methods of planning for the maintenance of behavior change, and these can be categorized as intermittent schedules, programming for naturally occurring contingencies, and the use of self-management procedures. The reader will note that there is some overlap between the strategies used to promote the maintenance of behavior and those used to promote generalization.

Intermittent Reinforcement Schedules

When students are learning new skills as part of a behavior support plan, teachers should provide preferred consequences (reinforcers) very frequently. As the student becomes competent in these skills, the frequency of positive consequences for engaging in the new behavior needs to be reduced systematically or placed on what is known as an intermittent schedule of reinforcement (see Chapter 2). For example, consider a student who was out of her seat 75% of the period at the beginning of the term. Her program consisted of teaching her how to monitor her own behavior with the provision of reinforcement for being in her seat throughout a 5-minute interval. At the beginning, when the student monitored her own behavior and was in her seat throughout a 5-minute span, she was reinforced. The time span was then increased from 5 minutes to 10 minutes and so on until the student was in her seat for the 40-minute class period before she received reinforcement. Once the student was able to self-monitor being in her seat throughout the period for three consecutive days, the contingencies for being in her seat were faded out completely. In this manner, reinforcement for her being in her seat was gradually decreased and eventually eliminated.

Use of Naturally Occurring Reinforcers

Another tactic to program for the maintenance of a behavior change is to ensure that the new behaviors come under the control of naturally occurring reinforcers (Cooper et al., 2007; Sulzer-Azaroff & Mayer, 1991). **Naturally occurring reinforcers** are consequences that are routinely available in the environment in which the new behavior will occur. If a new behavior can come under the control of naturally occurring reinforcers, there is no need to use contrived reinforcers (such as token economies) or to fade out the use of such contrived reinforcers eventually. Using naturally occurring reinforcers, such as positive teacher attention or breaks from difficult work tasks, can be a very powerful method for producing constructive and durable change in student behavior. It can also be a lot easier for teachers to learn to use naturally occurring reinforcers than to develop and accurately implement contrived consequence systems. With this tactic, maintaining behavior change is more likely.

Perhaps the most important aspect of programming for naturally occurring reinforcers is changing how others respond to student behavior. Many students who display problem behaviors may be social outcasts. Peers or teachers might not like these students much because they have a long history of causing problems for other students and educational staff. Therefore, it may be difficult to interact with these students in a positive manner. It is much easier to spot unwanted behavior from these students because teachers look for their unwanted behaviors. If long-lasting behavioral change is truly desired, however, other staff members must change the manner in which they interact with these students. **Positive scanning** or watching for positive and wanted behaviors displayed by these students should take the place of **negative scanning** or looking for unwanted behaviors. If we as educators can attempt to make our interactions with these students positive rather than negative, we can increase the likelihood that the behaviors we are trying to teach and reinforce will continue. In addition, if we can change the manner in which we engage these students and establish a more constructive and cooperative relationship with them, the students will be more likely to respond in kind.

Following is an example of using naturally occurring reinforcers to support a middle school student who displayed severe behavior problems (Martella, Leonard, et al., 1993). The teacher's main concern was with the number of negative statements the student made to other students and adults. This student displayed roughly 1.5 negative statements per minute in a class period. When he would say these negative things, the classroom staff and students would usually respond in a negative manner, such as by providing a reprimand or a "dirty look." Thus, almost all the student's interactions with others in the classroom were negative. Based on the definition of positive reinforcement, however, these "negative" interactions were positively reinforcing the student's unwanted negative statements. Once the behavior management program had been implemented, the student began to receive positive interactions with students and staff when he said something positive. The student's positive statements increased dramatically, whereas the negative statements decreased. Significantly, his use of positive statements continued long after the program was withdrawn, as did his avoidance of negative statements, which remained at zero levels. The reason this behavior change was maintained after the program was withdrawn was that the staff and students changed how they interacted with the student. This new interaction was essentially a built-in maintenance procedure in which naturally maintaining contingencies were introduced (i.e., you have positive interactions with people when you are nice to them).

The previous discussion about naturally occurring reinforcers leads to a related and equally important strategy called behavioral trapping (Cooper et al., 2007). In some situations, naturally occurring reinforcers may not be powerful enough initially to enable a person to develop and maintain new behavioral change. Therefore, contrived reinforcers may need to be introduced (e.g., a token system). Once the behavior has changed in a positive direction, then naturally occurring reinforcers are introduced (positive teacher praise) as the contrived reinforcers are thinned using an intermittent schedule. In this way, a wanted behavior becomes "trapped" within its natural setting or environment and behavioral trapping has occurred (i.e., the new behaviors eventually come under the control of naturally occurring reinforcers in that environment). **Behavioral trapping** has also been described in terms of teaching students to recruit normally occurring reinforcers in the classroom (Baer & Wolf, 1970; Cooper et al.; Kohler & Greenwood, 1986). Students can be taught how to seek out reinforcement for positive behaviors ("How am I doing on this worksheet?"), which should in turn "trap" or maintain the behavior.

A teacher can therefore teach the student specific behaviors that will prompt reinforcement. For example, individuals with developmental disabilities were taught how to avoid injuries at work (Martella et al., 1992). One part of the training was to report to the supervisor that something was done to avoid an injury (e.g., removing an object from an aisle). This instruction helped maintain the safe worker behavior by prompting the supervisor to praise the workers when they recognized and avoided injury. This concept can be used in the classroom as well. For instance, students who do not complete seatwork very often could be taught to tell the teacher when they do complete the work. Therefore, the students prompt the teacher to reinforce the work completion.

Use of Self-Management Procedures

Self-management procedures were presented earlier in this chapter as an intervention method. Self-management protocols are also very effective strategies to promote the maintenance of behavior change. When students learn to manage their own behavior, they become their own behavior change agents. Thus, the positive change achieved through self-management does not rely on external prompts from teachers or reinforcers.

For example, when students are taught to self-instruct, they use self-generated verbal prompts to engage in the targeted appropriate behavior. Therefore, the behavior may not come under the control of teacher prompts but under the control of the self-prompts. In this way, a self-management procedure such as self-instruction may allow the behavior to be maintained by reducing students' reliance on teachers.

What Is the Planning Process for Generalization and Maintenance?

Generalization and maintenance are critical aspects of a behavior support plan. If behavior change is not durable (i.e., if the individuals cannot maintain the change and generalize it to various settings and situations), then the veracity of the intervention is questionable. As discussed, there are several ways of programming for generalization and maintenance, but these methods take planning. According to Cooper et al. (2007), three steps should be considered. First, all the desired behavior changes must be listed. Second, a list must be created showing all the situations, settings, and places in which the wanted behaviors should occur as well as all the people with whom the wanted behaviors should occur. Finally, this list of behaviors, settings, and relevant persons must be shared with all of those key individuals who work with the student and who will be involved in supporting and promoting behavior change. Behavior change must be thought of as changing not only the student's behavior but also the behavior of all those working with the student. In other words, teachers must ask themselves what they must do to lead to an improvement in student behavior rather than only focusing on what students must do.

VIGNETTE REVISITED   Seeking Help From a Building Assistance Team

Ms. Armstrong presented the difficulties she was having with Juan to the building assistance team. She indicated that there was nothing Juan would work for, in terms of a reinforcer. One member of the team suggested that Juan would indeed work for something, and that was not interacting with the class. This teacher told Ms. Armstrong that, if she could decrease the amount of time Juan sat isolated from the class, she could use sitting alone as a reinforcer for becoming involved in class activities. The critical aspect of this technique was decreasing the amount of time Juan isolated himself from the class. This teacher also told Ms. Armstrong that she should start small, such as by requiring Juan to interact with the class for 5 minutes and then gradually "shaping" or increasing this time.

Ms. Armstrong decided to give it a try. The next day, she told Juan that he could sit alone and not be bothered during the class period if he became involved for 5 minutes in a class activity. She also told Juan that if he refused to become involved for 5 minutes, she would stand next to him while instructing the class. Wanting to be left alone, Juan agreed to become involved in the class activity (one she thought would be reinforcing for him). After 5 minutes, he went back to the corner of the room. Once Juan was regularly involved in the 5-minute class activity, Ms. Armstrong increased the required involvement in the class to 10 minutes. Over a period of five weeks, Ms. Armstrong was able to get Juan involved in all but the last 5 minutes of class, when Juan was allowed to sit in his corner uninterrupted.

Summary

In this chapter, we provided an overview of the strategies that can be used as part of a behavior support plan to increase adaptive behaviors for students. It is a central tenet of behavioral support that programs should focus on increasing skills rather than on decreasing problematic behaviors. Several strategies for increasing adaptive responding were described. Basic prompting strategies such as gestures, verbal instructions, and physical prompts can be used to increase appropriate responses for students. When adapting curricula and teaching strategies to support students with challenging behavior, teachers should also be aware of behavioral phenomena such as the Premack principle, behavioral momentum, and the impact of student choice and preference. We spent a large amount of time in this chapter discussing self-management strategies. These are very powerful behavior change techniques and are very much in line with a behavioral support ethic in that they enhance self-determination coupled with behavior change. A variety of self-management procedures were described including self-instruction, self-monitoring, and problem solving. A variety of consequence-based strategies were then discussed including contingency contracts and token economies. These strategies involve clarifying the nature and schedule of positive consequences for appropriate behavior. Finally, we described strategies that should be incorporated into a behavior support plan to foster generalization and the maintenance of behavior change. It is critical that these strategies be included in all behavioral support programs in order to produce durable behavior change.

Key Terms

Discussion Questions

1. Why is it critical to consider increasing wanted behavior versus simply decreasing unwanted behavior?

2. How can a teacher use different prompting strategies to get wanted behaviors to occur?

3. How can shaping be used to improve a behavior that is not occurring enough, such as on-task behavior? Provide an example.

4. How are the Premack principle and the response deprivation hypothesis similar? How are they different?

5. How can a teacher reduce a student's reluctance in responding to instruction by using behavioral momentum and preference and choice?

6. Why is the development of self-managed behavior a desirable goal for students? What skills can be taught to help a student become more self-managed?

7. How can correspondence training increase the likelihood that students will accurately report what they did or follow through on what they say they will do?

8. How can self-management techniques promote the maintenance of behavior change?

9. Describe the key components of a token economy.

10. How can teachers plan for the generalization and maintenance of behavior change?

6

Decreasing Undesirable Behaviors

Chapter Objectives

After studying this chapter, you should be able to

- describe the least restrictive, least intrusive, and most effective alternatives for decreasing undesirable behaviors,

- illustrate the cautions associated with the use of restrictive or intrusive procedures,

- depict the informal procedures one can use to respond to unwanted behavior,

- characterize level I behavior reduction procedures,

- describe level II behavior reduction procedures,

- explain what is meant by aversive-based procedures and describe their side effects,

- illustrate level III behavior reduction procedures,

- describe level IV behavior reduction procedures,

- explain how to decide which management procedure to use, and

- characterize how consequence-imposed behavior change is generalized and maintained.

VIGNETTE	**Reducing Swearing and Tantrums by Asking for a Break**

MS. JACKSON TAUGHT FOURTH GRADE. One student, Jackie, would frequently swear and have tantrums in class. Although Jackie's grades were slightly below average, she did not seem to have any particular weakness in any subject, but she did seem frustrated at times with some of her assignments (both group and individual). When Jackie became frustrated, she would become angry and begin to swear until she had a tantrum. Ms. Jackson would respond to these unwanted behaviors by sending Jackie to time-out for five minutes at a desk located in the classroom.

Following time-out, Jackie was required do the assignment once again. Ms. Jackson found that Jackie would often engage in tantrums again following a time-out. Sending Jackie to time-out did not seem to be having the desired effect. Unfortunately, Ms. Jackson was not sure why these swearing and tantrum behaviors were occurring.

Ms. Jackson became concerned enough to complete an FBA on Jackie. She had hoped that the assessment would not only reveal why Jackie was acting this way but also lead to an appropriate and effective solution. The result of the assessment suggested that Jackie was having tantrums or swearing during difficult tasks that lasted for several minutes. There did not seem to be a particular subject that was associated with the unwanted behaviors. These behaviors occurred during reading, math, and spelling. Based on this assessment, Ms. Jackson believed the function of Jackie's tantrum behavior was to escape from academic demands.

Overview

Recall that the first step in any behavior management program is to attempt to improve students' behaviors through reinforcement procedures. Unfortunately, not all students respond favorably to these attempts. For some students, procedures to decrease the likelihood of unwanted behavior need to be implemented. The difference between procedures aimed at increasing wanted behaviors and those aimed at decreasing unwanted behaviors has to do with the focus of the intervention. When focusing on increasing wanted behaviors, teachers hope that, if wanted behaviors are increased, they will take the place of unwanted behaviors. Unwanted behaviors, however, do not always go away with these attempts. Therefore, sometimes teachers need to focus specifically on decreasing unwanted behaviors.

In this chapter, several management methods used to decrease problem behaviors are outlined. The procedures discussed in Chapter 5 should be used in conjunction with the procedures discussed in this chapter. The concepts of least restrictive, least intrusive, and most effective approaches to the task of decreasing unwanted behaviors will be discussed here as well. Following this discussion, informal procedures will be described. Level I, II, III, and IV formal behavior-reduction techniques will also be highlighted. Finally, generalization and maintenance methods will be described.

What Are the Least Restrictive, Least Intrusive, and Most Effective Alternatives for Reducing Unwanted Behavior?

The procedures used in behavioral support that are designed to decrease behavior place some restrictions on students and are intrusive in some manner. Ethically, however, educators must use the least restrictive and least intrusive interventions possible while still providing effective supports. Teachers must understand what restrictiveness and intrusiveness mean. In addition, they must know their professional positions on the use of different management methods as well as fully understand the rules and regulations of particular states with regard to which procedures are considered more or less restrictive and intrusive. States set guidelines as to which procedures can be used with or without formal approval, and they place limits on the use of these procedures.

Restrictiveness

Restrictiveness involves the extent to which an individual is denied access to basic human freedoms, such as privacy, movement, or leisure (Cooper, Heron, & Heward, 2007; Kerr & Nelson, 2010; Wolery, Bailey, & Sugai, 1988). In general, methods that impinge the least on these freedoms should be used. For example, placing a student in time-out is technically considered more restrictive than providing a reprimand, physical restraint is more restrictive than a time-out, and overcorrection is more restrictive than extinction.

Intrusiveness

Intrusiveness involves the extent to which behavioral interventions affect a person's bodily or personal rights. Procedures associated with pain, discomfort, or social stigma are considered intrusive (Kerr & Nelson, 2010; Wolery et al., 1988). Thus, corporal punishment is more intrusive than a time-out, reprimanding a student in front of other students is more intrusive than reprimanding her when she is alone, and placing a student in exclusionary time-out is more intrusive than placing him in nonexclusionary time-out.

Effectiveness

As professionals, educators are obligated to use behavior management procedures that have been shown to be effective in the research literature (Cooper et al., 2007). If teachers are going to use an individualized management system, they should be confident that it will be effective because it has been shown to be effective in the past. If a procedure has not been shown to be effective or if there is not enough information to demonstrate its effectiveness with students, the principle of least dangerous assumption should be used (Wolery et al., 1988). The **principle of least dangerous assumption** "suggests that the strategy selected should produce the least amount of harm if the procedure is ineffective. This principle may be quite important when choosing between strategies that have not been used with a particular population, behavior problem, or setting" (Wolery et al., p. 370).

Teachers, then, must maintain a balancing act. They must choose the least restrictive and least intrusive alternatives while using the most effective procedures. At times, the most effective interventions will be more restrictive or intrusive. Ultimately, the decision concerning what interventions will be used may depend on what is allowed by state guidelines and what has been tried in the past (i.e., the teacher begins with the least restrictive and intrusive interventions and uses more restrictive or intrusive interventions if the first ones have failed).

The decision as to which behavior management procedure to use comes down to the right to effective interventions (see Chapter 1). Students have a fundamental right to receive the most effective behavior management programs available. Although the aim is to use preventive techniques and reinforcement-based systems, more restrictive and intrusive interventions may be needed.

Cautions With the Use of Restrictive or Intrusive Procedures

Kerr and Nelson (2010) discuss the need to protect students receiving restrictive or intrusive interventions. One critical aspect of protecting students' rights when using restrictive or intrusive interventions is to evaluate the efficacy of the intervention. Teachers must use the information obtained from ongoing evaluations to make decisions about future interventions. A second aspect in protecting students is to ensure adequate staff training and supervision. Restrictive or intrusive procedures can be misused and can violate the rights of students. The better the staff training in the use of restrictive and intrusive procedures and the more extensive the supervision, the less likely that the interventions will be misused. A third aspect is whether or not an FBA was implemented. The information obtained from such an analysis may decrease the need to resort to more restrictive and intrusive interventions in the first place. If it is determined that restrictive or intrusive interventions are required, however, this determination should result from an FBA.

Again, interventions designed to decrease behavior should be selected and monitored carefully. There are instances of abuse that have resulted from the inappropriate application of these interventions. For example, locking a student in a closet as a time-out is not supported in the scientific and educational communities and is considered abusive. Such an intervention should not be used. Similarly, berating a student or calling a student a derogatory name and terming the procedure "a reprimand" is not supported. The type and form of restrictive or intrusive techniques used should be shown to be effective in the scientific research literature. If the decision has been made to use restrictive or intrusive techniques, it is necessary to start from the least restrictive or intrusive approach before moving to more restrictive and intrusive interventions.

Conclusion

The major concern associated with the use of procedures to decrease unwanted behaviors is to protect students and preserve their rights as much as possible. Consequently, teachers should use procedures that are the least restrictive and intrusive before moving to more restrictive and intrusive methods. These procedures, arranged from the least restrictive and intrusive to the most restrictive and intrusive, are discussed next.

What Are Informal Procedures?

Informal procedures (also called *preventive strategies*) are those procedures that do not require explicit behavior management plans. That does not mean that these procedures do not take planning. A great deal of thought must be put into deciding which informal procedure to use, when to use it, and how it should be implemented. These informal procedures should be the first step in attempting to decrease unwanted behavior.

Situational Inducement

One effective method of decreasing the probability of unwanted behaviors is called situational inducement (Martin & Pear, 2007). **Situational inducement** involves manipulating contexts that already have a history of control over the behavior. We have all experienced situational inducement in our interactions in society. Police substations in communities tend to decrease the likelihood of crime in those areas. Cameras visible in stores make shoplifting less likely to occur. Cameras placed at intersections are used to decrease the running of red lights. Situational inducement can also be used to make other behaviors more likely to occur. For example, when you go into a supermarket for an item that people purchase frequently, such as milk, notice that you have to go to the back of the store. The reason is that when customers pass a large number of items in stores, they are more likely to buy something that they did not intend to buy initially. The items near a checkout line are also a situational inducement for buying something we may not need. When people are waiting in line, they are more likely to buy something than if they do not have to wait. Finally, go into a busy restaurant on a Friday evening and find out if there is music playing. If so, is it fast music? Music with a quick tempo tends to make people eat faster. Busy restaurants make more money if there is a fast turnover of customers, so inducing their customers to eat quickly is beneficial.

Situational inducement can work in the classroom to increase the likelihood of wanted behavior. Situational inducement can also be used in the classroom to decrease the likelihood of unwanted behaviors. When situational inducement procedures are used to decrease the likelihood of unwanted behaviors, they are used as an informal behavior management method. An example of situational inducement that decreases the likelihood of unwanted behaviors is moving a disruptive student from the back of the room to the front row or moving two disruptive students away from each other.

Therefore, one of the first considerations in terms of decreasing the likelihood of unwanted behavior is to determine if there is an informal procedure that can be used for a student engaging in the unwanted behavior. The effective use of such procedures may eliminate the need for more intrusive behavior management plans.

Redirection

Redirection is also an informal method of stopping a behavior. **Redirection** involves prompting students to do something that interferes with the unwanted behavior (Chandler & Dahlquist, 2010). In a sense, redirection is an attempt to get the students to take their "minds" off the unwanted behavior. For example, suppose students go off task during instruction. Redirection involves telling the students they need to get back to work. Another example involves asking students who are getting angry to talk about what they enjoy doing on weekends. Finally, a student who is out of her seat could be guided back to her desk. So when misbehavior occurs or if you sense one is about to occur, simply prompting the students back to the task or distracting them can decrease the unwanted behavior.

Chain Stopping

In Chapter 2, chaining was discussed in terms of how to teach a behavior. Behavior chains, however, can also be used to help with unwanted behaviors (Nelson & Roberts, 2000; Zirpoli, 2008). Like wanted behaviors, unwanted behaviors occur in chains. For example, Figure 6.1 shows a possible chain of behaviors for a student who is aggressive. Several behaviors occur before the aggressive episode. If the chain of responses can be determined, the teacher might be able to break it by intervening at one of its earlier "links" and preventing the aggression from occurring; this procedure is called **chain stopping**.

For example, consider a student with bulimia, an eating disorder. Bulimia is characterized by binge eating and purging (i.e., getting rid of the food in some manner such as vomiting). Part of the program designed to decrease this unwanted behavior was to define a chain of responses and then to break the chain before a binge and purge episode occurred. For this student, the behaviors or links in the chain included pacing, going to the bedroom door, opening the door a few times, going to the kitchen and back to the room a few times, going to the kitchen and opening the refrigerator, taking out food and then putting it back a few times, taking out the food and taking a bite, eating all the food (e.g., an entire jar of peanut butter), and then going to the bathroom and purging. This behavioral chain was stopped by having the student call a friend when the pacing began. The call was enough to stop the chain. If the pacing were to occur again, the student would again call the friend. (This step was only one component of the total intervention.)

Another example involves a high school student who engaged in severe destructive episodes when he became angry. Before he became angry, he would stomp his feet.

| Figure 6.1 | Chain-Stopping Procedure for a Noncompliant Student |

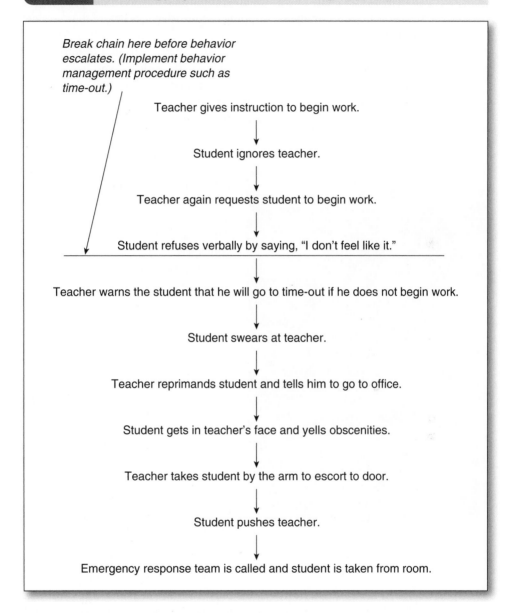

Break chain here before behavior escalates. (Implement behavior management procedure such as time-out.)

Teacher gives instruction to begin work.

↓

Student ignores teacher.

↓

Teacher again requests student to begin work.

↓

Student refuses verbally by saying, "I don't feel like it."

↓

Teacher warns the student that he will go to time-out if he does not begin work.

↓

Student swears at teacher.

↓

Teacher reprimands student and tells him to go to office.

↓

Student gets in teacher's face and yells obscenities.

↓

Teacher takes student by the arm to escort to door.

↓

Student pushes teacher.

↓

Emergency response team is called and student is taken from room.

He would sit in his chair and bring his foot down to the floor lightly, like a tap at first. Then the stomping would become more pronounced and louder, and he would bring his foot down with more and more force as he became more agitated. Chain stopping involved going over to the student, asking him what was the matter, and attempting to defuse the situation. Much of the time, the student was becoming frustrated with his seatwork. Therefore, the teacher provided assistance with the assignment so that the student would calm down. Chain stopping in this example prevented the problem behavior from occurring by stopping minor behaviors before they escalated into more severe behaviors.

In examples from the research literature, Nelson (1996b) and Nelson and Roberts (2000) have used chain stopping with students who have engaged in disruptive behavior. These authors have shown that problem behaviors later in the chain can be predicted by these prior minor behaviors. Therefore, teachers should respond to the minor behaviors before the behaviors become more severe. A positive aspect of chain stopping shown by Nelson and colleagues is that students are more likely to respond favorably to a behavior management intervention if the intervention occurs before the occurrence of the more severe behaviors. Not only is the likelihood of the target behavior decreased, but students can be taught more effectively what are appropriate and inappropriate behaviors. Chain stopping is a critical aspect of effective behavior management programs.

Teachers can use proximity control to keep students on task.

Proximity Control

Proximity control is a procedure often used by teachers in the classroom setting that has been shown to affect a student's behavior (Slavin, 2009). **Proximity control** involves decreasing unwanted behaviors by positioning the teacher somewhere next to the student (Zirpoli, 2008). The teacher's proximity to the student should decrease the probability of the unwanted behavior when this proximity is a signal that a negative consequence will occur if the behavior continues. Proximity control is an informal method of behavior management that uses a conditioned aversive situation (i.e., the closeness of the teacher) to stop the behavior. The teacher being close to the student, however, will not function as a conditioned aversive situation unless this close proximity has been conditioned in some manner. This conditioning could occur by following through with the management procedure in place, such as instituting a time-out from reinforcement (described later) if the behavior does not cease with a teacher's close proximity.

What Are Behavior Reduction Procedures?

Systematic behavior management procedures designed to decrease the likelihood of a problem behavior can, and in most instances should, involve the first level of restrictiveness (level I). These reinforcement-based procedures are considered the least restrictive methods of decreasing unwanted behaviors and involve stimulus control and differential reinforcement. (Other procedures discussed in Chapter 5, such as the Premack principle, self-management, and token economy systems, can also be used to reduce unwanted behavior and are considered least restrictive; these procedures and others like them, however, are categorized as techniques primarily aimed at increasing desirable behavior.) If level I procedures prove to be ineffective, it may be necessary to move to the next level of restrictiveness (level II), which involves extinction. The third level of restrictiveness (level III) involves the withdrawal of reinforcement for the problem behavior; these methods involve response cost and time-out. The fourth level (level IV) of management methods aimed at reducing unwanted behaviors involves the removal of an aversive stimulus if the student behaves appropriately (escape or avoidance conditions) or the presentation of aversive stimuli (reprimands, overcorrection, contingent exertion, negative practice, and physical restraint) contingent on inappropriate behavior. Table 6.1 shows a hierarchy of interventions based on

Table 6.1	Hierarchy of Interventions From Least to Most Restrictive

Level I Procedures (Presentation of Reinforcement)
- Stimulus control
- Differential reinforcement

Level II Procedure (Removal of Source of Reinforcement)
- Extinction

Level III Procedures (Removal of Reinforcing Stimuli)
- Response cost
- Time-out

Level IV Procedures (Presentation of Aversive Stimuli)
- Escape conditioning or avoidance conditioning
- Reprimands
- Overcorrection
- Contingent exertion
- Negative practice
- Physical restraint

their restrictiveness. Aversive procedures should be used as a last resort because of their potential negative side effects.

Level I Procedures (Presentation of Reinforcement)

Level I procedures are the least restrictive approaches aimed at reducing unwanted behavior (Alberto & Troutman, 2009). These procedures differ from the previously described informal procedures in that they are planned and implemented in a systematic fashion. Two level I procedures—stimulus control and differential reinforcement methods—are described here.

Stimulus Control. **Stimulus control** methods can be used to initiate behavior and also to stop or prevent behavior (Cooper et al., 2007; Sulzer-Azaroff & Mayer, 1991). Stimulus control methods should be planned and implemented formally. In terms of producing behavior, stimulus control methods involve presenting the discriminative stimulus (S^D) and reinforcing the appropriate behavior when it occurs in the presence of this stimulus. For example, telling the students it is time to work (S^D) will produce the behavior of students sitting down in their seats and then being reinforced in some manner, such as being praised (if praise is a reinforcer). When teachers prevent a behavior from occurring, they do not present the S^D (also called the S^Δ) and do not reinforce the student in its absence. For instance, if teachers did not present the instruction to get to work, they would not reinforce the student's "getting ready to do work behavior." To make sure that an S^D is in effect, teachers must be sure not to reinforce the student in the absence of the S^D. In addition, an unwanted behavior can be prevented or stopped from occurring by presenting an S^{D-} in which the stimulus presented is an indication that behavior other than the appropriate responding will be punished. For example, providing a start-up request such as "You need to get to work" could be an S^{D-} for working, and not getting to work will be punished in some manner. Thus, teachers should think of methods they can use to increase the likelihood of a behavior by reinforcing it in the presence of the discriminative stimulus (e.g., posting verbal rules on the walls). Also, teachers should withhold reinforcement or deliver punishment for unwanted behaviors in the presence of the discriminative stimulus.

Differential Reinforcement Procedures. **Differential reinforcement** procedures are those used to reinforce appropriate behaviors while withholding reinforcement for inappropriate behavior (Cooper et al., 2007; Sulzer-Azaroff & Mayer, 1991). Although differential reinforcement procedures can be thought of as attempts to increase wanted behaviors, their main focus is on decreasing unwanted behaviors. They are systematic applications of reinforcement. These procedures are rarely instituted for every student in a systematic manner. When a student needs an individualized behavior management program, however, teachers must become more explicit in their interventions. They can use these procedures to gain control over the unwanted behaviors and then to move to a more natural method of behavior management later. There are four differential reinforcement schedules: differential reinforcement of other behavior (DRO), differential reinforcement of incompatible behavior (DRI), differential reinforcement of alternative behavior (DRA), and differential reinforcement of low-rate behavior (DRL). See Table 6.2 for a summary of these schedules.

Table 6.2	Summary of Differential Reinforcement Schedules	
Schedule	**Definition**	**Example**
Differential reinforcement of other behavior (DRO)	Reinforce any behavior other than the target behavior, and extinguish the target behavior.	Praise the student every 5 minutes if hitting another student does not occur, and do not reinforce if hitting does occur.
Differential reinforcement of incompatible behavior (DRI)	Reinforce the opposite behavior of the targeted one, and extinguish the targeted behavior.	Praise on-task and ignore off-task behavior.
Differential reinforcement of alternative behavior (DRA)	Reinforce an alternative appropriate behavior, and extinguish the targeted behavior.	Allow a break for asking for one from work, and ignore tantrums to get out of work.
Differential reinforcement of low-rate behavior (DRL)	Reinforce low-rate behavior, and extinguish high-rate behavior.	Respond to a student's request for help only if these requests are limited to an agreed-on rate, and ignore inappropriate demands for help.
	Spaced responding: Reinforce only if a set time occurs between each behavior.	*Answer a question if the student waits 5 minutes between questions and ignore if less than 5 minutes.*
	Limited responding: Reinforce if a certain number of behaviors occur or fewer within a certain time period.	*Answer a question if the student has asked 10 or fewer questions per hour and ignore if the student asks more than 10 questions.*

Differential Reinforcement of Other Behavior (DRO). With **differential reinforcement of other behavior (DRO)**, which is also called differential reinforcement of zero rate behavior and omission training, reinforcement is provided if an unwanted (targeted) behavior has not occurred within an established time period. For example, a DRO-5-minute schedule means that if the unwanted behavior has not occurred during a 5-minute period, the student will be reinforced. If the unwanted behavior does occur, the unwanted behavior will not be reinforced, and the time is reset for another 5-minute period.

How often reinforcement will occur during DRO is determined by taking a baseline and calculating, on average, how much time elapses before each instance of an unwanted behavior. For example, if an individual displays the unwanted behavior 12 times per hour on average, the average rate of behavior is one every 5 minutes. Therefore, the time period is set at 5 minutes. Once the time interval has been set, the

DRO is implemented. If the behavior doesn't occur for a 5-minute period, then the student receives reinforcement. At the end of 5 minutes, the time starts over again. If an unwanted behavior occurs during the 5 minutes, say after only 2 minutes, the 5-minute time interval starts over then (see Figure 6.2).

When the student's behavior is observed consistently over the time period, a **whole-interval DRO** is being used (Sulzer-Azaroff & Mayer, 1991). Once the student reliably refrains from emitting the unwanted behavior (e.g., no unwanted behavior for three consecutive days), the 5 minutes can be increased to, say, 8 minutes, then 10 minutes, then 15 minutes, and so on. A momentary DRO can also be used in this circumstance. With a **momentary DRO**, at the end of the stated time period, say 5 minutes, the teacher looks over at the student to see if the misbehavior is occurring. If the behavior is not occurring, the student is reinforced. If the unwanted behavior is ongoing at that time, the student's unwanted behavior is not reinforced. The advantage of the momentary DRO is that the teacher does not have to observe the student's behaviors for the entire time but only at the end of the time period.

These DROs can be implemented at either fixed or variable intervals (Cooper et al., 2007). A **fixed-interval DRO** results in a student being reinforced if he or she refrains from the unwanted behavior for the entire interval (e.g., 5 minutes). The time stays the same for each interval. A **variable-interval DRO** results in a student being reinforced if he or she refrains from the unwanted behavior for an average amount of time. For instance, if the DRO were 5 minutes, the student may have to refrain from the behavior for 2 minutes at one time and 7 minutes the next. The average of the intervals, however, is 5 minutes. Likewise, a **fixed-momentary DRO** involves reinforcing the student at the end of a fixed time period (e.g., 5 minutes) for each interval. A **variable-momentary DRO** results in reinforcement for the student if there is a lack of unwanted behavior at the end of varying interval lengths.

Figure 6.2	Example of a DRO-5-Minute Schedule for an Observation Time of 20 Minutes

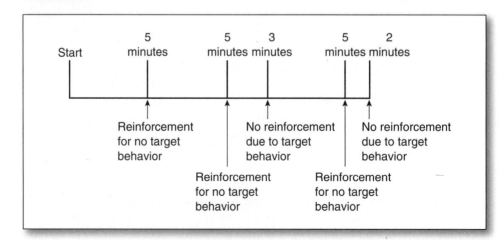

Any DRO requires some effort on the part of the teacher. The teacher must conduct a baseline observation, time the intervals, observe the student's behavior during intervals, and deliver reinforcement when appropriate. Using a momentary DRO can overcome many of these practical obstacles, however.

The use of DROs has been effective across a variety of settings and for a variety of problem behaviors (Miltenberger, 2007). There is, though, one problem with the use of the DRO. The DRO does not pass the "dead man's test" (Axelrod, 1987a; Cooper et al., 2007). It fails this test because it reinforces *not* doing something; a dead man, who exhibits no behavior at all, could receive reinforcement according to the DRO's requirements. In other words, the DRO fails the **dead man's test** because a lack of behavior on the part of the individual is reinforced; the student is required only to refrain from unwanted behavior to receive reinforcement. The DRO has no requirement for the student to engage in appropriate behavior to be reinforced, and there is no skill-teaching component incorporated as part of the intervention. So DROs should not occur in isolation in a behavior support plan but may be included as part of a program that also includes strategies to increase adaptive behavior.

Differential Reinforcement of Incompatible Behavior (DRI). **Differential reinforcement of incompatible behavior** (**DRI**) means reinforcing a behavior that is topographically incompatible with or opposite to the unwanted behavior while placing the unwanted behavior on a continuous schedule of extinction (Zirpoli, 2008). A DRI is used to teach an appropriate behavior or at least make a wanted behavior more likely. For example, the opposite behavior of being out of one's seat is being in one's seat. When an opposite behavior (i.e., being in one's seat) is increased, the other behavior (i.e., being out of one's seat) must decrease. The teacher must first determine the behavior to decrease, such as being off task. This behavior must be clearly defined. A clear definition of "out-of-seat" behavior might be, "student's buttocks are higher than two inches above the seat of the chair or one buttock is more than two inches off the chair (e.g., leaning to one side)." Once "out-of-seat" behavior has been defined, the opposite behavior must be determined. For example, in-seat behavior could be defined as having "both halves of the buttocks in the seat or lifted above the chair by less than two inches with both feet on the floor." During the DRI intervention, the out-of-seat behavior is either ignored or punished (e.g., mild reprimand) and the in-seat behavior is reinforced (e.g., praised). Reinforcement is given each time the student is observed to be engaged in the appropriate behavior. Data must be taken on the occurrence of these behaviors. Once in-seat behavior is occurring at a predefined level, an intermittent reinforcement schedule should be used. As the out-of-seat behavior decreases, the in-seat behavior increases. Obviously, a DRI passes the dead man's test because this protocol increases appropriate behavior in addition to reducing unwanted behavior. A time-based schedule can be used to implement DRI interventions. For example, teachers could find it feasible to implement a momentary DRI schedule similar to the one described previously.

Differential Reinforcement of Alternative Behavior (DRA). **Differential reinforcement of alternative behavior** (**DRA**) involves reinforcing a more appropriate form of an unwanted behavior. The behavior support plan shown in Chapter 4 (Figure 4.14), which reinforces a replacement behavior, is essentially a DRA. Individuals will engage in unwanted behaviors many times because they have a limited skill repertoire and lack appropriate skills. Take, for example, a young child who has limited verbal skills. Suppose this child is a year and a half old and wants a cookie. The child may go into the kitchen and begin to cry. When the parents try to discover what the child wants, she or he gets frustrated because the parents do not understand. As the parents frantically search for what the child wants, the child begins to cry more loudly until the episode turns into a tantrum. Finally, the parents grab the cookies and ask the child if this is what is wanted. The child stops crying and smiles and reaches a hand out for a cookie. Fortunately for the parents, they have found what the child wants and are able to stop the tantrum. Unfortunately, they have just reinforced the child's tantrum behavior and have made it more likely to occur the next time the child wants a cookie. How can this cycle be broken? The parents have taught the child that the way to get things is to have a tantrum. From an educational perspective, the child's tantrum can be seen as an opportunity to teach a valuable skill: communicating what we want. What are the parents to do?

As with any behavior program, the first step is to define what needs to stop; in this case, it is the tantrum. A tantrum can be defined as any whining, crying, screaming, hitting, or throwing of objects. The next step is to determine what the replacement behavior should be. In this case, an appropriate replacement behavior is asking for a cookie without having a tantrum. The child should be taught how to say something like "cookie please." When the child says "cookie please," the parents should provide the cookie immediately. If the child has a tantrum, however, it should be ignored, and the child should not receive a cookie. What should occur, eventually, is a decrease in the tantrums because they do not receive reinforcement, and saying "cookie please" should become more likely. At first, saying "cookie please" should be reinforced on a continuous reinforcement schedule. Once the child has learned how to ask appropriately and consistently for a cookie (e.g., five consecutive appropriate requests without a tantrum), an intermittent reinforcement schedule can be used.

Another example involves a student who becomes angry and swears when given seatwork during math. The teacher should consider what an appropriate alternative response would be for swearing. The first step is to determine the communicative intent. Based on the results of an FBA, the teacher might find that the communicative intent is to avoid the task for some period of time by being sent out of the classroom. Therefore, the teacher could teach the student a more appropriate method of avoiding the task than swearing, such as saying, "I need a break." The replacement behavior (asking for a break) serves the same purpose as the target behavior (swearing). Swearing is ignored and asking for a break is reinforced on a continuous reinforcement schedule initially and then on an intermittent schedule.

Obviously, DRIs and DRAs are similar in that the target behavior is ignored while a replacement behavior is reinforced. The difference is that the target behavior and the incompatible behavior cannot occur at the same time within the DRI schedule. However, with the DRA, the target behavior and the alternative behavior can be displayed at the same time. That is, the child can have a tantrum while asking for a cookie, and the student can swear when asking for a break.

Differential Reinforcement of Low-Rate Behavior (DRL). When teachers use DROs, DRIs, and DRAs, they are looking to eliminate the unwanted behavior altogether because any level of the target behavior is not appropriate. For example, a tantrum is never appropriate. At times, however, a particular behavior is not unwanted but occurs too often. In such cases, the goal is not to eliminate the behavior but to decrease its rate of occurrence. We all have experienced this behavior at some point in our lives. Think of people who simply talk too much. They talk all the time, and you can never get a word in edgewise. Or what about the student who asks too many questions during a class? How about the friend who asks to borrow things from you all the time? These behaviors may be acceptable many times, but when they occur too often, we become irritated. In the classroom, a high incidence of some of these necessary behaviors (e.g., asking for help) can be disruptive. To solve this problem, we attempt to reduce the level at which these behaviors occur. There are two methods of reducing, but not totally eliminating, a behavior through the **differential reinforcement of low-rate behavior (DRL)**: spaced responding and limited responding. (Note: These methods can be used to eliminate unwanted behavior as well.)

A **spaced-responding DRL** involves reinforcing a behavior if a certain amount of time has elapsed between responses (Ferster & Skinner, 1957). The period between responses is called the **interresponse time (IRT)**. For example, if there is an average of 5 minutes between a student's questions, the IRT is 5 minutes. The IRT is calculated by determining the rate of response. Thus, if a student has an average of 12 questions per hour, the IRT for each question is approximately 5 minutes. Now, suppose that a student asking 12 questions per hour on average is too much. One way to decrease the number of questions per hour is to increase the IRT. If the IRT is increased to 10 minutes, the target number of responses (i.e., questions) is now 6 per hour. Therefore, a teacher should first determine the maximum number of questions a student could ask per hour without interrupting the instruction. Once this number is determined, say, at 4 questions per hour, the IRT can be determined (e.g., 15 minutes). Then, the teacher only reinforces the student (by answering a question or calling on the student when she raises her hand) if there is the required IRT (15 minutes) between questions. Thus, a certain amount of time is required between the previous behavior and the current one for the behavior to be reinforced. If a behavior occurs before the required IRT is met (e.g., at fewer than 15 minutes of elapsed time between the previous behavior and the current one), the behavior is not reinforced (e.g., the question is ignored).

Informally, spaced-responding DRLs are used every day. For example, when a speaker asks the audience to withhold applause until all names have been called, a required IRT is being stated. If a professor says to withhold all questions until she has finished lecturing, an IRT is being required. The difference between what occurs in everyday life and a formal spaced-responding DRL is that the formal, spaced DRL is systematically determined.

One possible problem with the spaced-responding DRL involves setting the response time. If the required time between responses is too great, the student may not meet the criterion. For example, if the student is asking questions with a 5-minute IRT, setting the required IRT at 15 minutes may not work because the student may never go 15 minutes without asking a question. If the student is not able to meet the required IRT, it should be set at a lower, obtainable level. This level can be gradually extended to establish, eventually, an appropriate level of responding.

The limited-responding DRL has similar results to but is a different approach than the spaced-responding DRL. The **limited-responding DRL** involves providing reinforcement if a student emits a certain number of behaviors or fewer. The limited-responding DRL does not require a certain time period between each behavior; rather, the total number of behaviors allowed are determined and reinforced (Deitz & Repp, 1973). In the previous example of a student asking too many questions, if four responses per hour are determined to be acceptable, only the first four questions are reinforced and the others are ignored when a teacher uses a limited-responding DRL. It is appropriate to tell the student that she can ask only four questions; a good approach is to teach the student how to self-monitor the number of questions she asks (see self-management in Chapter 5). This approach was taken by Martella, Leonard, Marchand-Martella, and Agran (1993) in decreasing inappropriate verbalizations. A student was displaying up to 1.5 inappropriate verbalizations per minute (or 23 per 15-minute observation). Therefore, to decrease the number of inappropriate verbalizations, an upper number such as 16 per observation was allowed, and then the number was decreased each time the student met the criterion of having this number or fewer inappropriate verbalizations during an observation period for four consecutive days. (In this particular case, the limited-responding DRL was used to decrease the total number of inappropriate verbalizations to zero.)

Similar to the spaced-responding DRL, the limited-responding DRL must enable reinforcement; in other words, the number of allowed behaviors must be set at a level that the student can obtain. If the number is too low, the student will likely not meet the required level. For example, if the student with inappropriate verbalizations were required to have five or fewer inappropriate verbalizations in 15 minutes, the student would be unlikely to meet the level. If the level is set too low, the teacher will find the student is not meeting the criterion. If that occurs, the level should be changed to an obtainable one, so the behavior change desired can be supported.

Level II Procedure (Removal of Source of Reinforcement)

A **level II procedure** involves the removal of the source of reinforcement (Alberto & Troutman, 2009). This procedure is called extinction.

Extinction. Extinction procedures can be used to decrease the likelihood of a behavior being repeated again in the future (Skinner, 1953). As indicated in Chapter 2, extinction involves the permanent removal of the source of reinforcement for a particular behavior. Therefore, based on an FBA, the source of reinforcement for the behavior must be determined and removed, and the removal of this reinforcement will decrease the level of the behavior.

No matter what the reinforcer is, its removal will eventually decrease the level of the behavior. Sources of reinforcement are not always easy to identify or remove, however. For example, suppose the function of a behavior is negative reinforcement via the removal of the student from the classroom. The student's unwanted behavior may be negatively reinforced by what the teacher perceives to be a punishment in that there was something in the classroom that was aversive to the student, such as a particular task required of the student. Extinction in this circumstance involves the removal of the negative reinforcer by not allowing the student to escape or avoid the required task. How would that be accomplished? The choices regarding how to remove this reinforcer may not be all that pleasant. First, the teacher could force the student to accomplish the task through some form of prompting procedure (e.g., physically making the student go through the motions). Second, the teacher could tell the student that he cannot leave the situation until the task is accomplished. For some students, that might mean sitting in their seats for extended periods of time. Third, the teacher could attempt to punish the behavior first (for example, by sending the student to the principal's office) and then remove the reinforcer, perhaps by requiring the student to begin the task again once he comes back. This third option is the most viable of the three in that there is no physical interaction necessary, nor is there a battle of wills. The student, however, may still attempt to avoid the task each time he comes back. Also, the other students are likely to move on to another task, which puts the student behind his peers. The best options are to not allow the student to escape or avoid the task through an inappropriate behavior (extinction) and to teach an appropriate escape or avoidance response, such as asking for a break. The teacher should also determine what makes the task so aversive. Determining what makes the task aversive involves considering the academic and behavioral skill level of the student. Are we at the correct instructional level? Is there reinforcement being provided for the task? Are the lengths of the tasks short enough to prevent fatigue?

Another problem with the removal of reinforcement can be seen when teachers try to use this strategy to limit or extinguish attention-seeking behavior. The teacher may say, "I ignore the behavior, but it keeps occurring." The problem is that the attention may not be from the teacher but from the other students. Attention does not come from just the adults. If the student is being reinforced by peer attention, removal of this attention is difficult. The teacher may ask the other students to ignore the misbehaving student, which is not very likely to occur. A second option is to move the student away from the other students when the behavior occurs.

Overall, extinction procedures should be used if access to the source of reinforcement can be found and controlled. Also, if the extinction burst can be tolerated, extinction is a viable alternative. Caution should be used, however, because gaining access to the source of reinforcement is not always possible, and we may not be able to outlive the extinction burst. Additionally, even if the source of reinforcement can be identified and controlled, some extinction protocols may be quite intrusive (such as some of the escape extinction interventions mentioned earlier), and the behavior might be better controlled through antecedent interventions (e.g., modifying the curriculum to achieve a better fit between student skills and classroom requirements).

What Are Aversive-Based Procedures?

A decision practitioners must make is what type of consequence to provide for a student's behavior. Essentially, there are two choices: reinforcement and aversive-based procedures. The preferred method of behavior management uses positive reinforcement procedures (Alberto & Troutman, 2009). These procedures do not have the negative side effects that aversive procedures have (described later). If, and only if, positive reinforcement procedures prove to be ineffective, aversive-based procedures should be considered, starting with the least restrictive alternatives shown in Table 6.1 and moving to the more restrictive procedures only when necessary and appropriate.

Negative Side Effects

There are several possible side effects when aversives are used (Miltenberger, 2007). Table 2.1 (in Chapter 2) shows the possible negative side effects of aversive procedures (Sulzer-Azaroff & Mayer, 1991). The first negative side effect is that the student may tend to avoid contexts in which aversives are used. Recall from Chapter 2 that when an aversive (e.g., a reprimand) is paired with something (e.g., a teacher), this something can take on aversive properties. If a teacher notices the student is attempting to avoid or escape her presence, she is likely to be aversive to the student. The second potential negative side effect is that the student may become fearful of the punisher. When aversive methods are used, emotional responses may result. One such emotional response is to become afraid of the person providing the aversive stimulation. A third negative side effect is that aversive methods of behavior management may stop other behaviors; aversive procedures may have a generalized effect on the student's overall classroom performance. For example, if a teacher reprimands a student for talking out in class, the student may stop talking in class altogether. A fourth negative side effect is that the use of aversives by teachers models their use to the students. Essentially, there is a possibility that, when an aversive method such as a reprimand is used, students will learn to use the same method when interacting with their peers. This modeling is a main reason many experts attempt to get parents to stop spanking their children. The argument is that, when we spank our children, we are teaching them that physical aggression is acceptable behavior. The same phenomenon can occur in the classroom. Remember that teachers are critical in the learning processes of students, and when teachers react a certain way to misbehavior, they are essentially teaching their students that this response is an appropriate way to behave. The fifth negative side effect is that the use of punishment tends to promote negative self-esteem. When students are exposed to aversives, they tend to feel poorly about themselves.

The last three negative side effects are perhaps the most troublesome, especially in light of the growing problem of school violence. The use of aversive procedures tends to promote aggression toward the punisher or those associated with the punisher. Technically, this reaction is called **response-induced aggression**. Research has shown that the use of aversive stimulation increases the likelihood of aggression. Unfortunately, educators have not always taken the necessary steps to decrease the level of aversives in schools and classrooms. If students become aggressive to peers or school staff, it is possible that they are reacting to aversive procedures. Acts of aggression against others are not necessarily an indication of a student's personal flaw, ignorance, or mental disorder; they may indicate that the school context needs to be modified to minimize an aversive culture—the school may be teaching aggression.

Another negative side effect associated with the use of aversives is that they can be negatively reinforcing to the person providing them, and, as a result, they may be overused. The use of aversives tends to decrease the unwanted behavior quickly, whereas systems based on positive reinforcement tend to take longer to work. Therefore, teachers can get caught in a negative reinforcement trap: the more they use negative reinforcement, the less unwanted behavior they see, which increases the likelihood of their using aversive-based methods again when they intervene to control unwanted behavior. Unfortunately, aversive strategies on their own have only short-term advantages; in the long run, teachers are likely to see other unwanted and potentially more severe behaviors due to the previously described negative side effects.

Other negative side effects listed by Sulzer-Azaroff and Mayer (1991) but not presented in Table 2.1 include inappropriate generalization and influencing the social status of the recipient of the punishment. Inappropriate generalization can occur when the student's behavior generalizes to other situations or stimuli that were not related to the punishment initially. For example, if a student is presented with aversive consequences because of poor performance in reading, reading in general can become aversive. One of the authors was in a finance class in college. The professor in this class was extremely aversive and used threats and warnings to get students to perform (e.g., "Answer this question, or I will give you an F for your grade"). Unfortunately, finance itself became an aversive topic, which created some emotional upset when the author had to buy a house. Aversive procedures also carry the risk of decreasing the social status of the recipient of a punishment. Additionally, other students may become less likely to interact with the student who is always in trouble. On the other hand, some students may have their status enhanced if peers feel sorry for them. For example, peers may provide additional support to someone who is punished routinely. If that occurs, the peer support could counteract the effects of the punishment, possibly increasing the level of unwanted behavior.

With the understanding that aversive procedures should be used only as a last resort and that their use tends to bring about negative side effects, we present the more popular aversive methods of behavior control next.

Level III Procedures (Contingent Removal of Reinforcing Stimuli)

Level III procedures involve the contingent removal of reinforcing stimuli (Alberto & Troutman, 2009). These procedures are more restrictive and aversive than level I or II procedures. Nevertheless, parents and teachers frequently use level III procedures, such as response cost and time-out systems, in a variety of settings.

Response Cost. Response cost systems may be used in token systems (described in Chapter 5). Many of us have experienced response costs of some sort. For example, getting a parking ticket will result in a fine, and this fine is a response cost. **Response cost** involves the permanent removal of some portion of a reinforcer (Sulzer-Azaroff & Mayer, 1991) such as our money and can be called negative punishment. If a response cost system were paired with a token system, some of the tokens would be taken away from the student contingent on an unwanted behavior. There are three cautions with the use of such a system. First, consistency must be ensured. An adequate monetary system must be in place to track both the number of tokens earned and the number removed. Second, there must be a reserve of tokens; that is, the number of tokens removed for an unwanted behavior must not be so high that a negative balance will result. Thus, staff must determine how many tokens will be removed when a behavior occurs. If a student gets into a negative balance, the token system will probably not be successful. Finally, there is a high likelihood that the student will react against the removal of the tokens. This reaction could be in the form of aggression or an escalation of the unwanted behavior. One way to decrease this likelihood is to remove a certain number of tokens and then give some of those back to the student if the student accepts the removal appropriately. For example, if a teacher removes 10 tokens for swearing, and the student gives up those tokens without a "fight," the teacher could give 3 tokens back for the acceptance of the token removal.

Time-Out. **Time-out** is a technical procedure that involves the temporary removal of the source of reinforcement contingent on an unwanted behavior (Cooper et al., 2007; Sulzer-Azaroff & Mayer, 1991). Time-out can be considered a negative punisher. It is critical to understand that time-out is a procedure of removing reinforcement for a behavior; it is not a location or a place. Time-out is not placing a student in the corner, out in the hall, or behind a barrier. Time-out is not putting a student in a time-out room. If time-out is thought of as a place, mistakes will be made. As such, there are three categories of time-out: moving from the least restrictive to the most restrictive, these are nonexclusionary, exclusionary, and seclusionary.

Nonexclusionary Time-Out. **Nonexclusionary time-out** involves the temporary removal of the source of reinforcement contingent on an unwanted behavior without removing the student from the group or environment (Cooper et al., 2007). An example of a nonexclusionary time-out is a sit and watch or contingent observation procedure in which the student can be part of the group but not participate (Zirpoli, 2008). Missing a turn in a game for poor sportsmanship is another example. A third is the use of a time-out ribbon (Foxx & Shapiro, 1978). In this procedure, the student wears a ribbon while behaving appropriately. Attention is provided when the ribbon is worn. If a student misbehaves, the ribbon is temporarily removed, and the student is not provided attention during the time-out period. A third example would be to remove an item temporarily, such as a toy, book, or game, if the student is not behaving appropriately, such as when a toy is misused (Zirpoli). If time-out is used, nonexclusionary time-out would be the first choice since the student is still part of the group and does not miss out on the task or instruction.

Exclusionary Time-Out. Exclusionary time-out is the form most people think of when they hear the term. **Exclusionary time-out** is the temporary removal of the source of reinforcement contingent on an unwanted behavior by removing the student from the group or environment (Cooper et al., 2007). An example is placing the student in a corner, outside of the classroom door, behind a barrier, or in another part of the room. Exclusionary time-out is only effective if the source of reinforcement is removed. For example, if the student is in another part of the room but can still hear the other students laugh, attention may continue to reinforce the unwanted behavior. Also, if a student is in the hallway, he or she may get attention from students in other rooms or from people walking in the hallway (Cooper et al.).

Seclusionary Time-Out. **Seclusionary time-out** is the temporary removal of a student from the group to an isolated area. According to the Council for Children with Behavioral Disorders (CCBD), "Seclusion is the involuntary confinement of a student in a room or area from which the student is physically prevented from leaving" (CCBD, 2009b, p. 235). Seclusionary time-outs were normally used in institutional settings or in special circumstances when there was a need to prevent injury to others, to the persons themselves, or to property (Zabel, 1986). Unfortunately, seclusionary time-out booths are currently being used in some public school classrooms. There are state and professional restrictions on the use of seclusionary time-outs because they have an increased likelihood of being abused.

CCBD provides ethical statements regarding the use of seclusion. Any time a student is prevented from accessing instruction, is separated from his or her peers, and lacks the opportunity to leave the area, seclusion or aspects of seclusion are being used. Unfortunately, there is a lack of research demonstrating the effectiveness of seclusion in school settings (CCBD, 2009b). Essentially, CCBD recommends seclusion only for emergency events and not as an intervention designed to decrease problem behavior. Additionally, if seclusion is used, its use must be documented, and this documentation must include the names of those involved and the circumstances that resulted in its use. Parents should be informed when seclusion is used, and, within 48 hours, a debriefing meeting should take place to determine how to avoid the use of seclusion in the future. During the use of seclusion, a staff member should observe the entire procedure continuously. Finally, if staff members repeatedly use seclusion with a student, the behavior management program in place should be viewed as a failure and must be modified. CCBD does not view seclusion as part of the time-out continuum but as a form of restraint. Also, according to CCBD, there is a lack of research demonstrating the effectiveness of restraint when this procedure is used in school settings.

How to Use Time-Out Effectively. Several considerations should be made before time-out is used (Cooper et al., 2007; Sulzer-Azaroff & Mayer, 1991). (See Table 6.3 for various examples of effective time-out procedures.) First, time-outs can be time based or behavior based. A **time-based time-out** involves removing the source of reinforcement for a set amount of time. With time-based time-outs, a person's removal from time-out is based on time, not on behavior. A **behavior-based time-out** involves removing the source of reinforcement until the student is calm and ready to rejoin the

Table 6.3	Successful Use of Time-Out

Removal from the reinforcer for a short period of time is a time-out. Successful variations include

Time-based time-outs: 1 minute for every year of age of the student

Behavior-based time-outs: Behavior is appropriate before the student leaves from the time-out

Combination: 1 minute for every year of age of the student but ensure that, during the last 15 seconds of the time-out, the student is quiet

Other considerations:

Brief explanation (fewer than 10 words before time-out is given)

Removal of source of reinforcement

Immediate time-in after time-out

group. A combination of the two is to release a student from time-out after a certain time has elapsed, while requiring quiet behavior for the last few seconds of the time-out. For example, a time-out may occur for a period of 7 minutes, with the student being released after this time as long as the last 15 seconds of the time-out are quiet. If the student is not quiet for the last 15 seconds, the time-out remains in effect until the quiet behavior occurs. If a time-based time-out is used, the traditional time to use is one minute per year of age. The advantage of short-duration time-outs is that the student is away from class activities (if exclusionary time-out is used) for a shorter time.

Second, the amount of explanation given to the student when implementing a time-out should be kept to a minimum, preferably to fewer than 10 words. If more words are used, the student may be gaining unneeded attention. A statement such as, "John, you hit Susie, so go to time-out" is preferable to a long explanation and verbal reprimand. Consequently, prior to using this procedure, teachers should make sure that students are aware of the time-out protocol (when and how time-out will be implemented).

Third, reinforcement must be removed. If the source of reinforcement is attention from other students, and time-out is used in the class, teachers may not be removing the source of reinforcement for the behavior. In such a case, an out-of-class time-out may be necessary. If the reinforcement is not removed, the procedure is not a time-out.

Finally, there must be time-in. In other words, if there is not a reinforcing classroom environment, there will not be any reinforcement to remove. If a teacher uses many threats and warnings to control behavior, removal from that classroom may actually be a negative reinforcer of the student's misbehavior rather than the removal of a reinforcer—the student escapes the negative classroom by being placed in time-out. In addition, there must be time-in once the student is allowed back in the group. Teachers cannot and should not hold grudges. Once time-out is ended, a teacher should immediately get the student back into the routine and reinforcement of the class.

Why Time-Out Can Fail. Time-out can fail for two reasons: lack of time-in and not being able to remove the source of reinforcement. The first reason involves not having a reinforcing environment. If the classroom is aversive, the student may misbehave so as to escape it. In such a case, time-out is not time-out. Therefore, if teachers are to use time-out, they must make sure there are sources of reinforcement for the students in the classroom. Second, time-out can fail if the source of reinforcement is not removed. As an example of this sort of failure, imagine that a teacher places a student in a hallway by the classroom door as a time-out, but the student's unwanted behavior does not improve. Knowing that removing its source of reinforcement means that a behavior will decrease, the teacher reasons that the target behavior must still be getting reinforced in some manner. So the teacher decides to monitor what is occurring in the hallway. She discovers that the school's principal regularly comes by her class and asks the student why he is in the hall. So the teacher asks the principal to ignore the student when the student is in the hallway, which the principal does. The unwanted behavior soon decreases. In this instance, what the teacher thought was time-out was not because the source of reinforcement (i.e., attention) was not removed.

Level IV Procedures (Presentation of Aversive Stimuli)

Level IV procedures involve the presentation of aversive stimuli (Alberto & Troutman, 2009). These procedures are considered to be at the highest level of restrictiveness, and they increase the probability of negative side effects, such as aggressive responses on the part of the student. (See Table 2.1 for negative side effects associated with the use of aversive stimuli.) Therefore, these procedures should be used with caution and only after other procedures have been tried and have failed. Six level IV procedures are described: escape conditioning and avoidance conditioning, reprimands, overcorrection, contingent exertion, negative practice, and physical restraint.

Escape Conditioning and Avoidance Conditioning. Escape conditioning and avoidance conditioning involve using an aversive or the threat (warning stimulus) of an aversive to increase desired behavior. Escape conditioning and avoidance conditioning involve presenting a discriminative stimulus (S^{D^-}) that indicates that, if a response is emitted in the presence of the stimulus, it will be punished. Escape conditioning and avoidance conditioning are negative reinforcement procedures. In **escape conditioning**, an ongoing aversive is removed only if the student behaves appropriately. Nagging a student until she does what the teacher wants is an example. **Avoidance conditioning** is the prevention of an aversive only when the student acts a certain way. The student becoming compliant to avoid going to the principal's office is an example. Another is indicating to a student that, if his behavior continues, he will be sent to time-out or his parents will be called. When threats or warnings are used to get a behavior to occur or to stop, teachers hope that these statements will reduce the likelihood that some punishment procedure will need to be used. That is why some parents will count to three to get their children to behave. Escape conditioning and avoidance conditioning are used in our everyday lives. Unfortunately, they can result in unwanted side effects.

One side effect is conditioning new behaviors that are unwanted, such as lying. When students lie, they are attempting to avoid the negative consequences of telling the truth. Other negative side effects are the same as those listed previously in our discussion of aversive procedures. Therefore, teachers should be careful when using escape conditioning or avoidance conditioning. The temptation to use this type of conditioning can be great, but teachers must try not to use it so as to avoid the possible negative side effects that can result.

Reprimands. **Reprimands** are strong negative verbal statements that are contingent on the occurrence of an unwanted behavior. Examples are "No," "Don't do that," and "That was bad." Given that reprimands are provided when a behavior occurs, they are considered a positive punishment procedure. Reprimands are usually not considered highly restrictive as they usually consist of a brief verbal statement. However, the teacher giving the reprimand may use an aggressive tone or raise his or her voice, and reprimands sometimes include a negative statement about the student's behavior. Therefore, reprimands are considered a level IV procedure even though they can be mild.

Overcorrection. Overcorrection procedures have been shown to be effective methods for managing unwanted behaviors (Kazdin, 2001). These procedures were once thought to be educative in that they taught students what to do; as Foxx and Bechtel (1983) clearly indicate, however, **overcorrection** involves aversive procedures aimed at decreasing unwanted behaviors by requiring the student to engage in a behavior that is related to correcting the damage caused by the unwanted behavior (Cooper et al., 2007). These methods are based on positive punishment. Therefore, because overcorrection procedures can be viewed as aversive means of control, their use should be limited. Although the use of overcorrection procedures should be limited, it is important to know what they are and how they are used. There are two types of overcorrection: positive practice and restitutional overcorrection.

Positive Practice Overcorrection. **Positive practice overcorrection** involves having students engage in an alternative appropriate behavior instead of an inappropriate one (Miltenberger, 2007). For example, walking in the halls is an important behavior for students because running in the hall could result in injury. If a student runs in the hall, a teacher would require the student to walk down the hall appropriately three times, for example. The premise of positive practice overcorrection is that practicing an appropriate behavior over and over again is aversive. Therefore, the future probability of a student running in the hall would decrease. Another example is having a student who throws a chair pick up a chair and place it under a table. The teacher then takes another chair and places it on the floor; the student must again pick it up and put it under the table, and so on, for several repetitions.

Of course, the description of positive practice overcorrection is easier said than done. Because positive practice overcorrection works based on the presentation of an aversive stimulus, negative side effects are possible. One potential negative side effect is that the student may simply refuse to go along with the request. In such a case, the teacher is left with two choices. First, the student could be allowed to refuse the instruction, which could result in future occurrences of the same refusal behavior. Second, the teacher could physically prompt the student through the task several times. The difficulty with this choice is that once the student becomes resistive, there is a probability that someone will get injured. Therefore, before teachers use positive practice overcorrection, they must determine what they would do if a student refused to follow instructions.

Restitutional Overcorrection. **Restitutional overcorrection** involves having the student return the environment to a better state than it was in before (Miltenberger, 2007). When an unwanted behavior affects the environment, the student must overcompensate for the disruption to the environment. For example, suppose a student was writing on her desk. Restitutional overcorrection involves having the student clean off her desk with soap and water as well as all the other desks in the classroom. Another example is a student who puts chewing gum under her desk. The teacher then provides the student with a scraper and has the student scrape the gum off her desk as well as all the other desks in the classroom.

The difficulty with restitutional overcorrection is the same as with positive practice overcorrection. If a student refuses to follow the teacher's instructions, the teacher is left with two undesirable choices. Thus, before teachers decide to use restitutional overcorrection, they must make sure they understand the potential consequences of that decision.

Contingent Exertion. Contingent exertion (also called contingent exercise) has been used for several years by coaches, military officers, and teachers. **Contingent exertion** refers to the practice of requiring an individual to do some physically exerting behavior as punishment for an unwanted behavior (Cooper et al., 2007). (Whether or not contingent exertion or any other procedure is a punishment procedure will depend on how it affects the behavior.) For example, the football coach who tells a player to run five laps, the military officer who tells the recruit to do 50 push-ups, and the gym teacher who tells students to do 10 pull-ups are using contingent exertion.

Contingent exertion is a positive punishment procedure and can be very aversive to the individual being punished. The primary problem with contingent exertion is that the student may not follow the instruction to do the exercise. As with overcorrection, the teacher is left with two unpleasant options. Try to get someone to do sit-ups when he or she refuses to do so. Again, the use of a procedure such as contingent exercise should be used only with caution, if at all, and the possibility of student refusal should be considered.

Negative Practice. Some individuals will confuse negative practice with overcorrection (Alberto & Troutman, 2009). **Negative practice** is similar to overcorrection except that overcorrection requires a wanted behavior to be displayed repeatedly, whereas negative practice requires the negative or unwanted behavior to be practiced repeatedly. In negative practice, an unwanted behavior such as throwing a chair is required over and over again. The purpose of negative practice is either to decrease the unwanted behavior by requiring the repetition of behavior (positive punishment) or to satiate individuals with the behavior (nontechnically, to get it out of their system). Negative practice has not been researched to the same extent as overcorrection.

As with the previously described aversive procedures, negative practice can cause several negative side effects. Students may become resistant, and the teacher will either allow them to refuse to follow directions or will physically prompt them. Overall, negative practice is probably not worth the effort, and more positive procedures should be attempted.

Restraint. Restraint is a procedure that is used to prevent students from harming themselves or others. **Restraint** refers to limiting or restricting an individual from behaving in some way. There are three types of restraint: mechanical, chemical, and physical (CCBD, 2009a). **Mechanical restraint** involves the use of a device or object to limit bodily movement (CCBD). **Chemical restraint** involves the use of medication to control behavior or to restrict movement (CCBD). **Physical restraint** involves the restriction of a movement of a person's body (Flick, 2011). Similar to seclusion, restraint has a lack of research demonstrating its effectiveness in school environments (CCBD).

According to CCBD (2009a), restraint should never be used as part of a program to manage behavior. Restraint should be used only as an emergency procedure. School personnel who use restraint procedures should be specifically trained in their use. If teachers wish to become trained in physical restraint, they should contact their district for information on trainings and on district policies regarding the use of restraint. As with seclusion, the use of restraint must be documented including the names of those involved and the circumstances that resulted in its use. Parents should be informed when seclusion is used and, within 48 hours, a debriefing meeting should take place to determine how to avoid the use of seclusion in the future. Finally, if staff members repeatedly use restraint with a student, the behavior management program used should be viewed as a failure and must be modified.

How Do We Decide Which Procedure to Use?

Selecting which behavior management system to use is important in leading to behavior change. The first step anyone should complete is an FBA of what is maintaining the unwanted behavior. If the source of reinforcement can be found, this source should be removed. There are, however, negative side effects of extinction. Other behaviors must be taught so as to avoid some of these negative side effects. The decision of what and how to teach depends on the goals for the students. If there is a need for more independence, self-management procedures are a good option. If self-management procedures alone do not work, they can be combined with behavioral contracts. If self-management skills are not necessary, differential reinforcement schedules can be used to decrease unwanted behaviors and to improve the level of wanted behaviors. Token systems can also be effective in getting a behavior to occur; these systems, however, are contrived and difficult to maintain.

Mild aversive techniques can be added to reinforcement-based procedures, but only mild forms such as nonexclusionary or exclusionary time-out should be used first. If reinforcement-based and mild aversive procedures fail, other procedures can be tried only as a last resort and under the permission of administrators and parents. These procedures (e.g., seclusionary time-out, overcorrection, contingent exertion) increase the likelihood that abuse and injuries could occur. Advice from behavioral specialists should be sought before these procedures are used.

How Is Consequence-Imposed Behavior Change Generalized?

The concern for generalization was discussed in Chapter 5. Whenever unwanted behaviors are decreased, another behavior to take the place of those behaviors being eliminated must also be increased (called the fair-pair rule [Salend, 2011]). Once that is accomplished, generalization can be planned. The methods of planning generalization are the same as those described in Chapter 5.

How Is Consequence-Imposed Behavior Change Maintained?

Strategies for promoting maintenance of responding were discussed in Chapter 5. It is important to focus on behavior change and strategies to achieve such change (e.g., self-management) when implementing aversive interventions such as those described in this chapter. So the teacher must consider and implement strategies to increase and maintain adaptive behavior (discussed in Chapter 5) while also using strategies discussed in this chapter (if necessary) to reduce unwanted behavior.

VIGNETTE REVISITED	**Reducing Swearing and Tantrums by Asking for a Break**

Based on the results of the FBA, Ms. Jackson knew she had to decide on an appropriate management intervention. Therefore, she decided to teach Jackie to ask for a break when she began to feel agitated. If Jackie asked for a break without swearing or having a tantrum, she was allowed to take a 2-minute break. If Jackie swore, she was immediately redirected to the task and reminded to ask for a break in an appropriate manner. If her behavior escalated to a tantrum or if she continued to swear, she was sent to a time-out area for 10 minutes. When she was allowed to come out of the time-out area, Jackie was required to complete her work.

Jackie quickly learned to ask for a break. Ms. Jackson was pleased with the results of her management technique. After two weeks, however, Jackie began to ask for a break about 10 times every hour. Clearly, these frequent requests were becoming as much of a problem as the tantrums. Therefore, Ms. Jackson decided to restrict the number of breaks Jackie could ask for from 10 to 8 per hour. Once Jackie was requesting a break 8 times per hour or less for three consecutive days, the maximum number was reduced to 6, then 4, and then to the goal of 2 per hour. Ms. Jackson thought she had accomplished her goal of reducing Jackie's swearing and tantrums while also teaching her that she could ask for a break instead of displaying these unacceptable behaviors.

Summary

When teachers make the decision to develop an individualized behavior management plan based on the individual needs of the student, they must decide how they will approach the behavior change. They always want to complete an FBA first. They then must decide how to change the behaviors in question. They should always attempt to develop or teach skills students can use to make the unwanted behaviors unneeded. At times, however, increasing other behaviors may not be enough, and teachers may have to resort to behavior reduction strategies. When implementing behavior reduction strategies, always begin with the least restrictive and intrusive intervention, starting with informal strategies. Unfortunately, in some instances a teacher will have to move up the restrictiveness and intrusiveness scale to aversive-based strategies.

The major concern with the use of reduction-based strategies is teachers' need to protect the students' right to the most effective yet least restrictive and intrusive intervention possible. Reduction procedures, however, are never used in isolation. If they are used, teachers should combine these strategies with those strategies aimed at increasing desirable behaviors described in Chapter 5. Once the unwanted behavior has decreased to acceptable levels, teachers must be concerned with generalization and maintenance. Generalization and maintenance of behavior reduction should be planned in a similar manner to that used in planning generalization and maintenance of desirable behaviors.

Key Terms

avoidance conditioning   203

behavior-based time-out   201

chain stopping   186

chemical restraint   206

contingent exertion   205

dead man's test   193

differential reinforcement of alternative
 behavior (DRA)   193

differential reinforcement of incompatible
 behavior (DRI)   193

differential reinforcement of low-rate
 behavior (DRL)   195

differential reinforcement of other
 behavior (DRO)   191

differential reinforcement   190

escape conditioning   203

exclusionary time-out   201

fixed-interval DRO   192

fixed-momentary DRO   192

informal procedures   185

interresponse time (IRT)   195

intrusiveness   183

level I procedures   190

level II procedures   196

level III procedures   199

level IV procedures   203

limited-responding DRL   196

mechanical restraint   206

momentary DRO   192

negative practice   205

nonexclusionary time-out   200

overcorrection   204

physical restraint   206

positive practice overcorrection   204

Discussion Questions

1. How should teachers balance the concern over restrictive or intrusive interventions with the need to use the most effective intervention?

2. How can teachers use informal procedures to decrease unwanted behaviors?

3. Why should teachers begin with level I procedures before moving to more restrictive or intrusive interventions?

4. How can differential reinforcement procedures be used to improve the classroom behavior of students?

5. When would a teacher move to a level II procedure? What needs to be known before extinction can be used?

6. Why should teachers attempt to decrease the use of aversive procedures in schools?

7. How would a teacher decide on the type of time-out to use? What information must be taken into consideration?

8. How can a token economy system and response cost be combined in a behavior management program? Provide an example of such a system.

9. What needs to occur before a teacher moves to a level IV intervention? What can the teacher expect to occur?

10. Some people have indicated that overcorrection procedures are educational in nature. Is this statement true? Why or why not?

Part III

Classroom Supports

7

Preliminary Considerations

Chapter Objectives

After studying this chapter, you should be able to

- explain why it is important to have good classroom management skills,

- illustrate effective classroom arrangements,

- characterize nonverbal communication methods,

- depict how to set effective classroom rules,

- describe how rule-governed behavior is learned,

- illustrate how to establish routines,

- describe how to use precorrection,

- explain the importance of social skills training,

- depict the different group-oriented management approaches,

- explain how to implement the Good Behavior Game,

- describe how Think Time® can be used in the classroom,

- characterize the advantages and disadvantages of each of the group-oriented management approaches, and

- state the important considerations teachers should make when using group-oriented management approaches.

VIGNETTE

Establishing Rules and Routines to Prevent Misbehavior

MS. HERNANDEZ, A SEVENTH-GRADE TEACHER at Lincoln Middle School, is having increasing difficulties getting students to follow rules and routines in her classroom. Many students tend to move about the room and talk with others without her permission. She has noticed that those students who are most likely to disobey rules are the ones who were disruptive from the first day of class. She has also noticed other students following the lead of these few students as the school year progresses. Ms. Hernandez is finding more and more of her time is spent on disruptive behavior and less and less on actual instruction.

Ms. Hernandez is unsure what to do. She tries to respond the best she can to problem behaviors. She uses warnings to get students on task and has sent students out of the room on occasion, but she wonders if she can do more. She seems to be simply reacting to the students' misbehavior. She wonders if she can take specific steps to prevent these problems from occurring in the first place.

To find answers to her questions, Ms. Hernandez decides to attend behavior management workshops over the summer. She is hopeful she can find preventive strategies to use in the classroom that will allow her to spend less time on getting disruptive students on task and more time on instruction. She believes if she can spend more time on instruction, her students will get better grades in the classroom.

Overview

Behavior management is often thought of as a "student problem," but behavior management difficulties are often an indication of problems in the management procedures used in the classroom. These management problems should be seen as an opportunity to teach students how to behave appropriately rather than as the fault of individual students; teachers should not blame students or their parents for misbehaviors or low achievement (Colvin, Sugai, & Patching, 1993; Haydon & Scott, 2008). In a recent survey of educational professionals, Wilkins, Caldarella, Crook-Lyon, and Young (2010) found that the majority of respondents noted the importance of teaching civil behavior to students through **direct instruction** (showing students how to act and then giving them opportunities to practice the skills they learned). Further, many of these respondents reported the need for school professionals to model appropriate behaviors (see Chapter 8), focus on schoolwide positive behavior support (see Chapter 12), teach rules and expectations (see Chapter 8), and emphasize character education (see Chapter 1).

As stated by Bloom (1980), two categories of variables affect student achievement—nonalterable variables and alterable variables (see Table 7.1). **Nonalterable variables** are things we cannot change, such as ethnicity, socioeconomic status, gender, and home background. Hart and Risley (1995) describe how nonalterable variables can affect school success. They tracked the vocabulary levels of three groups of children: affluent, middle class, and poor (welfare). They reported that three-year-old children from poor backgrounds had fewer than 600 words in their vocabulary. Middle-class children had slightly fewer than 800 words by age three. Finally, children from affluent backgrounds had more than 1,000 words in their vocabulary. Thus, compared with affluent children, poor children had slightly more than half the number of words in their vocabulary. Clearly, teachers have a difficult responsibility in teaching students from such varied backgrounds. Making it even more problematic is that, as children from poorer homes progress through school, they tend to fall further and further behind their peers. "Moreover, if you want to know the single greatest predictor of academic and social failure in the public schools of the United States, look no further than poverty." (Sabornie & DeBettencourt, 2009, p. 47)

Obviously, educators must be concerned with the environments from which students come. However, it does no good to blame student deficiencies on the home environment. Instead, educators should focus on variables that can be controlled. The second category of variables that affect student achievement includes alterable variables. **Alterable variables** are things we can change, such as teaching skills, the quantity of teacher-to-student interactions, and the use of instructional time. Head Start is such an attempt. Educators provide young children with rich learning experiences before they enter school, so they can catch up to their peers. Teachers can enhance academic readiness and learning by providing better instruction and management in the classroom; these alterable variables are under their control.

Teachers can go a long way toward making these improvements by thinking of management problems in the classroom as a *classroom* issue rather than a *student* issue. Approaching behavior management in this manner allows teachers to plan how to prevent or respond to management issues as part of their overall classroom planning process. This chapter is concerned with three areas of alterable variables. First, teachers must consider preventive strategies that can be used in behavior management, including seating arrangements and the establishment of rules and routines. Second, teachers must consider the types of group contingencies to be used in the classroom. Third, teachers must consider methods of teaching appropriate behaviors to decrease the likelihood of unwanted behavior.

This chapter will cover several important concepts needed to support the classroom environment. These concepts relate to **classroom structure** and include such things as the seating arrangements, rules, and routines present in the classroom. A discussion will be provided on why classroom management is important. Next, effective classroom arrangements will be explained along with nonverbal communication

Table 7.1	Nonalterable and Alterable Variables

Nonalterable Variables	**Alterable Variables**
Ethnicity	Use of time
Socioeconomic status	Teaching skills
Gender	Quantity of teacher-to-student interactions
Home background	

SOURCE: Adapted from G. R. Patterson, *Coercive Family Process: A Social Learning Approach.* Copyright © 1982 by Castalia Publishing Co.

methods and guidelines for setting classroom rules and routines. Then, important instructional issues for students with behavior problems will be highlighted, including the precorrection strategy and social skills training. Finally, group-oriented management approaches will be described, specifically highlighting the Good Behavior Game and Think Time®.

Why Is Classroom Management Critical?

Although we are frequently tempted to explain away behavior difficulties by assuming they are developmental in nature and the student will eventually "grow out of them" or we frequently shrug our shoulders and say, "Boys will be boys," we must take each behavior problem seriously. The single best predictor of delinquency in adolescence is behavior difficulties exhibited in elementary school (Walker, 1997). Research also suggests behaviors do not simply disappear over time for those students who have the most severe problem behaviors. In fact, Walker indicates that the stability of aggressive behavior over a 10-year period is about the same as the stability of intelligence over the same time period. The stability of IQ scores is approximately .70, whereas the stability of aggressive behavior is .60 to .80. Therefore, problem behavior must be changed as early as possible in elementary school. If problem behavior persists after then, the likelihood of making successful changes later in a student's academic career diminishes radically (Walker). Thus, the teachers who should have the very best behavior management skills are those in the primary grades.

The early grades are so critical because that is where adults have the most influence over student behavior. Thereafter, peers take on a more important role. Patterson (1982a) devised a model to explain how behavior problems develop. As shown in Figure 7.1, problem behaviors frequently begin in the home. The process begins with family stressors that, in turn, put severe pressure on family members. These stressors then begin to escalate into negative-aggressive interactions, which then result in adults using coercive techniques to force children to submit. Aversive control is used in these families to control unwanted behaviors. Next, antisocial behavior patterns begin to emerge as the students enter school. **Antisocial behavior** violates socially prescribed norms or patterns of behavior. Antisocial behaviors begin to become problematic around age three or four. At this age, children who will exhibit antisocial behaviors later when they enter school can be fairly reliably identified. Once these students enter school, their antisocial behaviors are often fairly salient and become frequent in nature and occur under many different settings and in multiple forms. Teachers and peers begin to reject these students, so they begin to seek out other deviant students with whom to interact. By the time they enter the fourth and fifth grades, they begin to affiliate with a deviant peer group. Finally, by the time they are in the sixth to tenth grades, the students are affiliated with a delinquent gang and begin a violent and criminal lifestyle. Many drop out of school during this time. We must be cautious, however, not to blame the parents for the behavior problems of their children. According to Heward (2009), school personnel should work with parents to improve parental relationships with their children to prevent, or decrease the severity of, behavior problems.

Figure 7.1 The Development of Antisocial Behavior Patterns

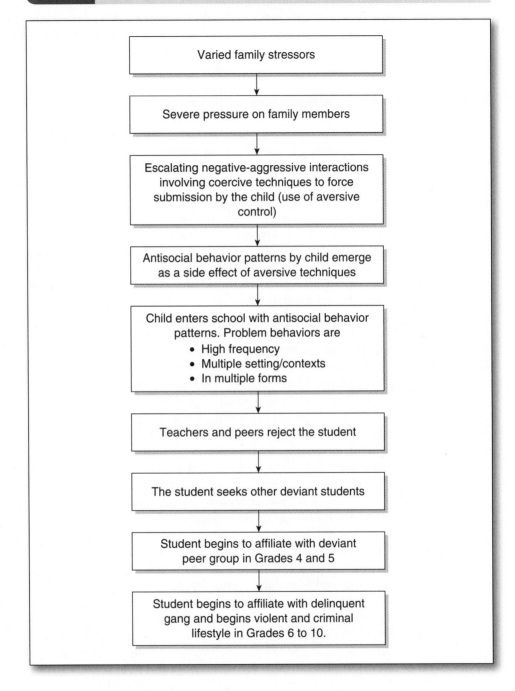

Although the progression of behavior problems is fairly obvious, school personnel may not respond in time to prevent this negative spiral. The positive side is that the negative progression can be stopped, but teachers must be ready and willing to set up their classrooms to break the cycle. Teachers cannot wait. They must begin to consider how they are going to prevent management problems from the first day of class. Make no mistake: more students with severe behavior problems are entering the general education classroom. Therefore, teachers need to be better at classroom management today than perhaps at any other time in educational history.

The first step at better classroom management is to prevent problem behavior from occurring in the first place. These preliminary steps to prevent management problems are discussed throughout the rest of this chapter.

What Are Effective Classroom Arrangements?

Teachers can use effective classroom arrangements to prevent the occurrence of behavior problems in the classroom. Clearly, many different classroom arrangements are effective for different grades. Lewis and Doorlag (2011) described six aspects to consider when designing the physical arrangement of the classroom (see Table 7.2). First, teachers should plan for a separation between quiet and noisier areas of the classroom. For example, if small group instruction is provided at a table at the back of the classroom, those completing individualized seatwork should be seated at the front of the classroom whenever possible to avoid distractions. Classroom partitions may be used in an advantageous manner to keep areas separate and more quiet.

The seating arrangement, such as the placing of desks in rows, should be considered depending on the type of instruction.

Second, teachers should consider placing equipment, supplies, and materials where they can be conveniently accessed. For example, placing workbooks on a table at the back or front of the classroom near the entrance could allow easier access when students first enter the room for instruction. Materials should be stored near where they will be used.

Third, teachers should plan for student traffic patterns. For example, there should be plenty of room for students to stand in line when entering or exiting the classroom. Further, there should be a direct route to high traffic areas such as the pencil sharpener or bathroom. Teachers might set up a self-checking station with a red pen and an answer key where students can check their answers. This station should be easy to access and away from students still completing their work.

Table 7.2	Six Aspects to Consider When Designing the Physical Arrangement of the Classroom

1. Plan for a separation between quiet and noisier areas of the classroom.
2. Consider placing equipment, supplies, and materials where they can be conveniently accessed.
3. Plan for student traffic patterns.
4. Be mindful of student mobility in the classroom.
5. Be flexible in the arrangement and rearrangement of the classroom.
6. Consider the population density of the classroom and student placement.

SOURCE: From S. C. Paine, J. Radicchi, L. C. Rosellini, L. Deutchman, and C. B. Darch, *Structuring Your Classroom for Academic Success* (1983, p. 21). Copyright © 1983 by the authors. Reprinted by permission.

Fourth, teachers should be mindful of their own mobility in the classroom. For example, if desks are in rows, teachers should be able to move through all rows to access students when they need assistance. There should be no space in the classroom that cannot be easily accessed by the teacher. The teacher's desk should be placed in one of the front corners of the room, facing the students. If an instructional aide's desk is in the room, it should be placed at the back of the room on the opposite side of the teacher's desk.

Fifth, teachers should be flexible in their arrangement and rearrangement of the classroom. For example, if the purpose of instruction is for students to work together, student groups should face one another rather than the teacher. If the purpose is to increase student interaction, using a circle, square, or U-shaped arrangement works well. During a teacher-directed lesson, the teacher should be the center of attention. Students should never have their backs to the speaker. All desks should face the front of the room. Desks should face away from the windows. Additionally, movable partitions can be used to restructure the classroom for specific teaching situations. If small group instruction is occurring, a partition on wheels can be moved easily to shield the small group from the larger group's activity. However the classroom is arranged, though, teachers should be able to see each student. Students should not be hidden by a permanent partition or a support beam in the room.

Finally, teachers should consider the population density of students and student placement in their classrooms. For example, students should not be crowded. They should have plenty of room to sit and complete their work. Further, the highest performing students should sit near the back of the class, and the lowest performing students and those with behavior difficulties should sit near the front of the class. This arrangement allows teachers to maintain the attention of all students.

Figure 7.2 shows an example of an effectively arranged classroom. Obviously, the classroom arrangement shown here may not be perfectly appropriate for all classrooms. It does, however, contain all of the essential elements of an effectively arranged classroom.

| Figure 7.2 | Physical Arrangement of the Classroom |

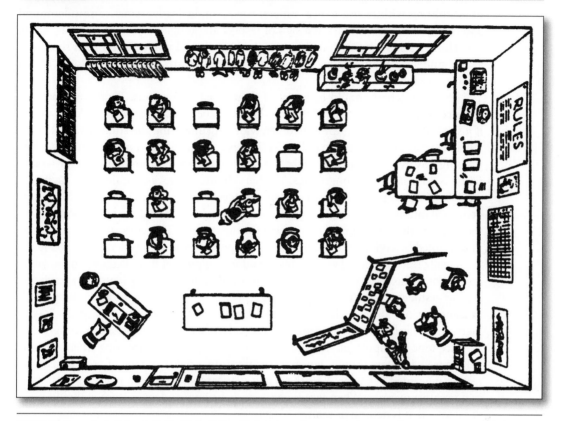

SOURCE: From S. C. Paine, J. Radicchi, L. C. Rosellini, L. Deutchman, and C. B. Darch, *Structuring Your Classroom for Academic Success* (1983, p. 21). Copyright © 1983 by the authors. Reprinted by permission.

What Are Nonverbal Communication Methods?

An important area of behavior management involves nonverbal communication on the part of teachers (Salend, 2011). Students respond not only to what is said but also to what is done in the classroom. It is interesting to observe the classroom dynamics that occur between students and teachers. Nonverbal cues can go far in producing positive and not-so-positive classroom behavior. Nonverbal communication involves several elements. First, the distance teachers are from the students when providing instruction can affect whether the students will respond favorably to instruction. In general, it is better to move closer to students when providing instruction, providing reinforcement for a positive behavior, and correcting unwanted behavior.

Second, teachers should provide eye contact with students. Eye contact allows teachers to inform students they are being spoken to. In addition, teachers should have the students provide eye contact to teachers (saying "All eyes on me" or "I need your attention"). Obtaining student attention allows teachers to increase the likelihood that students are attending to what is being said. Teachers, however, must be mindful of other cultures with regard to eye contact. For example, Native American students and adults may avoid eye contact as a sign of respect and religious custom (Zirpoli, 2008).

Third, teachers should face the students. They should not look over their shoulders at the students. Again, facing the students communicates they are the focus of the teachers' attention.

Fourth, teachers should be aware of their facial expressions. There must be congruence between what is said to students and a teacher's facial expression. For example, if a student engages in an unwanted behavior, reprimanding the student with a smile will likely decrease the reprimand's effectiveness. Likewise, frowning at a student while praising positive behavior can make the praise less effective. Smiling while providing praise is an instance of congruence. Teachers should, however, refrain from having an angry look on their faces when a student engages in an unwanted behavior. Many students will interpret such angry expressions as an indication that the behavior bothered the teacher, which may prove reinforcing for the student. Therefore, if students engage in unwanted behaviors, the teacher's facial response should be as neutral as possible.

Finally, teachers should vary the tone, loudness, or pitch of their voices when providing instructions. This vocal variation (called **pause and punch**) also provides additional information to students. For example, providing emphasis on one part of the instruction—such as using a pause and punch on the word *door*, as in "Close the . . . *door* please"—can increase the likelihood the student will respond. As with facial expressions, congruence of voice tone is important. Teachers should have a positive voice tone when students behave well; teachers should, however, refrain from a negative tone of voice when correcting unwanted behavior. A teacher's angry or sarcastic tone can make students react in a negative manner. When faced with a misbehaving student, a teacher should use a vocal tone that is neutral or matter-of-fact.

How Do We Set Effective Classroom Rules?

Rules are an important aspect of classroom management. **Rules** are statements that contain one or more of the three terms in the three-term contingency (i.e., antecedent, behavior, consequence; see Chapter 2). They provide students with the expectations of the teacher and other school personnel. As stated by Anderson and Spaulding (2007), "Classroom rules provide structure and consistency. Rules also allow a teacher to maintain a positive environment and to focus on academics. Finally, having a set of classroom rules provides legal, ethical, and professional accountability" (p. 28). Rules, then, are essentially attempts to prevent behavior problems from occurring, and effective teachers establish rules to prevent classroom management difficulties (Slavin, 2009). Unfortunately, all rules are not created equal. Many classrooms have rules that may be ineffective for several reasons.

It is important, therefore, to clarify what makes a good rule, what rules are, and how they work. One of the more significant steps that can occur in a student's life is the development of rule-governed behavior. **Rule-governed behavior** is behavior that is controlled by verbal or written rules. When we are born, our behaviors are determined by two major sources: genetics and direct consequences. Genetically, we are born with certain behaviors that allow us to survive. For example, the sucking response allows us to eat and obtain sustenance. From direct acting, we also learn the consequences of our early behaviors. When babies engage in the sucking response, the milk reinforces this action. Babies also quickly learn that crying will bring them food and other necessary comforts such as warmth. Very young infants, however, do not learn through rules. Telling a newborn that crying will not be tolerated will have little effect on the crying behavior. Likewise, telling a very young infant not to touch a hot stove will usually result in the child touching it, unless the child has learned to follow your rules. Thus, most, if not all, of our very early behaviors are not affected by rules at all. This situation changes as we get older. The older we get, the more important the role of rules in our lives. Most of us usually do not have to experience the direct consequences of all our behaviors. For example, if we only learned by experiencing the consequences, we would not learn to cross the street without looking both ways unless we got hit by a car or at least came close to getting hit.

Fortunately, we can tell children to look both ways before crossing the street, and they will do so. In this case, following rules allows for the avoidance of the serious consequences of not following rules. Indeed, most of our learning in society is dependent on rules. Rules are how the culture or society takes control of most of our behaviors. Now think of what goes on in the classroom. The most well-behaved students are those who follow the rules. Thus, we go through this very important transition as we grow older. This transition involves learning by experiencing the direct and positive consequences of behaving and *obeying* rules.

Unfortunately, some individuals do not follow rules. These individuals break rules (laws) and may have to experience the direct consequences of *not obeying* the rules (laws). Some students do not follow the rules of the classroom and may have to experience the direct consequences of not following these classroom rules. What can be done with these students? How can the likelihood of rule-following behavior be increased?

As previously stated, rules are statements that contain one or more of the three terms in the three-term contingency. For example, the rule "Walk in the hallway" contains the behavior. The rule "When you are in the school, walk in the hallway" contains the antecedent (when you are in the school) and the behavior. Finally, the rule "When you are in the school, walk in the hallway to avoid getting hurt" contains the antecedent, the behavior, and the consequence (not getting hurt). All of these aspects of a rule—its antecedent, the behavior it requests, and the consequences of following it or not—are important in establishing whether a rule obtains control over a behavior. When rules have obtained control over a behavior, that behavior is called rule governed. When rules fail to have an effect on a student's behavior, the rules have not enacted control over the behavior. This lack of control may be because the potential consequences are too improbable (when someone shoplifts, the probability of actually being caught may be remote), the engagement of the behavior opposed to the rule may be reinforcing (skipping class to go "on the town" may be just too tempting; recall the movie *Ferris Bueller's Day Off*), or the consequences of the rules may be too delayed (cheating now may result in a lack of skills later in life rather than immediate negative consequences). Whatever the reason for students not following rules, a teacher can still attempt to teach them rule-following behavior.

Developing Effective Classroom Rules

Rules are not developed overnight and put up on the board the first day of class. The development of effective rules contains several steps (see Table 7.3). First, teachers should discuss with the students the positive consequences that result when they follow the rules and the negative consequences that will occur when rules are not followed (Gable, Hester, Rock, & Hughes, 2009). This discussion should focus on telling students the importance of rules. For example, a statement such as "Rules allow all of us to know what is expected" could be used. A comparison between the classroom and society in general could be used. Laws are essentially the rules of society. Teachers could therefore talk about what would happen in society if there were no laws. For example, speed limit signs are statements of rules. A discussion on why it is important to have speed limits might be used to help students understand the necessity of rules.

Second, effective rules should be developed with student input; student commitment should be obtained (Gable et al., 2009). Getting student input allows students to have ownership over the classroom rules, and students will be more likely to follow rules if they have a say in their development. Students are also more apt to think a teacher respects what they have to say when they help develop the rules. This is not to say students have the final say in the development of classroom rules; ultimately, teachers have the final say. If, however, students disagree with a particular rule, it is much better to identify what the disagreement is early in the development of the rules rather than later, when the rules are already solidified. In addition, gaining student input

---

Table 7.3   Development of Effective Rules

1. Discuss the value of rules with students.
2. Gather student input to develop rules while keeping in mind the following:
   - Keep the number of rules to a minimum (i.e., four to five).
   - Use simple language.
   - State rules positively.
   - Use different sets of rules for different situations, if needed.
   - Keep class and school rules consistent.
3. Teach rules explicitly.
4. Post rules in a prominent location.
5. Monitor and review rule following.

allows teachers to provide rationales for each rule as it is being developed. Effective rules must be developed with the following in mind.

1. *Rules must be kept to a minimum.* The general advice is to keep the number of rules to four or five (Gable et al., 2009). A short list is important because students must be able to repeat the rules without referencing the written rules. They should be able to memorize the rules. Many students break rules because they do not know what the rules are. Therefore, keeping the list short will help avoid this problem.

   Many teachers will have difficulty limiting the list to only four to five rules. If this difficulty arises, it is likely the rules are too specific. Many rules can be combined into a more general rule. For example, if there are several rules such as "keep your hands to yourself," "say nice things to others," "keep negative comments to yourself," and "assist others who are in need of help," one general rule, such as "treat others with respect," could include all of them.

2. *Rules should contain simple language.* Teachers have a variety of students with different strengths and weaknesses. Clearly, rules should not contain language beyond what students can understand. For example, rather than saying "be altruistic," say "treat others with respect." Rules are not meant to be vocabulary lessons. Keeping the wording simple also allows students to remember the rules.

3. *Rules should be stated positively.* This principle is perhaps violated more than the others. Some teachers may tell students what they do not want them doing rather than what they do want them to do. For example, rather than having the rule "Do not disrespect others," teachers can say, "Treat others with respect." Instead of saying "No cheating," teachers can say, "Keep your eyes on your own work." Likewise, instead of saying "No running in the hall," a teacher can say, "Walk in the hall." This characteristic of effective rules should also spill over to those instances when instructions to students are provided. For example, rather than directing students "not to show up late to class," we should tell them to "get to class on time." The importance of this characteristic cannot be overstated; telling a student *what not to do* does not necessarily tell the student *what to do.* Telling a student not to use foul language does not tell a student to use appropriate language. Instead, this negative "rule" could result in the student simply not talking in class, which reduces foul language but does not improve the student's use of appropriate language. In addition, stating rules positively helps teachers scan for positive behaviors rather than negative ones.

4. *There may be different sets of rules for different situations, if needed.* For example, having a rule of walking in the classroom is not appropriate in physical education. Also, having a rule for students to keep their eyes on their own work is not relevant during cooperative learning groups, when the sharing of work may be wanted. Therefore, depending on the situation, some rules may be more appropriate in one context but not in another.

5. *Class rules and school rules must be consistent.* Obviously, if classroom rules were not aligned with school rules, students would not know how to react. Therefore, teachers should review the school rules and ensure these rules are consistent with the classroom rules. For example, a school may have an overall expectation of showing respect toward others. This expectation could become a rule in any particular classroom.

Third, once rules are developed, they should be deliberately taught (Anderson & Spaulding, 2007; Slavin, 2009). Following an "I do, we do, you do" procedure, the teacher can model following the rules ("I do"); practice rule following, providing feedback to students ("we do"); and give students opportunities to practice rule following on their own ("you do"). Role-playing is an excellent way to teach rules. Examples of following and not following rules can be discussed with students. For instance, for the rule "be respectful of others," examples of showing respect (e.g., asking politely for a piece of paper from another student) and of showing disrespect (e.g., taking another student's paper without asking) could be discussed. Teachers can also request examples from the students of obeying and disobeying rules. In addition, when examples of not following or of actively breaking rules are provided, the teacher should discuss what the consequence might be, such as being sent to time-out or accidentally hurting another student. Once it is apparent that students can tell the difference between the examples of following and not following rules, the rules can be displayed.

Fourth, rules should be posted in a prominent or easy-to-see location (Salend, 2011). This posting is a reminder to the students of what the rules actually are. The positioning also allows visitors to the classroom to learn what is expected of the students. In addition, posting rules allows other staff, such as substitute teachers, to know classroom expectations and to inform the students that visitors to the classroom also know what is expected.

Finally, rule following must be monitored and reviewed (Gable et al., 2009). Teachers should observe how the rules affect student behavior. If students begin to break rules consistently, the reason for the infraction should be determined. Many times, students, especially younger ones, simply do not remember what the rules are. To avoid or prevent this potential problem, rules should be reviewed on a consistent basis (e.g., once a week). Once students master the rules (i.e., can recite the rules without looking at the posted rules), the review can be faded. Students may also break rules because the rules are unclear. If this is the case, rules should be modified until all students can explain what is meant by each rule. Using unison responding provides all students an opportunity to say the rules back to the teacher. In addition, rules might not be followed because the teacher does not enforce them. The teacher might not reinforce rule following or might not punish rule violations. Teachers must reinforce rule following as immediately and consistently as possible. Once the students demonstrate rule-following behavior, reinforcement can be faded to an intermittent basis. Teachers must also make sure that they do not reinforce rule breaking at any time because doing so only makes breaking rules more likely in the future.

How Do We Establish Routines?

The development of rules is a critical aspect of preventing behavior management problems in the classroom. An equally important and sometimes overlooked area, however, is the teaching of routines. **Routines** are sets of actions students take to reach specific outcomes in the most efficient manner. For example, there should be a procedure for using the restroom or for sharpening pencils. There might be a routine for indicating whether a hot lunch is needed for a student at the elementary level. There can be start-up routines to get students ready for the day, such as having a short activity for students to begin while the teacher completes tasks such as taking role. If we were to observe an orderly classroom, we would see one in which the teacher has taken the time to teach students how to follow certain prescribed routines. Routines should be taught in any area that will help with the smooth flow of activities in a classroom. Routines are commonly related to the following, as noted by Gable et al. (2009):

1. Use of the restroom

2. Conduct at assemblies

3. Classroom transitions

4. Movement to the cafeteria

Additional routines might include how to behave at the beginning or end of class or the school day, how to respond to another student with disabilities, how to behave when a visitor is present, what to do during announcements, and how to be an effective member of a small group. Trussell (2008) also describes the importance of having a routine for how students reenter the classroom from individually determined activities. Is the student expected to join the group or begin a different activity?

The process for teaching routines is the same as for teaching any other task. First, the teacher should model what the procedure is for the students ("I do"). For example, the teacher could model taking the bathroom card from the wall and going from the classroom to the bathroom. The teacher in an elementary school might model how to flush the toilet and how to wash one's hands. Second, the teacher should take students and guide them through the routine while providing feedback along the way ("we do"). Third, the teacher should have each student practice the bathroom routine independently while again providing feedback ("you do"). Once the students have demonstrated the skill of the bathroom routine, another procedure can be taught. Finally, the teacher should continuously monitor the students in how they perform the procedure, providing positive and corrective feedback over time.

Although some teachers might not think of routines as an important behavior management tool, routine procedures that are adequately taught can have a dramatic impact on preventing student misbehavior (Salend, 2011). Many so-called misbehaviors are simply behaviors students display because they have not been taught the appropriate or expected procedures. Therefore, the time commitment involved in teaching procedures will be well worthwhile.

What Is Precorrection?

One fundamental assumption that can be made about classroom behavior problems is that they are learned. In addition, appropriate classroom behavior can be taught. Thus, problem behavior can be seen not only as a management issue but also as an instructional one

(Kauffman, Pullen, Mostert, & Trent, 2011). Colvin et al. (1993) developed the technique called precorrection. **Precorrection** involves active teacher supervision and effective instruction (Haydon & Scott, 2008), during which students are taught expectations, rules, and routines to prevent a misbehavior from occurring. This instructional approach is based on three assumptions. First, problem behaviors are learned through our interactions with our environments. Second, students need to learn appropriate behavior; thus, they need to be taught. Third, emphasis should be placed on teaching social skills. The idea here is that, if management problems can be corrected by instructional techniques, these problems can also be prevented by the same techniques. Essentially, precorrection is based on the concept that teachers can prevent management problems by anticipating where or when problems are likely to be encountered (e.g., during transitions) and then designing a lesson plan to teach the relevant skills to students to prevent these problem behaviors.

Colvin et al. (1993) describe the similarities of academic correction and behavior problem correction. For example, suppose a student writes a story and uses "it's" to refer to possession (it's cage is clean) instead of "its." The teacher could correct the error by explaining to the student that "it's" does not refer to possession but rather means "it is" (e.g., it is cage is clean). Then the teacher could have the student repeat what "it's" means and correct the mistake in the story, praising the student for the correction. Similarly, if a student swears at another student, the teacher could remind the student of the rule to treat others with respect, have the student repeat the rule, ask the student to apologize to the other student, and then praise the apology. Thus, the teacher treats the problem behavior as an opportunity to teach appropriate behavior.

Suppose the student is still having difficulty with discriminating when to use or not use "it's." Good teachers would take a step back and reteach the rule of when to use "it's" and "its." This reteaching would continue until the student could demonstrate mastery of the concept. Now consider the example of the student swearing at peers. What would happen if this student again directed swear words toward another student? Most teachers would attempt to punish this misbehavior in some fashion. If, however, an instructional method to solve problem behaviors were to be used, the teacher, rather than simply attempting to punish the swearing behavior, would take a step back with the student and reteach classroom rules until the student could demonstrate an understanding of the rules. Colvin et al. (1993) call the difference between these two methods of responding to behavior "correction" and "precorrection." As shown in Table 7.4, precorrection procedures are more instructional in nature.

Colvin et al. (1993) and Haydon and Scott (2008) describe a seven-step plan for precorrection. First, the context of the predictable behavior should be identified. Teachers should determine when and where problem behaviors are likely to occur. For example, based on experience, most teachers can predict that problem behaviors are most likely to occur during lunch, transitions, assemblies, or recess (for precorrection techniques used during recess at an elementary school, see Lewis, Colvin, & Sugai, 2000). Teachers can also document when and where behavior problems usually occur by using any of the assessment methods described in Chapter 4. Once they establish where and when problem behaviors are likely to occur, teachers should plan to address these problems by teaching or reteaching appropriate behavior. This planning is no different than planning for academic problems that students are likely to experience

| Table 7.4 | Comparison of Correction and Precorrection Procedures |

Correction	Precorrection
1. Is reactive	1. Is proactive
2. Involves a manipulation of consequences	2. Involves a manipulation of antecedents
3. May lead to negative teacher-student interactions	3. May lead to positive teacher-student interactions
4. Focuses on inappropriate behavior	4. Focuses on appropriate behavior
5. May lead to escalating behavior	5. May lead to appropriate behavior
6. Focuses on immediate events	6. Focuses on future events

SOURCE: From G. Colvin, G. Sugai, and B. Patching (1993) Precorrection: An Instructional Approach for Managing Predictable Problem Behaviors. *Intervention in School and Clinic, 28,* 143–150. Copyright © 1993 by PRO-ED, Inc. Reprinted by permission.

during certain academic tasks. In both cases, teachers consider ahead of time what they will do when a student has a problem and set out to prevent that problem from occurring, whether it is an academic or a behavior problem.

Second, the predictable and expected behaviors should be specified. For example, during transitions, teachers may predict that pushing is likely to occur. Then, they need to determine what behaviors are appropriate under the circumstances, such as "Keep your hands to yourself."

Third, teachers should consider how to modify the context of the situation. For example, proximity control can be used to prevent students from pushing during a transition. Teachers or other adults can be near the students during a transition to make the behavior less likely.

Fourth, teachers should rehearse the appropriate behaviors with the students. For example, before the students transition to lunch, the teacher could stand near the students and have them repeat the rule about keeping their hands to themselves. Reminders of appropriate behaviors before students have an opportunity to engage in unwanted behaviors can prevent the unwanted behaviors from occurring. Again, this step is similar to reminding students about the rules governing the use of "it's" and "its" before they begin to write.

Fifth, teachers should determine how they will reinforce appropriate student behavior. For example, when students transition to lunch appropriately, the teacher could reinforce the students by providing them with five extra minutes of free time when they reenter the room. Note that reinforcement does not always have to mean receiving something tangible or being allowed some activity; praise from teachers may also function as a strong form of reinforcement.

Sixth, expected behaviors should be prompted by teachers. That is, when students begin to break a rule, teachers should first attempt to bring about the appropriate behavior by prompting it to occur. For example, if a student begins to push another student during a transition, the teacher could say, "Remember the rule about keeping your hands to yourself." If the prompt does not work, and the student continues the unwanted behavior, the teacher should then have a predetermined response to this noncompliance. For instance, if the student continues to push, the teacher may need to remove the student from the group during the transition and provide a brief time-out.

Finally, the plan must be monitored. Teachers should continue to determine if appropriate behaviors are being exhibited. If a problem persists, an individualized intervention may be needed (described in Chapters 3–6).

Figure 7.3 shows a checklist and precorrection plan similar to those illustrated by Colvin et al. (1993), Haydon and Scott (2008), and Kauffman et al. (2011). As shown

| **Figure 7.3** | Precorrection Checklist and Plan |

Precorrection Checklist and Plan	Teacher: _____ Student: _____ Date: _____/_____/_____
☐ 1. Context Predictable behavior	
☐ 2. Expected behavior	
☐ 3. Context modification	
☐ 4. Behavior rehearsal	
☐ 5. Strong reinforcement	
☐ 6. Prompts	
☐ 7. Monitoring plan	

SOURCE: From G. Colvin, G. Sugai, and B. Patching (1993) Precorrection: An Instructional Approach for Managing Predictable Problem Behaviors. *Intervention in School and Clinic, 28,* 143–150. Copyright © 1993 by PRO-ED, Inc. Reprinted by permission.

in the figure, precorrection requires planning in a similar manner as would occur when a teacher prepares to teach an academic task. Notice that the example plan is for an individual student, but this plan can also be used for the entire class. Precorrection is placed in the classroom change section of this book because effective classroom change takes planning. The precorrection plan provides an excellent model for achieving the goal of designing a classroom environment that prevents or reduces the probability that management problems will occur.

What Are Social Skills?

To have meaningful relationships with their peers, teachers, and parents, students must acquire adequate social skills. According to Kauffman et al. (2011), "Without good social skills, students' academic progress is likely to be less than optimal, their future educational opportunities are likely to be restricted, and they are less likely to make a successful transition to adulthood and employment" (p. 104). Consequently, more educators are placing an emphasis on teaching social skills to their students (Kauffman et al.; Maag, 2006). According to Gresham, Cook, Crews, and Kern (2004), it could be argued that the primary reason for referring students to behavior services is their deficit in social skills. Thus, social skills training may be just as important as academic skills training in determining students' future success (Kauffman et al.). Unfortunately, Bellini, Peters, Benner, and Hopf (2007) and Maag (2006) indicate social skills training has resulted in only modest outcomes across various student populations. Regardless, Maag states that social skills training is an accepted practice when educators work with students who have behavioral disorders.

Social skills training often focuses on teaching students appropriate eye contact during social interactions, initiating and responding to social interactions, responding to authority figures in an appropriate manner, accepting criticism, and displaying appropriate affect (Kauffman et al., 2011). Social skills can be taught without specific programs or with published programs such as *First Step to Success* (Walker et al., 1997) or *Second Step* (Committee for Children, 1997). No matter which direction is followed, teachers should ask themselves the following (Kauffman et al.):

(a) What are the particular social skills that my students need to learn?

(b) Do my teaching strategies promote social competence?

(c) Do I teach social skills explicitly?

(d) Am I able to generalize training in social skills from simulated to actual social situations?

(e) Is my approach to social skills training consistent with the needs of students with mild disabilities and of students at risk?

Whatever the intervention chosen, students should first observe effective modeling of the skill to be learned, practice displaying the skill while receiving teacher feedback, and then have opportunities to display the skill independently in contrived or real-life contexts. Modeling can be demonstrated by adults, peers, or video-based models. As suggested by Gresham, Sugai, and Horner (2001), the effectiveness of social skills training can be improved by increasing the amount of training students receive, conducting training in natural settings, matching the skills taught with each student's deficit, and implementing social skills training with fidelity (i.e., implementing a program as it was designed to be implemented).

What Are Group-Oriented Management Approaches?

When setting out to prevent behavior problems in the classroom, teachers must determine how to respond to student behavior. Their response to student behavior should be well planned. A decision should be made regarding what type of group-oriented management approaches will be used in the classroom. **Group-oriented management approaches** involve providing consequences based on the behavior of one member of a group, a small number of students within the group, or all members of the group. Typically these consequences involve positive reinforcers; however, consequences serving as negative reinforcers or punishers can also be delivered. Although reinforcing or punishing student behavior is typically thought of as a procedure directed toward an individual student, group-oriented management approaches are in effect if all students in a group have the same expectations and are exposed to the same consequences. Group-oriented management approaches take advantage of peer pressure to improve student behavior (Kauffman et al., 2011). There are three categories of group-oriented management approaches: dependent, interdependent, and independent (Cooper, Heron, & Heward, 2007; Kauffman et al.). Each type has its advantages and disadvantages.

Dependent Group Management

Dependent group management provides consequences to the group based on the behavior of a selected group member or of a small number of members of a larger group (Kauffman et al., 2011). Consequences do not depend on every member's performance. Dependent group management can be readily seen in classrooms under certain circumstances. For example, if the teacher tells the students they can go out to recess as soon as everyone in the class finishes the assignment, when students go to recess is dependent on when the last student finishes. Therefore, recess is dependent on one member of the group. Another example occurs when an item is missing and the whole group is punished if the person who has taken the item does not come forward. Although the selected student is not known, the whole group faces the consequences of a particular individual. Yet another example is denying the class extra free time because two students did not behave well. A teacher saying no one can go out to play because Mary and Jacob were not in their seats illustrates dependent group management.

Dependent group management can be used to improve the classroom behavior of a student who behaves poorly. If a teacher places a low-achieving student in a cooperative learning group with higher achievers and says the group's grade is dependent on the lowest performer, dependent group management is being used to encourage the higher-achieving students to help the lower-achieving student.

Additionally, dependent group management can be used to improve all students' homework completion and accuracy. Lynch, Theodore, Bray, and Kehle (2009) compared three group-oriented management approaches to see their effects on the homework completion and accuracy of six elementary-aged students with learning disabilities or speech impairments. When the teacher used dependent group management intervention, the class was informed they could earn a reinforcer if the homework performance of one anonymous member of the class (selected randomly from a basket of student names) met a selected criterion. If the selected student met the criterion, the class earned the reinforcer; if the selected student did not meet the criterion, the class was not provided the reinforcer. The dependent group management approach resulted in improved homework completion and accuracy for all six students. (Note: All three group management approaches resulted in similar effects.)

Interdependent Group Management

Interdependent group management treats a group of students as a single individual. In other words, the same response requirements are set for all group members; consequences are delivered based on the performance of all members of the group (Kauffman et al., 2011). The students in a group are then interdependent, relying on each other for the consequences. Interdependent group management is typically built into cooperative learning groups (for a discussion of cooperative learning models, see Slavin, 2009). In such a group, the progress of the group as a whole accounts for the group's grade. Thus, each and every member of the group has an incentive to help others with the task.

Teachers can use interdependent group management to assist with classroom behavior management. In such an approach, teachers can reinforce a class as a whole on their behavior during a specified time. For example, if a substitute tells the teacher her students were well behaved during class when she was gone, the teacher could reinforce the class with extra free time when she returns. Therefore, every student in the class relies on the other students for access to the reinforcer. Interdependent group management uses the advantages of peer pressure to encourage good behavior on everyone's part.

The Good Behavior Game. An example of interdependent group management is the **Good Behavior Game** (Kauffman et al., 2011). Barrish, Saunders, and Wolf (1969) researched the game in the 1960s. The Good Behavior Game involves separating the students in a class into separate teams. Unwanted behaviors are targeted and defined. Next, a criterion level of maximum allowed behaviors is set. When any member of a team displays a target behavior, the team as a whole receives a mark. The team or teams with fewer marks than the criterion allowed or the team with the fewest marks wins the game. Consequences for winning often involve special privileges, such as extra recess or computer time. The losing teams would not be punished but would not receive the reinforcer. The Good Behavior Game can be used on a daily basis. Unless the class is especially unruly, however, playing the game over a week with consequences provided at the end of the week would be appropriate.

Sulzer-Azaroff and Mayer (1991) report that the Good Behavior Game may be set up to reduce disruptive behavior rather than to increase desirable behavior. Therefore, they describe an important modification: a process in which five to seven positive behaviors are targeted that can earn points and five to seven unwanted behaviors are targeted that can lose points. This modification is essentially a combination of the Good Behavior Game, a token system (see Chapter 5), and a response cost system (see Chapter 6). Before the last half-hour of the day, the team with the most points wins the game. Also, any team that has no negative points is awarded bonus points.

Independent Group Management

Independent group management involves the same response requirements for all students while providing individual consequences based on the behavior of each student (Kauffman et al., 2011). This approach is commonly used in the classroom, so we will provide an expanded example here. To use independent group management, teachers must set what the response requirement is for all students. For example, one such requirement would be a test that all students take but for which each student receives a unique grade. Criteria are set for varying levels of test scores (e.g., 90% = A, 80% = B). Students have the same response requirements. They all take the test. In addition, students can study together for a test. Consequences are based on individual performance, however. All students do not receive the same grade if all students do not score the same. Likewise, if a cooperative learning group were set up and students worked together on an assignment but had to turn in to be graded individual assignments resulting from the group work, each individual in the group would receive a score based on his or her own performance. The group as a whole would not suffer if one individual in the group scored poorly, nor would the group as a whole benefit if a member in the group scored particularly well. Both situations exemplify independent group management that aims to teach academic skills, but this technique can be used not only to improve student academic performance but also to reduce problem behavior in the classroom. One such independent group management approach used to reduce problem behaviors has been designated as an exemplary program by the U.S. Department of Education's Expert Panel on Safe, Disciplined, and Drug-Free Schools. It is called Think Time®.

Think Time®. Unfortunately, many classroom management systems or strategies used by teachers do not work well. Teachers often respond to a student's problem behavior by ignoring it until they can no longer stand it or by using elaborate warning systems such as checks after a name or pulling differently colored cards. These responses to problem behaviors often result in more persistent chronic behavior patterns or escalate minor behaviors into more severe forms. The varying staff responses to problem behaviors are especially troublesome for difficult-to-teach students who are experiencing or are at risk for school failure. These students often work with several professionals throughout the day, each with different responses to problem behaviors. Although many students can handle the wide range of responses from staff, some of the difficult-to-teach students with whom teachers struggle are unable to manage these varying teacher responses.

Classrooms have distinctive properties that greatly affect teachers, regardless of how they organize students for learning or what management systems they use (Doyle, 1986). In other words, a set of universal properties is in place in every classroom. These properties create constant pressures that shape teaching and classroom management. Although the intensity of their effects with regard to student behavior will vary with the particular conditions of every school, these pressures operate in all classrooms, regardless of how classrooms are organized and managed.

This discussion of the distinctive properties of classrooms comes first for a very important reason. Discussions of classroom management or the handling of misbehavior tend to emphasize the individual student as the target of the teacher's thinking and action, failing to capture the group or social dimension. Although the description of Think Time® is directed at how teachers respond to the problem behaviors of individual students, its effects must be viewed within the group dimension. Think Time® is designed to have a positive and powerful influence not only on individual students but also on the group dynamics of classrooms and schools.

Think Time® includes three interventions common to schools: (a) an effective request for appropriate behavior versus threats, ultimatums, warnings, or repeated requests; (b) **antiseptic bounding** (a quiet reflective period in which everyone disengages from the student); and (c) **behavioral debriefing** (i.e., the student's evaluation of his or her behavior). Think Time® requires teamwork between two or more teachers (i.e., the homeroom teacher and a cooperating teacher who provides the designated Think Time area). There are five interrelated steps in Think Time®: (a) catching problem behavior early, (b) moving to and entering the designated Think Time classroom, (c) experiencing the Think Time period and debriefing process, (d) checking students' debriefing responses, and (e) rejoining the class. Many of the steps presented here are restatements of Think Time® presented earlier, but it is critical to understand and implement the strategy appropriately for it to be effective.

Table 7.5 shows the four steps involved in preparing to implement Think Time®. First, a teacher should identify cooperating teachers. Think Time® requires teamwork between two or more teachers. The cooperating teacher's classroom (Think Time classroom) should be located in close proximity to its partner classrooms, thereby reducing the amount of travel time and the potential for problems during student transition to the Think Time® classroom.

Second, teachers should prepare the classroom. Typically, teachers will place two to three desks in a designated Think Time® area, an area free of visual distractions such as posters or traffic. Furthermore, this area should be located in a low-use region of the classroom, one that is not in close proximity to where the students in the classroom are working.

Third, teachers should inform parents of how Think Time® will be used in the classroom. Teachers should develop and send home a parent information letter.

Table 7.5	Four Steps in Preparing to Implement Think Time®

1. Teachers should identify cooperating teachers.

2. Teachers should physically prepare the classroom.

3. Teachers should inform parents regarding how Think Time® will be used in the classroom.

4. Students should be taught how Think Time® works in the classroom. Teachers should take the following steps:
   - Provide a rationale.
   - Teach that certain behaviors will result in the use of Think Time®.
   - Teach students how to move to and enter the designated Think Time® classroom.
   - Show what is involved during the Think Time® period and behavioral debriefing process.
   - Instruct students about how to rejoin the classroom.

Think Time® should also be discussed with parents during conference time or other informational meetings.

Finally, students should be taught how Think Time® works in the classroom. The method of teaching students about Think Time® is similar to the process of teaching rules and routines, which has been described previously (i.e., the "I do, we do, you do" procedure). There are five distinct parts to a teaching plan that addresses how Think Time® will be used in the classroom:

1. *Providing a rationale.* The rationale for Think Time® should focus on three areas. First, the teacher should communicate that the overall goal is for the students to succeed and enjoy the class. Teachers will not allow students to do anything that interferes with their or someone else's success. Second, teachers should communicate the importance of creating a safe and orderly learning environment to ensure everyone's success. They should indicate that a safe and orderly learning environment will set a positive tone for learning in the classroom. Finally, teachers must communicate that it is important for each member of the class to control his or her own behavior and that Think Time® will help all learn how to develop self-control.

2. *Teaching that certain behaviors will result in the use of Think Time®.* After describing the rationale for the use of Think Time®, teachers should discuss and model for students those behaviors that interfere with the learning and teaching processes. This discussion does not center solely on classroom rules. Rather, teachers should discuss with students the full range of behaviors that interfere with these processes. Teachers can brainstorm with students to identify these behaviors. Older students (second grade and up) are fully aware of behaviors that interfere with the teaching and learning processes.

3. *Teaching how to move to and enter the designated Think Time® classroom.* Teaching students to leave the room for Think Time® involves teaching them (a) the signal used to cue students to leave the classroom, (b) how they are to leave the classroom, and (c) how they are

to enter the designated Think Time® classroom. Teachers should discuss and model for the students the signal used to cue them to leave the room for Think Time®.

4. *Showing what is involved during the Think Time® period and behavioral debriefing process.* Teachers should discuss and model for students how they are to sit at the designated desk in the Think Time® classroom: e.g., sit quietly and wait for instructions from the teacher. The goal is to give students an opportunity to calm down and regain self-control. Keep in mind that, although students should sit quietly and wait for the teacher to give them instructions, teachers should limit the number of tasks students have to accomplish at the same time (e.g., it's probably best to forget about directing students to sit with their feet flat on the floor, back straight). Additionally, students should be taught how to fill out the debriefing form (see Table 7.6).

5. *Instructing students about how to rejoin the classroom.* Teaching the students to rejoin the class involves teaching them (a) to wait at the door in a controlled fashion until the teachers can check the accuracy of the debriefing form, (b) how the debriefing form will be handled, and (c) the reentry procedures the teachers will use to ensure that students are able to make up the work they missed.

Table 7.6	Behavior Debriefing Form

Name: _____   Date: _____

Teacher: _____   Grade: _____

Arrival Time: _____   Departure Time: _____

1. What was your behavior? _____

_____

_____

2. What behavior do you need to display when you go back to your classroom? _____

_____

_____

3. Will you be able to do it? ___Yes ___No ___I need to see the teacher

_____

_____

Table 7.7 shows an evaluation checklist for the implementation of Think Time®. Six major skills are listed for evaluation. These skills include (a) setting and implementing rules and routines, (b) appropriate behavior recognized and validated,

Table 7.7	Think Time® Evaluation Checklist

The Think Time® evaluation checklist is designed to assess a teacher's strengths when implementing Think Time®. The checklist can be used by an independent observer or can be completed by the teacher. The evaluation questions are provided as a guide to the primary behaviors that exemplify the effective use of Think Time®. Feel free to add evaluation questions if you think such additions will increase the practicality and sensitivity of the evaluation process. In addition, please make supporting notes that will help describe any problems in more detail.

Rating scale: 1, No change necessary; 2, Minor problems; 3, Major problems

Skill 1. Setting and implementing rules and routines

Evaluation Questions	Rating and Notes
a. Does the teacher provide a set of rules?	
b. Do the rules specify behaviors needed for productive instructional and classroom interactions?	
c. Does the teacher have well-established classroom routines?	

Skill 2. Appropriate behavior recognized and validated

Evaluation Questions	Rating and Notes
a. Is teacher praise specific and contingent?	
b. Is teacher praise delivered in a credible manner?	
c. Does the teacher recognize appropriate academic and classroom interaction?	

Skill 3. Prevention of problem behavior

Evaluation Questions	Rating and Notes
a. Does the teacher demonstrate increased vigilance at appropriate times?	
b. Does the teacher effectively use nonintrusive measures such as eye contact and physical placement to monitor students?	
c. Does the teacher coach and remind students to follow the classroom rules and routines?	

Skill 4. Responding to behavior efficiently

Evaluation Questions	Rating and Notes
a. Does the teacher use limited warnings, requests, and so forth?	
b. Are the teacher's reactions to misbehavior limited, unemotional, and matter-of-fact?	
c. Does the teacher use contingent and specific requests to encourage students to stop the misbehavior?	
d. Do the tone and content of the requests threaten or demean students?	

Skill 5. Managing the Think Time® period and debriefing process

Evaluation Questions	Rating and Notes
a. Does the placement of the Think Time® area limit social interactions with the teacher, other students, and materials?	
b. Are the rules for the Think Time® period unnecessarily restrictive?	
c. Does the teacher direct the student to the Think Time® area quickly and efficiently?	
d. Are the social interactions of the teacher during the debriefing process unemotional and matter-of-fact?	
e. Does the teacher keep Think Time® to a minimum?	

Skill 6. Managing the reentry

Evaluation Questions	Rating and Notes
a. Does the teacher respond quickly and efficiently to the student?	
b. Does the teacher demonstrate a willingness to engage the students positively?	
c. Does the teacher provide direction or strategies to the student regarding any missed work?	

(c) prevention of problem behavior, (d) responding to behavior efficiently, (e) managing the Think Time® period and debriefing process, and (f) managing the reentry.

Research Base for Think Time®. In contrast to common classroom management strategies, Think Time® treats the problem behaviors of difficult-to-teach students as a chain rather than an event. In other words, Think Time® is built on the premise that there is an interpersonal relationship between the problem behaviors of difficult-to-teach students and the responses of their teachers (i.e., a reciprocal effect between student-teacher behaviors) as well as an intrapersonal relationship across student and teacher behaviors (i.e., each individual's behavior serves as an antecedent for subsequent behaviors). The net result of these inter- and intrapersonal effects is that problem behaviors develop into chronic behavior patterns or minor problem behaviors escalate into more severe forms.

Also in contrast to traditional classroom management strategies, Think Time® minimizes verbal interactions with students. Students who exhibit problem behaviors tend to have language deficits that make it difficult for them to manage the excessive dialogue of teachers' attempts to adjust student behavior.

Six areas of research underpin Think Time®, including investigations pertaining to (a) developmental psychology, (b) families of children who exhibit antisocial behaviors, (c) individuals with developmental delays, (d) student-teacher interactions in the classroom, (e) the language deficits of students with social adjustment problems, and (f) research conducted on Think Time® itself. The first five areas of research focus on evidence supporting the premise that the problem behaviors of difficult-to-teach students should be viewed as chains rather than events. The last area focuses on studies conducted on Think Time®.

Taken together, research in developmental psychology—with families, with individuals with developmental delays, and in classrooms—on the reciprocal effects of child-adult behaviors suggests that the problem behaviors exhibited by difficult-to-teach students are dyadic events (chains of responses) rather than monadic ones (single events). Because such behaviors may be dyadic events, the intra- and interpersonal reciprocal influences that occur around minor problems may lead to more severe forms of challenging behaviors in the classroom. In addition, research on the language deficits of students with behavioral disorders suggests that many difficult-to-teach students are incapable of dealing with the excessive dialogue of teachers around incidents of problem behavior, resulting in frustration on the part of the students and an increased probability of severe challenging behaviors.

Based on this research, Nelson and his colleagues (Nelson, 1996a; Nelson, Martella, & Garland, 1998) hypothesized that teachers' responses to the minor infractions of students who exhibit behavior problems, responses that might include turning cards, checks after names, or repeated warnings and reprimands, may actually result in intra- and interpersonal reciprocal behavioral sequences in which the responses of both students and teachers become more intense and problematic. If that is the case, the minor classroom problems of students who exhibit unwanted behaviors may serve not only as antecedents for teachers' responses (e.g., reprimands) but also as antecedents for subsequent severe challenging behaviors (see Figure 7.4, left-hand side). Nelson

Figure 7.4 Traditional Classroom Management Systems Versus Think Time®

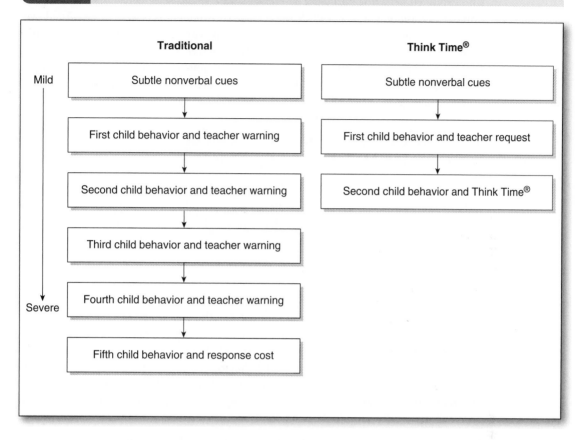

and colleagues also hypothesized that a teacher could cut off interaction to decrease the likelihood of student behavior escalation (see Figure 7.4, right hand-side).

Nelson (1996b) examined the effects of setting clear limits in combination with using Think Time® when trying to change problem behaviors related to the school survival skills, social adjustment, and academic performance of a group of difficult-to-teach students. Comparisons between target students (i.e., those with or at risk of emotional and behavioral disorders) and criterion students (i.e., those without and not at risk of emotional and behavioral disorders) indicated positive effects on the social adjustment (effect size = 0.81), academic performance (effect size = 0.92), and school survival skills (effect size = 0.84) of the target students.

Building on this work, Nelson, Roberts, and Smith (1998) conducted a component analysis to provide more conclusive information on the effects of Think Time® on severe challenging behaviors that require an administrative intervention (e.g., suspension). The results indicated that the strategy alone resulted in a 70% decrease in such behaviors. Finally, Nelson, Gutierrez-Ohrman, Roberts, and Smith (2000) examined the effects of Think Time® on the severe challenging behaviors (behavioral earthquakes) of

24 students with behavior difficulties. The results indicated that the group of students who exhibited behavior problems had fewer severe challenging behaviors following the implementation of Think Time®. If the average treatment effects were extrapolated over the course of the school year, the group of students with emotional and behavioral disorders would have exhibited more than 1,200 fewer severe challenging behaviors. Further, individual students would have exhibited approximately 20 severe challenging behaviors over the course of the school year, compared with more than 90 prior to the implementation of Think Time®.

What Are the Advantages and Disadvantages of Each Group-Oriented Management Approach?

The group management approaches described can be effective in managing a classroom. Each group management approach requires planning similar to planning for instruction. However, each approach has advantages and disadvantages that must be taken into account during the planning process.

Dependent Group Management

Advantages. Dependent group management has the advantage of using group pressure to aid the target student academically or to modify the behavior of a particular student. Dependent group management attempts to get the group as a whole to help the target student to exhibit improved behavior. Social reinforcement delivered by peers can be more powerful than reinforcement delivered by a teacher. Therefore, dependent group management takes advantage of the powerful influence peers can have over their fellow students' behavior.

Disadvantages. The one major disadvantage of dependent group management is the possibility that the target student will become the brunt of threats by his or her peers. The other students could chastise the target student because they all suffer if the target student misbehaves. This disadvantage may be serious enough to prevent teachers from using dependent group management.

Interdependent Group Management

Advantages. Interdependent group management has a long and successful history in education. Clearly, cooperative learning groups are popular in education, and these groups are frequently exposed to interdependent group management. Like dependent group management, interdependent group management, according to the evidence, encourages students to work together more closely, which promotes higher academic performance and cooperation compared with individual management approaches. Similarly, interdependent group management takes advantage of peer pressure to improve the behavior of students in the classroom.

Disadvantages. The disadvantages of interdependent group management are similar to those of dependent group management except that, as opposed to one particular student being the target of ridicule, any student in the group could be subjected to threats. The possibility of threats and ridicule, however, may be less overall for each student when interdependent group management is used than it is for the targeted student in dependent group management.

Independent Group Management

Advantages. Independent group management has several advantages. First, it allows teachers to individualize the consequences for wanted and unwanted behaviors. Some teachers might think it unfair to provide consequences to students for the behavior of others. Second, independent group management is already in practice in classrooms. Grades are based on individual performance. It is rare to see classroom teachers provide a subject grade based on classroom performance as a whole. Third, individual responsibility is usually expected of people in society. Thus, individual group management resembles the situation operating within society in general. Finally, individual group management is effective in changing unwanted behaviors and increasing desirable ones.

Disadvantages. The disadvantages of independent group management are that they do not foster group cooperation and they do not take advantage of peer pressure in solving behavior difficulties. In addition, some students are singled out for reasons other than simply their behavior. Some students may be treated differently due to things beyond their control, such as gender, ethnicity, or physical attributes. Of course, teachers should be aware of such biases and work to prevent them from occurring.

What Are Important Considerations When Using Group-Oriented Management Approaches?

Although each type of group-oriented management approach is different from the others, what ties them together is that they all require the provision of consequences as well as some degree of teacher-student interaction. Because of these similarities, it is possible to discuss in terms relevant to all group-oriented management methods the most appropriate approaches to their implementation. There are three important considerations.

Teachers Should Avoid Negative Traps

Negative traps involve the provision of punishment techniques in such a manner that the negative interactions escalate. For example, imagine that students are not listening to a teacher's instructions, so the teacher reprimands them. Unfortunately, reprimanding the class results in the students becoming more unruly. As the class becomes more unruly, the teacher threatens the students with having to stay after school. Some of the students continue to escalate further by arguing, and the teacher then begins to argue with these students. This escalation continues until the interaction gets out of hand. Figure 7.5 shows this trap, with the teacher and students becoming entangled in an almost endless tug-of-war. A much better response to the class would have been to provide a start-up request: for example, "Everyone's attention, please. Now, let's begin the unit on the Civil War." If a few of the students continue to misbehave, the teacher could then take them aside and handle the problem behaviors on an individual basis away from the class, or the teacher could praise those students who were on task. Traps shown to escalate behaviors include the following (Latham, 1992): (a) criticism (e.g., "You never listen to me"), (b) sarcasm (e.g., "You all are listening so well today"), (c) threats (e.g., "If you don't stop talking, I will keep everyone after school"), (d) logic (e.g., "You know, if you don't listen to me, you will not learn the material and will fail the class. Therefore, I need you all to listen so that you can learn what caused the Civil War"), (e) arguing (e.g.,

Figure 7.5 Reprimands: A Trap for the Unwary

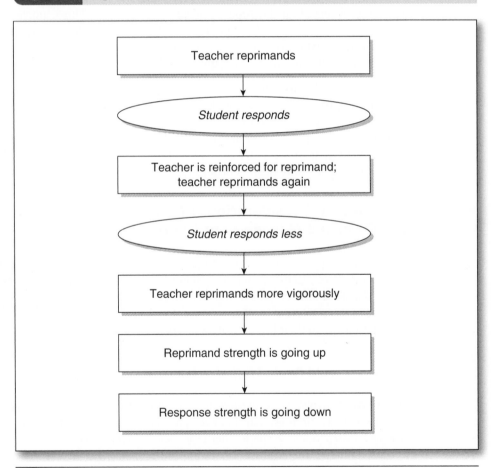

"I don't care if you find the Civil War boring"), (f) questioning (e.g., "How many times do I need to tell everyone to listen?"), (g) physical force (e.g., taking a student who is talking and physically turning her head toward you), and (h) despair or pleading and hopelessness ("I can't continue teaching this way. Could you all please just try for me?").

Teachers Should Actively Practice Positive Interaction Skills

Teachers must attempt to improve the atmosphere of the classroom. The way they can do so is by decreasing negative interactions with students and increasing positive ones. According to Latham (1992), teachers allow 90% of all appropriate behaviors to go unrecognized. Unfortunately, we too often become prone to **negative scanning**, to trying to find students misbehaving. Latham also indicates that teachers are five times more likely to respond to unwanted behaviors as they are to respond to wanted ones.

Teachers Should Use a Teaching Interaction Strategy When Attempting to Correct Unwanted Behavior

This interaction strategy can decrease the probability of a negative interaction with the student. First, teachers should say something positive (if possible) to the students, such as "You all did a good job on your homework." Second, they should briefly describe the problem behavior, saying something such as "Some of you are looking away when I am speaking." Third, teachers should describe the desired alternative behaviors, by saying, for example, "I would like everyone's attention when I am teaching." Fourth, they need to give a reason the new behavior is more desirable: for example, "If everyone listens, tonight's homework will not be too difficult." Fifth, teachers should have the students exhibit the desired behavior. Finally, they should provide positive feedback for the desired behavior, perhaps a praise statement such as "I appreciate you listening when I'm talking."

VIGNETTE REVISITED **Establishing Rules and Routines to Prevent Misbehavior**

After studying classroom management procedures, Ms. Hernandez realizes she should be spending more time teaching students how to behave properly in the classroom. Therefore, on the first and second days of class, she sits down with the students and develops a set of classroom rules. She also goes over classroom routines. Once the rules have been developed and the routines described, Ms. Hernandez models rule-following behavior, coming into the classroom and sitting at a desk ready to begin work. She also models routines such as what to do when one needs to sharpen a pencil or get a drink. Once Ms. Hernandez has modeled the rules and routines for the students, she asks several students to show her proper rule- and routine-following behavior while she discusses why the behavior shown by the students is correct. Ms. Hernandez also discusses examples of not following rules and routines and asks the students why it is important to follow the proper ones instead. Once she is confident all students know what the rules and routines are, she begins to focus on academics while continually reinforcing rule and routine following.

Although Ms. Hernandez has lost two days of instruction at the beginning of the year, she knows she will gain back those days and then some by having a well-managed classroom. Ms. Hernandez also knows that, unfortunately, there will always be a few students who do not follow the rules and routines. Therefore, she decides on the consequences for such behavior. Ms. Hernandez decides to approach such misbehavior as an instructional problem. She understands that only punishing infractions does not teach students what to do instead. Therefore, she establishes a seven-step precorrection routine, which she uses when students fail to follow rules and routines. She also plans to implement Think Time® as an independent group management program if students continue to misbehave.

Summary

Teachers are in a unique and important position to improve student classroom behavior. They are in control of the physical arrangements of the classroom, what the rules and routines will be, and how to respond to both positive and negative classroom behaviors. We know that the best way to improve the classroom behavior of students is to prevent unwanted behaviors from occurring in the first place. We also know that, for some of the students, it is critical to stop the progress of misbehavior as soon as possible. Therefore, teachers should plan how the classroom will be arranged to promote wanted behaviors and minimize unwanted ones, including how the students will be seated, what routines will be required, and how to teach appropriate behaviors through precorrection strategies and social skills training. Everything that happens in the classroom, including the teacher's nonverbal behaviors, will affect the likelihood students will display unwanted behaviors. Teachers must look at each of the aforementioned factors as part of their management plan for the classroom. Doing so will not eliminate all unwanted behaviors but will improve the probability of a positive classroom climate conducive to learning.

As indicated by Hofmeister and Lubke (1990), classroom management is not the creation of an orderly environment but the creation of a learning environment; classroom management does not involve the reduction of misbehavior but the increase of appropriate behavior. Teachers can achieve these goals by carefully planning before problem behaviors occur.

Teachers must also consider the role instructional variables have on student behavior. The next two chapters will describe how instruction can be planned to improve the academic performance and classroom behavior of students.

Key Terms

alterable variables   214

antiseptic bounding   233

antisocial behavior   215

behavioral debriefing   233

classroom structure   214

dependent group management   230

Discussion Questions

1. Why is it important for teachers to understand the concept of nonalterable and alterable variables when teaching students from families with low socioeconomic status (SES)?

2. Why is it critical to attack behavior difficulties in the early grades?

3. As someone who has recently learned about effective classroom design, how would you set up your classroom?

4. Briefly discuss the five main nonverbal communication methods teachers can use to help improve classroom environments.

5. Develop four effective rules. How do your rules have the characteristics of effective rules?

6. Why is it important for teachers to involve students in the rule-making process?

7. Discuss the seven steps involved in precorrection.

8. What are the three types of group contingencies? What are the advantages and disadvantages of each?

9. What are the critical differences between Think Time® and more common classroom management strategies?

10. Many of the students in Mrs. Allen's class have begun acting out at the start of her lesson. What are some ways she can avoid falling into a negative trap?

8

Instructional Variables

Chapter Objectives

After studying this chapter, you should be able to

- illustrate the levels of time,
- explain how teachers can improve their use of allocated time and improve students' engaged and academic learning times,
- depict how to plan for transitions,
- characterize what effective instruction involves,
- explain teaching functions,
- depict the stages of learning,
- illustrate different response prompting strategies,
- depict what an effective lesson plan format involves,
- describe three critical components for providing effective instruction,
- explain what is meant by the term mastery,
- describe differentiated instruction and how it can be used in the classroom,
- illustrate three teaching behaviors that can help reduce behavior problems,
- explain how to complete an academic functional assessment,
- characterize the different evidence-based practices, and
- depict the key features of effective instructional practices.

| **VIGNETTE** | **Improving Behavior by Focusing on Instruction** |

MR. THOMPSON, A FOURTH-GRADE TEACHER, is experiencing difficulty with student behavior in his classroom. He has trouble getting and keeping his students on task and has noticed they are not learning at the rate he would like. He thinks the problem with the students' academic progress has to do with his lack of instructional time. Mr. Thompson has also informally observed that most of the behavior problems he sees occur when there is downtime in the classroom. In other words, when there are managerial tasks to be done, during transitions from one academic topic to another, or during independent work time, there is a high likelihood of behavior problems.

A further difficulty is that students seem to take a long time to transition from an activity such as physical education or recess. He has observed students wandering around aimlessly as well as engaging in play behavior. Unfortunately, transitions are beginning to interfere with instructional activities because the class is constantly 10 to 15 minutes behind schedule.

To further complicate things, Mr. Thompson is concerned with the students who are academically at risk for failure. He is unsure what programs are available to help these students gain important reading skills. Mr. Thompson fears that if something is not done soon, student academic and classroom behavior will suffer. More important, he fears his fourth graders will not learn what they need to know to move to fifth grade. Therefore, Mr. Thompson has begun to look for solutions to his dilemma.

Overview

Classroom management has been considered separately from classroom instruction over the years, yet teachers should think of everything that goes on in the classroom as instruction. Behavior management involves the creation of a successful learning environment. Therefore, teachers should focus their attention on how they provide instruction. Specifically, teachers should instruct in a manner that is consistent with what has been found to be effective through empirical investigation. Teacher performance creates an environment for student learning experiences, which then contribute to positive or negative student performance. The reason it is important to consider student outcomes is that research has demonstrated a strong positive correlation between behavior problems and low academic achievement (Landrum, Tankersley, & Kauffman, 2003). In fact, Payne, Marks, and Bogan (2007) report that behavioral and academic problems are reciprocal in nature. In other words, behavior problems may cause a disruption in academic engagement and, as a result, students may fail to master skills. A classroom with high levels of academic achievement for all students will be a classroom with low levels of behavior difficulties. This point is critical. Students do not come to school hating to be there. Students learn to hate school because they experience more failure than success. As Scott, Nelson, and Liaupsin (2001) note, "academics become aversive" (p. 313). These failures are in large part determined by how well teachers provide instruction to their students. Also, be assured that the more students find the classroom aversive, the more likely they will be to exhibit unwanted behaviors (Payne et al.; Scott et al., 2001).

Effective instruction involves several components that are under a teacher's control, and we know what these components are because research into effective teaching has shown what excellent teacher performance is. Excellent teacher performance comes from having appropriate curriculum pacing, lesson pacing, and transition management (Hofmeister & Lubke, 1990; Marchand-Martella, Blakely, & Schaefer, 2004). As shown in Figure 8.1, these teacher behaviors contribute to instructional momentum. **Instructional momentum** means the students are moving quickly and successfully through the curriculum. Instructional momentum, in turn, reduces student misbehavior. This reduction in unwanted student behavior comes about for at least two reasons (Hofmeister & Lubke). First, when students are successful, they are less likely to misbehave. Second, when there is momentum, students have less time to misbehave. Stated another way, the more downtime (i.e., unstructured activities) students have, the more likely they will be to exhibit misbehavior; the less downtime students have, however, the less likely they will go off task (Hofmeister & Lubke; Witt, LaFleur,

| Figure 8.1 | Instructional Momentum |

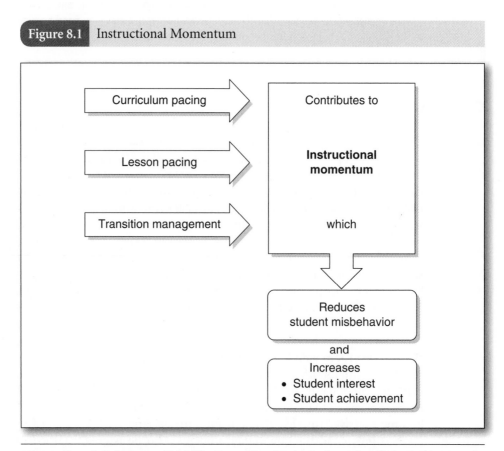

SOURCE: From A. Hofmeister and M. Lubke, *Research Into Practice: Implementing Effective Teaching Strategies.* Copyright © 1990 by Allyn & Bacon. Reprinted by permission.

Naquin, & Gilbertson, 1999). Instructional momentum also increases student interest and student achievement (Hofmeister & Lubke). Again, students who are interested in what is going on in the classroom and who are achieving at high levels are less likely to misbehave than other students. According to Slavin (2009), "Students who are participating in well-structured activities that engage their interests, who are highly motivated to learn, and who are working on tasks that are challenging yet within their capabilities rarely pose any serious management problems" (p. 329). Therefore, the goal for educators is to help students become successful in the classroom.

This chapter will discuss the methods of helping students become successful in the classroom. Here, the levels of time teachers have available and how that time can be maximized are discussed, and this discussion will focus on curriculum and lesson pacing and planning for transitions. In addition, effective instructional methods, teaching functions, and stages of learning will be highlighted. Other important concepts will be described, including response prompting strategies, developing an effective lesson format, and the critical components for effective instruction and mastery. Finally, three effective teaching behaviors that can help reduce behavior problems in the classroom will be discussed, as will academic functional assessments and evidence-based practices.

What Are the Levels of Time?

One of the most important aspects of teaching is the use of the time that teachers are afforded each academic day. The more teachers are able to use their time effectively and efficiently, the more students will learn, and the more progress they will make. "What seems to be important is how time is used in class" (Slavin, 2009, p. 330). Paine, Radicchi, Rosellini, Deutchman, and Darch (1983) liken time to money: (a) time is like money (it can be managed; it can slip through your hands; it is cumulative) and (b) time is money (it is the basic currency in education and is the only resource directly converted into student learning). As Paine et al. note, "You are wealthy or poor in this resource depending on how skilled or unskilled you are in managing your time" (p. 67).

If teachers manage their time well, students will make academic progress and will be less likely to have behavior problems in the classroom. As shown in Figure 8.2, there are four basic **levels of time**—available time, allocated time, engaged time, and academic learning time (Marchand-Martella, Blakely, & Schaefer, 2004).

Available Time

Available time involves the amount of time available for all instruction. In other words, if a school day is 6 hours, the total available time is 6 hours. Schools, however, never have 6 hours available for instruction. Students have recess or other types of breaks, such as lunch; assemblies also take away from available time. Therefore, the amount of time actually available for instruction is less than 6 hours. The amount of time left for teaching academic subjects is allocated time.

Figure 8.2	Levels of Time

Available time: The time available for all instruction
100% of available time = 6 hours

Allocated time: The time a teacher or school delegates for a content/subject area; 79% of available time = 4 hours and 44 minutes

Engaged time: The time students are actively engaged in learning activities; 42% of available time = 2 hours and 31 minutes

Academic learning time: The time when students are engaged in academic tasks and are successful; 17% of available time = 1 hour and 1 minute

Allocated Time

Allocated time is the amount of time a teacher or school delegates for teaching content, for example, for teaching in subject areas such as mathematics, language arts, science, or history. As shown in Figure 8.2, teachers use approximately 79% of the total available time (Hofmeister & Lubke, 1990). In other words, out of a 6-hour day, the amount of time actually allocated for instruction is 4 hours and 44 minutes. Thus, approximately 1 hour and 16 minutes is unused allocated time. Unfortunately, the amount of time *allocated* for content or subject area teaching is not the actual amount of time spent instructing students. Time for transitions (discussed in detail later), for the completion of classroom tasks (e.g., handing out papers or taking roll), and for handling disruptions take away from the teacher's instructional time (i.e., the amount of time the teacher spends providing instruction in one or various subject areas). Possibly due to these disruptions in allocated time, it is not strongly related to student achievement (Wolery, Bailey, & Sugai, 1988).

The problem with not using as much allocated time as possible is that the more downtime there is in the classroom, the higher the likelihood that students will misbehave (Hofmeister & Lubke, 1990; Slavin, 2009; Witt et al., 1999). Management issues also take away from a teacher's instructional time. As behavior problems persist and become worse, teachers have less time to teach and more unused allocated time. The more noninstructional time there is, the more behavior problems there are likely to be.

Fortunately, teachers can have a significant effect on the amount of time they have to instruct. Allocated time can be used fully or poorly, depending on factors such as teacher planning and behavior management skills. According to Hofmeister and Lubke (1990), there are four general areas in which teachers can better plan to use their allocated time. First, teachers should keep sufficient materials and supplies such as workbooks, pencils, paper, handouts, or other lesson materials available. When these materials are not available, teachers waste time locating ample materials for students. Before instruction begins, then, a teacher should prepare all materials and plan how to get them to students.

Second, teachers should have necessary equipment available before teaching a lesson. For example, audiovisual equipment should be in the classroom or be easily accessible. Also, the equipment should be tested before class to make sure it is working properly. Nothing is more frustrating than turning on a digital projector and having a burned-out bulb. Such delays only waste instructional time and allow students to go off task.

Third, materials should be stored in easily accessible areas in the classroom. The organization of materials is critical to preventing delays in finding these materials. Classroom materials should be filed in an orderly fashion that allows easy access for teachers and students. Paine et al. (1983) recommend designating an area in the classroom for collected work and materials and teaching rules for passing and collecting materials. These rules include the following: pass or collect materials quietly, have paper monitors (assigned helpers in the classroom), pick up materials quickly, have paper monitors pass or collect in their zone only, pass or collect materials keeping your hands to yourself, and have monitors return materials to the correct storage area. When one teaches these rules explicitly, students learn what is expected of them, which helps prevent difficulties when students and teachers manage materials in the classroom.

Fourth, the collection and correction of homework should be planned. Hofmeister and Lubke (1990) state that homework checking procedures should take less than five minutes. Paine et al. (1983) recommend a student self-correction station for homework or other seatwork done in the classroom. Again, rules should be developed and taught directly to students so that they can be more successful at the self-correction station. Rules include the following: only one person at each answer key, leave your pens or pencils at your desk (only correcting pens are allowed at the station), check your work quietly, and put all corrected work in the box.

Additional concerns related to allocated time include coming to class prepared and organized. Organized teachers are able to begin class on time and have a minimal number of delays before and during their instruction (Slavin, 2009). Further, Slavin notes that teachers may choose to put a "Do not disturb—learning in progress" sign on their classroom doors to prevent interruptions to instruction. Paine et al. (1983) also suggest finding effective ways to deal with student requests for assistance. If they don't teach students how to seek help, teachers may find that students raise their hands and wait for the teacher, losing precious time to work on other problems or to complete parts of their assignment that they can do at their desk and thus increasing the opportunities for misbehavior. Paine et al. developed an assistance card that could be taped to the end of each student's desk. On one side were the words "please keep working," and on the other were the words "please help me." The sign could be raised so that a person needing help would see the student prompt (please keep working), and the teacher would see his or her prompt (please help me). While waiting, students accessed a "surefire" work folder containing materials that could be done without teacher assistance. Students were taught to work on these materials until the teacher was able to provide assistance.

Engaged Time

Engaged time involves the amount of time students are actively engaged in learning activities; it is the time they spend doing assigned work (Slavin, 2009). Engaged time is also called on-task time. According to Hofmeister and Lubke (1990), students are actively engaged in learning activities an average of 42% of the day, with a range of 25% to 58% (see Figure 8.2). In other words, students spend approximately 2 hours and 31 minutes on task in a school day. Given that students are more likely to misbehave during downtime, teachers must be concerned with the amount of time students are *actually engaged*. Teachers should consider methods of getting and keeping students on task to maximize learning and prevent misbehavior.

Getting and Keeping Students On Task. Latham (1992) sets general guidelines for getting and keeping students on task. According to Latham, the sooner teachers can get students on task, the easier it is to keep them on task. It is also easier to get students back on task when the teacher attempts this as quickly as possible after they go off task. "Students should always have something to do and, once started working, are not interrupted" (Slavin, 2009, p. 333). Therefore, a key to increasing the likelihood of on-task behavior is to get students on task as soon as possible. To achieve this goal, teachers should begin instruction immediately. Unwarranted delays at the beginning of a class period only make off-task behavior more likely. To better manage on-task behavior, teachers should walk around during the instructional time. Paine et al. (1983) also recommend these four steps. First, teachers should "move" or circulate about the classroom in an unpredictable pattern. Second, teachers should scan the classroom, searching for students who are doing well. Third, teachers should use their attention to manage student behavior by praising students' efforts. Circulating and scanning can help achieve this end. Finally, teachers can use the **praise around technique** by praising students around the student who is off task and then, according to Paine et al., following up with the student by providing immediate praise when he or she comes back on task.

Latham (1992) outlines ways to increase the likelihood that students will get on task early in the period and maintain their on-task behavior. First, teachers should state and role-play their expectations. For example, a teacher could tell students that they are expected to work hard throughout the period. If they do so, they will be able to do something different sooner. Role-playing these expectations can be an important step, especially for younger students who can see what on-task behavior looks like. Second, teachers should state and apply consequences for on-task and off-task behavior. When students are on task, every attempt should be made to reinforce that behavior. Praising students for being on task is critical to keeping them on task over time. When students are not on task, a simple redirect to get them on task can be tried. In most instances, the redirect will work. The redirect (or start-up request) should state exactly the behavior the teacher wishes the student to perform, such as, "You need to be working on your math sheet." Finally, teachers should deal proactively with distracters. For example, moving students away from windows or from the back of the room to the front and telling students of the expectations before instruction begins can increase the likelihood of on-task behavior. Paine et al. (1983) recommend teaching rules (or expectations) for various activities in the classroom, modeling them for students, practicing them, and providing ample feedback to ensure that students have learned what to do. After they have learned expectations, a teacher can fade out these procedures, being sure to praise students intermittently when they do what they need to do in the classroom.

Academic Learning Time

Similar to engaged time, **academic learning time** is when students are actively involved in learning activities. Academic learning time, however, also involves the concept of students being *successful* in their learning. As Olson and Platt (2000) note, "For academic progress to occur, students must not only be on-task, but must also achieve at a high accuracy level" (p. 172). Academic learning time is the time when true learning takes place (Marchand-Martella, Blakely, & Schaefer, 2004). Simply being engaged does not mean that students are actually learning. Students can be engaged while making mistakes. When students are making mistakes, they are not learning. Therefore, the old adage that we learn through our mistakes is incorrect. When we make mistakes, we only learn how to make mistakes. On the other hand, when we respond correctly, we are learning how to make the correct response. Unfortunately, the amount of time that students are actually learning is small. As shown in Figure 8.2, academic learning time is approximately 17% of the school day, with a range of 10% to 25% (Hofmeister & Lubke, 1990). Latham (1992) estimates academic learning time at 18%. Therefore, in a school day, only slightly over 1 hour of a 6-hour school day is spent actually learning.

A misconception many have is that, as long as students are paying attention, they are learning. Another is that practice makes perfect. In truth, because we can practice the incorrect responses to a problem, practice does not make perfect. For example, if a student follows an incorrect process for answering math problems, the student could be making the same mistakes consistently. Unless some form of corrective feedback is provided, the student is unlikely to learn the correct process for solving these and similar problems. Once the student has learned the incorrect process of solving math problems, it is much more difficult to teach the student the correct process. Students then become frustrated, and this frustration could lead to unwanted classroom behavior. Instead of assuming that practice makes perfect, teachers would be better served by the saying "perfect practice makes perfect." With this perspective, teachers should aid students continuously in making correct or successful responses while decreasing the likelihood of mistakes. Thus, teachers must closely supervise their students and make sure that they are responding appropriately to assigned material. This supervision requires constant checking for student understanding.

Hofmeister and Lubke (1990) make several suggestions about how to increase the academic learning time of students. First, student involvement must be enhanced.

Teachers can enhance student involvement by connecting their instruction with the students' personal lives. For example, students could practice language arts by writing a story about what they did over the summer break. Second, teachers must make sure that students attend to initial presentations. For example, requiring eye contact during instruction and checking for understanding initially through questioning during a lesson will increase students' attention.

Third, students should be involved in the instructional activity. For example, students can be asked questions throughout instruction, or teachers can use unison responding (described later in this chapter) to engage an entire group of students in the learning process. Fourth, teachers should provide relevant lessons and assignments. Busywork should be avoided because students learn that this work is not very relevant to them. Unfortunately, this attitude could extend to more meaningful tasks. Teachers should attempt to build their instruction around student interests. For example, many students are interested in dinosaurs. Teachers could build a lesson on western geography around the locations where different dinosaur species lived. Also, teachers should focus their instruction on the skills that students most need in their daily lives. Telling time, counting money, and measuring objects are examples of critical skills for students. Finally, teacher instruction should be organized. Lessons can be scripted or outlined. They should be sequenced so there is a logical order to the tasks to be learned, keeping errors to a minimum. Also, instruction should be planned at the students' levels of skill development and rate of learning. Flexible skill grouping for instruction (described later in this chapter) could be used.

Academic learning time is perhaps the most important area of time usage for teachers. In fact, academic learning time "relates most strongly to achievement" in the classroom (Gettinger & Seibert, 2002, p. 3). Teachers can use efficiently all the allocated time available to them, but if students are not successfully engaged in academic learning, this time is wasted. To increase the time they have available to teach and the time during which students can participate in academic learning, teachers must also be aware of the curriculum, lesson pacing, and the time taken for transitions. As stated by Gettinger and Seibert, "Academic learning time is one of the most important correlates of achievement, and its linkage with learning is one of the most consistent findings in educational research" (p. 13).

What Is the Importance of Curriculum and Lesson Pacing?

Curriculum pacing and lesson pacing are important aspects of instruction. **Curriculum pacing** is concerned with the rate at which students progress through the curricula (e.g., basal reading series) or program used in the classroom. **Lesson pacing** deals with the pace at which teachers conduct individual or daily lessons. According to Hofmeister and Lubke (1990), "There is a direct relationship between the amount of material covered and the amount students learn" (p. 42). That is, the more the teacher covers, the more the students learn. The principal objective of both curriculum and lesson pacing, then, is to accelerate the performance of students. If students are accelerated in a particular skill, they become relatively "smart" compared with students who have not been accelerated (Adams & Engelmann, 1996). According to Adams and Engelmann, acceleration is possible if well-designed instruction—teaching more skills in less time with more substantial generalizations—is used. Just because students may be working below grade level does not mean that information should be presented at a slower pace (provided the students are appropriately placed in the curricula or program used).

Effective schools recognize that they must establish a well-defined, systematically developed, multiyear curriculum of goals and objectives that, when mastered, enables any student to perform at high (criterion) levels. To accommodate any student, such a curriculum must include multiple entry points determined by objective, clearly defined placement procedures; frequent assessments of mastery or progress to date; and built-in systems to allow for adequate practice, correction, and remediation as well as methods of acceleration for students learning at a quicker pace. To educate all students well, effective schools acknowledge that, in each subject area, there can be only one curriculum sequence to which all students and staff adhere. Other programs or technologies are valued only to the extent that they build on or extend the core curriculum. This additional effort might occur, for example, to meet unique assessment or standards requirements in a given state (Marchand-Martella, Blakely, & Schaefer, 2004, pp. 306–307).

How Do We Plan for Transitions?

Transitions, which occur for a variety of reasons throughout the school day, take up much of the allocated time. Witt et al. (1999) report that transitions occur an average of 15 times per day. If these transitions take an average of 10 minutes each, students spend 2.5 hours in transition. Therefore, transitions would take more than 2 hours away from students' academics. For example, transitioning from recess to the classroom takes time, and the time it takes for students to come in from recess and get seated and ready to work cuts into the teacher's allocated time. Likewise, lunchtime transitions also tend to decrease the amount of time available to instruct students. Transitions from one topic to another, such as from reading to math, can also adversely affect allocated time. Essentially, any time students break from one activity to go to another is considered noninstructional in nature. Interestingly, many behavior management problems occur during these noninstructional transitions (Witt et al.). "Transitions are the seams of class management at which classroom order is most likely to come apart" (Slavin, 2009, p. 334). Therefore, teachers should attempt to decrease their transition times as much as possible. Doing so achieves two things. First, decreasing transition times increases the time teachers have to instruct, which can enhance student learning. Slavin notes early research on the importance of managing transitions: teachers' efficiency at managing transitions between activities was positively related to their students' achievement. Second, decreasing transition times can decrease behavior management problems because students simply have less time to misbehave (Slavin; Witt et al.).

To help with these transitions, Paine et al. (1983) recommend teaching students how to transition and posting these expectations on a chart. Teaching students to move quietly, put books away and get what they need for the next activity, move chairs quietly, and keep hands and feet to themselves can actually decrease transition times because students learn what to do in an effective and efficient manner.

In addition, several other steps can be taken to decrease transition times (see Table 8.1). First, teachers should set a goal for the desired length of each transition (Witt et al., 1999). For example, a teacher may wish to decrease the time it takes for transitions by half, with the goal of having transitions completed within five minutes. Second, students should be prepared in advance for the transition (Hofmeister & Lubke, 1990). For example, students can be told that they will be transitioning in a few minutes. Third, the teacher should signal for student attention (Witt et al.). For example, the teacher could ask for all students to look at her, and once all students are attentive, she could then move to the next step. Fourth, the activity should be brought to a close (Hofmeister & Lubke). For example, the teacher should summarize the lesson and have students put materials away before the transition begins. Fifth, the teacher should tell the students what they need to do (Witt et al.). For example, he might give the following directions: "I need you to put your reading materials away and take out your math books" or "I need you to form a single line at the door and walk down the hall to the library when the bell rings." According to Hofmeister and Lubke, the same type of signal should be used for each transition. Sixth, the teacher should monitor the time it takes for the transition to occur (Witt et al.). Seventh, the teacher must monitor which students are following the instruction and prompt those who are off task (Witt et al.). Eighth, the teacher should provide feedback to the students who meet the time goal and instruct the students who were too slow to try to transition within the goal time (Witt et al.). For example, the teacher could say, "Great job to those of you who have your books on your desk and are ready to get started. Those of you who are not ready yet, let's try to beat the clock tomorrow." Finally, the teacher should begin the lesson when all students are ready to learn (Witt et al.).

Decreasing transition times can free up many hours for instruction. For example, if a teacher is able to decrease her transitions from 10 minutes to 5 minutes, the teacher gains

Table 8.1 Steps to Decrease Transition Times

1. Set a goal for the desired length of each transition.
2. Prepare students in advance for the transition.
3. Signal for student attention.
4. Bring the activity to a close.
5. Tell the students exactly what needs to be done.
6. Monitor the time it takes for the transition to occur.
7. Monitor which students are following the instruction and prompt those who are off task.
8. Provide feedback to students who meet the time goal, and instruct students who were too slow to try to transition within the goal time.
9. Begin the lesson when all students are ready to learn.

1 hour and 15 minutes of instructional time. Over a year, the teacher would gain approximately 237 hours of instructional time. Essentially, this gain in hours is equivalent to almost 40 extra days of instruction. Therefore, although moving from 10-minute to 5-minute transitions may seem like a small step, in the end a great deal of time is gained.

Figure 8.3 shows a transition-planning sheet developed by Hofmeister and Lubke (1990). As shown in the figure, two types of activities are to be listed (i.e., between and within activities). Between activities could include moving from math to reading, recess

Figure 8.3	Transitions

Time of day	Description of transition			Length of transition
	Between activities		Within activities	
	From	To	(Describe)	
	→			
	→			
	→			
	→			
	→			
	→			
	→			
	→			
	→			
	→			
	→			
	→			
	→			
	→			
	→			
	→			

School _____ Date _____

Teacher _____ Observer _____

SOURCE: From A. Hofmeister and M. Lubke, *Research Into Practice: Implementing Effective Teaching Strategies.* Copyright © 1990 by Allyn & Bacon. Reprinted by permission.

to music, or lunch to science. Within activities could include passing out independent reading assignments, passing out math worksheets, or returning graded homework assignments. On the planning form, the teacher documents the time of day the transition occurs, what the transition involves, and the length of time it takes for the transition. At the end of the day, the teacher calculates the total time it takes for transitions. Then, a teacher who wishes to decrease transition times can readily determine those transitions that take too much time. At this point, teachers would use the transition planning sheet shown in Figure 8.3 to go through the planning process.

What Is Effective Instruction?

There continues to be an intense concern about the need to improve education. The focus of this concern often centers on economic, cultural, and social issues. People tend to blame failures on the cultural and socioeconomic factors of our communities, a lack of support from parents or families, and other factors out of our direct control. Failures in the schools are often seen as student and family failures. Effective teachers, however, assume full responsibility for their students and classrooms and focus on variables over which they have control (Carnine, Silbert, Kame'enui, & Tarver, 2010; Heward, 2009; Marchand-Martella, Blakely, & Schaefer, 2004; Meese, 2001).

The cry for educational reform in both general and special education classrooms is heard across the United States; reform efforts tend to focus on evaluation methods, extended school days or years, reduced class size, increased teacher pay, technology in every classroom, and the like. Much of the failure seen in schools can be attributed to curricular and instructional deficits, however (Carnine et al., 2010; Marchand-Martella, Blakely, & Schaefer, 2004). Thus, attention must be paid to effective instructional practices and the teaching functions of which they are composed. Instruction does matter in the classroom; "setting up an effective learning environment is a matter of knowing a set of techniques that any teacher can learn and apply" (Slavin, 2009, p. 329).

What Are Teaching Functions?

Teaching functions are classroom experiences that move students from a lack of skill mastery (no or little knowledge) to mastery (demonstration of skills or knowledge at high levels) (Hofmeister & Lubke, 1990). In a synthesis of the research on effective teaching based on the work of Rosenshine and Stevens (1986), Hofmeister and Lubke consolidate teaching functions into five groups: (a) daily reviews and prerequisite checks, (b) presentation of new content, (c) guided practice, (d) independent practice, and (e) weekly and monthly reviews (see Figure 8.4). These teaching functions are known to affect student achievement in a positive manner (Sabornie & DeBettencourt, 2009). Each of these teaching functions is described below.

| Figure 8.4 | Major Teaching Functions |

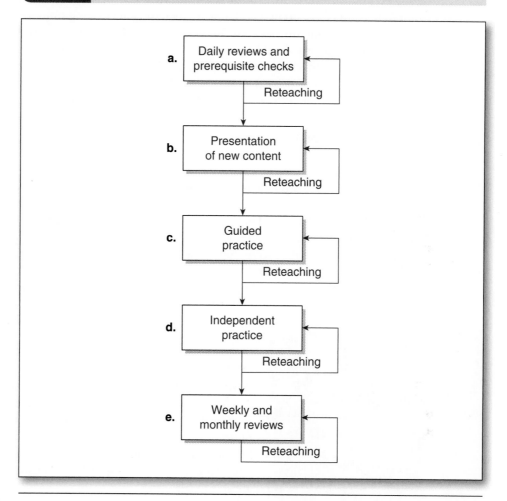

Daily Reviews

Effective teachers review material covered in previous lessons, check on homework completed the night before, check on the prerequisite skills needed for the upcoming lesson, and reteach, if necessary (Hofmeister & Lubke, 1990; Sabornie & DeBettencourt, 2009). To review material, teachers may provide several problems on the board or overhead that require written responses from students. This activity helps establish a work-oriented tone and gives students an opportunity to be successful (error rates should be low). Homework completed the night before should be checked promptly; going over homework serves as an additional review for students. Effective teachers try to prevent errors from occurring in upcoming lessons by making sure that the necessary prerequisite skills are mastered. For example, to solve more advanced word problems in math, students should have mastered basic math skills and more simplistic word problems. If students do not show mastery during the daily review, reteaching is necessary. It is better to delay the introduction of new material than to place students in a remedial situation, having them experience errors rather than successful learning.

Presentation of New Content

After the daily review, effective teachers present new content. They provide clear goals and objectives for the lesson, step-by-step instructions and directions, careful **modeling** (showing students how to do the skill), plenty of examples, and a check for student understanding (Hofmeister & Lubke, 1990; Sabornie & DeBettencourt, 2009). The presentation of new content is often referred to as teacher demonstration (Marchand-Martella & Martella, 2009; Meese, 2001), teacher modeling, or "I do." Effective teachers are clear about their objectives for the lesson. They organize material so that one step builds on the mastery of the previous step, giving clear and explicit instructions along the

Teachers should frequently check for student understanding of new content.

way. During modeling of new information, effective teachers model or demonstrate the skill (when appropriate). This step is called the "I do" step because the teacher is explicitly showing the students what to do ("Now watch me"). Numerous examples should be demonstrated to ensure that students are learning this new information. Checking for student understanding may involve having the students answer questions in unison (compared with saying, "Do you understand?"), having students summarize the main points, and reteaching if necessary (again based on what students are able to perform).

Guided Practice

Following the presentation of new content, effective teachers provide opportunities for guided practice. **Guided practice** is also called prompted practice (Meese, 2001), guided rehearsal (Sabornie & DeBettencourt, 2009), or the "we do" of instruction because the teacher is actively participating in the learning with the students ("let's do some together"). Guided practice is referred to as the "bridge" between the presentation of new information and independent practice (Hofmeister & Lubke, 1990). Students must traverse this bridge to ensure that they can perform the skill when they get to the other side (independent practice, or doing it on their own). Guided practice involves asking questions and giving feedback (Marchand-Martella & Martella, 2009; Meese). This acquisition stage of learning (during which students are first acquiring the skill) should have focused questions that have only one correct answer. Unison responding, response cards (preprinted cards with answers), or chalkboards or laminate boards on which students write their answers can be used to provide practice opportunities for students. These procedures focus on group responding, thereby giving everyone an opportunity to respond and receive feedback. Teacher feedback (praise or error corrections) is critical in guided practice, and, to ensure successful student learning, this feedback should be immediate (as close to the response as possible) and specific (telling the students what they have done the right way or what they need to do to remediate).

Independent Practice

According to Hofmeister and Lubke (1990), "The transition from guided practice to independent practice should not occur until students are at least 80% successful in their guided practice" (p. 61). That is, students should not move into the **independent practice** or "you do" phase of learning until they can demonstrate success with the teacher (during the "we do" phase). During independent practice, students may do seatwork tasks or other practice activities, such as working on the computer or reading to a peer tutor (Meese, 2001). Teachers must still actively monitor student performance and reteach if necessary (Sabornie & DeBettencourt, 2009).

Effective teachers provide homework only when students are successful, that is, during independent practice. Students should not receive homework that they do not know how to do. They should be able to do the work on their own with a high degree of success. New material should not be encountered; high error rates should not be shown (Hofmeister & Lubke, 1990). Likewise, cooperative learning activities (with students working together on a common assignment) should only be introduced when students have the skills to perform the task. Cooperative learning should be used during independent practice to ensure that all group members can work together and be successful when performing the activity.

Interestingly, Martella (2009) provided a high school student's perspective on homework. She noted three important points about assigning homework (Cooper, 1989, was cited as a foundational paper for these recommendations): (a) Homework should be sent home only after students have mastered the information in school, (b) homework should not exceed two hours per night, and (c) homework should not be assigned before a test day. She noted the stress that ensues when students bring home material they do not know how to do or have so much homework that they cannot possibly do it all and spend time with their families and friends or participate in extracurricular activities. Perhaps we should listen to our students more often.

Weekly and Monthly Reviews

Weekly and monthly **reviews** help ensure that students have opportunities to perform the skills over time so that skills are not forgotten (Hofmeister & Lubke, 1990). For example, weekly comprehensive mastery tests help students maintain skills. If skill atrophy is shown, reteaching is warranted. Reteaching involves all three learning phases—"I do, we do, you do"—and gives the students more opportunities to learn and practice the skills. It is critical to provide this distributed practice so that students have opportunities to perform the skill and receive feedback over time.

What Are the Stages of Learning?

In addition to the teaching functions, teachers should also keep in mind five **learning stages** when planning lessons for students. These learning stages are acquisition, proficiency, maintenance, generalization, and adaptation (Gargiulo & Metcalf, 2010). Figure 8.5 shows these stages of learning.

Figure 8.5	Stages of Learning

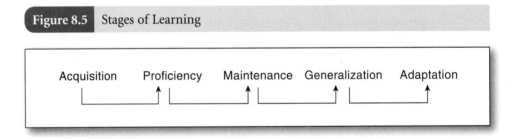

Acquisition Stage

The **acquisition stage** is the first stage of learning; it is the entry point when one learns a skill. Assessment scores in this stage may range from 0% to 80% (Gargiulo & Metcalf, 2010). Students typically have little or no knowledge about the task at hand and require some level of teacher assistance (Meese, 2001). The most effective way of getting students to learn a skill is by following the teaching functions noted previously, placing particular emphasis on the presentation of new content, guided practice, and independent practice. This stage of learning is highly teacher directed; unison responding and frequent teacher questioning are requirements to ensure increased opportunities for students to respond and receive feedback. When effective instruction is delivered at the acquisition stage of learning, errors are diminished and the chances of future generalization and mainte-nance of the skill are enhanced. At the end of the acquisition stage, students should perform the skill at a high rate of accuracy, usually 80% to 90% (Wolery et al., 1988). These students, however, may not be fluent in skill performance or able to perform the skill under different situations (generalization). For example, given a worksheet of 10 double-digit addition problems, the student completes the problems with two errors and takes five minutes to complete the activity. Therefore, once acquisition is achieved, students must move to the proficiency stage of learning.

Proficiency Stage

The **proficiency stage** of learning follows acquisition; that is, once students have acquired a skill, they must be able to perform the skill at a fluent or automatic level (Gargiulo & Metcalf, 2010; Meese, 2001). Teaching at this stage can incorporate drill and practice activities, fluency building (e.g., time trials using precision teaching), and less teacher-directed instruction. Peer tutoring or computer-assisted instruction may be used to provide additional feedback and practice to students. Students could engage in the repeated reading of a story to improve their reading speed. All these procedures help produce fluent student responding. Wolery et al. (1988) discuss such objectives as duration and latency of response during this stage of learning. Thus, the focus is on the rate of learning or the time it takes to perform a particular skill. Revisiting the previous example of a teacher giving a student a worksheet of 10 double-digit addition problems, we would see that a student in the proficiency stage would complete the problems in one minute with no errors.

Maintenance Stage

According to Meese (2001), "As students become proficient with a new skill or concept, teachers must help them retain the material over time" (p. 178). The **maintenance stage** of learning involves periodic practice and review of the skill to ensure that students maintain skill mastery over time. Instruction is no longer needed, but practice is important (Wolery et al., 1988). Homework and seatwork activities are provided to keep students practicing and familiar with the task at hand. Students must have opportunities to continue to perform the skill; if not, the skill may atrophy (Gargiulo & Metcalf, 2010). So a student in the maintenance stage of learning could be given that worksheet of 10 double-digit addition problems a week later to complete as homework.

Generalization Stage

Many consider the **generalization stage** to be the most important stage of learning because, in it, students use their newly learned skills in novel situations. Gargiulo and Metcalf (2010) refer to this stage of learning as the transfer of learning. If we were to extend the previous example, we would say that a student at the generalization stage is able to use the skills acquired from completing math worksheets to calculate the answers to double-digit addition problems in story problems or during a math fact game. Wolery et al. (1988) note that, for a skill to be considered mastered, the student must perform it in different settings (a student exhibits appropriate social skills in other classrooms and in the community), across different persons (a student is able to ask for help from another teacher and a job supervisor), across new or similar behaviors (a student exhibits a reduction in swearing after learning to self-manage talking outbursts), or with differing materials (a student is able to read the newspaper after being taught to read in a basal reader). Teachers may ask for the help of teachers, parents, or other students to prompt or praise others when skills are demonstrated in the natural environment (Meese, 2001).

Adaptation Stage

The fifth and highest stage of learning is the **adaptation stage,** in which students learn to "categorize, make decisions, see relationships/analogies, analyze, estimate, compare/contrast, show flexibility, and identify items that are irrelevant" (Gargiulo & Metcalf, 2010, p. 237). This problem-solving stage of learning requires the mastery of prerequisite skills. These skills build on one another and are utilized to solve more complex problems. Students learn to expand or extend their knowledge to do these higher-order thinking skills. At this stage, students should reflect or think about what they are doing and connect their learning to previous experiences (Gargiulo & Metcalf).

What Are Response Prompting Strategies?

Response prompting strategies are similar to what Vygotsky called "scaffolding." These strategies allow teachers to teach while decreasing the chances of students making errors and increasing their chances of success. As stated in Chapter 5, there are several prompting and fading strategies that can be used for behavior issues: antecedent prompt and test, most-to-least prompting, antecedent prompt and fade, least-to-most prompting, graduated guidance, and time delay. These strategies can also be used to teach academic skills.

Antecedent Prompt and Test Procedure

The **antecedent prompt and test procedure** can be used to teach academic skills: teachers prompt students during instruction and then provide them with practice or test trials after removing all prompts. As stated in Chapter 5, this procedure involves three steps: "I do" (model), "we do" (guided practice), and "you do" (independent practice). For example, the teacher presents a prompt such as "That word is *blue.*" Next, the teacher performs the skill or task with the student or presents a test or practice trial. This test or practice trial can occur immediately after the initial prompt or sometime later and could involve the teacher saying something like the following: "That word is *blue.* What word?" Correct independent responses are then reinforced: "Yes, that word is *blue.*" Incorrect responses are corrected and feedback is provided: "That word is *blue.* Say it with me. *Blue.* What word?"

Most-to-Least Prompting

As discussed previously, **most-to-least prompting** involves decreasing assistance to a student in a progressive fashion (Cooper, Heron, & Heward, 2007; Wolery et al., 1988) and creating a prompt hierarchy. For example, the teacher could begin by guiding the student's hand when the student writes the letter "A." Once the student is able to meet a predetermined criterion for this prompt (e.g., freely moves hand with teacher with no resistance for three consecutive trials), a less intrusive prompt in the hierarchy is provided, such as the teacher placing his or her hand on the student's elbow to guide the writing of the letter. This prompt continues until the student can perform the skill independently, with the least intrusive level of prompting, such as telling the student to write the letter on his or her own.

Antecedent Prompt and Fade Procedure

You will recall that the **antecedent prompt and fade procedure** involves providing a more intrusive prompt on initial instructional trials and then fading out the prompt in a systematic manner (Cooper et al., 2007; Wolery et al., 1988). For example, to teach a student to discriminate between *b* and *d*, the teacher could move from pointing to every *b* and asking the student to color each one red to pointing to just some of the *b*'s. As another example, imagine a teacher wants to teach a student how to write her name. Initially, the teacher physically guides the student's hand through the process. Once the student seems to be moving her hand appropriately to write her name, the teacher provides less pressure on the student's hand. Again, once the student is able to continue to write her name, the teacher provides even less pressure until the teacher's hand is moving just above the student's hand. If the student makes a mistake, the teacher provides an error correction, such as "You put the *m* before the *o* in your name. Let's go back and try again." The decision of when to move from one level of prompt to another is not typically defined (Wolery et al.). Therefore, this decision is based on teacher judgment. As stated in Chapter 5, a critical aspect of this strategy is to assess whether student errors increase as prompts are faded. If so, the more intrusive prompt may need to be re-implemented.

Least-to-Most Prompting

As you will recall, **least-to-most prompting** involves increasing assistance when a student does not perform a behavior (Cooper et al., 2007; Wolery et al., 1988). For example, a teacher could define a list of prompts from verbal (least) to full physical (most) prompts. The teacher may provide an instruction to copy the material from the board. The teacher waits for a predetermined time (response interval) to see if the student begins to copy the material. If the student makes a mistake or does not copy from the board, the teacher moves to the next level of prompt, such as a verbal and gestural prompt (e.g., verbalizing to the student to copy from the board while pointing to the board and then to the student's paper). If the student continues to make mistakes or does not begin copying within the response interval, the teacher moves to the next level of prompt, such as a verbal, gestural, and light physical prompt (e.g., touching the student on the shoulder). If the student copies the material from the board when the initial instruction to copy from the board is provided, the student is reinforced. In essence, the student determines the level of prompt that will be provided by his or her behavior.

Graduated Guidance

As you learned, **graduated guidance** is similar to the most-to-least prompting procedure except that it involves a more fluid movement from the highest level of prompt to the lowest level (Cooper et al., 2007; Miltenberger, 2007; Wolery et al., 1988). For example, when a student is being taught to write her name, the teacher provides a hand-over-hand physical prompt at first while the student is attempting to write. As soon as the student is writing more independently, the teacher immediately removes this level of prompt. The level of prompt provided is dependent on the student's level of need.

Time Delay

Recall that the **time delay** prompt involves presenting for several trials two prompts at the same time: an initial prompt and the prompt to which you ultimately want the students to respond (Wolery et al., 1988). Then, a time delay is provided between the two prompts (constant time delay), or the time delay between the two prompts is gradually increased (progressive time delay) on subsequent learning trials (Cooper et al., 2007; Wolery et al.). For example, suppose a student will not provide the answer to math problems unless the teacher specifically requests each answer. Initially, the teacher presents math division problems on cards and, at the same time, asks, "What is the answer?" After these beginning trials, the teacher holds up each card and waits for a response. If the student provides the correct response before the verbal prompt, the student is reinforced. If the student provides an incorrect response before or after the prompt, the teacher goes through an error correction procedure that includes modeling ("The answer is 12"), leading ("Say the answer with me. 12"), and testing ("What is the answer?") and then puts the card in the pile of problems to be retested. If the student does not respond within the delay period, the teacher provides the prompt (e.g., "What is the answer?"). If the student answers correctly after this prompt, the student is reinforced, but the response does not count toward the criterion for completion of the task (in other words, the cards can be put back into the pile of problems that have not been answered correctly before the prompt was provided). If the student still does not respond to the delayed prompt, whatever was used as a consequence for the correct responses should be reviewed.

With the progressive time delay procedure, the teacher may provide the instruction to provide an answer at 0 seconds initially over five trials, then at 1 second for three trials, then at 2 seconds for the next three trials, and so on.

What Is an Effective Lesson Plan Format?

Teachers use lesson plans to deliver instruction on a daily basis. One strategy helpful in the effective implementation of lesson plans is direct instruction, which emphasizes fast-paced and well-sequenced instruction typically delivered to small groups of students who are given many opportunities to respond and receive feedback (Adams & Engelmann, 1996; Marchand-Martella, Blakely, & Schaefer, 2004; Meese, 2001). Teachers use repetition and emphasize engaged time, pacing, and effective error corrections. An effective lesson plan format is shown in Table 8.2 (as noted by Meese). Its elements should be familiar, given the teaching functions previously described and the effective instructional cycle.

Table 8.2 Example of an Effective Lesson Plan Format

Lesson Plan Element	Contents
Opening the lesson	<ul><li>Gain student attention.</li><li>Review or summarize previous learning.</li><li>Remind students of important rules.</li><li>State the purpose of the lesson.</li><li>State why the skill should be learned.</li></ul>
Demonstrating the new skill or concept	<ul><li>Break the skill into a careful sequence of steps.</li><li>Model steps to students.</li></ul>
Giving guided practice	<ul><li>Provide numerous opportunities to practice.</li><li>Ask questions.</li><li>Use choral responding.</li><li>Give feedback.</li></ul>
Providing independent practice	<ul><li>Provide seatwork or other practice opportunities directly related to the lesson.</li><li>Actively monitor performance.</li></ul>
Closing the lesson	<ul><li>Review or summarize the main points learned.</li><li>Remind students of the usefulness of the information.</li><li>Provide specific directions on what will happen next.</li></ul>
Evaluating the lesson	<ul><li>Provide formative evaluation. (Have students accomplished the objectives of the lesson?)</li><li>Provide summative evaluation. (Have students accomplished the objectives of multiple lessons following a period of instruction?)</li></ul>

What Are Three Critical Components for Providing Effective Instruction in the Classroom?

Carnine et al. (2010) and Watkins and Slocum (2004) describe three critical components for providing effective instruction in the classroom. They are (a) organization of instruction, (b) program design, and (c) teacher presentation techniques. Each of these components is described below.

Organization of Instruction

Before focusing on the curricula and how to deliver effective instruction in the classroom, teachers must ensure that the organization of the classroom is efficient and appropriate for students. Three key elements should be considered: (a) time in the classroom, (b) scheduling, and (c) arranging materials. First, as previously noted, the time in the classroom (engaged time and academic learning time) needs to be examined and maximized to ensure better student outcomes. The more students are actively and successfully engaged, the more they will learn. Second, an emphasis must be made on academics and curriculum-related activities; thus, this time must be scheduled in the classroom. Finally, how the physical setting is arranged and how instructional materials are provided can also affect how instruction is delivered in the classroom. The organization of instruction can be compared to establishing and maintaining effective roadways. Without a safe place to travel, we would find driving our cars difficult, if not impossible.

Program Design

After teachers examine the organization of instruction (the "roadways for driving a car"), they should turn their attention to the programs or curricula used in the classroom ("the car"). The "car" should be reliable and run smoothly. It should be able to go down the road without fail and do so efficiently. The same is true of program design. The curricula teachers use in the classroom should have the following key elements for more effective use in the classroom: (a) specifying objectives, (b) devising strategies, (c) developing teaching procedures, (d) selecting examples, (e) sequencing skills, and (f) providing practice and review. First, the program should state what will be taught and describe teaching objectives using observable behaviors that are amenable to direct measurement (saying that students will learn to appreciate literature is not enough; it is better to specify reading rate per minute and accuracy levels, for example). Second, according to Carnine et al. (2010), students should rely on using strategies rather than memorizing information. These strategies (e.g., learning sounds and blending) can be used to tackle new learning tasks (e.g., sounding out unknown words), which increases general performance. When they teach strategies, teachers get much more learning from their students than if they taught one skill and got one skill; now, their students can do many more things than were actually taught.

Third, after specifying the objectives and devising the strategies, a good program specifies the formats for how teachers will actually present the information to students. This element relates to the teaching procedures used. These formats should be specific, so teachers do not have to guess how to present the information to students. Formats should be easy for students to understand and contain only one skill at a time so as to decrease the chance of student error. Some programs provide scripting for teachers to follow. Fourth, skills should be sequenced to avoid unnecessary errors and promote efficient learning. Carnine et al. (2010) recommend the following:

1. Preskills of a strategy are taught before the strategy itself is presented.

2. Instances that are consistent with the strategy are introduced before exceptions.

3. High-utility skills are introduced before less useful ones.

4. Easy skills are taught before more difficult ones.

5. Strategies and information likely to be confused are not introduced at the same time.

For example, teachers should not teach the letters and sounds "b" and "d" at the same time, because they look and sound similar and could promote confusion (and reversals!). Carnine et al. (2010) note that the most critical principle is teaching components of a strategy before the entire strategy is introduced.

Finally, the program should provide ample opportunities for practice and review. Repetitions are necessary because students are naive and need to practice correctly. (As previously discussed, it is perfect practice that makes perfect, not simply practice that makes perfect.)

Teacher Presentation Techniques

After examining the organization of instruction (the "roadways for driving a car") and program design ("the car"), we turn our attention to how to "drive the car." We can have the best car in the world and the smoothest and safest roadways around, but if we do not know how to drive the car, we cannot take the car down the road. Likewise, we could be the best driver in the world, but without a good car to drive, we cannot access the roadways. Teachers need all three components: good organization in the classroom, a good curriculum, and good instructional delivery. They can take a great curriculum and ruin it by not knowing how to present instruction to students. How teachers present instruction in the classroom includes many key elements: (a) small group instruction, (b) unison oral responding, (c) wait time, (d) pacing, (e) monitoring, (f) diagnosis and correction, and (g) motivation.

First, small group instruction should be used. These groups should be formed using homogeneous and **flexible skill grouping**. That is, students are grouped according to skill but can move into other groups depending on their skill performance. Grouping this way is very efficient for teachers; they have more engaged and academic learning time because students are being successful. Second, when small groups are used, **unison oral responding**, another opportunity for all students to respond together and to receive feedback from the teacher, should be conducted. Third, wait time is critical to the effective delivery of instruction. **Wait time** (also called "think time") gives students an opportunity to think about the answer before they actually say it. To provide wait time opportunities, teachers use signals (cues that prompt student responses). Without these cues, higher-performing students would monopolize the instructional sessions, jumping to the answer before other students could respond.

Fourth, pacing should be varied and fast (providing more opportunities for students to respond and receive feedback). So-called perky pacing contributes to better student achievement and decreased behavior problems. Students do not have time to go off task. Fifth, monitoring student performance is critical. Teachers can monitor student performance while students respond in unison (are they correct and responding together?). Individual turns should be provided after groups respond, and these individual responses should be firm (i.e., a student should say it like she or he knows it). This requirement helps teachers to check individual student performance (another monitoring approach). Names should always be used at the end of the instruction provided to individual students (e.g., "Read the next sentence, Joseph" rather than "Joseph, read the next sentence"). This tactic ensures that all students will pay attention to the task at hand. Sixth, diagnosis and correction should be maximized. **Error correction procedures** should focus on providing an effective model (e.g., "That word is *brother*"), a lead ("Say it with me. Brother"), a test (e.g., "What word?"), and a delayed test (e.g., "Starting over") to ensure firm responding. Other error correction procedures can be used for more advanced items but are beyond the scope of this book. Finally, increasing student motivation should be key to instructional delivery. Students respond well to praise. Saying "yes" to the correct answers provided by students provides them with yet another repetition of hearing the correct answer and tells them that what they said was correct ("yes, the word is *brother*" or "yes, *brother*"). Contrived reinforcers (as noted in Chapter 1) can be used initially and then faded out and replaced by more naturally occurring reinforcers to maximize student performance.

What Is Mastery?

Mastery involves performing skills at high, successful levels. Engelmann (2007) likens mastery to a stairway, saying "Mastery is the guarantee that students are able to reach each stair without falling" (p. 48). Effective teachers carefully design their instruction toward this goal (or use curricula specifically designed for this purpose). Engelmann recommends that teachers examine first-time corrects to ensure that mastery will be achieved. Each time a task is presented, students either respond correctly (in unison) or incorrectly (one or more students provide the wrong response or do not answer). Four criteria allow precise interpretation of how students respond during the lesson.

1. Students should be at least 70% correct on information that is being introduced for the first time. (If they are only at 50%, they are at chance level and are guessing.)

2. Students should be at least 90% correct on skills taught earlier in the program sequence (this assumes previous skill mastery).

3. At the end of the lesson, all students should be "virtually 100% firm on all tasks and activities" (p. 50).

4. Student error rates should be low enough to ensure that teachers have sufficient time to complete lessons.

To calculate **first-time corrects**, teachers count the number of tasks in which students provide responses and the number of times students respond correctly and then divide the correct responses by the total responses, multiplying by 100 for a percentage of first-time corrects. So, if a teacher provides 10 tasks and the students respond correctly to 8 of these tasks, the percentage of first-time corrects is 80%. Ensuring skill mastery leads to higher academic performance, which, in turn, leads to better behavior in the classroom. Students who are successful in school are less likely to be disruptive in class.

What Is Differentiated Instruction?

Differentiated instruction means teachers adjust instruction to meet the unique needs of students (Smith & Tyler, 2010). They "ramp up" their efforts when students are first learning skills and "ramp down" their efforts when students are performing skills independently. "Differentiated instruction focuses on whom we teach, where we teach, and how we teach. Its primary goal is ensuring teachers focus on processes and procedures that ensure effective learning for varied individuals" (Tomlinson & McTighe, 2006, p. 3). Teachers adjust instruction to address such things as student readiness, student interest, instructional formats, and time for learning; they provide frequent questioning strategies and deliver the presentation of information in different ways. An integral part of differentiated instruction is formative assessment, which means teachers monitor student learning progress on a frequent basis to make informed decisions about how effective their teaching is and how to improve it (Salend, 2011). One program, *Read to Achieve* (Marchand-Martella & Martella, 2010a; Marchand-Martella & Martella, 2010b) offers differentiated instructional guidelines for every unit across two courses of study—content area and advanced narrative text. Students are classified as at mastery or approaching mastery based on their performance on end-of-unit assessments, and instructional recommendations are provided based on how individual students do. Recommendations for differentiated instruction are also provided for the English language learner (ELL).

Teachers should think of differentiated instruction along a continuum, from more teacher-directed instruction when students are naive learners to more student-centered approaches when students have the skills to learn from these effectively. Two broad areas of differentiated instruction include multitiered interventions (described in Chapter 12) and technology integration, a strategy that infuses technology whenever possible because students find computers and other technological advances very reinforcing (Smith & Tyler, 2010). Differentiated instruction requires unique partnerships among general and special educators, related services personnel, parents, and students (Turnbull, Turnbull, & Wehmeyer, 2010). It should be an integral part of any classroom that incorporates best practices in effective instruction.

What Are Three Teaching Behaviors That Can Help Reduce Behavior Problems in the Classroom?

Martella and colleagues pinpointed three behaviors—giving appropriate instructions, specific praise, and appropriate error corrections—that should be taught to those interacting with students in the classroom. In order to teach classroom staff these behaviors, Martella, Marchand-Martella, Macfarlane, and Young (1993) and Martella, Marchand-Martella, Miller, Young, and Macfarlane (1995) recommend modeling appropriate use of these behaviors. Following that step, opportunities for guided practice (including role-playing) should be conducted. Feedback on the correct use of the behaviors and on corrective feedback should be provided. Finally, observations should be made.

Appropriate Instructions

Appropriate instructions (called *instructional commands* by Martella et al., 1995) include statements that express a command succinctly without phrasing it as a question (e.g., "Susan, tell me the word on this card" rather than "Can you tell me the word on this card?"); specify a desired motoric or verbal response (e.g., "Tom, erase the number 6 on your paper" rather than "Tom, erase it"); use a neutral or positive and pleasant tone of voice; and have a time delay of five seconds between commands, as opposed to having the instructor rapidly repeat the command several times (p. 54).

The performance criterion for appropriate instructions is 100%. The number of appropriate instructions is tracked, as are the number of inappropriate instructions. The total number of appropriate instructions is divided by the total number of instructions and multiplied by 100 for a percentage of appropriate instructions. For example, if 8 appropriate instructions are observed and 2 inappropriate instructions are observed, the percentage of appropriate instructions is 80% (8/10 × 100).

Specific Praise

Specific praise statements are "precise statements in a neutral or positive/pleasant tone of voice that reflect a positive response to a desired behavior" (Martella et al., 1995, p. 54). For example, a teacher could say "Good job putting your coat in the closet, Joe" rather than "Good job, Joe." The performance criterion for specific praise is 50%. That is, half of all praise statements should be specific rather than nonspecific (general to the task or behavior, such as "good" or "super"). To determine an educator's use of specific praise, one would track the number of specific praise statements and the number of nonspecific praise statements. The total number of specific praise statements is divided by the total number of praise statements and multiplied by 100 for a percentage of specific praise statements. For example, if 5 specific praise statements are observed and 5 nonspecific praise statements are observed, the percentage of appropriate specific praise statements is 50% (5/10 × 100).

Appropriate Error Corrections

Appropriate error corrections include a model, lead, test, and delayed test. Error correction procedures should be stated in a neutral tone of voice. Teachers should avoid using an inflected tone of voice that indicates negativity and saying phrases such as "That's not right," "You're guessing," or "You can do better than that" (Martella et al., 1995).

The performance criterion for appropriate error corrections is 100%. Performance is determined by tracking the number of appropriate error corrections and the number of inappropriate error corrections. The total number of appropriate error corrections is divided by the total number of error corrections and multiplied by 100 for a percentage of appropriate error corrections. For example, if 7 appropriate error corrections are observed and 3 inappropriate error corrections are observed, the percentage of appropriate error corrections is 70% (7/10 × 100).

What Is an Academic Functional Assessment?

An **academic functional assessment** helps determine the function or purpose of a student's behavior as it relates to his or her academic performance. (Chapter 4 presents a detailed description of FBAs.) Of course, if these reasons are not effectively remediated, behavior problems in the classroom often result. Instructional performance is closely tied to how students behave in the classroom. Witt and Beck (1999) analyze what happens before and after students' academic performance that can help or hinder how they do in the classroom. They recommend maximizing effective instructional activities before students engage in academic performance, as well as maximizing effective feedback (or consequences) after they perform. In addition, detractions, distractions, and disruptions should be minimized before academic performance occurs; consequences that may decrease how students do following academic performance (e.g., attention from peers for nonacademic behavior such as playing or whispering) should also be minimized.

According to Witt and Beck (1999), "There are two, and only two, reasons a student does not perform academic work: he can't do it or he won't do it. That means he either lacks the skills to do the work or he simply prefers not to do the work" (p. 46). One-minute functional assessments are recommended to determine the four basic reasons students fail to progress academically (Witt & Beck). These are (a) the student won't do the work (motivation problem), (b) the material is too hard (the student can't do the work), (c) the student needs more practice (the student can't do the work), and (d) the student needs more help (the student can't do the work).

One-minute functional assessments should be conducted to determine if students exhibit won't do or can't do deficits. These assessments include the following four key parts (Witt & Beck, 1999):

1. *Monitor student performance to get a baseline.* Data are taken on precision teaching charts (three-cycle academic charts) on rate of performance in academic areas such as oral reading; examples of student performance include flatlining, high variability, progress is too slow, and satisfactory.

2. *Evaluate student performance.* Students are expected to progress 25% per week. If they achieve more than 25%, progress is deemed satisfactory; if less than 25%, it is time to analyze the learner.

3. *Analyze the learner.* This step pertains to finding things under the teacher's control that can make a difference in academic performance, such as providing motivation if a student exhibits a "won't do" deficit or, for "can't do" deficits, testing the use of easier materials if the material is too hard, adding practice if more practice is needed, or providing assistance if a student needs more help. When these or other strategies are attempted, teachers should determine their corresponding effects.

4. *Teach with precision.* Link the assessment previously conducted with intervention ideas such as goal setting for motivation problems, peer tutoring for students who need more practice, interspersing easy work with more difficult work when material is too hard, and using response cards when students need more help; these interventions—along with many other good ideas—are provided by Witt and Beck (1999).

What Are Evidence-Based Practices?

Evidence-based practices must rest on the principles of the scientific method. The scientific method helps us gain an understanding of the world. It includes the following steps: (a) identification of a problem, (b) definition of the problem, (c) formulation of a hypothesis or research question, (d) determination of the observable consequences of the hypothesis or research question, and (e) testing the hypothesis or attempting to answer the research question (Martella et al., 1999). The scientific method helps describe, explain, predict, and improve the world around us (Martella et al.). It is important to use the scientific method to guide the selection of effective evidence-based programs and instructional practices in schools.

Key Features of Effective Programs

As noted by Adams and Engelmann (1996), an effective evidence-based program has seven key features. These features can serve as criteria with which to assess the effectiveness and possible adoption of programs used by schools. They include the following:

1. Would teachers, even those with below average teaching skills, be able to teach the program successfully after receiving relatively small amounts of training?

2. Does the program permit reliable predictions about how much student progress may be anticipated for a given period?

3. Is the sum of the "promised" skills relatively substantial compared with the sum of skills currently mastered by students during the same period?

4. Is there an analytical basis to suggest that these gains are at least plausible?

5. Are there sufficient tests of student performance to serve as a guide for adjusting the rate of presentation to students?

6. Do priority skills receive relatively more instructional attention than trivial skills?

7. Is there consumer protection information to suggest that the outcomes are possible? (Adams & Engelmann, 1996, p. 7)

Direct Instruction

One evidence-based program meeting all seven criteria is Direct Instruction (published by SRA/McGraw-Hill; see the Association for Direct Instruction for further details: *http://www.adihome.org*). **Direct Instruction** provides a model of instruction that increases student achievement through carefully focused instruction; its aim is to provide intense and efficient lessons that allow all students, even the lowest performing, to achieve mastery of academic skills. This program can be used with minimal training (of course, the more training, the better). It permits reliable predictions about student progress because of homogeneous and flexible skill grouping as well as a scripted presentation format, allowing predictions about what can be accomplished in an academic year. In addition, it has a wealth of published (empirically based) research and field testing documenting its use. It provides information on the scope and sequences of skills to be taught so that the sum of promised skills are substantial over time. Direct Instruction offers theoretical support and, more important, empirical evidence of the program's efficacy (see Marchand-Martella, Slocum, & Martella, 2004, for a comprehensive look at Direct Instruction programs and design features).

In addition, Direct Instruction offers multiple opportunities for students to respond (unison responding) and curriculum-based assessments to ensure program mastery. An emphasis on priority skills is a key feature of Direct Instruction. These skills are carefully sequenced so that higher-order thinking skills can be easily accomplished (based on the prior mastery of prerequisite skills). Finally, the main form of consumer protection available for Direct Instruction comes through empirical investigations comparing the program with other approaches. Again, the field-testing of Direct Instruction makes it one of the most widely researched programs in the country.

Key Features of Effective Instructional Practices

Effective instructional practices include these design features: big ideas, mediated scaffolding, conspicuous strategies, strategic integration, primed background knowledge, and judicious review (Harniss, Hollenbeck, & Dickson, 2004). Each of these features is described below.

Big Ideas. **Big ideas** are the underlying concepts or skills that allow students to apply or generalize what they learn. An example related to reading acquisition is phonemic awareness; directly teaching this skill has positive effects on early reading success (Armbruster, Lehr, & Osborn, 2006).

Mediated Scaffolding. **Mediated scaffolding** enables students to bridge the gap between their current skill levels and the goal of instruction. This scaffolding can be provided through the selection of content, tasks, materials, and instructional approaches that support initial skills instruction and facilitate student mastery of skills. One-to-one instructional formats are examples of mediated scaffolding. These formats enable teachers to adjust the level of scaffolding provided to individual students as they acquire skills and move through content.

Conspicuous Strategies. Related to mediated scaffolding, **conspicuous strategies** are explicit teaching strategies to ensure student mastery of skills. To make teaching strategies conspicuous, a program should stress teacher modeling and effective error corrections.

Strategic Integration. **Strategic integration** involves the integration of concepts, content, and skills that are mutually facilitative of each other or are arranged so that instruction communicates generalizations to new areas removed from the original area of instruction. For example, a lesson that integrates phonemic awareness, alphabetic understanding (the knowledge that words are made up of individual letters called graphemes), and automaticity (automatic decoding or fluency) is more effective for teaching beginning reading than instruction in alphabetic understanding alone (Armbruster et al., 2006).

Primed Background Knowledge. **Primed background knowledge** involves connecting new learning to the students' previously acquired knowledge of the skills about to be taught. For example, teachers can prompt students to use their segmenting and blending skills when decoding a new word, directing them to first break down words into component sounds (*m/a/n* would be the sounds said in *man*) and then running these sounds together without stopping between them to form a word (*mmmaaannn*). Primed knowledge also involves ensuring the teaching of prerequisite skills. A hierarchical structure of the scope and sequence of learning tasks ensures that students acquire prerequisite skills to enhance later learning of more complex skills.

Judicious Review. **Judicious review** refers to the sequencing and scheduling of opportunities for students to apply newly acquired skills and develop fluency with them. Programs should be structured to include immediate practice, varied review activities, and intermittent review to ensure that students fully acquire the skills being taught.

Other Resources

Other resources emphasizing evidence-based programs, strategies, and instructional practices include, but are not limited to, *Direct Instruction Reading* (Carnine et al., 2010),

What Works Clearinghouse (http://ies.ed.gov/ncee/wwc/), Best Evidence Encyclopedia (http://www.bestevidence.org), the Florida Center for Reading Research (*http://www.fcrr .org*), *Designing Effective Mathematics Instruction: A Direct Instruction Approach* (Stein, Kinder, Silbert, & Carnine, 2006), the Center on Instruction (*http://www.centeron instruction.org/*), National Registry of Evidence-Based Programs and Practices (*http:// www.nrepp.samhsa.gov*), Intervention Central (*http://www.interventioncentral.org/*), National Institute for Literacy (*http://www.nifl.gov/*), Alliance for Excellent Education (*http://www.all4ed.org/*), American Federation of Teachers (*http://www.aft.org/*), and the Carnegie Corporation of New York (*http://carnegie.org/*).

VIGNETTE REVISITED Improving Behavior by Focusing on Instruction

Mr. Thompson decides to research methods of improving the classroom behavior of his students and their academic progress. The first thing he decides to do is calculate how much of his instructional time is lost due to transitions. Once he realizes that a full 25% of his allocated time is spent trying to get students through their transitions, he considers methods of decreasing that time. He teaches his students how to transition (e.g., how to line up at the door, where to go upon entering the room).

Mr. Thompson also thinks he needs to increase the rate at which he provides instruction. He believes there is too much downtime during the day. Downtime occurs when he is prompting some students to get on task and conducting managerial tasks such as handing out papers. Therefore, Mr. Thompson modifies how he delivers instruction throughout the day by increasing the pace of his instruction, attempting to praise appropriate student behavior more specifically and frequently, and having student assistants help with managerial tasks, so these tasks can be completed in half the time.

With these minor changes, Mr. Thompson sees improved student behavior through higher percentages of on-task behavior and lower disruptions and higher student achievement after only two weeks.

Summary

Behavior management is frequently thought of separately from academic instruction. Unwanted behavior (e.g., acting out in class), however, is no different in form or function from academic behavior (e.g., reading). In other words, behaviors (both positive and negative) are affected by the same thing: what goes on in the classroom. Therefore, rather than thinking about unwanted behavior as separate and distinct from academic behavior, teachers should consider both as classroom behaviors. Once this consideration is made, they can investigate how instruction in the classroom positively or negatively affects the behavior of students. In general, the students who display behavior problems are frequently poor performers in the classroom. The connection can be explained in one of three ways. First, misbehavior adversely affects student academic performance. Second, poor academic performance adversely affects student behavior.

Third, something else such as dysfunctional family relationships adversely affects both. All three of these explanations have validity. Teachers, however, have little or no control over the third reason that some students display both academic and behavioral deficits; they do have control over the first two. Unfortunately, improving classroom behavior does not necessarily result in improved academic performance. Students still need to be instructed appropriately. On the other hand, improving academic instruction has been shown to improve classroom behavior. Therefore, one of the best methods of improving classroom management is to improve the way students are provided instruction.

In this chapter, several considerations teachers should make when planning their instruction and when considering their behavior management procedures were covered. Teachers owe it to their students to use the time available for instruction wisely. Also, as educators, teachers owe students the opportunity to be instructed in a manner that has been shown to be effective through the scientific research literature. This research has determined that effective instruction involves several important factors, including the use of scientifically validated curricular materials. If teachers work on improving their instruction, improved classroom behavior will result. There will still be unwanted behavior from time to time, and teachers must understand and use appropriate responses to these behaviors.

Key Terms

academic functional assessment   273

academic learning time   253

acquisition stage   262

adaptation stage   264

allocated time   250

antecedent prompt and fade procedure   265

antecedent prompt and test procedure   264

appropriate error corrections   273

appropriate instructions   272

available time   249

big ideas   276

conspicuous strategies   276

curriculum pacing   254

differentiated instruction   271

Direct Instruction   275

engaged time   252

error correction procedures   270

first-time corrects   271

flexible skill grouping   269

generalization stage   263

graduated guidance   266

guided practice   260

independent practice   261

instructional momentum   248

judicious review   276

learning stages   262

least-to-most prompting   265

lesson pacing   254

levels of time   249

maintenance stage   263

mastery   270

mediated scaffolding   276

modeling   260

most-to-least prompting   265

praise around technique   252

primed background knowledge   276

Discussion Questions

1. What are the four levels of time associated with each academic day?

2. Why is it critical for teachers to understand transitions in the schools?

3. How can teachers better manage their time with students during the school day?

4. Discuss the five teaching functions teachers should utilize and how they should utilize them in their classrooms.

5. How does most-to-least prompting differ from least-to-most? Provide examples for both types of prompting procedures.

6. What are the three components of providing effective instruction? How do these components tie together?

7. What is differentiated instruction? How can it be used in the classroom?

8. What are the three teaching behaviors that can help to reduce behavior problems in the classroom?

9. What is an academic functional assessment? Provide an example of how to conduct such an assessment.

10. Explain how Direct Instruction meets all seven criteria for an effective program.

Part IV

Schoolwide Supports

9

School Safety

Chapter Objectives

After studying this chapter, you should be able to

- characterize the problems that arise from misconceptions about school safety,

- describe whether schools are safe,

- depict inductive and deductive profiling processes,

- illustrate the problems with profiling,

- describe a fact-based approach to threat assessment,

- characterize the three levels of threats in a fact-based threat assessment,

- describe the importance of considering the level of detail in the attacker's plan,

- explain the three levels of threat,

- depict the personality area or prong considered in a fact-based threat assessment,

- illustrate the family dynamics area or prong considered in a fact-based threat assessment,

- describe the school dynamics area or prong considered in a fact-based threat assessment,

- characterize the social dynamics area or prong considered in a fact-based threat assessment, and

- explain what schools can do to prevent the likelihood of school violence.

| **VIGNETTE** | **Investigating Aspects of School Violence** |

MS. SALINIS IS STILL AFFECTED each time a school shooting is reported or there is media coverage of the anniversaries of school shootings, such as the one at Columbine High School. She wonders to what extent the Internet is having an effect on school violence. The extensive coverage of school shootings and cyber-bullying describes these events as "an all-too-familiar story" or "another in a recent trend." Experts interviewed after each shooting indicate that the student perpetrators had exhibited behavioral patterns school officials had overlooked.

Ms. Salinis has been teaching literature at an urban high school for 15 years. During this time, she has taught many students who exhibited problematic behavioral patterns. Until the ever-expanding national coverage of school shootings, she had not thought a great deal about whether school violence might be a problem in her school or whether her students could be at risk for committing violence. At the time of the Columbine shooting, her principal handed out copies of *Early Warning, Timely Response: A Guide to Safe Schools* (Dwyer, Osher, & Warger, 1998) and summaries about school violence published by the National School Safety Center and the National Center for Educational Statistics and encouraged staff to read them. Recently, the principal informed staff about the need for new policies on cyber-bullying and about the possibility of the school installing security cameras and profiling potentially violent students to ensure that "a school shooting will not happen here." Parents also continue to talk to Ms. Salinis about their fears that a school shooting or other forms of violence might occur at school. As one parent put it, "It scares me to death that I'm sending my child to school to get an education and that she may be exposed to violence."

Ms. Salinis decides to look at the school violence problem more closely. She is interested in finding out whether school violence is a problem and whether she can detect students at risk of committing violent acts.

Overview

Although violence in schools has been declining, policy makers and parents are still concerned about the safety of children in today's schools. This decline in school violence may be affected by the expansion of problematic policies across the United States. For example, although the removal of students who pose a danger to others is justifiable, it is not uncommon now for students to be expelled for relatively minor acts, such as having problematic interactions with peers and adults, under the guise of improving school safety (Dupper, Theriot, & Craun, 2009). In 1997, 3.1 million students were suspended from school, most for nonviolent, noncriminal acts (Brooks, Schiraldi, & Ziedenberg, 2000). Students face greater risks of dropping out permanently and becoming entangled in the courts when they are excluded from school (American Academy of Pediatrics, 2003). A growing body of research has explored individual factors associated with school exclusion. This research consistently highlights that minority students and students with disabilities are bearing the brunt of these new exclusion policies. More than 30 years of data have shown African Americans, Latinos, and students with disabilities are suspended from school at several times the rate of white students (Skiba & Rausch, 2006). It has also been reported that, relative to other students, African American students receive more frequent and harsher sanctions, and they receive them for more subjective reasons (Raffaele Mendez & Knoff, 2003). Additionally, research indicates school factors are also associated with the greater use of exclusion. Exclusion is more likely to occur in schools having lower school attendance rates, higher percentages of students living in poverty, and higher percentages of nonwhite students (Bruns, Moore, Stephan, Pruitt, & Weist, 2005).

This research suggests the larger threat comes not from school violence but from the policies and practices being implemented in our schools. These failed policies may cause schools to neglect the development and implementation of schoolwide positive behavior intervention and support programs. As Americans soberly reflect on the needless loss of life that occurs anytime there is a school shooting, there is a need to take a closer look at school safety.

This chapter will focus on school safety. A description of school safety is followed by a discussion of the consequences of misconceptions about school safety. This discussion is followed by a description of how to conduct a fact-based assessment of threats of violence.

Are Schools Safe?

In this section, the extent to which schools are safe is examined. To outline the various facets of school safety, we use comprehensive reviews of school safety conducted by a number of organizations, such as the National School Safety Center, the National Center for Education Statistics, the Institute of Education Sciences, and Centers for Disease Control. The reviews detail information about school-related violent deaths; weapons and physical fights; students' perceptions of safety in and away from school; bullying at school and cyber-bullying anywhere; and teachers' perceptions of student misbehavior, tardiness, and class cutting.

School-Related Violent Deaths

We might think it would be relatively straightforward to determine the rate of school-related violent deaths occurring in any given year. Unfortunately, no reliable, scientific counts are maintained regarding the true number of children killed in schools in the United States each year (Donohue, Schiraldi, & Ziedenberg, 1998). The best data on the annual rates of school-associated violence are compiled by the National School Safety Center (*http://www.schoolsafety.us/*). It is important to note, however, that there are two primary methodological flaws to consider if we want to use this data to estimate the true number of students killed in schools each year and whether there is a trend over time.

First, the National School Safety Center uses a broad definition of school-associated violent deaths. It records any violent deaths that occur on school property, including suicides and the deaths of both adults and children, as well as any violent deaths that occur while people are on their way to or from school or a school-related activity. The definition is as follows:

> A school-associated violent death is any homicide, suicide, or weapons-related violent death in the United States in which the fatal injury occurred:
>
> 1. on the property of a functioning public, private or parochial elementary or secondary school, Kindergarten through grade 12 (including alternative schools);
>
> 2. on the way to or from regular sessions at such a school;
>
> 3. while a person was attending or was on the way to or from an official school-sponsored event;
>
> 4. as an obvious direct result of school incidents, functions or activities, whether on or off school bus/vehicle or school property. (National School Safety Center, 2010)

Thus, some of the deaths are included in the count simply because they occurred on or near a school property. For example, a teacher was shot and killed in an Alabama high school parking lot by her husband in January 2010. A similar killing occurred on the premises of an elementary school in Washington State. Consequently, of the seven "school-related violent deaths" that occurred in the 2009–2010 school year, three adult deaths accounted for 43% of the total. Only one of these adult deaths was at the hands of a student.

Second, the National School Safety Center relies on newspaper clippings as its data source for school-related violent deaths. Thus, the number of school-related violent deaths may be dependent on the extent to which the issue of school violence is on the media's "radar screen" from year to year. For example, although homicides in the United States dropped by 13% between 1990 and 1995, coverage of homicides on ABC, CBS, and NBC evening news programs increased by 240% (Donohue et al., 1998). As a result, the National School Safety Center statistics are influenced by changes in the frequency with which school-related violence is reported, reducing the accuracy of its data.

The number of school-related violent deaths from the 1992–1993 to 2009–2010 school years by school type is presented in Table 9.1. To reiterate the discussion above, we remind you that these numbers also include suicides and deaths of adults or children that were caused by adults or children in, near, or on the way to school. Thus, the relatively low numbers of school-related violent deaths are inflated (mean number of school-related violent deaths across the years = 24.96). Inspection of Table 9.1 reveals not only that the relative number of school-related violent deaths is relatively low but also that this number has varied widely over the years ($SD = 15.82$; Range = 3 to 56). For example, during the 2004–2005 school year, the Center reported 27 deaths. This represented a 68% decline from the previous year.

Table 9.1	Number of School-Related Violent Deaths From 1992–1993 to 2009–2010 (From National School Safety Center Data)					
School Year	Elementary	Middle	High	Alternative	Other	Total
1992–1993	3	7	42	2	2	56
1993–1994	12	7	32	2		53
1994–1995	1	3	17			21
1995–1996	1	8	22	4	1	36
1996–1997	4	3	18	1		26
1997–1998	5	6	42	1	3	57
1998–1999		5	24	2		31
1999–2000	5	6	17		4	32
2000–2001	3	3	17	1		24
2001–2002		2	2	2		6
2002–2003	2	7	12		1	22
2003–2004	9	4	27		2	42
2004–2005	3	1	22		1	27
2005–2006		1	4			5
2006–2007	2	1	10		7	20
2007–2008		1	1	1		3
2008–2009	1	1	11			13
2009–2010	1	1	5			7

Weapons Possession and Physical Fights in Schools

Each year Centers for Disease Control (CDC) conducts a nationwide Youth Risk Behavior Survey. The survey, which monitors priority health-risk behavior and the prevalence of obesity and asthma among youth and young adults, includes a national school-based survey that identifies the percentage of students who report carrying a weapon (e.g., gun, knife, or club) to school during the 30-day period before they complete the survey (*http://cdc.gov/healthyyouth/yrbs/*). The survey is conducted every other year. The biannual percentage of students reporting they had carried a weapon to school for the 1991 to 2007 period is presented in Table 9.2. The results show a continuing decline in student-reported risk factors between 1991 (26.1%) and 1999 (17.3%). There was essentially no change between 2001 and 2007.

With regard to other violence-related risk factors, between 1991 and 2001, there was a decline in the number of students who reported they were in a physical fight in school during the 12-month period before they completed the survey. The biannual percentage of students reporting they were in a physical fight in school for the 1991 to

Table 9.2	Biannual Percentages of Students Reporting They Carried a Weapon to School, 1991–1992 to 2007–2008

School Year	Percentage
1991	26.1
1993	22.1
1995	20.0
1997	18.3
1999	17.3
2001	17.4
2003	17.1
2005	18.5
2007	18.0

Table 9.3	Biannual Percentages of Students Reporting They Were in a Physical Fight, 1991–1992 to 2007–2008

School Year	Percentage
1991	42.5
1993	41.8
1995	38.7
1997	36.6
1999	35.7
2001	33.2
2003	33.0
2005	35.9
2007	35.5

2007 period is presented in Table 9.3. Similar to the data on weapons carrying, the statistics on fighting show that the percentage of students reporting they were in a physical fight declined from 1991–2001 and remained relatively stable for the 2003–2007 period.

Students' Perceptions of Personal Safety at School and Away From School

The National Center for Education Statistics (NCES), the Institute of Education Sciences (IES) in the U.S. Department of Education, and the Bureau of Justice Statistics (BJS) prepare an annual report on school crime and safety. One element of the report, the National Crime Victimization Survey, focuses on the perceptions of personal safety that students aged 12 to 18 have at school and away from school (*http://nces.ed.gov/programs/crimeindicators/*). Between 1995 and 2007, the percentage of students who reported that they feared attack or harm at school decreased from 12% to 5%. There appeared to be no pattern of increase or decrease in the percentages of students who reported they feared attack or harm away from school between 1999 and 2007.

Students' reports on their fears about safety vary by race or ethnicity and school type. For example, in 2007, smaller percentages of white (4%) and Asian (2%) students reported being afraid of attack or harm at school relative to their black (9%) and Hispanic (7%) peers. In contrast, a smaller percentage of white students (3%) than black (5%) and Hispanic (6%) peers reported being afraid of attack or harm away from school. Students attending public schools (6%) were more likely to report being afraid of attack or harm than their peers attending private schools (2%). There was no statistically significant difference in the percentage of public and private school students who reported being afraid of attack or harm away from school.

Bullying at School and Cyber-Bullying Anywhere

Students aged 12 to 18 were asked if they had been bullied at school or had experienced cyber-bullying anywhere during the year. Bullying behavior includes being made fun of; being the subject of rumors; being threatened with harm; being pushed, shoved, tripped, or spit on; being pressured into doing things one does not want to do; being excluded; and having property destroyed on purpose. In the most recent survey (2007–2008), approximately 32% of students reported having been bullied at school. Twenty-one percent of students said they had experienced bullying that consisted of being made fun of; 18% reported being the subject of rumors; 11% said they were pushed, shoved, tripped, or spit on; 6% said they were threatened with harm; 5% said they were excluded from activities on purpose; and 4% was the statistic reported for being pressured into doing things one doesn't want or for having one's property destroyed on purpose. Additionally, 63% of students said they had been bullied once or twice during the school year, 21% had experienced bullying once or twice a month, 10% reported being bullied once or twice a week, and 7% said they had been bullied almost daily. Only 36% of students who were bullied notified a teacher or another adult at school about the event(s).

A newer form of bullying (i.e., cyber-bullying) may occur on the computer.

Students who had experienced cyber-bullying were defined as those who responded that another student had posted hurtful information about the respondent on the Internet; made unwanted contact by threatening or insulting the respondent via instant messaging; or made unwanted contact by threatening or insulting the respondent via text (SMS) messaging. Overall, approximately 4% of students reported having been cyber-bullied anywhere during the 2007 school year. Two percent of students said they had experienced cyber-bullying that consisted of another student posting hurtful information about them on the Internet; and 2% of students reported unwanted contact, including being threatened or insulted, via instant messaging by another student.

Student reports of bullying and cyber-bullying vary by student characteristics. Females (33%) were more likely than males (30%) to report being bullied at school and cyber-bullied anywhere during the school year (5% versus 2%). Additionally, more white students (34%) reported being bullied at school than Hispanic (27%) or Asian (18%) students.

Teacher Reports on Student Misbehavior, Tardiness, and Class Cutting

Public and private school teachers were asked if student misbehavior, student tardiness, and class cutting interfered with their teaching (*http://nces.ed.gov/programs/crimeindicators/*). The percentage of teachers who reported that student misbehavior interfered with their teaching fluctuated between 1987–1988 and 2007–2008 (Range = 33.8% to 41.4%). The percentage of teachers reporting that student tardiness and class cutting interfered with their teaching remained stable between 1999–2000 and 2007–2008 (Range = 32.4% to 34.3%). Furthermore, there were no measurable differences in the percentage of teachers reporting that student misbehavior or tardiness and class cutting interfered with their teaching between the two most recent survey years, 2003–2004 and 2007–2008.

The percentage of teachers who report that student misbehavior, class cutting, and tardiness interfered with their teaching varies by teacher and school characteristics. For example, in 2007, public school teachers were more likely than private school teachers to report that student misbehavior (36% versus 21%) and student tardiness and class cutting (33% versus 18%) interfered with their teaching. A higher percentage of secondary school teachers than elementary school teachers reported that student misbehavior (39% versus 33%) and student tardiness and class cutting (45% versus 26%)

interfered with their teaching. Additionally, a greater percentage of teachers in urban schools (40%) relative to teachers in suburban (32%), town (34%), or rural (31%) schools reported that student misbehavior interfered with their teaching in 2007. Thirty-eight percent of teachers in city schools reported that student tardiness and class cutting interfered with their teaching compared with 29%, 32%, and 27% of teachers in suburban, town, and rural schools, respectively.

Safety and Security Measures Taken by Schools

Schools have implemented a number of safety and security measures in response to concerns regarding school violence. Students aged 12 to 18 were asked about whether their school used a variety of safety and security measures (*http://nces.ed.gov/programs/crimeindicators/*). In 2007, a majority of students indicated their school had a code of student conduct (96%) and a requirement for visitors to sign in (94%). Ninety percent of students reported the presence of school staff or other adult supervision in the hallway, and 69% reported the presence of security guards and/or assigned police officers. Sixty-one percent reported locked entrance or exit doors during the day, 66% reported the use of security cameras at their schools, and 54% of students reported locker checks. Twenty-four percent of students reported that badges or picture identification was required for entrance to the school. Only 10% of students reported the use of metal detectors at their school. It appears schools are increasingly controlling access by locking or monitoring doors (74.6% in 1999 versus 89.5% in 2007), using security cameras (19.4% in 1999 versus 55.0% in 2007), and providing telephones in the classroom (44.6% in 1999 versus 71.6% in 2007). No significant differences were detected in the percentage of students who reported metal detectors, locker checks, the presence of security guards and/or assigned police officers, the requiring of badges or picture identification, or the existence of a code of student conduct in their schools across all survey years.

Profiling Students at Risk of Targeted Violence

As a 1993 report on violence and youth by the American Psychological Association stated, "Our schools and communities can intervene effectively in the lives of children and youth to reduce or prevent their involvement in violence. Violence involving youth is not random, uncontrollable or inevitable" (p. 3). Trust in such statements makes the use of profiles only more enticing and tempting.

The media often portray children who commit violent acts as troubled children who exhibited unrecognized warning signs in their behavior and actions before they exploded in violence. Nancy Gibbs, in her 1999 article in *Time* magazine, refers to these troubled children in reference to the Columbine school shooting, for instance, as the "monsters next door." In her article and in countless accounts of school shootings, extensive descriptions of the shooter's activities prior to the shooting are provided, and we are left with the notion that educators, parents, and others should have seen the signs of future violent acts. In other words, we begin to think that profiling might be the solution to predicting violent behavior and apprehending criminals.

Profiling students involves identifying students at risk of engaging in violence through the use of checklists and warning guides listing characteristics and behaviors that could potentially lead to violence. Next is an overview of the origins and uses of profiling, of research on school shooters conducted by the U.S. Secret Service, of the weaknesses of profiling, and of the implementation implications of profiling.

Origins and Uses of Profiling. Since 1969, the Federal Bureau of Investigation (FBI) has conducted criminal profiling and provided results to criminal investigators and criminologists in the United States (Fey, Nelson, & Roberts, 2000). A profile is a set of behavioral indicators forming a characteristic pattern of actions or emotions that tend to point to a particular condition. To arrive at the characteristics composing a specific profile, a person's behavior is compared with case studies and evidence from other profiles (the results of this process conducted by the FBI in relation to school shooters is detailed below).

Essentially, two different types of criminal profiling methods exist: inductive and deductive. In **inductive criminal profiling**, the profiler looks for patterns in the data and induces possible outcomes (possible acts of targeted school violence committed by students who fit the pattern). This strategy is used to predict behavior and apprehend potential offenders before they commit a crime. Formal and informal studies of incarcerated criminals, the practical experiences of the profiler, and public data sources, such as media reports, are used to create profiles. General profiles are assembled relatively quickly and include general characteristics on a one- or two-page list.

There are two obvious problems with the use of inductive profiling. First, the generalizations made to construct the profile stem from limited and often very small population samples. Inductive profiles also take into account only the characteristics of apprehended offenders and neglect offenders who are at large. There is little question that the characteristics of unapprehended offenders are likely to be missing from the profiles. Second, in inductive profiling, behavior and motivations are assumed to be constant over time. When one is trying to predict student violence, this assumption neglects the very nature of changes in children's behavior over time. To justify the use of inductive profiling, we need to answer these questions in the affirmative: "Could the targeted acts of violence committed by the students in Santee, Littleton, Jonesboro, and Springfield have been predicted with the use of inductive profiling? Did previous incidents in other schools point undoubtedly to the occurrence of these tragedies or allow the construction of a profile that would have identified the students involved in the incidents?"

Deductive criminal profiling involves interpreting forensic evidence from a crime or crime scene to reconstruct behavior patterns and to deduce offender characteristics, demographics, emotions, and motivations. Most FBI profiling is deductive in nature. Anyone who has read Sherlock Holmes stories has encountered deductive profiling. Holmes uses physical evidence, gut feelings, and his work experience to deduce a profile of the criminal. Deductive profiling requires a great deal of effort, skill, and specialized training in forensic science and crime scene reconstruction.

There is one obvious problem with deductive criminal profiling. Although an offender for a particular crime might be successfully identified through deductive profiling, it does not enable us to develop a reliable base of generalizations to use in the identifications of other offenders. For deductive profiling, the question arises whether the targeted acts of school violence that have occurred allow us to construct a general behavioral profile that could be used for the identification of students at risk for violent behavior.

Research on School Shooters. The U.S. Secret Service initiated a Safe School Initiative in an effort to determine if schools could prevent targeted violence (Vossekuil, Reddy, Fein, Borum, & Modzeleski, 2000). Targeted violence is a term developed by the Secret Service to refer to any incident of violence where a known (or knowable) attacker selects a particular target prior to his or her violent attack. The target may be an identified (or identifiable) person (e.g., teacher or classmate), or it could be a school building itself. Although, as discussed above, acts of targeted violence are declining, the Secret Service studied the most recent school shooters in an effort to help schools consider the steps they can take to prevent incidents of targeted violence. The remainder of this section summarizes the results of the Secret Service's Safe School Initiative on targeted violence in schools (Vossekuil et al.).

The Safe School Initiative is a collaborative partnership with the U.S. Department of Education's Safe and Drug Free Schools Program. The overall goal of the initiative was to provide information to educators, law enforcement professionals, and others interested in preventing incidents of targeted violence in schools. Personnel from the Secret Service National Threat Assessment Center studied documented school shooting incidents. School shootings were only included if the attackers were current or recent students at the school and they chose the school for a particular purpose. School shootings were not studied if they were clearly related to gang or drug activity or were due to an interpersonal dispute that just happened to occur at the school.

Researchers reviewed primary source materials (i.e., investigative, school, court, and mental health records) for each incident. Information gleaned from these sources included facts about the attacker's development of an idea and plan to harm the target, selection of the target, motivation for the incident, communications about ideas and intent, acquisition of weapons, and demographic and background information about each attacker. In addition, researchers conducted in-depth interviews with 10 of the attackers to get their perspectives on their decision to engage in the attack. The primary attributes of the incidents are as follows:

1. Thirty-seven incidents, involving 41 attackers, met the study criteria.

2. Targeted violence at school is not a new phenomenon. The earliest documented case occurred in 1974, when a student set off the fire alarm and shot the janitors and firefighters who responded.

3. The incidents took place in 26 states, with more than one incident occurring in Arkansas, California, Kentucky, Missouri, and Tennessee.

4. Males committed all the incidents.

5. The targets of the attacker included almost an equal number of students and school officials (i.e., school administrators, teachers, or other staff).

6. Students or school officials were killed in more than 66% of the incidents. Handguns, rifles, and shotguns were the primary weapons used.

7. More than 50% of the attacks occurred in the middle of the school day.

The results revealed that there is no accurate profile of the school shooter. A summary of the characteristics of the attackers includes the following:

1. The ages of the attackers ranged from 11 to 21, and they came from a variety of racial and ethnic backgrounds.

2. They came from a variety of family situations (e.g., intact families, single-parent families).

3. Their academic performance ranged from poor to excellent.

4. Their friendship patterns ranged from socially isolated to popular.

5. Their behavioral histories ranged from no problems to multiple problems.

6. Attackers tended not to show any marked change in academic performance, friendship status, interest in school, or disciplinary problems at school.

7. Attackers were rarely diagnosed with any mental disorders prior to the attack.

8. Fewer than 33% of attackers had histories of drug or alcohol abuse.

Several findings suggest incidents of targeted violence at school are rarely impulsive. First, in most cases, the attacker decided to harm the target before the attack, and more than 50% did so at least two weeks prior to the attack. Second, in 75% of the cases, the attacker planned the attack, and more than 50% developed a plan at least two days prior to the incident. Third, 66% had multiple reasons for the attack, and more than 50% had revenge as a motive. Finally, more than 75% of the attackers held a grievance at the time of the attack and communicated this grievance to others prior to the attack.

The implications of the above findings are twofold. The *first implication* centers on the potential risks involved in using any given profile to identify students at risk for committing targeted violence. There are four potential risks associated with such profiling. First, the use of behavioral profiles is not effective for identifying these students. Knowing a student exhibits characteristics consistent with the behavioral profiles detailed in *Early Warning, Timely Response: A Guide to Safe Schools* (Dwyer et al., 1998) or the National School Safety Center's *Checklist of Characteristics of Youth Who Have Caused School-Associated Violent Deaths* (National School Safety Center, 1999) will not help educators and others determine whether a student is at risk of committing an act of targeted violence. (Table 9.4 presents profiling lists by the U.S. Department of Education and the National School Safety Center.) On the one hand, there is little question that using any given profile to identify these students would lead to overidentification because the majority of students who fit the profile will not actually pose a threat. On the other hand, the use of any given profile will fail to identify some students who in fact pose a risk of violence but share few, if any, of the characteristics.

Table 9.4	Profiling Lists by the U.S. Department of Education and the National School Safety Center

U.S. Department of Education	National School Safety Center
1. Social withdrawal	1. Has a history of tantrums and uncontrollable angry outbursts
2. Excessive feelings of isolation and being alone	2. Characteristically resorts to name-calling, cursing, or abusive language
3. Excessive feelings of rejection	3. Habitually makes violent threats when angry
4. Being a victim of violence	4. Has previously brought a weapon to school
5. Feelings of being picked on and persecuted	5. Has a background of serious disciplinary problems at school and in the community
6. Low school interest and poor academic performance	6. Has a background of drug, alcohol, or other substance abuse or dependency
7. Expression of violence in writings and drawings	7. Is on the fringe of his or her peer group, with few or no close friends
8. Uncontrolled anger	8. Is preoccupied with weapons, explosives, or other incendiary devices
9. History of discipline problems	9. Has previously been truant, suspended, or expelled from school
10. Past history of violent and aggressive behavior	10. Displays cruelty toward animals
11. Intolerance for differences and prejudicial attitudes	11. Has little or no supervision and support from parents and caring adults
12. Drug use and alcohol use	12. Has witnessed or been a victim of abuse or neglect in the home
13. Inappropriate access to, possession of, and use of firearms	13. Has been bullied and/or bullies or intimidates peers or younger children
14. Serious threats of violence	14. Tends to blame others for difficulties and problems he or she causes
	15. Consistently prefers television shows, movies, or music expressing violent themes and acts
	16. Prefers reading materials dealing with violent themes, rituals, and abuse
	17. Reflects anger, frustration, and the dark side of life in school essays or writing projects
	18. Is involved with a gang or an antisocial group on the fringe of acceptance
	19. Is often depressed or has significant mood swings
	20. Has threatened or attempted suicide

SOURCE: U.S. Department of Education (1998) and National School Safety Center (1999). Used with permission.

Second, special services will be in demand as students are identified through profiling as being at risk for committing targeted violence. Will the students identified as potentially violent receive all their instruction away from the other students, or will services for these students be limited to intervention programs conducted as part of the regular school day? What will the interaction between these students and the other students in the school be like? What demands will be placed on school personnel, including increased responsibilities and necessary training?

Third, in lieu of or in addition to special programs for students at risk for committing targeted violence, suspensions and expulsions might be used to deal with the identified students. Educators will have to decide whether students who supposedly or actually exhibit the behavioral characteristics described in any given profile would benefit from being excluded from the education process or would be more likely to commit violent acts as a consequence of their exclusion from school.

Finally, aside from policy implications at the school system level, some issues arise regarding the treatment and rights of students when profiling is implemented. These issues include student privacy rights and related legal implications. Stereotyping, discriminating, and the wrongful identification of potential perpetrators are ethically unjustifiable, even if the intentions are to protect students from harm. Student privacy rights are likely to be violated with the use of profiling. Educators could face legal action in the form of civil rights lawsuits and possibly class action suits, as well as negative media attention, especially if a student has been wrongfully identified as at risk for committing targeted violence.

The *second implication of the findings* focuses on the key issues educators should consider for preventing targeted violence. Rather than using behavioral profiles, educators should focus on students' behaviors and communications to determine if they appear to be planning an attack. Educators should use a fact-based rather than a trait-based approach to identify whether students are preparing an attack. The findings highlighted above suggest that students often communicate their plans in advance and have access to weapons. Thus, educators should take seriously students' verbal communications regarding a potential attack (in many cases students were communicating their plans to others, and many knew the attackers' plans in advance), and they should assess whether students have access to weapons (most attackers had access to weapons). Although a comprehensive description of key factors to consider in a fact-based approach is provided in the next section of this chapter, here are some key questions for educators to include in their fact-based assessment:

1. Have the students developed a plan and communicated it to others? In a majority of cases, students have communicated in advance their plans to commit a targeted act of violence.

2. Have students been bullied? More than 66% of the attackers reported they had been bullied, threatened, attacked, or injured by others prior to the incident.

3. Have students engaged in behaviors that cause concern or indicate a need for help (e.g., efforts to get a gun, disturbing behaviors such as threats of homicide and suicide)? Most attackers have engaged in behavior that caused others to be concerned. Educators have

expressed concern for the attackers in more than 75% of the cases. The attackers were of concern to more than one individual in more than 50% of the cases.

4. Do the students have access to weapons? The attackers got the guns they used in their attacks from their own homes or from those of relatives in more than 66% of the cases.

Finally, although it may appear to be relatively straightforward to conduct a fact-based assessment of the extent to which students are at risk of committing targeted violence, it is difficult to identify students who are planning an attack. In cases where there is a concern that students are planning an attack, the inquiry should focus on their difficulty coping with major losses, their perceived failures or injustices, and whether or not they have access to weapons. In addition, educators should develop a plan for how they will respond to students once they have been identified as being at risk for committing targeted violence. Although there are no definitive guidelines for how schools should respond to such students, we recommend that educators work with law enforcement and other social service agencies to develop an effective and supportive response to these students and their family members.

How Do We Conduct a Fact-Based Threat Assessment?

All threats should be assessed in a timely manner, and decisions regarding how they are to be handled must be made quickly. This is not to say that all threats should be treated the same. As discussed previously, it is easy for educators to run the risk of over- or underestimating threats, of unfairly punishing or stigmatizing students who are in fact not dangerous, or of missing the signs that a student is contemplating violence. The goal of the FBI's threat assessment approach is to make an informed judgment on two questions. How credible and serious is the threat itself? To what extent do the students appear to have the resources, intent, and motivation to carry out the threat? To help educators answer these two questions and thereby evaluate which students are at risk for committing targeted violence, the FBI developed a risk assessment approach for schools (O'Toole, 2000). In this section, we detail the key elements of the FBI's risk assessment approach, beginning with a discussion of some key concepts and ending with a description of the FBI's four-pronged, fact-based threat assessment approach. The **fact-based threat assessment** approach evaluates the likelihood that students will actually carry out a threat; it is used to make an informed judgment on how credible and serious the threat is.

Key Concepts

There are five key concepts in the FBI's risk assessment approach (summarized in Table 9.5): (a) threat, (b) motivation, (c) signposts, (d) level of detail in the attackers' plan, and (e) level of threat.

Table 9.5	Key Concepts in the FBI's Risk Assessment Approach

1. Threat (type)
   - Direct threat
   - Indirect threat
   - Veiled threat
   - Conditional threat

2. Motivation

3. Signposts

4. Level of detail in the attacker's plan

5. Level of threat
   - Low-level threat
   - Medium-level threat
   - High-level threat

Threat. A **threat** is an expression of intent to do harm or act out violently against someone or something. A threat can be spoken, written, or symbolic (e.g., motioning with one's hands as though shooting at another person is a symbolic threat). There are four **types of threats**: direct, indirect, veiled, and conditional.

A **direct threat** identifies a specific act against a specific target and is delivered in a straightforward, clear, and explicit manner (e.g., "I am going to kill John"). The communication suggests the targeted violence *will* occur.

An **indirect threat** tends to be vague, unclear, and ambiguous. The plan, the intended victim, the motivation, and other aspects of the threat are phrased tentatively (e.g., "If I wanted to, I could kill everyone at this school!"). The communication suggests the targeted violence *could* occur.

A **veiled threat** is one that strongly implies but does not explicitly threaten violence (e.g., "We would be better off without you around anymore"). The communication *hints* at a possible violent act but leaves it to the potential victim to interpret the meaning of the message.

Finally, a **conditional threat** warns that a violent act will happen unless a demand or set of demands is met (e.g., "If you don't pay me one million dollars, I will place a bomb in the school"). The communication suggests the targeted violence is *contingent* on a demand or set of demands.

Motivation. **Motivation** is the reason behind the threat. Threats are made for a variety of reasons. A threat may be a warning signal, a reaction to fear of punishment or some other anxiety, or a demand for attention. The motivation may be to taunt; intimidate; assert power or control; punish; manipulate or coerce; frighten; terrorize;

compel someone to do something; strike back for an injury, injustice, or slight; disrupt someone's or some institution's life; test authority; or protect oneself.

Signposts. **Signposts** are the behaviors that indicate students are planning a targeted act of violence. The actual act of targeted violence is just the end observable behavior of an evolutionary path toward it; most students do not "just snap" or decide impulsively to commit an attack. Common signposts in the evolutionary path include a frustration and brooding about failures and disappointments, fantasies about the destruction of specific individuals, and the development of a detailed plan. These behaviors are often evident in students' conversations, writings, drawings, and other actions.

Level of Detail in the Attacker's Plan. The higher its degree of **specificity and plausibility**, the more problematic the threat of targeted violence. A high degree of specificity and plausibility indicates students have thought a great deal about and planned for the targeted violence. Specific details can indicate that substantial thought, planning, and preparatory steps have been undertaken by the student, suggesting there is a higher risk this student will carry out the targeted violence. Detailed plans may include the identity of the victim or victims; the reason for making the threat; the means (e.g., weapon and method); the date, time, and place; and plans or preparations that have already been made. Plans that are more likely to be carried out also tend to have a high degree of plausibility; in other words, these plans appear to be realistic and attentive to practicalities. Likewise, a lack of specificity or plausibility indicates students have not thought a great deal about the targeted violence. In such cases, students are just responding to a frustration or attempting to intimidate or frighten a particular student or disrupt a particular school event. Plans with limited specificity or plausibility tend to be general in nature (e.g., "I'm going to blow up the gym . . .") and implausible (e.g., ". . . with a nuclear bomb").

In addition to specificity and plausibility, it is important to consider the emotional content of the threat and any precipitating stressors that may increase its seriousness. The degree of emotionality embedded in the content of the threat should be examined to assess the temperament of students. Although emotions provide important information regarding a student's temperament, they provide little information with which to assess the degree of threat. Precipitating stressors can serve as catalysts for an act of targeted violence. The impact of a precipitating event may depend on the personality traits, characteristics, and temperament of students.

Level of Threat. In general, there are three **levels of threat**: low, medium, and high. The overall content of a **low-level threat** suggests that students are unlikely to carry it out. The information is vague, indirect, inconsistent, or implausible, and it lacks detail or realism. An example is the threat, which a student writes in his or her journal, to kill everyone in the gym with a nuclear bomb.

The overall content of a **medium-level threat** suggests students could carry it out, but it does not appear entirely realistic. The information is more direct and more concrete than a low-level threat; it indicates that students have given some thought to how the act will be carried out. Further, the information provides an indication of a possible place and time (although not a detailed plan); it does not provide a strong indication students have taken preparatory steps (although there may be some veiled reference or ambiguous or inconclusive evidence to this effect). Finally, the information contains a specific statement seeking to convey that the threat is not empty (e.g., "I'm serious!"). An example is a threat, communicated to a friend, that an individual knows the specific times a particular group of students hangs out in the gym and is going to kill them someday.

The overall content of a **high-level threat** suggests students are likely to carry it out. The information is direct, specific to the victim, and plausible. Further, this information shows that concrete steps have been taken toward carrying the threat out (e.g., students have acquired or practiced with a weapon or have had the victims under surveillance). Finally, a specific place and time of the threat is provided. An example is a threat, communicated to friends, to kill a particular group of students in the gym with a shotgun at 11:00 AM on Wednesday.

In summary, the overall goal is to recognize and act on the most serious threats in a decisive manner and to address those less serious in a standardized and timely fashion. In many cases, the distinction between the levels of threat will not be obvious. Nevertheless, it is important for educators to understand that the higher the degree of specificity and planning, the more serious the threat.

Four-Pronged Threat Assessment Approach

The FBI uses a **four-pronged threat assessment** model to evaluate the likelihood students will actually carry out a threat. The model is designed to provide educators with a framework for evaluating students to determine if they have the motivation, means, and intent to carry out a proclaimed threat. The assessment is based on the "totality of the circumstances" known about a student in four major areas or prongs: (a) personality of the student, (b) family dynamics, (c) school dynamics and the student's role in those dynamics, and (d) social dynamics.

The first step involves a preliminary or rapid assessment of the content of the information included in the threat itself. This assessment can be conducted by the school psychologist, counselor, or other individuals trained to conduct the threat assessment. The goal is to identify the level of the threat (i.e., low, medium, or high).

The rapid assessment can include the collection of information in all four areas or prongs if the identities of the students are known. Information can come from a variety of sources including teachers, staff, students, and other outside sources, such as law enforcement agencies or mental health specialists. Threats assessed as medium or high and made by students who have serious problems in the majority of the four prongs should be taken more seriously. Appropriate intervention by school officials and law enforcement should be initiated immediately.

The following section outlines factors (summarized in Table 9.6) to be considered in each of the four prongs, including some of the types of behavior, personality traits, and contexts that should be considered seriously by school officials, law enforcement agents, and others. These variables should be used only in a fact-based threat assessment process and should not be used to profile students at risk for committing targeted violence. Furthermore, they are interconnected, and no trait or characteristic

Table 9.6	Four-Pronged Threat Assessment Approach Factors

Personality of the Student	
<ul><li>Leakage</li><li>Low tolerance for frustration</li><li>Poor coping skills</li><li>Lack of resiliency</li><li>Failed love relationship</li><li>Injustice collector</li><li>Signs of depression</li><li>Narcissism</li><li>Alienation</li><li>Dehumanizes others</li><li>Exaggerated sense of entitlement</li><li>Attitude of superiority</li><li>Exaggerated or pathological need for attention</li><li>Externalizes blame</li></ul>	<ul><li>Masks low self-esteem</li><li>Anger management problems</li><li>Intolerance</li><li>Inappropriate humor</li><li>Attempts to manipulate others</li><li>Lack of trust</li><li>Closed social group</li><li>Change of behavior</li><li>Rigid and opinionated</li><li>Unusual interest in sensational violence</li><li>Fascination with violence-filled entertainment</li><li>Negative role models</li><li>Behavior appears relevant to carrying out a threat</li></ul>
Family Dynamics	
<ul><li>Turbulent parent-child relationships</li><li>Acceptance of pathological behaviors</li><li>Access to weapons</li><li>Lack of intimacy</li></ul>	<ul><li>Student rules the roost</li><li>No limits or monitoring of television and the Internet</li></ul>
School Dynamics and the Student's Role in Those Dynamics	
<ul><li>Attachment to school</li><li>School tolerance for disrespectful behavior</li><li>Inequitable discipline</li></ul>	<ul><li>Inflexible culture</li><li>Pecking order among students</li><li>Code of silence</li><li>Unsupervised computer access</li></ul>
Social Dynamics	
<ul><li>Media, entertainment, and technology</li><li>Peer groups</li><li>Drugs and alcohol</li></ul>	<ul><li>Outside interests</li><li>Copycat effect</li></ul>

should be considered in isolation or given more weight than the others. All the characteristics can be identified in students not at risk for committing violence.

Personality of the Student. **Personality** is the pattern of traits or behaviors that characterize individual students. A **trait** is a psychological characteristic of a person, including dispositions to discriminate between or among different situations similarly and to respond to them consistently despite changing conditions. These dispositions are thought to be a product of inherited temperament and environmental influences. Assessing the personality of a student who has made a threat of violence requires knowledge of this individual's behavior over time and in a variety of contexts. Thus, it is important to identify individuals who have had extensive contact with the student when assessing this person's personality or how he or she will discriminate between and respond to different situations. Key dispositions include (a) coping strategies (i.e., the skill to deal with conflicts, disappointments, failures, and insults); (b) expression of emotions (i.e., the skill to express internal behaviors such as anger, sadness, or frustration); (c) empathy (i.e., the skill to demonstrate compassion for the feelings and experiences of others); (d) resiliency (i.e., the skill to come back after a setback, a failure, perceived criticism, disappointment, or another negative experience); (e) responsiveness to authority figures (i.e., the skill to follow rules and instructions); and (f) self-image (i.e., perceptions about self and about how she or he appears to others). Key personality characteristics that may be associated with a predilection for violence include the following:

Leakage. The student reveals clues to feelings, thoughts, fantasies, attitudes, or intentions that signal an incident of targeted violence. These clues may be in the form of spoken statements, stories, diary entries, essays, poems, letters, songs, drawings, doodles, tattoos, or videos. Another form of leakage occurs when a student tries to get unsuspecting friends or classmates to help with preparations for an incident of targeted violence.

Low Tolerance for Frustration. The student is easily bruised, insulted, angered, and hurt by real or perceived injustices done to him or her by others.

Poor Coping Skills. The student shows exaggerated, immature, or disproportionate responses to frustration, criticism, disappointment, failure, rejections, or humiliation.

Lack of Resiliency. The student has little capacity to bounce back (even when some time has elapsed) from a setback, putdown, or frustrating or disappointing experience.

Failed Love Relationship. The student feels rejected or humiliated after the end of a love relationship and is unable to accept or come to terms with the rejection or humiliation.

Injustice Collector. The student will not forget or forgive real or perceived injustices or the persons he or she believes are responsible; an injustice collector might keep a hit list of these individuals.

Signs of Depression. The student shows signs of depression, such as lethargy, physical fatigue, a morose or dark outlook on life, a sense of malaise, and a loss of interest in activities once enjoyed. Other signs of depression can include unpredictable and uncontrolled outbursts of anger, a generalized and excessive hatred toward everyone, feelings of hopelessness, agitation, restlessness, inattention, and sleeping and eating disorders.

Narcissism. The student lacks insight into others' needs or feelings and blames others for failures and disappointments. This lack of insight manifests itself in several ways. A student might (a) embrace the role of a victim to evoke sympathy and to feel temporarily superior to others, (b) display signs of paranoia and assume an attitude of self-importance that masks feelings of unworthiness, or (c) be either very thin-skinned or very thick-skinned in response to criticism.

Alienation. The student feels different or estranged from others. This isolation goes beyond being a loner and involves feelings of isolation, sadness, loneliness, not belonging, and not fitting in.

Dehumanizes Others. The student does not see others as fellow humans; they are nonpersons or objects to be thwarted.

Exaggerated Sense of Entitlement. The student expects special treatment and consideration and reacts negatively when either is not offered.

Attitude of Superiority. The student feels superior and presents himself or herself as smarter, more creative, more talented, more experienced, and worldlier than others.

Exaggerated or Pathological Need for Attention. The student shows an exaggerated or pathological need for positive or negative attention regardless of the situation.

Externalizes Blame. The student does not take responsibility for actions and faults others, events, or situations for his or her failures or inadequacies. This student seems impervious to rational argument and common sense when placing blame.

Masks Low Self-Esteem. The student masks a low self-esteem by displaying an arrogant, self-glorifying attitude and by avoiding high visibility or involvement in school activities.

Anger Management Problems. The student tends to burst out in temper tantrums or melodramatic displays or to brood in sulky, seething silence. The student's anger is noticeably out of proportion to the cause or is redirected toward people who had nothing to do with the original incident. This anger may also be accompanied by expressions of unfounded prejudice, dislike, or hatred toward individuals or groups.

Intolerance. The student often expresses (through words, slogans, symbols, or artwork) racial, religious, and other intolerant attitudes toward minorities.

Inappropriate Humor. The student tends to display humor that is macabre, insulting, belittling, or mean.

Attempts to Manipulate Others. The student tries to manipulate others in an effort to win their trust, so he or she can rationalize any aberrant or threatening behaviors.

Lack of Trust. The student is untrusting and chronically suspicious of others' motives and intentions. This lack of trust can approach a clinically paranoid state. The student may express the belief that he or she must deal with matters personally and alone because there are no trustworthy mechanisms to achieve justice or resolve conflicts.

Closed Social Group. The student appears introverted and has no close friendships or associates only with a single small closed social group that excludes everyone else. (A student who threatens or carries out a targeted act of violence is not necessarily a loner in the classic sense because he or she *does* associate with a small group of other students.)

Change of Behavior. The student's behavior changes (e.g., decline in academic performance, disregard for school rules).

Rigid and Opinionated. The student is rigid, judgmental, and cynical; voices strong opinions on subjects about which he or she has little or no knowledge; and disregards facts, logic, and reasoning that might challenge these opinions.

Unusual Interest in Sensational Violence. The student has an unusual interest in school shootings and other heavily publicized acts of violence. He or she will demonstrate this interest by declaring admiration for those who committed the acts or by criticizing them for their incompetence, for example, for failing to kill enough people. The student may express a desire to carry out a similar act in his or her own school.

Fascination With Violence-Filled Entertainment. The student has an unusual fascination with and spends an inordinate amount of time entertained by violent movies, television shows, computer games, music, or other forms of media that focus intensively on themes of violence, hatred, death, and destruction.

Negative Role Models. The student is drawn to negative role models associated with violence and destruction, such as Adolf Hitler and Satan.

Behavior Appears Relevant to Carrying Out a Threat. The student is occupied in activities that could be related to carrying out a threat (e.g., spending unusual amounts of time practicing with firearms or on learning about combat, bomb construction, or other aspects of how to perpetrate violence). The time occupied in these activities results in the exclusion of normal everyday pursuits such as homework, attending classes, going to work, and spending time with friends.

Family Dynamics. **Family dynamics** are the patterns of behaviors, relationships, thinking, beliefs, traditions, and crises that make up a family. The assessment of family dynamics includes determining each family member's opinion of the interrelationships among all family members. It is also important to identify key events that place a student at risk for psychiatric disorders. Key variables that have been found to be associated with child psychiatric disorders include (a) severe marital discord, (b) low socioeconomic status, (c) large family size, (d) a father with a criminal history, (e) maternal psychiatric problems, and (f) admission to care by authorities (Patterson, 1982b). Although exposure to any one of these variables does not necessarily place a student at risk for psychiatric disorders, there is an exponential increase in their likelihood with this exposure (Patterson, 1982b). The key characteristics in family dynamics are as follows:

Turbulent Parent-Child Relationship. The student has a difficult or turbulent relationship with his or her parents, expresses contempt for them, and dismisses or rejects their role in his or her life. Factors such as multiple moves, the loss of a parent, or the addition of a stepparent can underlie this turbulent relationship.

Acceptance of Pathological Behaviors. Parents do not react or appear to be unconcerned about behavior that most parents would find disturbing or abnormal. The parents appear unable to recognize problems in their children and respond in a defensive manner to any criticism of their child. When contacted by school officials, the parents appear unconcerned, minimize the problem, or reject the reports of their child's troubling behaviors.

Access to Weapons. The student has access to weapons or explosive materials in the home. The weapons and explosive materials are treated carelessly (e.g., guns are not locked away and are left loaded). Parents may handle the weapons or explosive materials casually or recklessly, conveying to their children that a weapon can be a useful and normal means of intimidating someone else or settling a dispute.

Lack of Intimacy. The family appears to lack intimacy and closeness. The family has moved frequently or recently.

Student Rules the Roost. The parents do not set limits on their child's conduct, regularly give in to this child's demands, and seem to be intimidated by him or her. In other words, the traditional family roles are reversed, with the child being the authority figure. The student insists on an inordinate degree of privacy, and the parents have little information about this child's activities, school life, friends, or other relationships.

No Limits or Monitoring of Television and the Internet. Parents do not limit or monitor this child's television watching or use of the Internet. The student may have a television in his or her own room or is otherwise free to decide how much time to spend watching television or surfing the Internet rather than engaging in activities with the family or with friends.

School Dynamics and the Student's Role in Those Dynamics. **School dynamics** are the patterns of behaviors, relationships, thinking, beliefs, and traditions that make up the school culture. There is no research on the relationship between school dynamics and threat assessment; nevertheless, these patterns have an effect on the behaviors of students, their feelings about themselves, their outlook on life, and so forth. The assessment of school dynamics involves evaluating the behaviors that are formally and informally reinforced in the school and the role that a student making a threat has within the school culture.

The assessment should examine the perceptions of school staff and students because there may be significant discrepancies between the views of each group. The key characteristics of school dynamics are as follows:

Attachment to School. The student appears detached from school and to have no or limited attachments to other students, teachers, and school activities.

School Tolerance for Disrespectful Behavior. The school does little to prevent or punish disrespectful behavior between individual students or groups of students. Bullying is part of the school culture, and school officials appear oblivious to it. The school atmosphere promotes racial or class divisions or allows them to remain unchallenged.

Inequitable Discipline. The use of discipline is inequitably applied, or staff and students perceive that this is the case.

Inflexible Culture. The school's culture (i.e., official and unofficial patterns of behaviors, values, and relationships among students and staff) is static, unyielding, and insensitive to the changing needs of newer students and staff.

Pecking Order Among Students. Certain groups of students are officially or unofficially given more prestige and respect than others. Staff and students treat those students in the high-prestige groups as though they are more important or more valuable than the other students.

Code of Silence. A code of silence prevails among the students. Little trust exists between staff and students. As a result, few students think that they can tell staff if they are concerned about the behaviors or attitudes of another student.

Unsupervised Computer Access. Students have unsupervised access to computers and the Internet. Students are able to play violent computer games or explore inappropriate websites (e.g., those that promote violent hate groups or give instructions on making bombs).

Social Dynamics. **Social dynamics** are the patterns of behaviors, relationships, thinking, beliefs, and traditions that make up the larger community in which students live and go to school. Students' behaviors, beliefs, opinions, choice of friends, feelings about themselves, outlook on life, and attitudes toward drugs, alcohol, and weapons will be shaped to some degree by the social dynamics of the community. Of particular interest in threat assessment is the student's peer group, because the student's relationship with this group will provide important information regarding the likelihood that a threat will be carried out. The key characteristics of social dynamics are as follows:

Media, Entertainment, and Technology. The student has unmonitored and easy access to movies, television shows, computer games, and Internet sites with themes and images of extreme violence.

Peer Groups. The student is intensely and exclusively involved with a group of peers who share a fascination with violence or extremist beliefs. The group excludes others who do not share its interests or beliefs. Thus, the student spends little or no time with others who think differently and is shielded from a reality check that comes from hearing others' views or perceptions.

Drugs and Alcohol. Knowledge of the student's use of and attitude toward drugs and alcohol can be important.

Outside Interests. The student's interests outside the school are important to consider. These interests can either mitigate or increase the level of concern.

Copycat Effect. Copycat behavior is very common. Thus, school shootings and other violent incidents that receive intense media attention can generate threats or copycat violence elsewhere. Staff, students, law enforcement agents, and parents should be more vigilant in the days, weeks, and even months following a heavily publicized incident elsewhere in the country.

Vignette Revisited — Investigating Aspects of School Violence

Ms. Salinis is surprised to find it is next to impossible to determine how many school shootings actually occurred in a given school year. She thought it would be relatively straightforward to determine the annual rate of school-related violent deaths, but it proved difficult to obtain such figures. She did find, however, that school-related deaths are not only relatively rare but appear to be declining. She also found that the number of fights and gun possessions at school has been declining over recent years and students and teachers feel safe at school. These findings are in direct contrast with the picture painted by the media's national coverage of school violence. She is not surprised to see that cyber-bullying represents a new form of school violence.

Ms. Salinis is also surprised to discover that students who commit school shootings do not exhibit identifiable behavior problems. In contrast to the picture presented by experts interviewed after each of the school shootings, school shooters do not follow identifiable behavioral patterns or fit into specific profiles. The ages, ethnicities, behavioral histories, friendship patterns, and academic performance of the attackers vary widely. Rather than looking for behavioral patterns, Ms. Salinis has learned she should conduct fact-based threat assessments.

Ms. Salinis has decided it is important for her to take threats of violence seriously. She now knows, however, that she should focus more on the characteristics of the threat than on the characteristics of the student. Ms. Salinis should focus on the degree of specificity and plausibility of the threat. A high degree of specificity and plausibility in the threat indicates the student has thought a great deal about and planned a violent incident. On the other hand, a low degree of specificity or plausibility in the threat indicates the student has not thought a great deal about committing targeted violence.

Summary

Violence is a complex issue with complex causes and consequences. As a result, school leaders face the difficult decision to implement strategies to prevent violence, such as schoolwide positive behavior intervention, and to support programs in schools in response to pressures from parents, politicians, and the public. Schools are one of the safest places for students. Overall, the level of violence in U.S. schools is low and is declining. The number of violent deaths at schools during the 2007–2008 academic year was seven.

We outlined profiling as a strategy and methodology to such an extent here that the decision to use or not use profiling will be facilitated for school leaders. The decision to use profiling reaches beyond pragmatic implementation issues and touches on the very core of what schools should and will look like with or without its use. The use of profiling in schools carries with it serious considerations. Its use can be justified neither by deferring to a climate of public pressure nor by using it as an emergency response to heightened concerns by parents and the general public about school safety.

Students will continue to make threats in schools (and, fortunately, most will never carry them out). Thus, we outlined the FBI's fact-based threat assessment approach to help schools assess the degree of risk that a threat poses. Although there is a clear need to field test, evaluate, and further develop the fact-based threat assessment approach, the four-pronged assessment detailed in this chapter provides clear guidelines. The threat assessment model can be used to identify and evaluate which students are at high risk for committing an act of targeted violence.

Finally, we clarified key issues, concepts, and practices related to school safety so that teachers can better focus on how to create safe and disciplined learning environments that work for all students. In Chapter 10, we will detail how to develop, implement, maintain, and evaluate a schoolwide positive behavior intervention and support program. The goals of such programs are to establish effective policies and procedures that create positive norms for behaviors, to improve the ecological arrangements of the school, and to identify and select evidence-based programs and strategies. A systematic process for planning, selecting, implementing, and evaluating evidence-based programs and strategies is covered in Chapter 11. Implementing evidence-based programs and strategies is important because not everything that is done in schoolwide discipline or violence prevention shows promise.

Key Terms

conditional threat   297

deductive criminal profiling   291

direct threat   297

fact-based threat assessment   296

family dynamics   303

four-pronged threat assessment   299

high-level threat   299

indirect threat   297

inductive criminal profiling   291

levels of threat   298

low-level threat   298

medium-level threat   298

motivation   297

personality   300

school dynamics   304

signposts   298

social dynamics   305

specificity and plausibility   298

threat   297

trait   300

types of threats   297

veiled threat   297

Discussion Questions

1. Discuss some of the misconceptions associated with school safety.

2. Discuss the mentality of students, teachers, and the general public in regard to overall school safety and the likelihood that a catastrophic event (e.g., the Columbine shooting) will occur in their schools.

3. Define bullying as discussed in this chapter. What are some of the behaviors associated with bullying and cyber-bullying?

4. Compare and contrast the differences between inductive and deductive criminal profiling.

5. What are the four key questions for educators to include in their fact-based assessment of school violence?

6. Discuss the four types of threats.

7. Discuss the three levels of threat.

8. Discuss some of the problem areas looked at when examining school dynamics using the four-pronged threat assessment model.

9. Briefly discuss the five key concepts in the FBI's threat assessment approach for schools evaluating students at risk for committing targeted violence.

10. Discuss the four major areas assessed in the four-pronged threat assessment approach.

10

Schoolwide Positive Behavior Intervention and Support

Chapter Objectives

After studying this chapter, you should be able to

- depict the theoretical foundation and goals of schoolwide positive behavior interventions and supports,

- illustrate the key elements of schoolwide positive behavior interventions and supports,

- characterize the six organizational systems that make up a schoolwide positive behavior intervention and support program,

- describe the seven key attributes of the leadership organizational system,

- illustrate the four key attributes of the schoolwide organizational system,

- describe the four key attributes of the nonclassroom organizational system,

- characterize the five key attributes of the classroom organizational system,

- depict the four key attributes of the individual organizational system,

- explain the three key attributes of the academic support system,

- describe the *School-wide Evaluation Tool* measure, including its uses, and

- explain the *Benchmarks for Advanced Tiers* measure, including its uses.

VIGNETTE	**Establishing a SWPBIS Program**

MATHEMATICS TEACHER JEFF GAVIN appealed to his middle school students in a big way. Turnout for sporting events had reached an all-time high in the six years since he had arrived at Lemuria, a middle school in a mostly Hispanic section of a large metropolis. Education carried a great deal of influence in the school community, and Lemuria provided students with unity and pride. Mr. Gavin's fellow faculty members had adopted a schoolwide program to identify problematic student behavior and to implement discipline policies on which all teachers and support staff could agree. Thus, the stage was set to help students toward prosocial, cooperative behavior and to contain any possible deterrents to student learning.

Zach Garcia and his buddies signed up for Mr. Gavin's mathematics class. Zach struggled with mathematics, but his influence and leadership among his group of friends gave him some real social leverage. Most of the boys in Zach's group received free or reduced-price lunches, came from homes where English wasn't usually spoken, and had difficulty achieving high grades in school. To them, school was a place for social interaction within their group.

In Mr. Gavin's mathematics class, Zach and his friends felt they were treated fairly. Grades depended in part on effort expended and personal progress. Attendance also figured into grading. For these reasons, as well as because of the contractual grading, each boy, even those who struggled with the mathematics concepts, could improve his grade based on personal efforts and attendance. Personal attention from Mr. Gavin felt good to them; his sense of humor, his warmth, and his equitable treatment of each member of the class according to the contract he developed assured the students in Zach's group they were on equal footing with others who were more successful in the class. Attention paid to creating a safe and disciplined learning environment had definitely paid off at Lemuria.

Overview

Concern about and a focus on the roles of schools in reducing problem behavior is not new (McPartland & McDill, 1977). Schools that promote prosocial, cooperative behavior and academic success are central to preventing problem behavior (Nelson, 1996b; Nelson, Duppong-Hurley, Synhorst, Epstein, & Stage, 2009; Nelson, Martella, & Marchand-Martella, 2002; Sugai & Horner, 2009). For approximately 180 days per year and six hours each day, educators strive to provide environments that are conducive to learning. Unfortunately, schools face significant contemporary challenges that make it increasingly difficult to achieve such learning environments.

The challenges are many. First, schools are asked to do more each year with fewer resources. To improve the academic achievement of all student groups, meet state and federally mandated accountability standards, infuse information technologies, and facilitate school-to-college transitions are just a few of the challenges being added to the list of demands schools are expected to meet. Second, schools must educate an increasingly heterogeneous population of students. Growing numbers of students in schools have limited English proficiency; significant learning and behavioral problems; and families in need of financial, social, and mental health support (Capps, Fix, Ost, Reardon-Anderson, & Passel, 2004; Knitzer, Steinberg, & Fleish, 1990; Stevens & Price, 1992).

Third, schools struggle to meet the needs of students who exhibit severe problem behavior (Nelson et al., 2009; Walker, Colvin, & Ramsey, 1995). Such students often account for a majority of the behavioral incidents handled by principals and support staff in schools, even though they represent only 1% to 5% of the school population (Sugai & Horner, 2009). Further, many of these students need comprehensive and time-consuming interventions such as wrap-around planning and supports that involve families, schools, and communities (Eber & Nelson, 1997). Finally, schools often lack the capacity to identify, adopt, and maintain policies and practices that meet the needs of all students (Nelson et al., 2009; Nelson, Martella, & Marchand-Martella, 2002; Sugai & Horner, 2009). Schools often provide staff with professional development opportunities on behavioral interventions and supports in a piecemeal fashion with little concern regarding their "contextual fit" to the needs and attributes of the school. Such professional development models lead to a fragmentation in the knowledge and competencies of school staff working within a school and ultimately to less than optimal outcomes for all students (Nelson et al., 2009; Sugai & Horner, 2009).

The focus of this chapter is on creating safe and disciplined learning environments. The goal here is to maximize student learning rather than simply reduce discipline problems. Although, as noted in Chapter 9, 96% of students report that their school has discipline and conduct policies, few schools have achieved safe and disciplined learning environments that fully maximize student learning. Thus, all schools, regardless of whether or not they are experiencing high rates of discipline-related problems, should develop a schoolwide positive behavior intervention and support (SWPBIS) program to ensure the school environment maximizes student learning.

Although the school is the primary context of interest, the SWPBIS planning process requires schools to examine the communities in which they are located; the nature of the surrounding social context has a significant influence on the intensity and structure of the SWPBIS program. In addition, the surrounding social context will affect the types of community-based behavior interventions and supports that can be provided to students who exhibit severe problem behavior and their families.

This chapter describes the attributes of SWPBIS, including its goals, elements, and organizational systems. This discussion is followed by a description of the two evaluation tools that can be used to guide the development, refinement, evaluation, and maintenance of SWPBIS.

What Is Schoolwide Positive Behavior Intervention and Support?

Schoolwide positive behavior intervention and support (SWPBIS) is the application of positive behavior interventions and supports to achieve socially important behavior change across all the school environments (described later). Further, improving student academic and social behavior outcomes requires that schools use and accurately implement evidence-based effective practices and interventions. SWPBIS is a decision-making framework or process used to guide the development or selection, integration, and implementation of evidence-based academic and behavioral practices and interventions for improving student academic and social behavior outcomes. SWPBIS is not a specific curriculum, intervention, or practice. Rather, SWPBIS is guided by the following principles.

1. Use data to make decisions and solve problems.

2. Develop strategies with reference to a continuum of evidence-based behavior (and academic) practices and interventions with a focus on teaching prosocial skills and behavior. This continuum typically includes three tiers or levels of practices and interventions: primary or tier 1, secondary or tier 2, and tertiary or tier 3 (see Figure 10.1). Refer to Chapter 12 for a complete description of response to intervention (RTI) and the multitiered continuum of practices and interventions.

3. Implement practices and interventions.

4. Monitor student performance and progress.

In any school, three types of students can be identified: *typical students* not at risk or at low risk for learning or behavior difficulties, *students at risk* of developing learning

---

Figure 10.1 Three-Tier Behavior Model

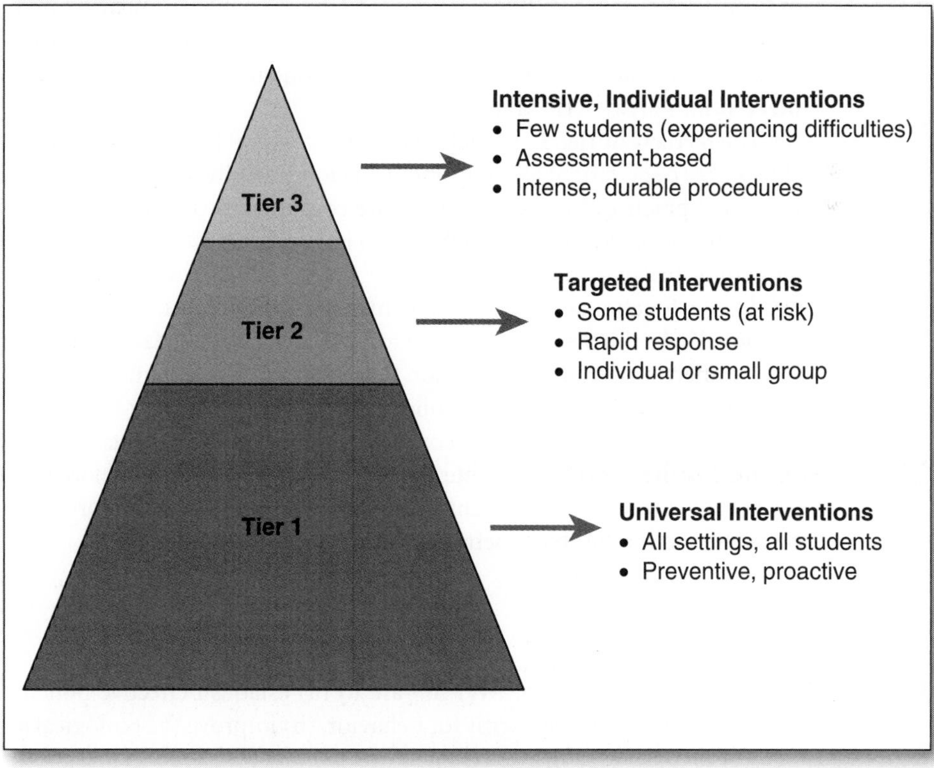

Intensive, Individual Interventions
- Few students (experiencing difficulties)
- Assessment-based
- Intense, durable procedures

Tier 3

Targeted Interventions
- Some students (at risk)
- Rapid response
- Individual or small group

Tier 2

Universal Interventions
- All settings, all students
- Preventive, proactive

Tier 1

or behavior difficulties, and *students who are at high risk of developing or show signs of life-course-persistent* learning and behavior difficulties (Moffitt, 1994; Nelson et al., 2009; Sugai & Horner, 2009). Members of each group are candidates for differing levels or types of intervention that represent greater specificity, comprehensiveness, expense, and intensity (Reid, 1993; Nelson et al., 2009; Sugai & Horner, 2009). The interventions appropriate for each student group are primary, secondary, and tertiary forms or levels of instructional or behavior supports. The **primary or tier 1** instructional and behavioral focus is on a schoolwide basis so that students do not become at risk for learning difficulties. Instructional and behavioral practices used for primary prevention are universal in that all students are exposed to them. SWPBIS is focused on school- and classroomwide systems for all students. Teaching and reinforcing students for displaying the schoolwide expectations and classroom management are considered to be primary practices delivered to every student in every setting. SWPBIS increases the probability that the majority of students will act according to expectations and is a proactive approach for students with or at risk of developing behavior difficulties.

The **secondary or tier 2** instructional and behavioral focus is on providing academic and behavioral support to students at risk for learning and behavior difficulties. Students who do not respond to the primary instructional practices or who demonstrate too many specific risk factors (e.g., poverty, poor school attendance) are candidates for secondary-level instructional and behavioral practices. At this level, SWPBIS is directed at students who are at risk for learning and behavior difficulties. Secondary interventions within SWPBIS are conceptualized as efficient instructional and behavioral change strategies that are implemented in a similar manner across all students receiving the intervention. Examples of secondary-level academic and behavioral interventions are described in Chapter 12.

The **tertiary or tier 3** instructional and behavioral focus is on students who display a life course of persistent learning and behavior difficulties. Successful instructional and behavioral practices for these students are comprehensive, intensive, and collaborative across professionals. At this level, SWPBIS is directed at students with or at high risk of developing behavior difficulties. Tertiary interventions within SWPBIS are generally based on a functional behavior assessment (Horner, Sugai, & Anderson, 2010). The functional behavior assessment (FBA) focuses on identifying factors in the environment that are affecting a student's behavior. Results of the FBA are integrated with other academic and social information to build a comprehensive tertiary-level behavior support plan. The support plan typically consists of multiple components, including strategies to influence the larger social context around a student, prevent the occurrence of problem behavior, teach new skills, ensure appropriate behavior is reinforced, and minimize the likelihood that problem behavior is reinforced (Horner et al.).

Goals

The three primary goals of SWPBIS are to (a) establish effective policies and procedures that create positive norms for behavior, (b) improve the ecological arrangements of the school, and (c) identify and select a continuum of evidence-based behavior practices and interventions. SWPBIS applies a behaviorally based systems approach to enhance the capacity of schools, families, and communities to design school environments that improve the fit or link between evidence-based behavior practices and interventions and the environments in which teaching and learning occur. The SWPBIS approach involves examining the environments in which problem behavior is observed; developing practices and interventions that consider the consequence variables that maintain occurrences of problem behavior; selecting practices and interventions that give careful scrutiny to the range of possible lifestyle outcomes (e.g., personal, health, social, family, work, recreation); and determining the acceptability of procedures and outcomes by students, families, and the community.

Key Elements

The SWPBIS approach represents the integration of four key elements: a science of behavior, evidence-based and practical interventions, attention to social values, and a systems approach. A description of these elements follows.

1. SWPBIS is founded on a science of human behavior (applied behavior analysis [ABA]) emphasizing that much of human behavior is learned, comes under the control of environmental factors, and can be changed. As our understanding of human behavior increases, so does our ability to teach and encourage more adaptive behavior.

2. SWPBIS emphasizes the adoption and maintained use of evidence-based and practical interventions. Although procedures to prevent and reduce the likelihood of occurrences of problem behavior are often associated with behavioral practices and interventions, SWPBIS emphasizes strategies that use assessment information (such as an FBA) to arrange learning and living environments so that factors likely to trigger or maintain problem behavior are less likely to be present and adaptive behavior is more likely to be taught, occasioned, and supported.

3. SWPBIS emphasizes the improvement of the living and learning options available to students, their peers, and their families. Thus, a central tenet of SWPBIS is that behavior change and the means by which behavior change is achieved need to be socially significant by being comprehensive, in other words, by considering all parts of a student's day (before, during, and after school) and important social contexts (home, school, neighborhood, and community). Both also need to be durable, so change lasts for long periods of time, and relevant by enhancing prosocial behavior that affects living and learning opportunities (academic, family, social, work).

4. SWPBIS emphasizes a systems approach, which considers the many contexts or organizational systems in which adaptive behavior is required. In schools, six organizational systems (described later) must be considered. A systems approach also focuses on prevention-based practices, team-based problem solving, active administrative support and participation, data-based decision making, and a full continuum of behavior support to accommodate the range of intensities of problem behaviors that occur in schools.

What Are the Organizational Systems Within a SWPBIS Program?

Six organizational systems are included within a SWPBIS program. These organizational systems focus on (a) leadership, (b) schoolwide systems, (c) nonclassrooms, (d) classrooms, (e) individual students, and (f) academic support systems. Each is described below (see Table 10.1 for a list of these systems).

Table 10.1	The Organizational Systems Within a SWPBIS Program

Leadership Organizational System

- Administrator support and representation
- Parental involvement
- Behavioral capacity
- Building-level status
- Support and commitment of staff
- Sustained effort
- Centrality within school's improvement goals

Schoolwide Organizational System

- Schoolwide guidelines for success
- Strategies for teaching staff, students, and families
- Clearly defined discipline roles and responsibilities
- Clearly defined crisis response plan

Nonclassroom Organizational System

- Behavioral expectations linked to the schoolwide guidelines for success
- Strategies for teaching behavioral expectations to students
- Ecological arrangements that maximize positive student behavior
- Training staff in active supervision and discipline procedures

Classroom Organizational System

- Curricula that focus on achieving academic success for all students
- Behavioral expectations that are linked to the schoolwide guidelines for success
- Consistent discipline procedures used by teachers
- Teacher access to effective assistance and recommendations for student behavioral and academic concerns
- Teacher access to ongoing staff development activities

Individual Organizational System

- Evidence-based practices and interventions for students who are at risk of or are experiencing learning and behavioral difficulties
- A common "solutions"-focused language or conceptual lens used by all staff to develop effective prevention and intervention practices

- An established, easily accessed behavior support team seen as more than a step in the special education referral process
- The use of community resources as prevention and intervention practices for students and families

Academic Support System

- Evidence-based primary-, secondary-, and tertiary-level instructional practices and interventions
- Primary-, secondary-, and tertiary-level instructional practices and interventions are coordinated and integrated with one another
- Early identification procedures

Leadership Organizational System

A **leadership organizational system** examines the school's role in developing a leadership team that implements a continual strategic planning process to achieve a safe and disciplined school environment maximizing student learning. This system is central to the development, implementation, maintenance, and evaluation of SWPBIS. Although not necessarily distinct from other leadership activities used to direct and support the school's efforts, this system focuses on establishing positive teaching and learning environments within all systems in the school: schoolwide (i.e., all students, all staff, and all settings), nonclassroom (i.e., particular times or places where supervision is emphasized), classroom (i.e., instructional settings), and individual student support (i.e., specific supports for students who are at risk of or engage in chronic problem behavior). The goal of the leadership organizational system is to improve the school's vision and organization; stakeholder involvement and communication; the allocation of resources (human, fiscal, and time); the development, implementation, and maintenance of systems to support positive teaching and learning environments; and continual self-assessment.

There are seven key attributes of the leadership organizational system. These attributes are (a) administrator support and representation, (b) parental involvement, (c) behavioral capacity, (d) building-level status, (e) the support and commitment of staff, (f) sustained effort, and (g) centrality within the school's improvement goals.

Administrator Support and Representation. The first key attribute of the leadership system is the support of the administrator. Support here is necessary because the administrative staff is

A leadership team will need to become engaged in the strategic planning process.

central to discipline policies and procedures, and its members provide a vision for all aspects of the school. In addition, the leadership team should be representative in terms of the key areas addressed by SWPBIS (e.g., administration, certified and uncertified teachers, support staff). It is, however, important not to include too many members. Six to eight members usually help to ensure the representativeness of the leadership team and its efficiency.

Parental Involvement. Parental involvement is important for two primary reasons. First, parental involvement plays an important role in establishing community support and commitment for SWPBIS. The community can provide many valuable resources and improve SWPBIS outcomes. Second, parental involvement will facilitate communication of the goals, procedures, and practices of SWPBIS with families and others.

Behavioral Capacity. The third key attribute of the leadership system is behavioral capacity. At least one member of the team should have training and experience in the behavioral model. Furthermore, the members of the leadership team should have broad and complementary expertise, particularly when developing SWPBIS, because its successful development involves academic, social, family, and community factors. All members of the leadership team should be knowledgeable in the subject of evidence-based academic and behavioral practices and interventions. It is difficult for the team to develop an effective SWPBIS program if the members are unfamiliar with basic ABA and evidence-based practices and interventions.

Building-Level Status. The leadership team must have building-level status, which simply means that the leadership team developing SWPBIS must be a key part of the school's organizational structure. Because SWPBIS affects essentially all areas of the school (e.g., curriculum), it is important for the leadership team to be coordinated with the remaining functions of the school's overall organizational system. In addition, the team should not be seen as temporary or tangential to the organizational structure of the school.

Support and Commitment of Staff. The support and commitment of the staff make up another attribute of the leadership system. The leadership system should not be based on a top-down process to build SWPBIS; rather, the teams should work to build consensus on all SWPBIS policies, procedures, interventions, and practices. Although there is no set standard, schools generally try to achieve 80% consensus among staff prior to implementing any aspect of the SWPBIS program.

Sustained Effort. Sustained effort on the part of the leadership team is also necessary to develop, implement, maintain, and evaluate SWPBIS. Building SWPBIS is an ongoing refinement and maintenance process that requires sustained effort. Effective SWPBIS policies, procedures, interventions, and practices are developed over time. Given the comprehensive nature of SWPBIS, it is beyond the capacity of staff to develop and implement SWPBIS in less than two to three years. This time frame, coupled with changes in staff and the need to update the current staff's knowledge of SWPBIS, requires sustained effort.

Centrality Within the School's Improvement Goals. The final attribute of the leadership system is that developing a SWPBIS program should be seen as central to achieving school improvement goals. Achieving a school environment that maximizes the learning of all students should be a key part of these goals. The efforts of the leadership team must also be linked and coordinated to school reform efforts and activities and maintained over time. Further, as noted earlier, achieving a safe and disciplined learning environment that maximizes student learning is a process of continual refinement.

Schoolwide Organizational System

The **schoolwide organizational system** is defined as involving all students and staff in all settings within a school. The goals of the schoolwide organizational system are to create a common language among staff, students, and families regarding the school's culture; to clarify staff roles in regard to discipline issues, problems, and crisis procedures; and to provide feedback to staff on a regular basis.

There are four key attributes of the schoolwide organizational system. They are (a) schoolwide guidelines for success (e.g., be safe, be responsible, and be respectful); (b) strategies for teaching staff, students, and families the guidelines for success; (c) clearly defined discipline roles and responsibilities; and (d) a clearly defined crisis response plan.

Schoolwide Guidelines for Success. The first key attribute of the schoolwide organizational system is a list of guidelines for success. These guidelines are a limited set of general expectations that represent the overall culture the school wants to achieve. Because of the general nature of the guidelines for success, they serve not only to encompass many behaviors but also to provide the flexibility necessary for staff to connect more specific nonclassroom and classroom expectations to them. The guidelines for success provide a "common language" that staff can use to communicate with students and among themselves about behavioral issues (e.g., Was that safe, was that respectful, or was that responsible?). Using a common language improves the predictability of day-to-day interactions between students and staff as well as among staff. In addition, the guidelines for success provide a common language or foundation with which to connect nonclassroom and classroom rules or expectations.

Strategies for Teaching Staff, Students, and Families. Strategies for teaching staff, students, and families the guidelines to success and associated nonclassroom and classroom expectations form the second key attribute of the schoolwide organizational system. Developing and implementing such teaching strategies is critical because educators often assume that students already know what appropriate school behavior is. Indeed, this is one of the most unchallenged assumptions in schools today. Related to this issue is the notion that telling students the guidelines for success and the associated nonclassroom and classroom expectations is the same as teaching students what is expected. Effective schools acquaint students with the key areas of the school (e.g., gym, cafeteria, and break areas) and actively teach the guidelines for success and associated nonclassroom and classroom expectations (see *http://www.wapbis.org* and *http://www.pbis.org* for examples).

Clearly Defined Discipline Roles and Responsibilities. The third key attribute of the schoolwide organizational system is a system of defined discipline roles and responsibilities. It is important for all staff to understand the problem behavior they are expected to handle and their role in doing so. For example, problem behavior requiring an administrative response and the respective roles of the administrator and staff should be clearly defined. Clearly defined discipline roles and responsibilities reduce staff conflicts and improve communication among administrators, students, staff, and families. Often, schools divide problem behavior into two categories to improve disciplinary consistency across students and teachers: minors and majors (Vincent, Cartledge, May, & Tobin, 2009). Minor problem behavior includes low-intensity defiance, low-intensity disruption, inappropriate language, and inappropriate physical contact. Major problem behavior includes abusive language, insubordination, sustained disruption, and fighting.

Clearly Defined Crisis Response Plan. A crisis response plan is the fourth key attribute of the schoolwide organizational system. When a school achieves an "exemplary" level of implementation in each of the six organizational systems (described later), the occurrence of crisis is reduced. Crisis, however, can happen at any time, anywhere. The crisis response plan should help schools prepare for and resolve a range of crisis situations. Although the number of crisis events or situations that can be included in the response plan can vary, many schools focus on school-level events (e.g., anonymous threats to school safety and warnings about school shootings), nonclassroom and classroom level situations (e.g., defiance and verbal or physical aggression), and student-level events (e.g., suicide threats). The crisis response plan should clearly define the roles and responsibilities of all school staff, establish an effective communication system, and establish an efficient process for securing support (internally and externally when needed). Most schools are required to have in place a crisis response plan to ensure student and staff safety during a crisis.

Nonclassroom Organizational System

The **nonclassroom organizational system** is defined as involving particular times or places outside of the classroom where supervision is emphasized (e.g., hallways, cafeteria, playground, and bus). The goals of the nonclassroom system are to improve the predictability of the day-to-day interactions between staff and students and among staff by ensuring that the behavioral expectations are linked to the schoolwide guidelines for success, to increase the participation of all staff in creating safe and disciplined nonclassroom areas, to maximize the ecological arrangements of the nonclassroom areas of the school to promote positive student behavior, and to ensure the active supervision of students and the effective use of discipline procedures by supervisory staff.

The key attributes of the nonclassroom organizational system are (a) behavioral expectations that are linked to the schoolwide guidelines for success, (b) strategies for teaching behavioral expectations to students, (c) ecological arrangements that maximize positive student behavior, and (d) staff training for active supervision and discipline procedures.

Behavioral Expectations Linked to the Schoolwide Guidelines for Success. The
first key attribute of a nonclassroom organizational system is the linkage of the behavioral expectations of the nonclassroom areas with the schoolwide guidelines for success.
This linkage is more general and flexible in nature and improves the predictability of
the day-to-day interactions between students and staff as well as among staff. Example
behavioral expectations for the common areas of the school linked to the "be safe," "be
responsible," and "be respectful" guidelines are presented in Table 10.2 (see *http://www
.wapbis.org* and *http://www.pbis.org* for additional examples).

Table 10.2 Example of Schoolwide Expectations Linked to Guidelines for Success

Guidelines	Schoolwide Expectations		
	Arrival and Dismissal	**Hallways**	**Lunch**
Be Safe	• Follow crossing guard and staff directions • Keep hands, feet, and objects to self • Cross only in crosswalks • Use safe routes • Walk at all times	• Follow staff directions • Keep hands, feet, and objects to self • Walk at all times	• Follow staff directions • Keep hands, feet, and objects to self • Police area and throw trash in can • Walk at all times
Be Respectful	• Use appropriate language • Respect yourself, others, and property • Respect personal space and feelings of others	• Use appropriate language • Respect yourself, others, and property • Respect personal space and feelings of others	• Use appropriate language • Respect yourself, others, and property • Respect personal space and feelings of others • Wait for your turn in line
Be Responsible	• Follow crossing guard and staff directions • Arrive and leave at the designated times	• Follow staff directions • No talking or quiet voices when appropriate • Stay in single file • Carry hallway pass during class time	• Follow staff directions • Use conversational voices • Police area, return trays and utensils, and throw trash in can • Use designated seating areas

NOTE: This example does not include all schoolwide areas.

Strategies for Teaching Behavioral Expectations to Students. The second key attribute of the nonclassroom organizational system involves strategies for teaching staff and students expectations for each of the nonclassroom areas. Establishing strategies for teaching students, regardless of age, is critical to creating a safe and disciplined learning environment that maximizes student learning. Again, staff members who work with older students often mistakenly assume students already know the expectations required of them. Although the teaching strategies often differ (e.g., less rehearsing with older students), all staff should commit time at the beginning of the school year to teach students the expectations associated with each nonclassroom area of the school. Planned booster sessions should be conducted on a regular basis (see the following example of a school plan for teaching expectations). In addition, the behavioral expectations for each nonclassroom area should be linked to the guidelines for success when teaching and correcting students (see Table 10.3). The following is an example of a school plan for teaching expectations.

Table 10.3   Example of Classroom Expectations Linked to Guidelines for Success

Guidelines	Classroom Expectations		
	Large Group Work	**Small Group Work**	**Independent Work**
Be Safe	• Follow teacher directions • Keep hands, feet, and objects to self	• Follow teacher directions • Keep hands, feet, and objects to self	• Follow teacher directions • Keep hands, feet, and objects to self
Be Respectful	• Use appropriate language • Ask questions by raising hand • Respect personal space and feelings of others • Listen to others • Do your best work	• Use appropriate language • Ask questions by raising hand • Respect personal space and feelings of others • Listen to others • Do your best work	• Use appropriate language • Ask questions by raising hand • Wait for your turn when asking a question • Respect personal space and feelings of others • Do your best work
Be Responsible	• Follow teacher directions • Use learner position • Look at the focus of instruction • Use classroom voice • Finish work neatly and completely	• Follow teacher directions • Use learner position • Look at the focus of instruction • Use classroom voice • Finish work neatly and completely	• Follow teacher directions • Use conversational voices • Complete silence when working independently • Use designated seating areas

NOTE: This example does not include all classroom times (e.g., entry to classroom).

The staff will focus on teaching students the school expectations during the first week of school. The staff will conduct booster sessions the first week of every month and following each major holiday break. An automated telephone call will be made and a flyer will be sent home to parents or guardians prior to the start of school and will be given out to parents or guardians when they enroll their student during the school year.

Ecological Arrangements That Maximize Positive Student Behavior. The third key attribute of the nonclassroom organizational system is adjusting the ecological arrangements of the nonclassroom areas of the school to maximize positive student behavior. The basic assumption is that the proper design and effective use of the school environment reduces the incidence of problem behavior in the nonclassroom areas of the school. Critical examination of the ecological arrangements is difficult because the human tendency is to overlook obvious solutions to problems. Clichés such as "If it had been a snake it would have bit me!" apply to the ecological arrangements of the school. Staff members need to view the ecological arrangements through a different lens and take advantage of the solutions that are inherent in the school environment itself.

Typical modifications to the ecological arrangements in the nonclassroom areas of the school include eliminating or adjusting unsafe physical arrangements and improving the scheduling and use of space. Eliminating or adjusting unsafe physical arrangements involves actual structural changes and adjustments in the use of the space. Although each site plan is unique, some problems could occur. First, campus and specific area borders are sometimes poorly defined. Even when fencing is used, it is sometimes obscured by foliage that shields the campus from natural surveillance. Second, undifferentiated campus areas (e.g., a hidden corner of the playground) present opportunities for informal gathering areas for students that are out of sight from adult supervision. These areas not only are used for prohibited activities but also have a tendency to increase the incidence of problem behavior. Third, building layout and design often produce isolated spots (e.g., the end of a hallway) where students gravitate and may commit prohibited activities or be exposed to victimization. Finally, bus-loading areas are often in direct conflict with traffic flow or create conflict and congestion with automobile parking areas. These zones also tend to be in direct conflict with the flow of students leaving or entering the school grounds for extracurricular activities. Congestion created by traffic and student flow provides the occasion for problem behavior and increases safety concerns.

One of the most effective ecological strategies for promoting positive social behavior centers on improving the scheduling and use of space. For example, if lunch is scheduled in the cafeteria at the same time for all students and staff, it not only takes longer to get groups through the lunch line because of congestion but also provides the occasion for more physical and undesirable social interactions between and among students as well as students and staff. In elementary schools, reversing lunch and recess as well as mixing grades may eliminate many problems typically associated with the lunch or recess period. Although there are no set rules, general guidelines can be used to improve the scheduling and use of space. These guidelines include reducing the density of students by using all entrances and exits to a given area; increasing the space between groups, lines, and classes, and mixing age-groups as the density of students increases; keeping wait time to a minimum; decreasing travel time and distance as much as possible; using physical signs such as clearly marked transition zones to indicate movement from less controlled to more controlled space or behavioral expectations for the common areas of the school; and sequencing events in common areas designed to facilitate the type of behavioral momentum desired (e.g., going to recess before lunch rather than going to lunch before recess results in students being better prepared for instruction).

Training Staff in Active Supervision and Discipline Procedures. Training supervisory staff to supervise and use the discipline procedures is the final key attribute of the nonclassroom organizational system. Both certified and classified staff need training because the ratio of students to staff is the highest in the nonclassroom areas. Given this ratio, the possibility that staff can correct student behavior in a positive fashion is greatly decreased. Teaching staff to move among, observe, and engage students when they are exhibiting positive or problem behavior is key to creating positive nonclassroom areas. In addition, supervisory staff needs to understand the disciplinary procedures in place for each of the common areas and how to challenge in a nonconfrontational and unemotional manner students exhibiting problem behavior. Additionally, as noted previously, it is useful for staff to understand how to respond to problem behavior categorized as either minor (e.g., low-intensity defiance, low-intensity disruption, inappropriate language, inappropriate physical contact) or major (e.g., abusive language, insubordination, sustained disruption, fighting).

Classroom Organizational System

The **classroom organizational system** is defined as involving instructional settings in which teachers supervise and teach groups of students. The goals of this system are to ensure student learning outcomes, to improve the predictability of the day-to-day interactions between staff and students as well as among staff, and to build staff knowledge of and competencies in effective teaching and behavioral interventions and supports.

There are five key attributes of the classroom organizational system. They are (a) curricula that focus on achieving academic success for all students, (b) behavioral expectations that are linked to the schoolwide guidelines for success, (c) consistent discipline procedures used by teachers, (d) teachers having access to effective assistance and recommendations for student behavioral and academic concerns, and (e) teachers having access to ongoing staff development activities.

Curricula That Focus on Achieving Academic Success for all Students. The first key attribute of the classroom organizational system is a curricula focus on achieving positive student outcomes. This attribute not only focuses on the overall curriculum but also on establishing a full continuum of academic supports (e.g., small group and one-to-one instruction programs) to ensure the success of all students. Reflecting back on our brief description of three-tiered intervention models, we would expect that the core curricular approach being used by the school should be effective for at least 80% of the student population in a given school (Nelson et al., 2009).

Behavioral Expectations That Are Linked to the Schoolwide Guidelines for Success. Classroom behavioral expectations should be linked to the schoolwide guidelines for success. The linkage of each teacher's specific expectations to these guidelines, which are more general and flexible in nature across individual teachers than the schoolwide expectations, improves the predictability of day-to-day interactions between students and staff as well as among staff. That is not to say that every teacher has to have the same expectations. Rather, the linkage of each teacher's expectations to the schoolwide guidelines for success provides a common language with which to discuss student behavior (both appropriate and inappropriate). Example classroom expectations linked to schoolwide guidelines for success are presented in Table 10.3 (for additional examples, see the following websites: *http://www.wapbis.org* and *http:// www.pbis.org*).

Related to classroom expectations is the important task of altering or removing factors that trigger problem behavior. Teachers can increase the occurrence of positive behavior and reduce the occurrence of problem behavior by rearranging the classroom environment, schedule, or learning activities to better meet the needs of students.

Consistent Discipline Procedures Used by Teachers. The third key attribute of the classroom organizational area of the school is the use of consistent disciplinary procedures for common classroom problem behavior (e.g., off-task behavior and noncompliance). The goal is to provide a common disciplinary response by teachers to improve predictability in the day-to-day interactions between teachers and students. This predictability is extended throughout the school by linking these common disciplinary responses to the behavioral expectations associated with the schoolwide guidelines for success. Although there are numerous common disciplinary responses, effective ones tend to reduce or eliminate warnings, provide the student a chance to regain control, and plan or problem-solve alternative responses. It is important to maintain flexibility in administrative and classroom disciplinary responses to more severe problem behavior (e.g., fighting and defiance). Such responses should be adjusted given the context associated with the problem behavior.

Teachers Have Access to Effective Assistance and Recommendations for Student Behavioral and Academic Concerns. Ensuring that teachers have access to effective assistance and recommendations for student behavioral and academic concerns is the fourth key attribute of the classroom organizational system. Schools must develop efficient and simple structures (e.g., common planning time once a week focused on academic and behavioral concerns) to support problem solving by teachers. Schools must also develop the knowledge and competencies of key members of their staff to ensure that teachers have access to evidence-based practices and interventions. That is, a number of staff should have in-depth knowledge of academic and behavioral interventions and supports as well as the collaborative skills necessary to work with staff.

Teachers Have Access to Ongoing Staff Development Activities. Finally, staff should have access to ongoing staff development opportunities. These opportunities should be designed to sustain current practices in the school as well as to explore potential additions. Staff development activities should be targeted and strategic in nature if they are to facilitate the implementation, refinement, and maintenance of SWPBIS. There is a growing recognition that effective staff development is continuous and ongoing, enabling teachers to develop the skills necessary to implement interventions or practices. One-shot professional development activities tend to achieve limited effects.

Individual Organizational System

The **individual organizational system** is defined as specific supports for students who are at risk of or are experiencing learning and behavioral difficulties. The goals of this system are to establish preventive intervention procedures (academic and social) for students who are at risk of school failure and to provide individualized interventions and supports to students experiencing school failure.

Key attributes of the individual organizational system include (a) evidence-based practices and interventions for students who are at risk of or are experiencing learning and behavior difficulties, (b) a common "solutions"-focused language or conceptual lens used by all staff to develop effective prevention and intervention practices, (c) an established **behavior support team** that is easy to access and is not seen solely as a step in the special education referral process (this collaborative team should be comprised of teachers, administrators, and support staff who possess the knowledge and competencies necessary to address complex student problems by analyzing and designing interventions and supports to improve student outcomes), and (d) the use of community resources as prevention and intervention practices for students and families.

Evidence-Based Practices and Interventions for Students Who Are At Risk of or Are Experiencing Learning and Behavioral Difficulties. The first key attribute of the individual organizational system is the use of evidence-based practices and interventions. Evidence-based practices and interventions are punctuated by all the federal agencies (e.g., National Institutes of Mental Health, Institute of Education Sciences) and professional organizations (e.g., National Association for School Psychologists) having established criteria to determine whether a particular intervention or program is evidence based or not. Establishing these criteria was done because schools tend to apply interventions that are not evidence based. Chapter 11 describes in detail how to develop or select evidence-based practices and interventions. The term **evidence-based research** means research that involves the application of rigorous, systematic, and objective procedures to obtain reliable and valid knowledge relevant to educational activities and programs.

A Common "Solutions"-Focused Language or Conceptual Lens Used by All Staff to Develop Effective Prevention and Intervention Practices. Second, a common language or conceptual model with which to view problem behavior should be established. If staff members use different conceptual models, it is difficult not only to assess problem behavior but also to develop effective behavior support plans to treat the problem behavior. An effective conceptual model for viewing problem behavior should have principles and concepts that are easily understood. If the concepts are too complex, they will be difficult to use with all staff in a school setting. The conceptual model should also naturally lead to school-based interventions. A conceptual model is of little use if it does not logically connect to variables that can be manipulated in a school setting. Finally, the conceptual model should be legally defensible. Courts will look closely to see if schools have applied evidence-based processes and practices if a legal issue should arise in the treatment of a student. We believe the only conceptual model that meets all three criteria is the one used as the foundation for this book: a behavioral model based on ABA. Some of the more common conceptual models do not meet the criteria for an effective conceptual model. These include the psychoanalytic (i.e., behaviors are the function of the constant interplay of unconscious processes within the individual), the psychoeducational (i.e., similar to the psychoanalytic except that the focus of treatment is on the volitional aspect [ego] of the unconscious processes), and control theories (i.e., behaviors are internally controlled and not influenced by external events or individuals). Table 10.4 presents an analysis of these common conceptual models, including the behavioral model, relative to the basic attributes of an effective model.

An Established, Easily Accessed Behavior Support Team Seen as More Than a Step in the Special Education Referral Process. The third attribute of the individual organizational system is an established behavior support team that is easy to access and is not seen solely as a step in the special education referral process. To ensure easy and efficient access, the team should be integrated into the organizational structure of the school. Behavior support teams are composed of teachers, administrators, and support staff who possess the knowledge and competencies necessary to address complex student problems. The team works collaboratively with teachers to analyze problems and to design interventions and supports to improve student outcomes (academic and social). The team should use the FBA processes and procedures described in Chapter 4 as a problem-solving framework to address student problem behavior. In addition, the team should receive ongoing staff development to expand its capacity to address such behavior.

The Use of Community Resources as Prevention and Intervention Practices for Students and Families. Fourth, community resources should be used in individual organization systems. The educational focus and training in today's schools often limit a school's ability to respond to the most serious needs of some students. Thus, schools must establish collaborative relationships and procedures to access those agencies in the community charged with meeting the more complex needs of students and families.

Table 10.4 Comparative Analysis of Common Conceptual Models

	Conceptual Model			
Attribute	**Psychoanalytic**	**Psychoeducational**	**Control**	**Behavioral**
Easy to understand	No	No	Yes	Yes
Leads naturally to effective school-based interventions	No	No	No	Yes
Legally defensible	No	No	No	Yes

Procedures should be developed to improve communication and networking among social service agencies, law enforcement, the juvenile justice system, and other relevant community resources. The use of community resources to address student problem behavior is the final attribute of the individual organizational system. The problems presented by students experiencing learning and behavior difficulties and by their families are often complex and require resources beyond those provided by the school. The educational focus and staff training of educators limit the schools' ability to respond to the most serious needs of some students. Thus, schools should establish collaborative relationships and procedures to readily access community agencies charged with meeting the more complex needs associated with students and their families, needs that are beyond the scope of the school. Community resources can provide a wide range of services to students and families, from mentoring programs to multisystemic approaches to therapy.

Academic Support System

The **academic support system** is defined as the integration of evidence-based academic skill support practices and interventions in three key skill areas (i.e., beginning reading, language, and mathematics) at the secondary and tertiary levels (i.e., for students who are at risk of developing learning problems and for students who are experiencing learning problems, respectively). The secondary- and tertiary-level academic programs should build on the existing primary universal curriculum delivered to all students. In other words, these programs should align and fit contextually within the primary universal curriculum program provided to all students. Furthermore, the interventions should address key skill areas in reading, language, and mathematics rather than the entire set of skills.

There are three key attributes of the academic support organizational system: (a) evidence-based primary-, secondary- and tertiary-level instructional practices and interventions; (b) coordinated and integrated primary-, secondary-, and tertiary-level instructional procedures; and (c) early identification procedures.

Evidence Based Primary-, Secondary-, and Tertiary-Level Instructional Practices and Interventions. The first attribute of the academic support organizational system is the use of evidence-based primary-, secondary-, and tertiary-level instructional practices and interventions. The general attributes of academic programs at these three levels are depicted in Table 10.5. Primary practices are focused on meeting the instructional needs of a majority of the students (80% or more). The primary level is comprised of three elements (Vaughn, Wanzek, Woodruff, & Linan-Thompson, 2007). These elements include an evidence-based core curriculum, screening and benchmark assessment of students at least three times per year, and ongoing professional development to ensure teachers have the tools necessary to deliver the core curriculum with integrity. The secondary-level program is directed at those students for whom the primary-level instruction is insufficient. Secondary-level intervention is typically small group supplemental instruction in addition to instruction in the primary core curriculum. The

Table 10.5	General Attributes of Primary, Secondary, and Tertiary Academic Programs				
	Attribute				
Tier	**Focus**	**Program**	**Grouping**	**Assessment**	**Interventionist**
Primary	• All students	• Core, scientifically based	• Flexible grouping	• Benchmark assessment at the beginning, middle, and end of the year	• General education teacher
Secondary	• Students at risk of learning difficulties	• Specialized, scientifically based	• Homogeneous small group (4–6 people)	• Progress monitoring 2–4 times per month	• Personnel determined by the school
Tertiary	• Students with learning difficulties	• Intensive, scientifically based	• Homogeneous small group or individual (1–3 people)	• Progress monitoring 4–8 times per month	• Personnel determined by the school

tertiary-level program is focused on students for whom the other two levels of instruction have proven insufficient. Tertiary-level instruction is typically one-to-one or very small group intensive and strategic instruction.

Selecting such instructional practices is critical because these students with or at risk for learning problems need intensive sequenced instruction. Chapters 8 and 11 describe these evidence-based instructional practices and interventions.

Coordinated and Integrated Primary-, Secondary-, and Tertiary-Level Instructional Practices and Interventions. The second attribute of the academic support organizational system is the integration and coordination of primary-, secondary-, and tertiary-level instructional practices and interventions. The overall goal of establishing these three levels is to provide an interconnected continuum of support for students with or at risk for learning problems rather than distinct approaches. In other words, the secondary- and tertiary-level instructional practices and interventions should target key skill areas necessary for students to access the curriculum, which is at the primary level.

Early Identification Procedures. The final attribute of the academic support organizational system is the early identification of students with or at risk for learning problems. The goals of early identification are to prevent the emergence of learning difficulties and to provide early intervention. Universal screening involves assessing student performance and progress on a regular basis and in a systematic manner (see Chapter 12 for a description of screening procedures). Universal screening relies on assessment procedures that are characterized by the administration of quick, low-cost, and repeatable evaluations of critical academic skills. Educators administer the universal screeners to all students, typically three times a year. The data from the screening measures are used for two purposes. The first purpose is to assess the effectiveness of the core curriculum and instruction being provided to all students. It is expected that approximately 80% or more of all students in the school should be showing adequate progress in the core curriculum. The second purpose is to identify students who are not making adequate progress in the core curriculum. These students need instruction in addition to that provided in the core curriculum to make adequate progress; they need secondary- and tertiary-level interventions (see Chapter 12 for a discussion of the RTI model).

What Is the *School-wide Evaluation Tool*?

The *School-wide Evaluation Tool (SET)* (Sugai, Lewis-Palmer, Todd, & Horner, 2001) is used to assess and evaluate the critical features of the primary level of SWPBIS. Research suggests the *SET* is a reliable and valid instrument for guiding the development, refinement, and evaluation of SWPBIS (Horner et al., 2004). The *SET* is administered prior to the implementation of SWPBIS to identify elements of SWPBIS in place and those that need to be developed and implemented. It can be administered on a regular basis to guide the continual refinement and maintenance of SWPBIS. The *SET* is available at *http://www.pbis.org/*. Specifically, the *SET* data are used to (a) assess features of SWPBIS that are in place, (b) determine annual goals for SWPBIS, (c) evaluate ongoing efforts toward SWPBIS, (d) design and revise procedures as needed, and (e) compare efforts toward SWPBIS across the year. The goal for schools is to achieve 80% or more of the points on the teaching of expectations and 80% or more of the total points on the *SET* (Horner, Sugai, Todd, & Lewis-Palmer, 2005).

The *SET* consists of 28 items organized into 7 subscales that represent key features of the primary level of SWPBIS. Scoring for the *SET* involves assigning a value of 0, 1, or 2 for each of the 28 items. Subscale summary scores are the percentage of possible points for each of the 7 features. Reviewing the data and scoring the *SET* takes two to three hours. The *SET* gathers information from multiple sources, including the review of permanent products, observations, and student (minimum of 15) and staff (minimum of 10) interviews or surveys. Permanent products that are reviewed include the school's (a) discipline handbook, (b) school improvement goals, (c) annual action plan for meeting SWPBIS goals, (d) social skills instructional materials and implementation time line, (e) behavioral incident summaries or reports (e.g., office discipline referrals, suspensions, expulsions), (f) office discipline referral forms, and (g) other related information. The *SET* subscales and associated items are included in Table 10.6.

Table 10.6	The *SET* Subscales and Associated Items

A. Expectations defined.

1. Is there documentation that staff has agreed to five or fewer positively stated school rules/ behavioral expectations? (0 = no; 1 = too many/negatively focused; 2 = yes)

2. Are the agreed-on rules and expectations publicly posted in 8 of 10 locations? (See interview and observation form for selection of locations). (0 = 0–4; 1 = 5–7; 2 = 8–10)

B. Behavioral expectations taught.

1. Is there a documented system for teaching behavioral expectations to students on an annual basis? (0 = no; 1 = states that teaching will occur; 2 = yes)

2. Do 90% or more of the staff asked state that teaching of behavioral expectations has occurred? (0 = 0–50%; 1 = 51–89%; 2 = 90–100%)

3. Do 90% or more of team members asked state that the schoolwide program has been taught/ reviewed with staff on an annual basis? (0 = 0–50%; 1 = 51–69%; 2 = 70–100%)

C. Ongoing system for rewarding behavioral expectations.

1. Is there a documented system for rewarding student behavior? (0 = no; 1 = states to acknowledge, but not how; 2 = yes)

2. Do 50% or more of the staff asked indicate they have delivered a reward (other than verbal praise) to students for expected behaviors over the past 2 months? (See interview and observation form for selection of locations). (0 = 0–25%; 1 = 26–49%; 2 = 50–100%)

3. Do 90% or more of staff asked indicate they have delivered a reward (other than verbal praise) to students for expected behavior over the past 2 months? (0 = 0–50%; 1 = 51–89%; 2 = 90–100%)

D. System for responding to behavioral violations.

1. Is there a documented system for dealing with and reporting specific behavioral violations? (0 = no; 1 = states to document, but not how; 2 = yes)

2. Do 90% or more of staff asked agree with administration on what problems are office-managed and what problems are classroom-managed? (0 = 0–50%; 1 = 51–89%; 2 = 90–100%)

3. Is the documented crisis plan for responding to extreme dangerous situations readily available in 6 of 7 locations? (0 = 0–3; 1 = 4–5; 2 = 6–7)

4. Do 90% or more of staff asked agree with administration on the procedure for handling extreme emergencies (stranger in building with a weapon)? (0 = 0–50%; 1 = 51–89%; 2 = 90–100%)

(Continued)

Table 10.6 (Continued)

E. Monitoring and decision making.

1. Does the discipline referral form list (a) student/grade, (b) date, (c) time, (d) referring staff, (e) problem behavior, (f) location, (g) persons involved, (h) probable motivation, and (i) administrative decision? (0 = 0–3 items; 1 = 4–6 items; 2 = 7–9 items)

2. Can the administrator clearly define a system for collecting and summarizing discipline referrals (computer software, data entry time)? (0 = no; 1 = referrals are collected; 2 = yes)

3. Does the administrator report that the team provides discipline data summary reports to the staff at least three times/year? (0 = no; 1 = 1–2 times/yr; 2 = 3 or more times/yr)

4. Do 90% or more of team members asked report that discipline data is used for making decisions in designing, implementing, and revising schoolwide effective behavior support efforts? (0 = 0–50%; 1 = 51–89%; 2 = 90–100%)

F. Management.

1. Does the school improvement plan list improving behavior support systems as one of the top three school improvement plan goals? (0 = no; 1 = 4th or lower priority; 2 = 1st–3rd priority)

2. Can 90% or more of staff asked report that there is a schoolwide team established to address behavior support systems in the school? (0 = 0–50%; 1 = 51–89%; 2 = 90–100%)

3. Does the administrator report that team membership includes representation of all staff? (0 = no; 2 = yes)

4. Can 90% or more of team members asked identify the team leader? (0 = 0–50%; 1 = 51–89%; 2 = 90–100%)

5. Is the administrator an active member of the schoolwide behavior support team? (0 = no; 1 = yes, but not consistently; 2 = yes)

6. Does the administrator report that team meetings occur at least monthly? (0 = no team meeting; 1 = less often than monthly; 2 = at least monthly)

7. Does the administrator report that the team reports progress to the staff at least four times per year? (0 = no; 1 = less than 4 times per year; 2 = yes)

8. Does the team have an action plan with specific goals that is less than 1 year old? (0 = no; 2 = yes)

G. District-level support.

1. Does the school budget contain an allocated amount of money for building and maintaining schoolwide behavioral support? (0 = no; 2 = yes)

What Are the *Benchmarks for Advanced Tiers?*

The ***Benchmarks for Advanced Tiers (BAT)*** (Anderson et al., 2009) is a self-assessment measure of the implementation status of secondary (tier 2) and tertiary (tier 3) behavioral support systems within schools. School SWPBIS team members complete the *BAT*, which is available at *http://flpbs.fmhi.usf.edu/ProceduresTools.asp*.

Specifically, *BAT* data are used to (a) assess features of secondary and tertiary practices and interventions that are in place, (b) determine annual goals for these practices and interventions, (c) design and revise procedures as needed, and (d) compare efforts toward the secondary and tertiary practices and interventions across the year.

The *BAT* consists of 56 items organized into 10 subscales that represent key features of the secondary- and tertiary-level SWPBIS. The first subscale (implementation of schoolwide PBIS) includes three items that are scored based on information from the *SET* or three other measures not described in this chapter (see *www.pbis.org* for a description of other measures of SWPBIS). Scoring for the *BAT* involves assigning a value of 0 (not yet started), 1 (partially in place), or 2 (fully developed) for each of the 56 items. Subscale summary scores are the percentage of possible points for each of the seven features. The *BAT* gathers information from members of the teams involved with the secondary and tertiary practices and interventions. The *BAT* subscales and associated items are shown in Table 10.7. These subscales and associated items address three questions: (a) Are the foundational (organizational) elements in place for implementing secondary and tertiary behavioral support practices? (b) Is a tier 2 support system in place? and (c) Is a tier 3 system in place?

Table 10.7	The BAT Subscales and Associated Items

A. Tier 1 implementation of schoolwide PBS.

1. Schoolwide PBS, tier 1/universal intervention is in place as measured by scores on the *SET* (three other measures are noted).

2. Team members agree that schoolwide PBS is in place and is implemented consistently by teachers and staff.

3. A data system is in place for documenting office discipline referrals that include (a) problem behavior, (b) time of day, (c) location, (d) possible motivation, (e) others involved, and (f) administrative decision taken as a result of the problem behavior.

(Continued)

Table 10.7 (Continued)

B. Commitment.

4. There is crossover membership and/or communication that informs the tier 1 team of the status of tier 2 and 3 supports.

5. A team/individual makes decisions about students receiving tier 2 and tier 3 supports.

6. The number of students, program fidelity, and progress of students receiving tiers 2 and 3 are reported to faculty.

C. Student identification.

7. The school uses a data-based process for identifying students who may need tier 2 and tier 3 supports.

8. All school staff have been trained in and know the process for requesting tier 2 and tier 3 support for students.

9. Decisions about whether students get additional behavior support are made in a timely manner and staff are notified of decisions.

10. Students receive support in a timely manner.

D. Monitoring and evaluation.

11. The teacher(s) directly involved with students receiving tier 2 and tier 3 supports are notified about impact and changes to strategies.

12. The primary family members of students receiving tier 2 and tier 3 supports are notified about impact and changes to strategies.

E. Tier 2 support systems.

13. The administrator is updated about which students receive tier 2 supports.

14. The tier 2 team meets frequently.

15. The tier 2 team is formally trained on practices and systems required for implementation of tier 2 support.

16. Students receiving a tier 2 strategy have full access to tier 1 supports.

17. Tier 2 strategies are evaluated and updated regularly.

F. Main tier 2 strategy implementation (specific strategy used by the school).

18. There are personnel identified to coordinate and deliver the tier 2 strategy.

19. The tier 2 strategy is consistent with schoolwide expectations.

20. The tier 2 strategy is established within the school and does not need unique development for each participating student.

21. The tier 2 strategy includes a formal process for teaching appropriate behaviors.

22. The tier 2 strategy includes regular opportunities for students to perform appropriate behaviors.

23. The tier 2 strategy uses accurate and objective data to adapt, modify, and improve support.

24. The tier 2 strategy includes frequent communication with the family.

25. The tier 2 strategy has written materials that describe the core features, functions, and systems of the strategy.

26. The tier 2 strategy includes orientation material and procedures for the staff, substitutes, families, and volunteers.

27. The tier 2 strategy is efficient.

G. Main tier 2 strategy monitoring and evaluation.

28. An information system is used to monitor the impact of the tier 2 strategy.

29. There are documented decision rules to decide which students access the strategy, and the process is implemented consistently.

30. Documented decision rules are used to monitor, modify, or discontinue student involvement in the tier 2 strategy.

31. Fidelity of the tier 2 strategy is assessed.

H. Tier 3 intensive support systems.

32. A team builds and implements tier 3 behavior support plans.

33. The tier 3 support team includes individuals with knowledge about the school systems, the student, and behavioral theory (e.g., student, teacher, family member, administrator, behavior specialist, advocates).

34. A person is identified to coordinate tier 3 supports.

35. The administrator is a member of the tier 3 implementation team.

36. Tier 3 team members have sufficient formal training in implementation of the tier 3 support system.

37. The tier 3 team receives annual staff development in tier 3 procedures.

38. The team has an efficient and accurate data system for monitoring tier 3 impact.

39. The team reviews the tier 3 process and considers modifications, as needed.

40. The school has personnel to implement tier 3 supports.

41. The school facilitates the involvement of family members of students receiving tier 3 supports.

42. All faculty and staff are oriented to tier 3 support implementation.

43. Students receiving tier 3 support also have access to tier 1 and/or tier 2 supports.

(Continued)

Table 10.7 (Continued)

I. **Tier 3 assessment plan development.**

44. The problem behaviors are operationally defined.

45. The problem statements (summary statements) define three components: antecedent(s), behavior(s), and consequence(s).

46. Behavior intervention plans (BIPs) are developed by a team of individuals with documented knowledge about (a) the school context, (b) the student, and (c) behavioral theory.

47. The tier 3 approach includes procedures that allow a continuum of strategies to match student needs (e.g., single-element interventions, multi-component interventions, wrap around, life-style enhancement, medical supports).

48. Behavior intervention plans (BIPs) include a problem statement (summary statement) with (a) operational definition of problem behavior(s), (b) antecedent events, and (c) consequences that maintain problem behavior.

49. Based on an FBA, the BIPs include strategies for preventing problem behavior, if appropriate.

50. Based on an FBA, the BIPs include strategies for minimizing reward of problem behavior, if appropriate.

51. Based on an FBA, the BIPs include strategies for rewarding appropriate behavior, if appropriate.

52. Based on an FBA, the BIPs include strategies for ensuring physical safety, if appropriate.

53. BIPs include a formal action plan for developing, teaching, coaching, and supporting the core elements of the tier 3 strategies.

J. **Tier 3 monitoring and evaluation.**

54. The team formally progress monitors impact of each tier 3 support plan.

55. Data collected on student behavior is used to assess intervention effects and make modifications as needed.

56. Intervention plans include a process for monitoring fidelity of implementation.

Vignette Revisited   Establishing a SWPBIS Program

Several student behavioral incidents showed the staff how important it was to develop a schoolwide positive behavior intervention and support program that was supported by the community. In addition, the staff members were supported in their efforts to teach without having distracting discipline incidents. The consistent way in which behavioral incidents were handled enhanced teachers' feelings of being supported by disciplinary policies and being firmly linked to community values at the same time.

Mr. Gavin believed one critical factor in the implementation of this program was the information given to students concerning schoolwide expectations for their behavior and the consequences of both meeting and violating these expectations. This information was dispersed at the beginning of each semester by every teacher on the staff. Students were made aware of acceptable levels of behavior, of the process that would be followed if those standards were violated, and of consequences imposed. Therefore, when Mr. Gavin walked across a parking lot on Tuesday afternoon with some of his colleagues, he was surprised to see Zach and a couple of his friends gathered at the base of the bleachers. This territory was definitely off limits to students during the school day, and, for months, no violation of this nature had occurred. The ruling was usually easy to enforce because the distance from the school to the bleachers was too great for "between class" gatherings. When Zach saw Mr. Gavin, he gave recognition that he'd been caught and began a slow saunter back to the "slab" area with his friends in tow.

This slab was just that: a huge section of concrete flooring with vending machines, picnic tables, and benches for students to occupy as they took breaks, waited for buses, or visited before and after school. Mr. Gavin caught up with the boys and asked them their purpose in being so far from the building and in a restricted area. As they answered, he noticed dilated pupils and caught what he thought was a faint smell of marijuana coming from their padded jackets. As they talked, Mr. Gavin discovered that the boys had skipped their third-period class but fully intended to attend his class, which happened during fourth period, following the lunch break.

According to the schoolwide positive behavior intervention and support program adopted by Lemuria Middle School, these students—Zach and his buddies—were students who showed signs of life-course-persistent delinquent acts. The policies used to enforce their break with behavioral expectations of the school were predetermined, equitable, and clear. Mr. Gavin and the students were clear about the next steps. Rather than Mr. Gavin and other school authorities using punitive, exclusionary policies to address this aberrant behavior, they were able to treat these students according to the schoolwide plan that the school staff taught all members of the school community thoroughly at the beginning of each semester.

Summary

The development of SWPBIS programs represents one of the more important shifts in approaches to school discipline that have occurred in recent years (Lane, Wehby, Robertson, & Rogers, 2007). For the most part, traditional approaches to school discipline were based on punitive and exclusionary policies developed in the early 1900s, when schools were oriented toward academically inclined and socially acceptable students. Success in school was not necessary to obtain a job. Times have changed, though. Without a high school education today, a person tends to have very poor prospects for life success. Although times have changed, many schools have not. Administrators and teachers talk of lists of prohibitive rules and a series of increasingly severe punishments for the violators of these rules.

SWPBIS programs provide to schools a systematic process with which to apply positive behavioral interventions and supports across all school organizational systems. The goal of a SWPBIS program is to apply a behaviorally based systems approach to enhance the capacity of schools, families, and communities to design school environments that improve the fit or link between research-validated practices and the environments in which teaching and learning occur. The practices and processes of the SWPBIS approach emphasize the systematic examination of the environments in which problem behaviors are observed; the development of proactive evidence-based interventions and supports; and the importance of the acceptability of procedures and outcomes by the school staff, families, and community members.

The *SET,* which incorporates the key attributes of the primary level of SWPBIS, provides staff an efficient process with which to develop, implement, maintain, and evaluate this level of the positive behavior support program. The *SET* serves several important functions. First, it can be used to assess features of SWPBIS that are in place. Second, based on this assessment, staff can determine annual goals for the development of SWPBIS. Third, the *SET* can be used in ongoing efforts toward developing SWPBIS, guiding the design and revision of procedures as needed. Finally, the *SET* can be used to compare efforts toward SWPBIS across the year.

Similarly, the *BAT,* which incorporates the key attributes of the secondary and tertiary levels of SWPBIS, provides staff an efficient process with which to develop, implement, maintain, and evaluate the tier 2 and 3 positive behavior interventions and supports. The *BAT* essentially is designed to address three questions:

1. Are the foundational (organizational) elements in place for implementing secondary- and tertiary-level behavioral support practices?

2. Is a tier 2 support system in place?

3. Is a tier 3 system in place?

Together, the *SET* and *BAT* support data-based decision making regarding the current status of, the analysis of service gaps in, and the evaluation of the implementation and maintenance of SWPBIS. The organizational systems are designed to support staff in the implementation of safe school practices, which are designed to influence student behavior positively. In addition, the ongoing evaluation and planning process embedded within the *SET* and *BAT* ensure that the policies and practices adopted are "contextually fitted" to the school.

Key Terms

academic support system   326

behavior support team   324

Benchmarks for Advanced Tiers (BAT)   331

classroom organizational system   322

evidence-based research   324

individual organizational system   324

leadership organizational system   315

nonclassroom organizational system   318

primary or tier 1   312

School-wide Evaluation Tool (SET)   328

schoolwide organizational system   317

Schoolwide positive behavior intervention and support (SWPBIS)   310

secondary or tier 2   312

tertiary or tier 3   312

Discussion Questions

1. How do the key elements of SWPBIS help it obtain its goals?

2. Explain the role of the leadership organization system in a SWPBIS program.

3. Explain the role of the schoolwide organizational system in a SWPBIS program.

4. Explain the role of the nonclassroom organizational system in a SWPBIS program.

5. Explain the role of the classroom organizational system in a SWPBIS program.

6. Explain the role of the individual organizational system in a SWPBIS program.

7. Explain the role of the academic support system in a SWPBIS program.

8. Which tier does the *SET* assess, and how can it be used to evaluate a SWPBIS program?

9. How is the *BAT* used to evaluate the secondary and tertiary levels of SWPBIS in schools?

10. What are some challenges a team might face when attempting to implement SWPBIS in a school?

11

Evidence-Based Interventions and Programs

Chapter Objectives

After studying this chapter, you should be able to

- illustrate a strategy, an intervention, and a program,
- depict the relationships among strategies, interventions, and programs,
- describe the criteria for defining an evidence-based intervention,
- illustrate the process used to identify evidence-based interventions,
- describe how to determine the magnitude of the effects of an intervention,
- illustrate where to find evidence-based interventions,
- characterize the process for developing the capacity of the school to implement and sustain interventions, and
- explain the process for evaluating the implementation and outcomes of interventions.

VIGNETTE	Making a Difference in the Life of a Student Through Focused Intervention

FRED HELWIG GREW UP in a neighborhood in which the children had just about anything they wanted. Both his mother and father worked hard and made a respectable living. However, the family budget did not leave much room for any extras. Rather than ask for the "extras" he wanted to gain status with his classmates,

Fred's answer was simply to "take" what he needed from the lockers and backpacks of his fellow students. Fred's good looks and well-chosen wardrobe presented him as "respectable," although he was a loner at his upscale elementary school. In addition to his stealing from his classmates, which was becoming more apparent to the teaching staff, his skill levels in reading and math were far behind the norm. Thus, he was unable to be successful in the classroom.

Fred became increasingly unhappy in school because of his academic and social difficulties. Once in a while, he even began playing "hooky," coming home early to watch television. Always a bit of a loner, he now became almost sullen in his approach to the teaching staff and to his fellow students. His former attempts to fit in were replaced by disinterest in his peer group. As a result, the other students sensed his hostility and began to leave him to himself, both on the playground and in the classroom.

On one occasion, when he was placed in a cooperative learning group for a science project, Fred refused to join the other children and instead worked alone at his desk until the teacher intervened. Mr. Allen, Fred's fifth-grade teacher, felt empathy for the boy even though he knew of Fred's stealing from classmates and saw his struggle to integrate into the class. Mr. Allen mentioned Fred to the school leadership team and was told that Fred had shown few signs of overt problematic behavior other than a general failure to thrive and an occasional bout of stealing from his classmates. He probably qualified for a secondary intervention to enhance his reading skills.

The inability to read on or near his grade level showed up on Fred's standardized tests that year. Not surprisingly, his scores showed him to be capable but a nonachiever. Fred also began to demonstrate behavior that verged on hostility. His stealing came to a head one day when a classmate, Jonathan, caught Fred taking a pocket speller from the backpack in Jonathan's locker. Jonathan went to Mr. Allen and demanded that Fred be sent to the office or kicked out of the class.

Mr. Allen avoided a fight by bringing the boys together and talking to Fred about the theft. He asked Fred why it was important to own the speller instead of just borrowing it and encouraged Fred to apologize. Jonathan's anger dissipated when he had a chance to confront Fred. After school, though, Mr. Allen called Fred's parents and scheduled a conference with both parents and son for the following afternoon.

Overview

The three primary goals of SWPBIS programs are to (a) establish effective policies and procedures that create positive norms for behavior, (b) improve the ecological arrangements of the school, and (c) identify and select evidence-based interventions. The focus of this chapter is how to plan, select, implement, and evaluate primary-, secondary-, and tertiary-level interventions that have been validated through experimental studies or rigorous evaluation designs. The emphasis is on selecting evidence-based secondary- and tertiary-level interventions. (Tertiary or individual support interventions in this chapter refer to targeting groups of students who are experiencing behavior difficulties and designing interventions for all the targeted individuals. Chapters 3 through 6 specifically describe interventions for individual students experiencing behavior difficulties.) Research has demonstrated schools should be cautious when selecting interventions because not everything done in the name of improving the learning and behavior outcomes of students shows promise. For example, the most common treatment for students who exhibit problem behavior is insight-based counseling, even though past research has demonstrated that it is ineffective (Sherman et al., 1998).

Students who experience learning and behavior difficulties are at risk for school failure. Although such students are consistently among the highest priorities of schools and communities, they tend to be the least well-served segment of the school population. For example, it has been conservatively estimated that approximately 8% of school-age students have significant emotional and behavioral disorders (Walker, 2000). Furthermore, the results of the National Assessment of Educational Progress (NAEP; National Center for Education Statistics, 2009b), a longitudinal study of educational progress, indicate that 33% of fourth graders in the United States are at risk because they do not read well enough, quickly enough, or easily enough to ensure their success in school. (The NAEP is a nationally representative and continuing assessment of what America's students know and can do in reading, mathematics, science, writing, the arts, civics, economics, geography, and U.S. history.) The response of schools to these problems tends to be reactive rather than proactive. This reaction is unfortunate because we have the means with which to respond effectively to the learning and behavior difficulties that place students at risk for school failure.

In most cases, the failure of schools to plan, select, implement, and evaluate interventions actively occurs, at least in part, because establishing an effective system of intervention appears to be an overwhelming task for schools to undertake. That is especially the case if the schools have never been involved in such an effort. In this chapter, the steps schools can use to plan, select, implement, and evaluate evidence-based interventions are described. It is important for schools to remember that, as long as they fail to address learning and behavior difficulties, they will continue to plague the daily operation of the schooling process. Moreover, failure to address these problems proactively will result in a massive waste of human potential, with all its accompanying problems.

This chapter describes the process for selecting interventions to prevent and remediate learning and behavior difficulties and for implementing and evaluating their use in schools. The differences between a strategy, an intervention, and a program, including their relationship to one another, are discussed. These discussions are followed by a description of the process used to plan, select, implement, and evaluate evidence-based interventions.

What Are a Strategy, an Intervention, and a Program?

It is important to define how the terms *strategy, intervention,* and *program* are used in the prevention field and throughout this chapter (see Figure 11.1). These terms underlie the terms *evidence-based practices* and *interventions* that we used when discussing SWPBIS.

| Figure 11.1 | Strategy, Intervention, Program: A Chain of Relationship |

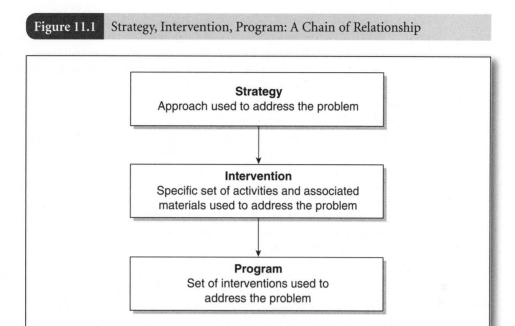

Strategy

A **strategy** is a general conceptual approach or framework for preventing or remediating learning and behavior difficulties. The defining attribute of a strategy is that it is a general or conceptual approach rather than a specific set of activities and associated materials or procedures (i.e., interventions). Often, schools will initially identify a strategy that is then used to guide the selection of an intervention or set of interventions. For example, conflict resolution (strategy) can be used to enhance students' social and problem-solving skills, or small group instruction (strategy) in reading can offer basic training in key beginning reading skills for students. These strategies would then be used by the school to guide their selection of interventions to enhance students' social and problem-solving skills or beginning reading skills.

Intervention

An **intervention** is a specific set of procedures or practices and associated materials developed to prevent or remediate learning and behavior difficulties. The defining attribute of an intervention is that it is a specific set of activities and associated materials or procedures rather than a general or conceptual approach (i.e., strategy). An intervention may be small in scope (e.g., the use of positive reinforcement to promote prosocial behavior), a modest bundle of procedures that address a narrow outcome (e.g., time out from reinforcement to reduce playground aggression), or a large package of procedures that collectively target a major social issue (e.g., a bundle of 20 interventions designed to prevent aggression). For example, *Promoting Alternative Thinking Strategies* (*PATHS*) (Greenberg, Kusche, & Mihalic, 1998) promotes the prevention of violence, aggression, and other behavior problems; the improvement of critical thinking skills; and the development of emotional literacy, social problem-solving skills, and interpersonal competence for all students in all settings in Grades K–6. Enhancing student social and emotional development is the general strategy underlying *PATHS*. The *PATHS* intervention is organized into three units: self-control, feelings and relationships, and interpersonal cognitive problem solving.

1. *Unit 1: Self-Control.* This unit focuses on introducing *PATHS* and enhancing students' self-control in the intrapersonal domain. The unit consists of a series of structured lessons accompanied by a reinforcement program that is individually tailored to the classroom teacher. Through a series of lessons, students are told a metaphorical story about a young turtle that has both interpersonal and academic difficulties that arise because the turtle does "not stop and think." These problems manifest themselves in the young turtle's aggressive behavior and associated uncomfortable feelings. With the assistance of a "wise old turtle," the young turtle learns to develop better self-control. A set of drawings is used in conjunction with the script for the turtle story to illustrate key concepts.

2. *Unit 2: Feelings and Relationships.* This unit focuses on improving students' emotional and intrapersonal understanding. The lessons focus on 50 distinct affective states, which are taught in a developmental hierarchy beginning with basic emotions (e.g., happy, sad, angry) and moving on to more complex emotional states (e.g., jealousy, guilt, pride). The lessons include group discussions, role-playing skits, art activities, stories, and educational games designed to teach students to label both emotional states and cues for the self-recognition of their own feelings and for the recognition of emotions in others. Students also receive training in affective self-monitoring techniques, in attributions that link causes and emotions, in perspective-taking skills that emphasize how and why to consider another's point of view, in empathic realization or how one's behavior can affect other people, and in how the behavior of others can affect oneself.

3. *Unit 3: Interpersonal Cognitive Problem Solving.* This unit focuses on enhancing students' interpersonal problem-solving skills. The problem-solving sequence taught includes these steps: (a) Stop–What is happening?—i.e., stopping and thinking, problem identification, feeling identification; (b) Get Ready–What could I do?—i.e., deciding on a goal, generating alternative solutions, evaluating the possible consequences of these solutions, selecting the best solution, planning the best solution; (c) Go!–Try my best plan—i.e., trying the formulated plan; and (d) Evaluate–How did I do?—i.e., evaluating the outcome, trying another solution and/or plan, or alternatively reevaluating the goal, if an obstacle results in failure to reach the intended goal.

In addition, as described in Chapter 10, in any school, three types of students can be identified: (a) *typical students* not at risk for learning and behavior difficulties, (b) *students at risk* for developing learning and behavior difficulties, and (c) *students who show signs of life-course-persistent* learning and behavior difficulties (Moffitt, 1994; Nelson, Duppong-Hurley, Synhorst, Epstein, & Stage, 2009; Nelson, Martella, & Marchand-Martella, 2002;

Sugai & Horner, 2009; Walker et al., 1996). Schools must consider whether the intervention(s) will be used at the primary, secondary, or tertiary levels.

Program

A **program** is a grouping of interventions designed to prevent or remediate learning and behavior difficulties. The defining attribute of a program is that it includes a set of interventions or practices rather than an individual intervention. SWPBIS is a program. For example, Nelson and colleagues (2009) developed and evaluated a SWPBIS program that included interventions at all three levels or tiers. The respective primary, secondary, and tertiary interventions included *Behavior and Academic Support and Enhancement (BASE*; Nelson, Martella, & Marchand-Martella, 2002), *First Step to Success* (Walker et al., 1997), and *Multisystemic Therapy (MST*; Henggeler, Schoenwald, Borduin, Rowland, & Cunningham, 1998). The primary-level intervention had three main components: (a) common area procedures and behavioral expectations (including active teaching, supervision, and reinforcement), (b) Think Time® (a consistent classroom management strategy applied schoolwide; see Chapter 7), and (c) a continuum of administrative disciplinary responses.

The secondary-level intervention, *First Step to Success,* consisted of three modules implementing a series of activities designed to be applied in concert with each other. The modules include (a) proactive, universal screening of all kindergarten and first-grade populations, (b) consultant-based school interventions involving the target student, peers, and teachers, and (c) parent training in caregiver skills for supporting and improving the student's school adjustment performance in the home (see Chapter 12 for a complete description).

MST, the tertiary-level intervention, views individuals as being surrounded by a network of interconnected systems that encompass individual, family, and extra-familial factors (peer, school, neighborhood) and recognizes that intervention is often a necessary combination of these systems. The primary goals of *MST* are to reduce the frequency and severity of mental health problems and other types of antisocial behavior as well as to achieve these outcomes at a cost savings by decreasing rates of incarceration and out-of-home placements. *MST* achieves these goals through adherence to nine *MST* treatment principles: (a) The primary purpose of assessment is to understand the fit between the identified problems and their broader systemic context; (b) therapeutic contacts emphasize the positive and use systemic strengths as levers for change; (c) interventions are designed to promote responsible behavior and decrease irresponsible behavior among family members; (d) interventions are present focused and action oriented, targeting specific and well-defined problems; (e) interventions target sequences of behavior within and between multiple systems that maintain the identified problems; (f) interventions are developmentally appropriate and fit the developmental needs of the students; (g) interventions are designed to require daily or weekly effort by family members; (h) intervention effectiveness is evaluated continuously from multiple perspectives with providers assuming accountability for overcoming barriers to successful outcomes; and (i) interventions are designed to promote treatment generalization and long-term maintenance of therapeutic change by empowering caregivers to address family members' needs across multiple systemic contexts.

In summary, strategies, interventions, and programs not only are related to one another but also depict the evolution of the comprehensiveness of a SWPBIS program being developed and implemented in the school. Typically, initial discussions within schools focus on the strategy or approach used to address a particular problem. Once a strategy is identified and adopted by schools, then schools plan, implement, and evaluate particular interventions. Over time, schools' efforts lead to the development of a comprehensive SWPBIS program that includes several interventions to address the full array of factors underlying the academic and behavior problems faced by the school.

What Are the Criteria for Being Defined as an Evidence-Based Intervention?

A growing emphasis is being placed on the criteria for the implementation of **evidence-based interventions** (Flay et al., 2005). Regardless of the size or scope of the intervention, the following six criteria (shown in Table 11.1) serve to define a practice or intervention that is under review for consideration as evidence based (Horner, Sugai, & Anderson, 2010).

Table 11.1	Six Criteria That Define a Practice or Intervention as Evidence Based

1. The intervention is operationally defined.
2. The qualifications of people who may use the intervention with success are defined.
3. The outcomes that may be expected from using the intervention are defined.
4. The settings (or contexts) in which the intervention is expected to be effective are defined.
5. The target population or populations for whom the intervention is effective are defined.
6. The conceptual theory and basic mechanisms framing the intervention are defined.

The Intervention Is Operationally Defined

An **operational definition** requires that the specific elements of the intervention can be observed and counted. In other words, the intervention must be described at a level that would allow others to implement it. It is important to note that descriptions of interventions presented in most research journals do not provide a complete operational definition of an intervention. Schools seeking to implement a particular intervention will need to consult information sources such as implementation manuals to understand the elements of an intervention. The operational definition should include a detailed description of the intervention's content and organization, its duration, the amount of training required to enable implementation, a determination of completeness of adoption, and an assessment of treatment implementation integrity.

The Qualifications of People Who May Use the Intervention With Success Are Defined

Teachers should have the training or expertise to run an intervention.

Some interventions may be used by anyone in an educational setting, while others (e.g., instructional assessment, FBA) are intended to be used only by individuals with specific training. If successful use of an intervention requires specific training or expertise, the qualifications of implementers should be clearly defined, and tools or measures for assessing implementation integrity also should be recommended and described. For example, the *First Step to Success* program is designed for use by a wide range of educators, including classroom teachers, resource teachers, and paraeducators (Walker et al., 1997). It is important for schools to keep in mind that researchers often conduct extensive training of implementers to ensure high degrees of implementation integrity. Schools may struggle to provide the same intensive level of professional development.

The Outcomes That May Be Expected From Using the Intervention Are Defined

Among the most important criteria for evidence-based practice is designation of the measurable outcomes that can be expected if the intervention is used with integrity. It is desirable that the outcomes include proximal measures (i.e., linked closely with the expected intervention outcomes) as well as distal measures (i.e., not linked closely with the expected intervention outcomes). For example, Walker and colleagues (2009) used behavioral observations of academic engaged time to assess the proximal effects of the *First Step to Success* program. The parent and teacher forms of the Problem Behavior scale of the *Social Skills Rating System* (Gresham & Elliott, 1990) were also used. It is also desirable that the long-term follow-up outcomes be reported. The reporting of long-term outcomes is especially critical when the outcomes be interventions may decay (e.g., reward system). Also, in some cases, documented benchmarks or criteria (e.g., 80% of students) and possible side effects or hypothesized effects (e.g., escape-related behaviors) should be described. The outcome measures should be psychometrically sound and accepted by the field.

The Settings (or Contexts) in Which the Intervention Is Expected to Be Effective Are Defined

If an intervention is designed for a specific setting, the relevant features of that setting should be stipulated. Practices that are uniquely designed for elementary school contexts, for example, may not be appropriate for high school. For example, Check-in/Check-out (CICO), also known as the "Behavior Education Plan" (Crone, Horner, & Hawkin, 2004), is designed for use in schools regardless of their structure (e.g., grade level, staffing, student population).

The Target Population or Populations for Whom the Intervention Is Effective Are Defined

Some interventions target students showing a general set of problems (e.g., classroom deportment problems); others focus only on students with specific characteristics (e.g., conduct disordered). If an intervention is designed primarily to address the needs of a specific population of students, the specific characteristics of that population should be indicated in the description of the intervention. For example, the authors of *Check & Connect* designed the program for K through 12 students with learning and/or behavior difficulties (Christenson et al., 2008).

The Conceptual Theory and Basic Mechanisms Framing the Intervention Are Defined

Defining the conceptual theory underlying an intervention provides the framework for assessing not only if an intervention works, but why. Defining an intervention in terms of a conceptual body of knowledge should serve to guide ongoing development, adaptation, and improvement. For example, a description of the conceptual theory for *MST* (Henggeler et al., 1998) indicates antisocial behavior is multidetermined and linked with characteristics of the individual youth and his or her family, peer group, school, and community contexts. As such, *MST* interventions aim to attenuate risk factors by building youth and family strengths (protective factors) on a highly individualized and comprehensive basis. The provision of home-based services circumvents barriers to service access that often characterize families of serious juvenile offenders. An emphasis on parental empowerment to modify the natural social network of their children facilitates the maintenance and generalization of treatment gains.

How Do Schools Identify Evidence-Based Interventions?

One of the greatest challenges facing schools seeking to implement evidence-based interventions is that the field of education contains a vast array of interventions, all claiming to enhance the educational outcomes of students and to be evidence based. Unfortunately, the evidence for many of these interventions comes from poorly designed or advocacy-driven research. Schools must sort through these claims to decide which interventions merit consideration for their use. The United States Department of Education created a guide that walks educators through the process of finding evidence-based practices: *Identifying and Implementing Educational Practices Supported by Rigorous Evidence* (Coalition for Evidence-Based Policy, 2003). We detail the three steps for identifying an evidence-based intervention highlighted in this guide in the remainder of this section (see Table 11.2).

Table 11.2	The Three Steps for Identifying an Evidence-Based Intervention

Step 1. Is the intervention backed by strong evidence of effectiveness?

Step 2. If the intervention is not backed by strong evidence, is it backed by possible evidence of effectiveness?

Step 3. If the answer to the questions in steps 1 and 2 is no, one may conclude the intervention is not supported by meaningful evidence.

Step 1. Is the Intervention Backed by Strong Evidence of Effectiveness?

The first step involved in evaluating whether an educational intervention is supported by rigorous evidence is to determine whether the intervention is backed by "strong" evidence of effectiveness. Randomized controlled trials that are well designed and properly implemented are considered the gold standard for evaluating the effectiveness of an intervention. Furthermore, the randomized trial should be conducted in the school and classroom settings for which the intervention is designed and in which it will be implemented.

Randomized controlled trials are studies that randomly assign students to an intervention group or to a comparison condition (often referred to as a control group) to measure the effects of the intervention on specified student outcomes. For example, Walker and colleagues (2009) assessed the effects of *First Step to Success* with a diverse sample of kindergarten and first-grade students at risk for behavior disorders. Participating students were randomly assigned to intervention or control groups. The treatment integrity was assessed to ensure the experimental condition was implemented as prescribed. Because of the random assignment process, differences in the social outcomes between the experimental and control conditions represented the effects of the program.

The process of randomly assigning students to either an intervention or comparison group ensures, to a high degree of confidence, that there are no systematic differences between groups in any observed and unobserved characteristics except participation in the experimental condition being tested. There are, of course, multiple variations on the basic concept of randomized controlled trials. Sometimes, individuals, entire classrooms, schools, or school districts are assigned randomly to intervention and control groups.

Although randomization should result in the creation of similar experimental and control groups, attrition from these groups may create differences. Thus, it is important to consider the potential influence of attrition on the study outcomes. Attrition results when an outcome variable is not available for all participants initially assigned to the experimental and comparison conditions. Schools should be concerned about overall attrition as well as differences in the rates of attrition for the experimental conditions. High levels of attrition may compromise the initial equivalence of the experimental conditions and the intervention effects may be biased. Studies with high levels of attrition should demonstrate the equivalence of the experimental conditions. The process for identifying the influence of attrition and equivalence, as recommended by the U.S. Department of Education's What Works Clearinghouse, involves considering the study design standards depicted in Figure 11.2 (What Works Clearinghouse, 2008).

| Figure 11.2 | Study Design Factors Considered by the What Works Clearinghouse |

Other organizations seeking to identify evidence-based interventions, such as Blueprints for Violence Prevention (*http://www.colorado.edu/cspv/blueprints/*), also distinguish between randomized controlled trials and other types of evidence supporting the use of an intervention. Thus, the emphasis on randomized controlled trials is not unique to the U.S. Department of Education's What Works Clearinghouse.

Key items to look for in assessing whether a randomized controlled trial is well designed include the following:

1. Does the study describe the intervention, including who administered it, who received it, how the experimental conditions differed from one another, and the logic of how the intervention is designed to affect student outcomes?

2. Were reliable and valid outcome measures used?

3. Was there any indication that attrition was a problem?

4. Were data reported on the proximal, distal, and long-term effects?

5. Were the studies conducted in settings targeted by the intervention for implementation?

6. Was the pre-intervention equivalence of the experimental and control groups established?

Step 2. If the Intervention Is Not Backed by Strong Evidence, Is It Backed by Possible Evidence of Effectiveness?

There is substantial evidence that well designed and implemented randomized controlled trials are superior to other study designs in measuring the effects of an intervention. It is clearly established that randomization is possible in many contexts and situations. For some interventions where randomization is impossible or if an intervention has not yet been studied using a randomized controlled trial, other designs are acceptable when used with caution and when careful attention is given to ruling out plausible alternative explanations for outcomes.

Quasi-experimental comparison designs (in which participants are not randomly assigned to the experimental and comparison groups, but the groups are equated) can be used effectively to establish the outcomes for an intervention. These designs, however, are credible only when adequately powered tests demonstrate the pretest equivalence of both groups, an equivalence that is naturally occurring rather than achieved through statistical techniques. It is also important that the assignment to experimental and comparison groups was not by self-selection.

Well-conducted regression discontinuity designs can be convincing also because the selection model is completely known. **Regression discontinuity designs** are designs in which participants are assigned to the intervention and the comparison conditions based on a cutoff score on a pre-intervention measure that typically assesses need or merit. This measure should have a known functional relationship with the outcome of interest over the range relevant for the study sample.

Well-conducted single-case designs can also be convincing for establishing intervention outcomes. Single-case designs involve repeated measurement of a single case (e.g., a student or a classroom) in different conditions or phases over time (single-case designs are described in more detail in Chapter 3). Single-case studies are especially relevant in assessing interventions that are small in scope (e.g., the use of positive reinforcement to promote prosocial behavior) or that target special populations of students (e.g., those with autism). Nevertheless, the rationale for the use of single-case methodology should be specified. This involves defining the strengths and weaknesses of the particular single-case design being used.

Types of studies that do not comprise possible evidence include pre-post studies, quasi-experimental comparison-group studies in which the equivalence of the experimental conditions was not established, and meta-analyses that include the results of low-quality studies. Pre-post studies assess whether participants in an intervention improve or regress during the course of an intervention. The central problem with this type of study is that, without reference to a comparison group or extended baseline data and replication of intervention effects across phases, they cannot establish whether the participants' improvement or regression would have occurred anyway even without the intervention.

Many quasi-experimental comparison-group studies also produce erroneous conclusions because the equivalence of the experimental conditions was not established. Rather, researchers use statistical techniques to create a comparison group that is matched with the intervention group on one or more factors (e.g., socioeconomic status). The primary problem is that there are often unobservable differences between participants of the experimental and comparison conditions. This problem typically occurs because intervention participants self-select themselves into the intervention group. Thus, for example, the motivation of participants rather than the intervention may account for the student outcomes.

Investigations using meta-analysis, which is a quantitative technique for combining individual studies, may produce erroneous conclusions because they include the results of poorly conducted individual studies. Combining the results from poorly conducted studies, such as randomized controlled trials with significant flaws, poorly matched comparison group studies, and pre-post studies, often leads to erroneous conclusions regarding intervention outcomes.

The following are key items to look for in assessing whether quasi-experimental comparison studies, regression discontinuity experiments, and single-case studies are well designed.

1. For all study types:
   - Does the study describe the intervention, including who administered it, who received it, how the experimental conditions differed from one another, and the logic of how the intervention is designed to affect student outcomes?
   - Were reliable and valid outcome measures used?
   - Was there any indication that attrition was a problem?
   - Were data reported on the proximal, distal, and long-term effects?
   - Were the studies conducted in settings targeted by the intervention for implementation?

2. Quasi-experimental comparison-group studies:
   - Was the pre-intervention equivalence of the experimental and comparison groups established, or were they matched very closely in academic achievement, social behavior, demographics, and other characteristics prior to the intervention?

- Was membership in the intervention and comparison groups assigned rather than self-selected?

3. Regression discontinuity:

   - Was assignment to the intervention based on a clearly defined index measure (e.g., a specified benchmark for reading difficulties) with a known cutoff for eligibility (who the intervention is targeted for)?
   - Was the index measure correlated with the intervention (no or low correlation is equivalent to random assignment)?

4. Single-case studies:

   - Was the baseline condition described in detail, and did it ascertain a pattern of responding to enable prediction of future performance if no intervention is provided?
   - Were the intervention effects demonstrated at three different points in time with a single participant or across different participants?

5. Meta-analyses:

   - Did the meta-analysis exclude poorly designed studies (e.g., pre-post studies) or differentiate intervention effects by design type?

Step 3. If the Answer to the Questions in Steps 1 and 2 Is No, One May Conclude the Intervention Is Not Supported by Meaningful Evidence

The reasons that studies do not meet the U.S. Department of Education's What Works Clearinghouse standards are listed below. Schools should consider these same reasons when evaluating intervention studies. A study may fail to meet the What Works Clearinghouse standards in the following circumstances:

1. It does not include a valid or reliable outcome measure or does not provide adequate information to determine whether it uses an outcome that is valid or reliable.

2. It includes only outcomes that are over-aligned with the intervention or measures in a way that is inconsistent with the protocol.

3. The intervention and comparison groups are not shown to be equivalent at baseline.

4. The overall attrition rate exceeds the What Works Clearinghouse standards for an area (see *www.ies.ed.gov/ncee/wwc/* for standards).

5. The differential attrition rate exceeds the What Works Clearinghouse standards for an area (see *www.ies.ed.gov/ncee/wwc/* for standards).

6. The estimates of effects did not account for differences in pre-intervention characteristics while using a quasi-experimental design.

7. The measures of effect cannot be attributed solely to the intervention—there was only one unit of analysis in one or both conditions.

8. The measures of effect cannot be attributed solely to the intervention—the intervention was combined with another intervention.

9. The measures of effect cannot be attributed solely to the intervention—the intervention was not implemented as designed.

How Do Schools Assess the Magnitude of the Effects of an Intervention?

There are two different approaches to assessing how large the effects of an intervention are—statistical significance and effect size.

Statistical Significance

Assessing the **statistical significance** of the intervention effects is one approach used to assess their magnitude. Statistically significant intervention effects are often mistakenly assumed to be large or important; whereas, statistically nonsignificant intervention effects are often assumed to be small or unimportant. The problem with this approach is that intervention effects of the same size can sometimes be statistically significant and at other times nonsignificant. Alternatively, effects that don't matter much can be statistically significant, while effects that matter a great deal can be statistically nonsignificant. This confusion occurs because tests of statistical significance actually confound two independent pieces of information: the magnitude of the intervention's effects and the size of the sample. Thus, it is important to keep in mind when reviewing research studies that statistical significance tells us very little about the magnitude or practical significance of the intervention effects and should not be used as a stand-alone measure of the importance of the intervention.

Effect Size

Calculating an effect size is another approach that can be used to assess the magnitude of the effects of an intervention. In contrast to the statistical significance approach, effect sizes do not confound the magnitude of an intervention's effects with the size of the sample. **Effect size** simply quantifies the difference between the experimental and control/comparison groups in experimental studies (single-case effect sizes are described later). The effect size provides a clear measure of the magnitude of the effects of an intervention. An effect size measurement uses the idea of a "standard deviation" to contextualize the difference between two groups. In general, an effect size is the difference between the mean values of the experimental and control/comparison groups divided by the standard deviation of the control/comparison group or the pooled standard deviation of the experimental and control/comparison groups. Before going on, it is important to note that there are multiple ways to estimate effect sizes in cases in which the means or standard deviations for the experimental and control/comparison groups are not reported. Additionally, reporting effect sizes in research studies is now considered best practice. Thus, in most cases, it is not necessary to calculate effect sizes given that researchers will most likely provide them for you.

How does one interpret effect sizes? There is no universally accepted set of criteria. Although larger is generally better, the quality of the research design and the relative experience of the two participant groups are equally important to consider. In other words, effect size estimates tend to be context dependent. For example, a large randomized controlled trial obtaining an effect size of .25 is more important than a small quasi-experimental comparison groups study with an effect size of .50. Cohen's (1988) recommendation—that effect sizes of .20, .50, and .80 are considered small, moderate, and large, respectively—is often used. Another way to interpret the magnitude of intervention effects indicated by an effect size is to consider the improvement in percentile score that would take place if an intervention with a given effect size were implemented (see Table 11.3).

Visual analysis has been the prominent technique for judging the magnitude of the intervention effects from single-case studies (Horner, Carr, et al., 2005; Matyas & Greenwood, 1990). **Visual analysis** requires assessment of all conditions within the design. Each design (e.g., multiple baseline, withdrawal) requires a specific data pattern for the researcher to claim that change in the dependent variable (what you are measuring, such as out-of-seat behavior) is a function of the independent variable (your behavior management program, such as self-management). More specifically, visual analysis involves looking at the level, trend, and variability of performance during baseline and

Table 11.3	Effect Sizes and Associated Change in Percentile Scores
Effect Size	**Increase in Percentile Scores**
+0.10	50 to 54
+0.20	50 to 58
+0.30	50 to 62
+0.40	50 to 66
+0.50	50 to 69
+0.60	50 to 73
+0.70	50 to 76
+0.80	50 to 79
+0.90	50 to 82
+1.00	50 to 84

intervention conditions (Horner, Carr, et al.). Level refers to the mean performance during a condition or phase of the study. The trend references the rate of increase or decrease in the slope (best-fit line) of the data within a condition or phase. Variability refers to the degree to which performance fluctuates around a mean slope during a condition or phase. In addition, visual analysis requires judgment of the immediacy and magnitude of effects following the onset or withdrawal of the intervention, the proportion of data points in adjacent conditions or phases that overlap in level, and the consistency of data patterns across multiple presentations of intervention and nonintervention conditions.

The integration of all of this information is used to judge if a functional relationship exists between the intervention and outcome measures, that is, whether the intervention appears to produce the changes in student behavior. The documentation necessary for an evidence-based intervention requires a compelling demonstration that a functional relationship exists. Demonstration that a functional relationship exists is compromised when a long time elapses between manipulation of the independent variable and changes in the dependent variable, when mean changes in conditions are small or similar to changes with condition, and when, following introduction of the intervention, trends fail to conform to those predicted (Horner, Carr, et al., 2005).

More recently, effect size estimates are being used as an adjunct to visual analysis (Parker & Hagan-Burke, 2007). When used in this way, effect size provides a measure of intervention strength, a summary when visual judgments do not agree, and a method for comparing relative intervention success across studies (Parker & Brossart, 2006). Some single-case effect size indices include (a) Cohen's (1988) "Percentage of Nonoverlapping Data" (CPND); (b) Parker, Hagan-Burke, and Vannest's (2007) "Percentage of All Nonoverlapping Data" (PAND); (c) Rosenthal, Rosnow, and Rubin's (2000) "Binomial Effect Size Display" (BESD) and "Percentile Rank in Control Group" (PR); (d) McGraw and Wong's (1992) "Common Language Effect Size" (CLES); and (e) Parker, Vannest, and Brown's (2009) "Nonoverlap of All Pairs" (NAP). It is important to note that established guidelines for interpreting the magnitude of effect sizes for single-case studies are not available. Thus, the use of effect sizes in evaluating the magnitude of intervention effects from single-case studies is still at the beginning stages of development. Guidelines for interpreting the magnitude of effect sizes for single-case studies will likely emerge as meta-analyses are conducted for interventions directed at specific learning and behavior difficulties.

Where Can Schools Find Evidence-Based Interventions?

As noted in Chapter 8, there are a number of organizations formally assessing the supporting evidence for interventions. The following websites can be useful in finding evidence-based academic and behavioral interventions. These sites use varying criteria for determining which interventions are supported by evidence. We recommend, however, that, when navigating these websites, you keep in mind the factors discussed previously. Note that the lists are updated on a regular basis.

1. Best Evidence Encyclopedia: *http://www.bestevidence.org/*

2. Center on the Social and Emotional Foundations for Early Learning: *http://www.vanderbilt.edu/csefel/wwb.html*

3. Division of Early Childhood of CEC—Recommended Practices: *http://www.dec-sped.org/About_DEC/Recommended_Practices*

4. National Autism Standards Project: *http://www.nationalautismcenter.org*

5. National Secondary Transition Technical Assistance Center: *http://www.nsttac.org/ebp/ebp_main.aspx*

6. NICHY Research to Practice Database: *http://www.nichcy.org/Research/Summaries/Pages/Default.aspx*

7. Promising Practices Network: *http://www.promisingpractices.net/*

8. Research and Training Center on Early Childhood Development: *http://www.researchtopractice.info/index.php*

9. What Works Clearinghouse: *http://ies.ed.gov/ncee/wwc/*

How Do Schools Develop the Capacity to Implement Interventions?

After interventions have been identified, the school must develop the capacity to implement them. A school must assess its organizational capacity in terms of both what resources (i.e., human, technical, physical, fiscal) are currently in place and whether the required resources necessary to implement interventions will be in place when needed.

The organizational capacity of schools is crucial to the scope of the interventions that can be undertaken and ultimately sustained. What are the barriers to implementing and establishing interventions? Will there be enough staff? Do staff members have the specialized technical knowledge necessary to implement the interventions? Are there resources for staffing, space, and materials? Differing interventions require differing levels of resources, and schools need to determine what is available in advance of implementing any intervention. These resources constitute the school's assets. Often, schools will be faced with deciding which interventions can be dropped to accommodate others as needs and resources change. A school must constantly reassess its assets or organizational capacity, as it adds or subtracts programs. There are four areas of capacity to consider: human, technical, physical setting, and funding capacity.

Human Capacity

Human capacity refers to the staff and volunteers who are currently available or could be available to implement the interventions. Schools should consider both which staff members are potentially available to implement the interventions and which are needed to operate the organizational capacity necessary to implement them. In addition, staff members who could be available for the management, implementation, evaluation, and fundraising (human and fiscal) activities associated with implementing interventions should be identified.

The extent to which schools have the capacity to initiate, mobilize, and sustain interventions should also be considered. Effective schools promote communication, decision making, and conflict resolution to ensure that interventions are implemented properly.

Finally, volunteers often are the fuel that will support interventions and keep them operating. They provide a bridge between community and school and give much needed support to the work. Volunteers can supplement staff at any level of work, from intervention facilitation to clerical work associated with the implementation (e.g., summarizing and graphing student progress monitoring data). They should be involved and committed, which a school can facilitate by providing them with proper training and feedback for the tasks they are asked to accomplish. All volunteers should have a well-defined task; if they are busy and think they are an integral part of the school, they are more likely to stay involved. Volunteers have varying interests and time constraints that must be taken into consideration. A periodic review of each volunteer's task and time commitment gives both the volunteer and the staff an opportunity to evaluate and make changes in a positive way.

Technical Capacity

Technical capacity refers primarily to the administrative and specialized support necessary to implement interventions. Administrative support provides the means for establishing the facility management, communications, operations, and logistics for implementing interventions. Specialized support refers to the kinds of knowledge infrastructure that may be needed for specialized interventions. Given the complexity of the factors underlying many problems addressed by contemporary schools, it is important to assess the school's technical capacity to determine whether any staff members have specialized knowledge related to an identified intervention and associated problem. It may be necessary for the school to bring in an individual from the community or identify a consultant to provide the technical knowledge necessary to support the selection and implementation of an intervention in an effective and efficient manner.

Physical Capacity

Physical capacity involves schools selecting the setting in which the interventions will occur. Selecting the setting requires the school to consider the characteristics of the target group and the interventions and programs to be provided. Although the context for providing primary-level interventions is logical, it is not always obvious in the case of secondary and tertiary interventions.

For example, at first blush, implementing a secondary-level small-group behavioral intervention for students with behavioral difficulties seems straightforward. Selecting a setting, however, is difficult. Take the case of the Check & Connect program (Christenson et al., 2008). Will the mentoring sessions be conducted in the student's classroom, potentially disrupting the ongoing instructional activities provided to the remaining students? Or will the mentoring sessions be conducted in the hallway, administrative offices, or empty classrooms, which would present a new set of concerns (e.g., transition time)?

It is clear that selecting the setting in which the interventions will occur can be rather difficult. The school may find it challenging to determine where the interventions can be carried out most effectively and efficiently. These issues become even more problematic if the interventions are multifaceted in nature.

Funding Capacity

Funding capacity refers to fiscal resources available to implement interventions. Inadequate funding is often the reason the implementation of new interventions fails. Assessing funding capacity means determining how much funding is available to be allocated toward the implementation of selected interventions. It also means devising strategies for reorganizing current interventions to match available funding resources. Most important, it means putting resources into the development of a long-term funding strategy for sustainable implementation of the selected interventions. Finally, it is important to examine external resources that can be used to support the implementation of interventions. External resources include not only external funding for the specific intervention but also services, equipment, and general funding support that will enable the school to leverage its internal resources to greater benefit.

How Do Schools Implement and Sustain Interventions?

After the interventions and the capacity of the school are developed, schools must set some implementation goals and objectives. The goal is a broad statement of what the members of the leadership team would like to accomplish. Objectives are the sequence of activities and tasks that must be accomplished to implement interventions and, in turn, to achieve the goal. Laying out a set of sequential objectives provides the school a means with which to track the implementation of interventions. Implementation objectives should identify (a) who is responsible, (b) what activities and tasks must be carried out, (c) where they are carried out, and (d) the anticipated completion date. A sample goal and its associated implementation objectives for a schoolwide discipline program are presented in Table 11.4.

It is important to limit the number of implementation objectives to make it easier for the school staff and other key stakeholders to identify the accomplishments. Furthermore, implementation objectives are not static. Objectives should be modified

Table 11.4	Sample Implementation Goal and Associated Objectives

Goal

Reduce the number of formal disciplinary office referrals.

Objectives

1. Establish effective ecological arrangements to achieve a safe school environment.

    Who: Members of the leadership team.

    What: Conduct site analysis, eliminate or adjust unsafe physical arrangements, and improve the scheduling and use of space.

    Where: Entire school campus.

    Date: Fall 2011

2. Establish consistent behavioral expectations and provide active supervision.

    Who: Entire school staff.

    What: Develop consensus among staff on behavioral expectations and levels of supervision.

    Where: Entire school campus.

    Date: Fall 2011

3. Implement Think Time® for responding to problem behaviors.

    Who: Entire school staff.

    What: One 2-hour training session with two 1-hour problem solving sessions.

    Where: School library.

    Date: Winter 2011

4. Establish behavior support team.

    Who: Members of the behavior support team.

    What: Three 2-hour training sessions on functional behavior assessment and behavior intervention plans.

    Where: School library.

    Date: Winter 2011

as resources change, activities proceed faster or slower than planned, or new information becomes available. Some guidelines for you to keep in mind include the following:

1. Ensure that the objectives are realistic and match the available resources and the capacity of the staff to implement interventions.

2. Ensure that input is obtained from outside agencies that will assist with the implementation of interventions and will make certain that implementation objectives are consistent with those of the agencies.

Establishing realistic implementation goals and associated objectives will ensure that interventions are implemented in a systematic fashion. The implementation objectives will not only clarify the tasks to be done but also provide the school a means with which to track the implementation of interventions. It is important to make mid-course changes in the implementation objectives, if necessary.

Schools should also ensure the sustainability of interventions. **Sustainability** means that an intervention is durable and likely to continue over a period of time—and has the resources to support it. Of course, schools should first ascertain if interventions should be sustained. Changes in circumstances, staff, and school needs might suggest that the intervention is not a good "fit" for the school. Perhaps the desired outcomes were not achieved. The careful planning that was undertaken to select interventions in the first place, however, suggests the likelihood that sustaining them will be a priority. Moreover, ending an intervention that achieves positive results is counter-productive if the problem for which it was chosen still exists. Creating interventions requires significant start-up costs that can be amortized over future years if continued. If interventions are successful but not sustainable, future ones may meet staff resistance. Some things for schools to consider with regard to the sustainability of interventions include the following:

1. Making sure the assessed needs of the school are continually driving the intervention.

2. Ensuring through a high-quality evaluation process that the intervention is producing desired outcomes.

3. Assessing capacity to identify natural supports for the intervention.

4. Preparing clear plans for sustaining the intervention.

5. Creating a strong organizational base for the intervention.

6. Considering integration of specific interventions into a comprehensive program.

7. Considering a scaled-down version of the intervention or program that will still be effective.

How Do Schools Evaluate Interventions and Programs?

Even after evidence-based interventions have been selected and used, it is important for schools to evaluate them. The two goals of the evaluation are to provide feedback to staff regarding the implementation of interventions (process evaluation) and to determine the extent to which interventions have accomplished their established goals (outcome evaluation). **Process evaluations** focus on fidelity of implementation (i.e., the extent to which the intervention is delivered as intended). **Outcome evaluations** center on whether or not interventions are effective and meet the established goals. Conducting process and outcome evaluations is complex. Thus, this section is not meant to be a comprehensive discussion of evaluation methodologies but rather a brief overview of the focus of process and outcome evaluations.

Process Evaluations

Process evaluations should focus on the extent to which the interventions have been implemented as intended. Measuring fidelity of implementation is critical to making judgments regarding the general evaluation of interventions. Research has confirmed the importance of fidelity of implementation to enhance program effectiveness (Benner, Nelson, Stage, & Ralston, 2011; Foorman & Moats, 2004). For example, Walker and colleagues (2009) reported that overall fidelity of implementation of the *First Step to Success* program delivered to elementary students was significantly related to change in student outcomes. The obtained correlations were considered to be within the medium to large effect size range. These results indicate that the quality of implementation has a practically significant effect on student outcomes.

When schools implement an intervention, it is critical to know whether it is being implemented as designed so that if the intervention is not producing positive student outcomes, schools can remedy the deficiency rather than abandoning the intervention. Checking fidelity of implementation for an intervention can be a complex and resource-intensive process. The tools to assess fidelity of implementation can be divided into two categories (Gresham, 1989): direct and indirect.

Direct Assessment. Direct assessment of the implementation of an intervention requires that its components be specified in operational terms. Doing this is much like performing a task analysis of each of the components of the intervention. A qualified staff member observes the intervention and counts or rates the occurrence of each of its components to determine the extent to which these are implemented; the observer also identifies those interventionists in need of retraining. For example, Nelson and colleagues (2009) used parent observations of the implementation of *First Step to Success*. Independent observations by project staff were conducted to determine the extent to which the coach implemented 18 components (i.e., occurred, did not occur) of the intervention (e.g., operating the program daily, awarding praise and points according to program guidelines and contingent on student performance).

Indirect Assessment. The second category of tools to assess fidelity of implementation is indirect assessment. The approaches included in this type of assessment are self-reports, interviews, and permanent products. Permanent product assessment is thought to be the most reliable and accurate of the indirect methods. Permanent products may include samples of student work or performance on assessments of instructional sessions. For example, Nelson and colleagues (2009) used self-evaluations by schools to assess the fidelity of implementation for a tier 1 SWPBIS program. Each project year, all staff members at each of the participating schools were asked to complete an eight-item questionnaire regarding whether the *BASE* implementation phase was followed. Staff rated each item on a 3-point Likert-type scale (i.e., low, medium, high). Each member completed the questionnaire independently in the second month of the school year. The eight items focused on key elements of *BASE* (e.g., the extent to which staff taught and reviewed the common area and disciplinary procedures with students, communicated with parents about expectations, and applied active supervision). The mean aggregate score ranges for all criteria on the survey were less than 12 for poor, 12 to less than 16 for limited, 16 to less than 18 for adequate, 18 to less than 22 for good, and greater than or equal to 22 for excellent (the total scale score range was 8 to 24). Each school was assigned a convergent evidence scale score ranging from 1 (poor implementation) to 5 (excellent implementation).

Proactive practices that help schools to ensure fidelity of implementation include the following:

1. Define the intervention operations, techniques, and components.

2. Define the responsibilities of the individuals responsible for implementing the intervention.

3. Create a system for measuring intervention operations, techniques, and components.

4. Create a system for feedback to the implementers to correct any implementation problems that arise.

Outcome Evaluations

Outcome evaluations focus on the effectiveness of interventions or the extent to which they are meeting the established goals. In other words, outcome evaluations are summative in nature and provide information with which to judge the value of interventions. Furthermore, outcome evaluations can take on several levels of complexity. At the first level, an outcome evaluation might be designed only to determine whether the target population has improved. At the second level, an outcome evaluation might be designed to determine whether the target population has improved relative to a similar group not receiving services. At the third level, an outcome evaluation might be designed to compare the relative effectiveness of two different types of interventions. Some guidelines for conducting evaluations of interventions are as follows:

1. *Decide what to assess.* Focus on what the intervention can realistically accomplish. For example, it would not be realistic to have the parents or guardians and all of the teachers complete norm-referenced behavior rating forms to assess the effects of a mentoring-oriented program such as Check & Connect (Christenson et al., 2008) on middle school students at risk for learning and behavior difficulties. Rather, monitoring the students' office discipline referrals would be more appropriate.

2. *Use several outcomes.* It is usually better to use several measurable outcomes when assessing interventions. For example, schools can use office disciplinary referrals but should add other measures such as level of violence in the school, in-class behavior for specific students, student absences, and student grades. Once the outcomes are selected, deciding on an evaluation design and creating data-collection methods will be much easier.

3. *Select an evaluation design to fit the intervention.* It is important to select an evaluation design that will provide a clear picture of the extent to which any changes can be attributable to the intervention. For example, single-case designs, such as a multiple baseline design across classrooms or students, are relatively easy to use and may fit naturally in the initial implementation sequence for an intervention. Of course, the strength of the evaluation design will enhance confidence in the findings.

4. *Determine when to assess.* The timing of measurements is important and will result from the evaluation design. For example, if the design uses a pre- and posttest, the measurements must be conducted before the implementation of the intervention and after it. Additionally, progress monitoring should be conducted to measure student performance throughout the intervention (see a discussion of progress monitoring in Chapter 12).

5. *Gather the data.* Decide who will collect the data and how the data will be collected. For example, it is important to identify someone who neither has a vested interest in the outcomes nor plays a direct supervisory role with the individuals implementing the intervention. The person selected to collect the data may affect the results. Will the members of the target population feel comfortable with the person? Can the person gathering data be as objective as the task requires? Some important issues that might arise include consent, confidentiality, and anonymity if the data are to be presented in professional venues (e.g., conferences). These issues must be considered carefully prior to collecting any data.

6. *Analyze the data.* Just as there are quantitative and qualitative data-collection methods, there are quantitative and qualitative data-analysis methods. The data-analysis procedures used should be consistent with the evaluation design and measures used. For example, as already noted, visual analysis of the level, trend, and variability of office discipline referrals or other forms of data during baseline and intervention conditions can be used to determine the effectiveness of the intervention.

7. *Interpret the data.* The process and outcome data obtained through the evaluation must be interpreted to guide improvements in interventions as well as improve them over time. The data should be interpreted against the established goals or benchmarks and the results weighed against the intervention's cost. For example, a school might monitor its implementation of the SWPBIS program using the *SET* relative to the established criteria of 80% or more total points (described in Chapter 10).

VIGNETTE REVISITED — Making a Difference in the Life of a Student Through Focused Intervention

Having handled the incident well, Mr. Allen now thinks it's time to submit Fred to the leadership team as a genuine and immediate problem. The school has spent the last several years identifying and implementing behavioral and learning interventions to address the needs of students such as Fred more directly.

During that time, the school focused on identifying interventions that had been developed and validated with students using high-quality experimental designs showing evidence of practically significant effects. The school focused on these interventions because they typically meet the twin goals of validated practice and consumer friendliness.

The school, having built a capacity to address problems such as Fred's, begins a tertiary intervention with Fred, a student the leadership team considers "severely involved." Rather than focusing on punitive behavior, the team arranges for Fred to have one-on-one tutoring in reading and math. In addition, Fred's parents attend a family management program through which they learn how to meet their needs as well as Fred's.

Gradually, through the monitoring by teachers and parents, Fred begins to emerge as a capable student. His acceptance is not complete until the end of his sixth-grade year, yet some improvement is noticed almost immediately. Knowing how to read and being competent in math seems to help Fred's confidence level. His stealing from classmates, another problem that had led to Fred's untrustworthiness in the eyes of other students, decreases as his social acceptance begins to increase.

Summary

In summary, schools should consider four standards for the selection of evidence-based programs. First, interventions should be considered only if they have been validated with well-implemented, high-quality experimental designs. Second, interventions should be considered only if they have produced practically significant effects. Third, interventions should be viewed more positively if they have been replicated at multiple sites with demonstrated effects. Finally, interventions should be viewed more positively if they have demonstrated durable effects (e.g., sustained for at least one year after the intervention).

One of the three primary goals of schoolwide positive behavior intervention and support programs is to identify and select evidence-based interventions. This chapter focused on how to plan, select, implement, and evaluate interventions (i.e., the fifth and sixth organizational systems of SWPBIS) that have been validated through experimental studies or rigorous evaluation designs. Planning, selecting, implementing, and evaluating evidence-based interventions are important to achieving an effective SWPBIS program.

The key terms underlying the entire process used to plan, select, implement, and evaluate evidence-based interventions are strategy, intervention, and program. Strategies, interventions, and programs are not only related to one another; they also depict the evolution of the comprehensiveness of a schoolwide positive behavior intervention and support program over time. Identifying a strategy or conceptual approach to address the problem is important in guiding the selection of interventions. Furthermore, selecting a set of primary-, secondary-, and tertiary-level interventions to address a problem leads to the development of an effective and comprehensive program.

Schools use six steps to plan, select, implement, and evaluate evidence-based interventions. First, schools should determine whether the intervention being considered meets the criteria for being defined as an evidence-based intervention. Second, schools must identify evidence-based interventions. Third, schools must assess the magnitude or practical significance of the intervention effects. Fourth, schools could identify evidence-based interventions that have been identified by other organizations. Nevertheless, schools must still evaluate the selected interventions closely. Fifth, schools must develop a strategic plan to implement and sustain the intervention. The plan should consider the capacity of the school to ensure that the implementation goals and objectives can be realistically met. Finally, the leadership team must conduct a process and outcome evaluation of the intervention. Conducting an evaluation of the intervention is important to ensure that it meets established goals.

Key Terms

effect size   352

evidence-based interventions   344

funding capacity   357

human capacity   355

intervention   341

operational definition   344

outcome evaluations   359

physical capacity   356

process evaluations   359

program   343

regression discontinuity designs   349

statistical significance   352

strategy   341

sustainability   359

technical capacity   356

visual analysis   353

Discussion Questions

1. Compare and contrast a strategy, intervention, and program.

2. Why is it difficult for schools to know which intervention to implement?

3. What are the criteria for defining a program as an evidence-based intervention?

4. Why is it important for schools to choose interventions that are evidence based?

5. Why is it important for an intervention to be operationally defined?

6. What are randomized controlled trials, and why should they be used when evaluating interventions?

7. What are the two ways to calculate the magnitude of an intervention's effect?

8. Briefly discuss the four areas of capacity schools must consider before implementing a program.

9. Why is it critical for schools to set up implementation goals and objectives for interventions?

10. What are the goals of evaluating an intervention, and how are these goals measured?

12

Response to Intervention (RTI) and SWPBIS Models

Chapter Objectives

After studying this chapter, you should be able to

- describe where response to intervention (RTI) models originated,

- explain the primary differences between three-tier intervention models in the behavioral and public health fields,

- summarize the influence of education policy on the development and use of RTI models,

- identify research strands and educational practices that have shaped current conceptualizations of RTI,

- describe the expected effects of RTI intervention models,

- note the differences between problem-solving and standard protocol approaches,

- determine the differences between response to intervention and resistance to intervention,

- explain the differences between response to intervention and responsiveness to intervention,

- summarize the differences between instruction and intervention,

- describe the key elements of RTI intervention models, and

- depict the link between RTI and SWPBIS.

VIGNETTE	**Investigating the Impact of an Effective RTI and SWPBIS Approach**

MR. GONZALES IS WONDERING whether two new initiatives to improve student outcomes being implemented by his school staff at Elliot Elementary School have any common elements. The two initiatives are RTI and SWPBIS. Mr. Gonzales is concerned staff may be overwhelmed by trying to implement these initiatives if they do not link with one another. The school staff is implementing RTI in the literacy area to prevent reading difficulties and to improve overall literacy outcomes. The principal has also indicated staff will explore the use of RTI to identify students with learning disabilities.

At the same time, the school staff is implementing SWPBIS to prevent behavior difficulties and to improve the social outcomes of students. The number of administrative actions and referrals to special education for behavioral disorders has increased over the years. School staff members believe it is important for them to develop a comprehensive approach to improve the social behavior of the school.

Mr. Gonzalez decides to look more closely at RTI and SWPBIS. He is interested in finding out whether these initiatives will require distinct efforts on the part of staff or whether they have common elements for implementation.

Overview

Schools are under increasing pressure to improve the outcomes of students in all areas. Recent updates to the Individuals With Disabilities Education Improvement Act of 2004 (IDEA; P.L. 108-446) and the Elementary and Secondary Education Act (ESEA)–No Child Left Behind Act (NCLB) of 2001 encourage schools to turn toward proactive and preventive approaches that match the services students receive with their level of need. There is little doubt this focus will remain unchanged in future reauthorizations of these federal education laws. One such approach being advocated by educators is response to intervention. **Response to intervention (RTI)** is an initiative aimed at providing a high-quality continuum of instruction and interventions matched to student need and monitoring progress frequently to make decisions about changes in what students need to be successful (Fuchs, Fuchs, & Stecker, 2010). RTI uses a problem-solving approach that considers environmental factors as they apply to students' learning difficulties and provides instructional interventions as soon as the students demonstrate a need. RTI has emerged as the new approach for both early intervention and disability identification in learning disabilities.

Similarly, SWPBIS encourages schools to use a comprehensive early intervention approach to prevent behavior difficulties. SWPBIS uses a problem-solving approach and a continuum of behavioral interventions that are consistent with the guiding principles of RTI (Sugai & Horner, 2009). These interventions are systematically applied to students based on their demonstrated level of need and address the role of the environment as it applies to the prevention and improvement of behavior difficulties.

This chapter will focus on the link between RTI and SWPBIS. A discussion of where RTI and multitiered intervention models originated is followed by an overview of the models' expected effects at each of the intervention levels. This overview is followed by a discussion of conceptual issues that arise within RTI intervention models. A description of the key elements of these models is provided. Finally, a discussion of the link between RTI and SWPBIS is presented.

Where Did RTI and Multitiered Intervention Models Originate?

It is important to understand the origins of the current conceptualizations of the RTI and multitiered intervention models being used by schools. Originally, RTI intervention models arose from the behavioral and public health fields. Within each of these fields, three-tier intervention models were conceptualized differently (Mrazek & Haggerty, 1994). In the *behavioral health* field, three-tier behavior models were correlated directly with the levels of risks in target populations (Mrazek & Haggerty). The three tiers in the behavioral health field were categorized as universal, selected, and indicated. This categorization of tiers was based on a classification system proposed more than a decade earlier (Gordon, 1983). Still today, universal interventions are directed at the general population. Selected interventions are directed at targeted groups at greater risk than the rest of the population. Indicated interventions are directed only to high-risk individuals and those who are experiencing a disorder, to reduce its severity and duration. The three-tier behavior model from the behavioral health field uses information on degree of risk to identify the appropriate intensity of intervention for the general, at-risk, and high-risk or disordered populations. This model is commonly referred to as a risk factor matching model of intervention delivery. Demographic factors, family functioning, past and current levels of behavioral and academic functioning, and other relevant risk variables may indicate the degree of risk. Thus, in almost all cases, students are immediately assigned to and experience a selected or indicated intervention based on their degree of risk. This is not to say students who are unresponsive to a particular level of intervention would not be moved to another level (e.g., universal to select). Rather, an attempt is made initially to match the intensity of the intervention to the individual needs of the student. It is important to note that students who receive the selected and indicated interventions also receive the universal intervention, given that it is delivered to all students.

In the public health field the three tiers are categorized as primary, secondary, and tertiary. Primary prevention is directed at preventing a potential problem, secondary prevention is directed at early detection and intervention to delay onset of or to mitigate a problem, and tertiary prevention is directed at minimizing and avoiding relapse of a problem. The three-tier model from the public health field is consistent with most RTI intervention models being used by schools, which involve moving to more intensive levels of treatment when the interventions from the less intensive tier do not produce the desired outcomes (e.g., Gresham, 2004; Horner, Sugai, Todd, & Lewis-Palmer, 2005; Sugai, 2007). Thus, in almost all cases, before a student would be assigned to and experience a tertiary intervention, a secondary intervention would have been applied and determined not to work. Additionally, as with the behavioral health model, students who receive the secondary and tertiary interventions also receive the primary or universal intervention, given that it is delivered to all students.

The behavioral and public health multitier intervention models are both focused on prevention and effective for systematically organizing and implementing tiers of interventions. The use of the term *RTI* to refer to tiered intervention models arose out of special education policy. Importantly, although it does not mention the term *RTI*, IDEA (P.L. 108-446) permits educators to use RTI as a substitute for or supplement to the IQ-achievement discrepancy method for identifying students with learning disabilities (LD). As regulatory language in IDEA states,

> In determining whether a child has a specific learning disability, a local educational agency may use a process that determines if the child responds to scientific, research-based intervention as a part of the evaluation procedures described in paragraphs (2) and (3). (p. 60)

The allowance within IDEA to enable the use of RTI arose from work done through the "Learning Disabilities Initiative" (Bradley, Danielson, & Hallahan, 2002) instituted by the Office of Special Education Programs in the U.S. Department of Education. One of the main outcomes of this initiative was the establishment of a number of consensus statements about learning disabilities—in particular, about the need for ways other than using an achievement discrepancy formula to identify students with LD. Response to scientifically based, effective intervention was emphasized as a promising and practical means for identification and for improving instructional outcomes. This approach was referred to as "response to intervention," or RTI. The hope of policy makers was that RTI would not only encourage and guide schools to intervene earlier with scientifically based interventions for students at risk of school failure but also represent a more valid method of LD identification (Fletcher, Coulter, Reschly, & Vaughn, 2004). This identification would decrease the number of students labeled as LD due to poor quality instruction rather than a true learning disability.

RTI and tiered intervention models began to play a critical role in general education because of the intent to more directly align IDEA with provisions of the amended Title I of the ESEA–NCLB (NCLB, 2001). Given that the term *RTI* was not identified in IDEA, it also did not appear in the amended Title I of the ESEA. The 10 alignment areas between ESEA–NCLB and IDEA emphasized by the U.S. Department of Education (Office of Special Education Program, 2005) include the following:

1. Definitions (e.g., "core academic areas," "Limited English Proficient," "highly qualified," "scientifically based research")

2. Allowable use of funds for state-level activities

3. Allowable use of funds in schoolwide programs

4. Allowable use of funds by a local education agency (LEA) in ESEA activities

5. Qualifications required of special education teachers

6. Performance goals and indicators

7. Reporting requirements

8. Development of alternative assessments

9. Linking of records of migratory students across states

10. Eligibility determination with respect to lack of appropriate instruction

In addition to work conducted in the behavioral and public health fields and in public education policy, a number of other research strands and educational practices have served to shape current conceptualizations of RTI intervention models (Sugai & Horner, 2009). These conceptualizations include the following (see also Table 12.1):

1. *Prereferral interventions and teacher assistance teaming.* Teachers identify and request assistance for students who are not benefiting from the existing curriculum. The teacher works with a team comprised of individuals with intervention expertise to address the academic difficulties or behavior problem. If student progress is not improved sufficiently, a referral for more specialized assistance is requested.

2. *Behavioral problem solving.* School consultation around academic and behavior problems involves a five-step problem-solving process: (a) problem identification, (b) problem clarification, (c) intervention development, (d) intervention implementation, and (e) evaluation.

3. *Diagnostic and prescriptive teaching.* Focus is on the learner as the source of at-risk performance. Analysis concentrates on the appropriateness of the curriculum, the integrity of its presentation, and the nature of the student's responsiveness to the curriculum and its presentation.

4. *Curriculum-based measurement.* **Curriculum-based measurement (CBM)** is a standardized method teachers use to assess how students are progressing in basic academic areas such as math, reading, writing, and spelling. CBM can be used to inform decisions related to screening and instructional planning, adaptation, and evaluation.

5. *Precision teaching.* **Precision teaching** involves standardized methods with which to evaluate the effectiveness of instruction and the curriculum in a formative fashion. The emphasis is on directly observable behavior, frequency as a measure of student performance, and standard "celeration" or behavior charts.

6. *Effective teaching research.* The effective teaching research demonstrated that student achievement is linked to teacher competence, explicit instructional presentation, review, skill practice, teacher questioning techniques, scaffolded instruction matched to student skill, and discipline practices.

7. *Direct instruction.* Direct instruction is a model for teaching that emphasizes standard protocol curriculum programs planned around sequential and clearly defined skills and associated teaching tasks.

8. *Applied behavior analysis.* Behavioral principles are applied to enhance student outcomes. Emphasis is placed on how the environment affects behavior.

Table 12.1	Research Strands and Educational Practices That Have Served to Shape Current Conceptualizations of RTI Intervention Models

1. Prereferral interventions and teacher assistance teaming

2. Behavioral problem solving

3. Diagnostic and prescriptive teaching

4. Curriculum-based measurement

5. Precision teaching

6. Effective teaching research

7. Direct instruction

8. Applied behavior analysis

What Are the Expected Effects of RTI Intervention Models?

Henceforth, we will use the term *RTI* to include multitiered intervention models. RTI intervention models promote the use of primary (universal), secondary (selected), and tertiary (indicated) interventions that are organized to respond to students' increasing support needs. More specifically, RTI has six general defining features that are applicable across academic areas and social behavior. (For more on these defining features, see, for example, Fuchs, Mock, Morgan, & Young, 2003, and Vaughn, Linan-Thompson, & Hickman, 2003.) Here are the six characteristics of RTI:

1. Use of screening measures for early identification of students at risk for school failure

2. Use of scientifically based interventions

3. Use of a tiered continuum of interventions (e.g., primary, secondary, tertiary) that increase in intensity (e.g., frequency, duration, individualization, specialized supports)

4. Use of a problem-solving protocol for assessment and instructional decision making

5. Use of explicit data-based decision rules and graphing for assessing student progress and making instructional and intervention adjustments

6. Use of treatment integrity measures to ensure high-quality implementation of interventions

RTI and multitier intervention models are expected to achieve a range of important student outcomes in relationship to the primary-, secondary-, and tertiary-level interventions (also called universal, selected, and indicated interventions, respectively). Primary interventions are expected to prevent the development of academic difficulties and problem behavior in a majority of students in the school altogether. The primary intervention should also sustain reductions in academic achievement difficulties and problem behavior achieved by the secondary and tertiary interventions. Secondary interventions are assumed to prevent the onset of significant academic difficulties and problem behavior for students at risk of school failure through the application of interventions early enough to make intervention efforts effective. Tertiary interventions are expected to decrease the severity or duration of the significant academic difficulties and problem behaviors of students experiencing or at high risk of school failure.

There is evidence that RTI intervention models achieve these expected effects (Nelson, Duppong-Hurley, Synhorst, Epstein, & Stage, 2009). Nelson and colleagues used a cohort longitudinal design to assess the extent to which a three-tier behavior intervention model (based on a behavioral health model) achieved the expected outcomes of RTI intervention models. The respective universal, selected, and indicated interventions included Behavior and Academic Support and Enhancement (Nelson, Martella, & Marchand-Martella, 2002), *First Step to Success* (Walker et al., 1997), and *Multisystemic Therapy* (Henggeler, Schoenwald, Borduin, Rowland, & Cunningham, 1998). A total of 407 K–3 elementary students from one of four longitudinal cohorts participated. The results of a two-level (student and school levels) linear growth analysis indicated the universal intervention prevented the onset of problem behavior in a majority of students altogether and sustained improvements in student social behavior outcomes by the selected and indicated interventions.

As indicated by this study's results, RTI and tiered intervention models appear to be effective in improving the outcomes of students at risk of school failure. In contrast to the use of a wide range of isolated interventions, RTI and tiered intervention models provide a systematic approach with which to integrate research-based universal, selected, and indicated interventions or primary, secondary, and tertiary interventions in the case of three-tier models based on the public health model. The results of this study also suggest schools can expect interventions validated in isolated studies to produce similar positive outcomes when they are integrated with one another within RTI and tiered intervention models. Thus, initiatives to identify scientifically based interventions aimed at improving student outcomes, such as the What Works Clearinghouse (*www.whatworks.ed.gov*) and the Blueprints for Violence Prevention programs (*http://www.colorado.edu/cspv/blueprints/*), can be used reliably by schools to identify interventions that can be integrated within RTI and tiered intervention models.

What Are Some Conceptual Issues That Arise Within RTI Intervention Models?

Before we describe the key elements of RTI intervention models, we must consider the conceptual issues associated with the discussion of these models and acknowledge that these issues derive, in part, from the history and development of RTI. Remember, although schools have only begun to use RTI intervention models relatively recently, these models have been used in education for years (Fuchs et al., 2003). Also, although their use in education focuses prominently on improving instruction and learning (specifically, on extending literacy), they were used originally, as previously stated, in the behavioral and public health fields (Gordon, 1983; Mrazek & Haggerty, 1994). Christ, Burns, and Ysseldyke (2005) identified four conceptual issues associated with discussions of RTI intervention models: problem solving and standard protocol, response and resistance to interventions, response and responsiveness to intervention, and response to instruction and intervention.

Problem Solving and Standard Protocol

In general, problem solving describes any set of activities designed to "eliminate the difference between 'what is' and 'what should be' with respect to student development" (Deno, 2002, p. 38). On the other hand, **standard protocol** refers to any set of activities designed to evaluate the effects of instruction or intervention on student achievement (Fuchs et al., 2003). Although problem solving and standard protocol represent distinct processes that may converge in some ways, they are not necessarily one and the same.

According to Fuchs et al. (2003), there are two groups of RTI advocates. The first group is behaviorally oriented school psychologists who advocate problem solving, and the second is early interventionists who recommend the use of standardized and validated standard treatment protocols. Although there appear to be conceptual distinctions between the problem solving and standard protocol approaches, the fundamental difference is the level of individualization and depth of problem analysis that occurs prior to the selection, design, and implementation of an intervention. Thus, both approaches fit within a problem-solving framework.

An RTI problem-solving intervention model is a more flexible process with an emphasis on individualized interventions that are derived from an in-depth analysis of the instructional and environmental conditions as well as skill deficits (Nelson et al., 2009; Tilly, Reschly, & Grimes, 1999). In contrast, an RTI standard protocol intervention model relies on minimal analysis of the skill deficit to identify the most appropriate standard, empirically supported instructional approach, such as the direct instruction of phonics skills. Despite this difference, both RTI problem-solving and standard protocol approaches are designed to prevent or remediate academic (or social) problems. Indeed, these approaches are combined in RTI intervention models implemented in schools (Fuchs & Fuchs, 2007; O'Shaughnessy, Lane, Gresham, & Beebe-Frankenberger, 2003). Fuchs and Fuchs recommend schools rely on a combination of both approaches—specifically, standard protocols have been shown to be highly effective for academic deficits, and problem-solving approaches are aimed at motivational and behavioral issues: "We recommend that schools rely on a combination of approaches with a standard treatment protocol used for academic difficulties and a problem-solving approach used for obvious behavior problems" (Fuchs & Fuchs, p. 16).

Response to Intervention and Resistance to Intervention

The "R" in RTI refers to response (as we reference in this book) or resistance. The distinction between response and resistance is important because the purpose, procedures, and conclusions of each of these intervention models are different (Christ et al., 2005). Within response models, academic (or social) performance is related to environmental events. The emphasis is on identifying the conditions necessary for students to benefit from instruction (Gresham, 2001). In contrast, resistance models relate academic (or social) performance to within-student deficits (Gresham). The emphasis is on identifying within-student deficits, deficiencies, disorders, or disabilities that impede achievement. The focus of **resistance to intervention** models on the identification of effective treatments is not inconsistent with diagnostic-oriented decisions. In contrast, response models are premised on the recognition that the identification of effective treatments precedes and supersedes diagnostic and categorical labels.

Response to Intervention and Responsiveness to Intervention

The "R" in RTI may also represent response or **responsiveness to intervention** (Christ et al., 2005). Although this distinction may not be evident on the surface, it parallels directly the difference between "response" and "resistance." As detailed above, the emphasis within response models is on identifying the conditions necessary for students to benefit from instruction. In contrast, the emphasis within responsiveness models is on identifying within-student deficits, deficiencies, disorders, or disabilities that impede achievement.

Instruction and Intervention

The "I" in RTI represents instruction or intervention. **Response to instruction** is the referent when RTI procedures are designed to evaluate students' responses to core instruction and primary or universal programming. The evaluation of students' responses to core educational practices relative to standards or benchmarks is used to guide decisions regarding students who should be considered for secondary- and tertiary-level interventions. In contrast, response to intervention is the referent when RTI procedures are designed to evaluate students' responses to a secondary- or tertiary-level intervention itself. The distinction between response to instruction and response to intervention centers on the intensity of intervention and the density of the formative assessment schedule. In RTI intervention models, assessment and evaluation activities become more frequent with the progression from primary to secondary to tertiary levels (Christ et al., 2005).

What Are the Key Elements of RTI Intervention Models?

The commonly described uses of RTI in schools include the prediction of at-risk students, the prevention of academic or behavioral difficulties, intervention for students with academic or behavioral difficulties, and the determination of LD (Fuchs et al., 2003). Although there is no single, absolute RTI intervention model, such models are comprised of four defining characteristics (Brown-Chidsey & Steege, 2005; Christ et al., 2005; Fuchs et al., 2003; Gresham, 2005; National Association of State Directors of Special Education, 2006). These include universal screening, a data-based problem-solving process, a continuum of scientifically based interventions, and progress monitoring.

Universal Screening

Students should take a universal screening assessment.

Learner performance and progress are reviewed on a regular basis and in a systematic manner to identify students who are progressing as expected, at some risk for school failure, and at high risk of or experiencing school failure. **Universal screening** relies on assessment procedures that are characterized by the administration of quick, low-cost, repeatable evaluations of critical academic skills. Educators administer the universal screeners to all students, typically three times a year. The data from the screening measures are used for two purposes. The first purpose is to assess the effectiveness of the core curriculum and instruction being provided to all students. In RTI intervention models, it is expected that approximately 80% or more of all students in the school should be showing adequate progress in the core curriculum and instruction program (tier 1). The second purpose is to identify students who are not making adequate progress in the core curriculum and instruction program. These students need supplemental instruction (secondary intervention or tier 2) in addition to the core curriculum and instruction program to make adequate progress.

The way schools identify students for secondary or tier 2 intervention varies. Consistent with the behavioral health model described above, schools may use a direct route approach. With this approach, students identified by a screening process as being at risk for reading difficulties are immediately provided a tier 2 intervention. In contrast, schools may use a progress monitoring approach, which aligns with the public health intervention model described above. With this approach, the progress of students identified as at risk for reading difficulties is monitored for several weeks. Whether these students receive tier 2 instruction depends on their rate of growth on a progress monitoring measure. The progress monitoring approach yields marginally better identification accuracy than the direct route approach. However, the direct route results in students being provided intervention earlier. Screening measures are available at the following websites:

https://dibels.uoregon.edu/ (literacy)

http://easycbm.com/ (literacy, mathematics)

http://www.aimsweb.com/ (literacy, mathematics, spelling, written expression)

http://www.interventioncentral.org/ (literacy, mathematics, spelling, written expression)

Data-Based Problem-Solving Process

Data that directly relate to student learning are used to guide intervention development or selection, intervention implementation, and intervention adaptations and modifications if applicable, as well as to evaluate intervention effectiveness. Typically, schools follow at least four steps when addressing large groups (district or school), smaller groups (classroom or grade level), or individual students:

1. *Problem identification.* This step entails identifying the problem and the desired behavior for students experiencing academic or behavioral difficulties.

2. *Problem analysis.* This step involves analyzing why the problem is occurring by collecting data to determine possible causes of the identified problem.

3. *Intervention selection or design.* This step entails selecting or developing scientifically based interventions, which are then implemented with integrity.

4. *Evaluation of intervention.* This step involves evaluating the effectiveness of interventions. It is commonly referred to as "response to intervention."

Continuum of Scientifically Based Interventions

Scientifically based interventions are the cornerstone of RTI models. Education policy and practice define the criteria for scientifically based interventions as (a) employing systematic, empirical methods that draw on observation or experiment; (b) involving rigorous data analyses that are adequate to test the stated hypotheses and justify the conclusion drawn; (c) relying on measurements or observational methods that have provided valid data across evaluators and across multiple measurements and observations; and (d) having been accepted by a peer-reviewed journal or approved, after a comparably rigorous, objective, and scientific review, by a panel of independent experts. The continuum of interventions typically includes primary (provided to all students), secondary (supplemental intervention provided to students at some risk of school failure, i.e., primary + secondary interventions provided), and tertiary (supplemental specialized and intensive intervention provided to students at high risk of or experiencing school failure, i.e., primary + tertiary interventions provided). The entire continuum of primary-, secondary-, and tertiary-level interventions must be implemented with integrity.

We described the steps for identifying evidence-based interventions in Chapter 11. We also listed a number of websites that present examples of evidence-based interventions. Although these sites do not provide exhaustive lists of all available interventions, the interventions they do list represent the current thinking around what works for students. Note that the lists are updated on a regular basis.

Progress Monitoring

Progress monitoring is the ongoing use of formative assessment procedures to determine the extent to which students are benefiting from classroom instruction and for monitoring the effectiveness of the core curriculum and instruction program as well as of secondary- and tertiary-level interventions. A fundamental assumption of RTI is that students will benefit from high-quality instruction. That is, a majority of students will learn and achieve the skills and content taught in the core curriculum and instruction program. For students who are not responsive to the core curriculum and instruction program, secondary- and tertiary-level interventions can be provided, and, again, students' responses to these interventions can be monitored. Progress monitoring is a valid and efficient tool for gauging the effectiveness of instruction, determining whether instructional modifications are necessary, and providing important information for eventual classification and placement decisions. Information about progress monitoring is rapidly expanding.

The National Center on Student Progress Monitoring, sponsored by the U.S. Office of Special Education Programs (OSEP), provides an array of free, web-based progress monitoring resource materials (www.studentprogress.org). We describe progress monitoring at the primary (tier 1), secondary (tier 2), and tertiary (tier 3) levels.

1. *Tier 1.* At the tier 1 level, schoolwide screening and progress monitoring serve a similar function. Screening of all students is used to determine those students who may be at risk of academic or behavioral difficulties by comparing their performance relative to a criterion measure. Progress monitoring displays student growth over time across the three screening periods (fall, winter, spring). This monitoring enables one to assess whether students are progressing as expected in the core curriculum and instruction program. The assumption underlying progress monitoring measures is that the alternative forms of the assessment are comparable in difficulty. For example, a CBM oral reading fluency measure is based on passages at the same reading grade level. If the oral reading fluency scores are increasing, this trend indicates an improvement in students' reading skills. If the scores are remaining the same or decreasing over time, this trend indicates no benefit from the core curriculum and instruction program.

2. *Tiers 2 and 3.* In tiers 2 and 3, the purposes of progress monitoring shift slightly. The primary purpose at these intervention levels is to determine whether the intervention is effective in improving the students' learning rate to an appropriate level. Decision rules are used to determine when students might no longer require tier 2 or 3 interventions and when the interventions need to be modified or changed. The following three recommendations are made for progress monitoring at these intervention levels. First, educators should establish an expected growth rate in a specified period of time. Second, they should assess student progress in tiers 2 and 3 twice per week. Third, educators should chart the results and analyze student progress on a regular basis. Finally, they should use preset rules to determine when a student is not adequately responding to an intervention (the common rule is that four consecutive data points below a goal line warrant a change in intervention; four above the goal line warrant raising the goal or decreasing the amount of time to achieve the goal). Today, educators have available to them a number of free or commercially available graphing programs. In these programs, educators can, for example, enter a student's name and grade, the type of CBM measure administered, goal lines, the dates of periodic progress monitoring, and the progress monitoring data (see Figures 12.1 and 12.2). Additionally, educators can track when instructional or goal line changes are made. The program can be printed easily and serves as a communication tool for educators, students, and parents.

| Figure 12.1 | Example of Progress Monitoring Graph When the Student Is Responding to a Tier 2 or 3 Intervention |

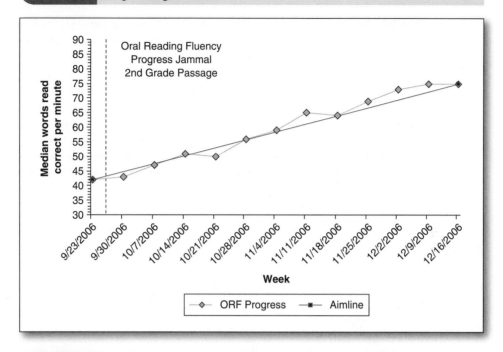

| Figure 12.2 | Example of Progress Monitoring Graph When Student Is Not Responding to Tier 2 or 3 Intervention |

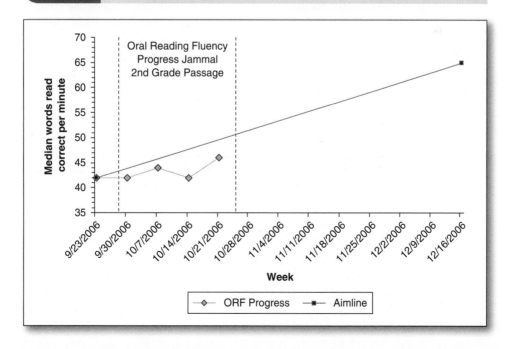

What Is the Link Between RTI and Schoolwide Positive Behavior Intervention and Support (SWPBIS)?

It should be apparent that academic success and student behavior go hand in hand. "Combining behavior support and effective instruction may be an important theme for school reform in the United States" (Horner, Sugai, et al., 2005, p. 382). This combination can be achieved by providing integrated three-tier academic and behavior models that target those students who lack the necessary academic and behavioral skills needed to succeed in school (Simonsen et al., 2010; Stewart, Benner, Martella, & Marchand-Martella, 2007; Stewart, Martella, Marchand-Martella, & Benner, 2005). As stated by Sprick (2009),

> If schools apply scientifically derived methods to create safer, more positive school climates through positive behavior support (PBS) and combine that effort with changes in the way they deliver services to at-risk students through response to intervention (RTI), they can reduce student misbehavior and increase student responsibility, motivation, and academic achievement. (p. 20)

Schools that implement only schoolwide academic models and those that implement only schoolwide behavior models may not see the kinds of results evidenced by those schools that combine both models. In a meta-analysis that compared schools implementing only schoolwide reading or behavior models or a combination of the two, Stewart et al. (2007) found clear differences in outcomes. Schools that implemented only schoolwide reading models found small to moderate effects on reading performance. Those schools did not track the impact on schoolwide behavior. Schools that implemented only schoolwide behavior models found small effects on reading and small to moderate effects on behavior. Schools that implemented a combination of the two models found a large effect on reading and a moderate effect on behavior. The results of this analysis show the implementation of schoolwide programs addressing both academic and behavior outcomes to result in much larger effects than the implementation of one model or the other. The remainder of this chapter will discuss the link between RTI and SWPBIS.

SWPBIS shares three of the commonly prescribed uses of RTI—namely, the prediction of at-risk students, the prevention of academic and behavior problems, and intervention for students with behavioral difficulties. The problem-solving model used in RTI plays the same crucial role in SWPBIS and offers a tiered range of interventions that are systematically applied to students based on their demonstrated level of need (Sandomierski, Kincaid, & Algozzine, 2010). Both RTI and SWPBIS identify factors and components critical to the primary (tier 1), secondary (tier 2), and tertiary (tier 3) levels. Note that Sugai and Horner (2009) consider SWPBIS to be an application of RTI. They suggest RTI is an "umbrella of guiding principles for improved assessment and intervention decision making" (p. 223) and SWPBIS is an example of its use for dealing with student behavior issues. We describe the key RTI and SWPBIS features associated with the primary, secondary, and tertiary intervention levels. The parallel attributes of tiered academic and behavior intervention models are depicted in Figure 12.3. Many of

| Figure 12.3 | Tiered Academic and Behavior RTI Intervention Models |

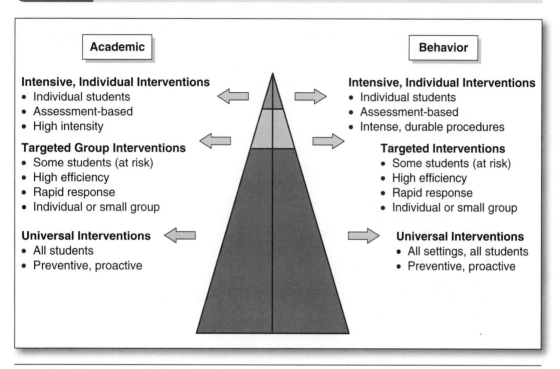

SOURCE: Office of Special Education Programs Center on Positive Behavioral Interventions & Supports (www.pbis.org).

the important aspects of RTI academic intervention models are not currently available for SWPBIS, including simple and efficient screening procedures and associated performance benchmarks in social behavior across the grades, as well as growth measures. There is also limited availability of easily implemented standard protocol interventions that target specific social behavioral difficulties.

Primary (Tier 1)

Both RTI and SWPBIS support a preventive approach to teaching academic and social behavior. RTI requires students to have adequate exposure to quality curricula and instruction to ensure their academic success and to prevent achievement difficulties. For example, Marchand-Martella, Ruby, and Martella (2007) described the use of intensifying reading instruction within a three-tier model at a Title 1 elementary school. At the primary level (tier 1), *Reading Mastery Plus* published by SRA/McGraw-Hill was the core reading program used with all students in Grades K through 3 (total students = 235). Independent reading was facilitated by the school's adoption of Scholastic's *Reading Counts!* program. The *Dynamic Indicators of Basic Early Literacy Skills (DIBELS)* and the

Scholastic Reading Inventory served as the reading assessment. Students received 90 minutes of reading instruction, five days per week. Students were grouped into flexible skill groups. Decisions for group movement were predominantly data driven, based on performance evidenced on within-program assessments. Treatment fidelity was ensured by coaching and monitored through observations conducted by an educational consultant.

For SWPBIS, the primary curriculum consists of the schoolwide expectations, rules, and procedures as well as the lesson plans used to teach them. An important contribution of SWPBIS has been the elevation of behavior curricula, which incorporate the instruction of expectations, rules, and procedures, to levels of interest and importance that are similar to those found within academic programs (Sandomierski et al., 2010). The practice of teaching and reinforcing students for displaying the schoolwide expectations and classroom management are considered to be primary interventions that are delivered to every student in every setting. Educators' use of SWPBIS increases the probability that the majority of students will act according to expectations, and it functions as a proactive intervention for students with or at risk of behavior difficulties. Furthermore, educators can begin to identify students in need of additional support when the primary intervention is implemented with fidelity. These are the students who fail to respond to the primary intervention that is effective with a majority of students.

Within RTI, universal screening and benchmark assessments are used to identify students who fail to respond to the primary-level program. At the primary level, the collection and use of office discipline referrals (ODRs) commonly inform programmatic decisions in SWPBIS (Kaufman et al., 2010). Educators review ODRs on a regular basis to identify students who need additional support to be successful; students who have a high number of ODRs relative to the rest of the school's population are identified as having a poor response to the universal intervention. It is important to note that while ODRs may be used to identify students with **externalizing behaviors** (i.e., directed outwardly by the student toward the external social environment), they are not sufficient for identifying students who have **internalizing behaviors** (i.e., directed inwardly and representative of problems with self) or who have less severe externalizing behaviors (Clonin, McDougal, Clark, & Davison, 2007; Severson, Walker, Hope-Doolittle, Kratochwill, & Gresham, 2007). Additionally, a concern is raised with using ODRs as a diagnostic measure given that they are used more frequently with African American students than with students from other ethnic groups (Kaufman et al.). The reliability and validity of ODRs have also been questioned (Martella et al., in press; Nelson, Benner, Reid, & Epstein, 2002).

Nevertheless, more formal screening processes, such as the *Systematic Screening for Behavior Disorders (SSBD)* system (Walker & Severson, 1992), can be used in a multiple-gating procedure (see Figure 12.4) to identify students at risk of externalizing and internalizing behavior. A **multiple-gating procedure** involves a series of assessments designed to screen out in a systematic fashion students with or at risk of learning or behavior problems. For the *SSBD,* teachers are given a description of typical characteristics of these two behavioral categories and asked to look at the list of students in their classrooms, to consider each student's characteristics, and then to list the 10 students

| Figure 12.4 | Multiple-Gating Assessment Procedures |

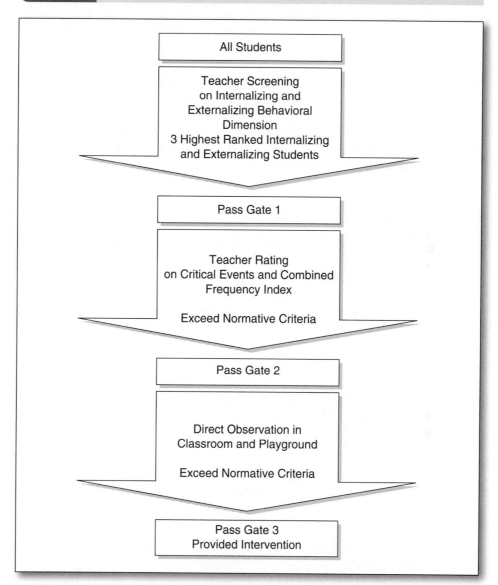

who best exemplify a description of externalizing characteristics and the 10 who best exemplify a description of internalizing characteristics. The two lists are mutually exclusive, so a student can only be put on one of the lists. This approach is a universal procedure because each student is considered and has an equal chance to be identified for further assessment. The students in the lists of 10 are then rank ordered according to how closely they match the profile of an internalizer or an externalizer. The three students with the highest ranks for internalizers and the three students with the highest ranks for externalizers are said to pass through Gate 1. These six students per class, who are nominated by their teachers as being potentially at risk for behavior problems, enter Gate 2 assessment. At Gate 2 of the *SSBD*, each student is rated by his or her teacher on the *SSBD* Adaptive Behavior, Maladaptive Behavior, and Critical Events scales. The teacher marks a Likert-like scale for the occurrence and frequency of specific behaviors. Data from the development of the *SSBD* indicate that, typically, in every two or three classrooms, at least one student per class is at risk for severe externalizing behavior problems (e.g., aggressive, disruptive, oppositional) and one student is at risk for severe internalizing behavior problems (e.g., fearful, depressed, anxious, neglected by peers). The final gate of the *SSBD* involves direct observations of students who meet the designated *SSBD* criteria on the Adaptive Behavior, Maladaptive Behavior, and Critical Events scales.

Secondary (Tier 2)

Secondary-level interventions are designed for students who are not responding to the primary level of support. Students receiving secondary interventions continue to participate in the primary intervention. Both RTI and SWPBIS use scientifically based interventions for students who have been identified as needing secondary-level support and monitor student progress. Within RTI, a standard protocol intervention is typically provided to small groups of students, and CBM measures, benchmarks, and instructional decision rules are used. Additionally, it is important to monitor implementation integrity.

Marchand-Martella et al. (2007) described the use of daily, 30- to 40-minute double dosing/reteaching sessions of *Reading Mastery Plus* in small groups of K–2 students as their secondary-level intervention (tier 2). Third graders received *Corrective Reading,* an SRA/McGraw-Hill program, as their secondary intervention, which was presented in a before-school tutorial three days per week (35 minutes per session). Sixty-four students benefited from this additional tier of support beyond their primary-level reading instruction. Decision making as to who received this additional level of instruction was data driven, being based on students' within-program performance in the primary-level program. Treatment fidelity was ensured at this level of instruction as well.

Secondary interventions within SWPBIS are conceptualized as intervention strategies made up of efficient behavior change procedures implemented in a similar manner across all students receiving the intervention. Examples of frequently implemented standard protocol secondary interventions include (a) Check & Connect (Sinclair, Christenson, & Thurlow, 2005), (b) Check-in/Check-out (Crone, Horner, & Hawkin, 2004), and (c) *First Step to Success* (Walker et al., 1997). Following are descriptions of these three standard protocol interventions.

Check & Connect. The Check & Connect model relies on a monitor to facilitate students' connection with the school. The monitor's primary goal is to promote regular school participation and to keep education a salient issue for students, parents, and teachers. The monitor extends the school's outreach services to the student and family in an effort to better understand the circumstances affecting their connection to school and works with them to overcome barriers that have kept them estranged from school and learning. Here are some of the overall goals of the mentor:

1. *Relationship Building*—establish mutual trust and open communication, nurtured through a long-term commitment focused on students' educational success.

2. *Routine Monitoring of Alterable Indicators*—systemically check warning signs of withdrawal (attendance, academic performance, behavior) that are readily available to school personnel and that can be altered through intervention.

3. *Individualized and Timely Intervention*—ensure support tailored to individual student needs, based on level of engagement with school, associated with influences of home and school, and achieved through leveraging of local resources.

4. *Long-Term Commitment*—commit to students and families for at least two years, and follow highly mobile youth from school to school and program to program.

5. *Persistence Plus*—provide a persistent source of academic motivation, a continuity of familiarity with the youth and family, and a consistency in the message that "education is important for your future."

6. *Problem Solving*—promote the acquisition of skills to resolve conflict constructively and to look for solutions rather than a source of blame.

7. *Affiliation With School and Learning*—facilitate students' access to and active participation in school-related activities and events.

The monitors' interactions with students, parents, educators, and others are guided by the "check" and "connect" components of the model. The "check" component is designed to facilitate the continuous assessment of student levels of engagement with the school and to guide intervention. Student levels of engagement are systematically monitored monthly and documented using a monitoring sheet. Engagement at school and with learning is measured according to several indicators that are *alterable*—that is, factors within the power of educators and parents to change. Alterable indicators include attendance (tardy to school, skipping classes, absenteeism), social/behavior performance (out-of-school suspension, other disciplinary consequences such as behavior referrals, detention, in-school suspension), and academic performance (course failures, accrual of credits). The monitors obtain attendance information and the other indicators of participation primarily from school records, attendance clerks, teachers, and assistant principals. These individuals, as well as the student or parents, are also consulted to clarify contradictory information.

The "connect" component includes two levels of student-focused interventions developed to maximize the use of finite resources: *basic interventions*, which are the same for all students, and *intensive interventions*, which are more frequent and individualized. All students receive basic interventions (even if receiving intensive interventions), whereas indicators of student engagement are used to guide who receives intensive interventions. The individual needs of the student dictate what specific intervention strategy is used. The two levels of intervention help the monitors to manage their time and resources with efficiency and responsiveness. The basic intervention is administered to all targeted students. Basic intervention uses minimal resources in an effort to keep education a salient issue, especially after a working relationship has been established between the monitor, the student, his or her parents, and school staff. Basic interventions begin with introductions and sharing general information about the monitor's role and the Check & Connect model with the student and his or her family. When on site at the school building, monitors routinely interact with students, at least weekly at the secondary level and up to daily at the elementary level. However, the substance of basic intervention is a deliberate conversation with each student—at least monthly for secondary students and weekly for elementary students. The conversation covers the student's progress in school, the relationship between school completion and the "check" indicators of engagement, the importance of staying in school, and the problem-solving steps used to resolve conflict and cope with life's challenges. For problem solving, students are guided through real and hypothetical problems using a five-step, cognitive-behavioral, problem-solving strategy:

1. "Stop. Think about the problem."

2. "What are the choices?"

3. "Choose one."

4. "Do it."

5. "How did it work?"

Intensive interventions are administered for students showing high risk in relation to any of the early warning signs of withdrawal. Typically, about two-thirds to three-quarters of the students receive intensive intervention at any given time. Connection strategies correspond to key indicators of student engagement (e.g., participation in or identification with school) and are developmentally appropriate to grade levels. Existing services are used as much as possible to avoid the development of a separate set of duplicative services.

Here are some examples of intensive interventions for elementary students:

1. *Participation*—calling the student in the morning to make sure he or she is out of bed and getting ready for school

2. *Student Initiative and Responsibility*—helping students regularly apply organizational skills

3. *Academic Competence*—working with students and parents to establish effective homework completion strategies

Some examples of intensive interventions for the secondary student include the following:

1. *Identification*—encouraging active student and parent participation in the transition planning process for students with disabilities and facilitating interagency participation in the development and implementation of relevant transition goals and objectives

2. *Social/Behavioral Competence*—role-playing the use of problem-solving steps to manage conflict and think about alternative actions

3. *School Support for Learning*—negotiating with school administrators for alternatives to out-of-school suspension and administrative transfers

Communication and collaboration between home and school is an integral component of the Check & Connect model and most explicit at the elementary level. Strategies used to enhance communication between home and school regarding students' educational progress range from frequent telephone calls to home visits or meetings at a neutral community setting or the school. A critical goal of parent-connect efforts, particularly at the elementary level, is working with families as partners to increase their active participation in their children's education. Essentially, the monitors build trusting relationships with families by affirming the importance of the role played by parents and by helping parents gain the skills and confidence to take initiative with the schools and to help their children be consistent learners.

Check-in/Check-out. Key features of Check-in/Check-out (CICO), also known as the "Behavior Education Plan" (Crone et al., 2004), include (a) being readily available, (b) increasing monitoring and adult contact, (c) providing contingent and frequent feedback, and (d) increasing coordination between school and home support. After a brief, initial meeting of a behavior support team or a teacher assistance team to clarify the nature of the behavioral issues for each student, students participating in CICO typically follow the routine listed below each day.

1. Each morning the student checks in with a designated school staff person (e.g., teacher, secretary, counselor, educational assistant). That check-in determines if the student has the materials needed for class and is physically prepared to attend classes. The student is then given a form (e.g., point sheet or card) to use throughout the day that lists the student's behavioral goals and a matrix showing classes or time periods. This check-in usually takes less than five minutes and includes verbal prompts and encouragement.

2. Teachers continually monitor the behavior of the student throughout the day. Each class period (or at other designated times), the student brings the form to the teacher, who marks a rating of how well the student met his or her behavioral goals. In some cases, the student also self-monitors.

3. At the end of the school day, the student takes the form back to the staff person who conducted the morning check-in and who then begins the afternoon check-out, which consists of a quick review of the form, verbal feedback, and, in some cases, small reinforcers if certain goals have been met (e.g., 80% of possible points on the teachers' ratings). The afternoon check-out typically takes less than five minutes.

4. The student takes the form (sometimes called a daily behavior report card) home to show his or her parents, who then sign it. The form is returned to school the next day. The school staff member who is monitoring the student maintains a record of progress, which can be charted and used to make decisions about maintaining, fading, or strengthening the intervention over time.

First Step to Success. *First Step to Success* consists of three modules implementing a series of activities designed to be applied in concert with each other. The modules include (a) proactive, universal screening of all kindergarten and first-grade populations; (b) consultant-based school interventions involving the target student, peers, and teachers; and (c) parent training in caregiver skills for supporting and improving the student's school adjustment performance in the home.

Screening Module. The *SSBD* (described earlier) is used to identify students at risk for behavior difficulties.

School Module. The school module of *First Step to Success* is an adapted version of the *Contingencies for Learning Academic and Social Skills (CLASS)* program by Hops and Walker (1988). *CLASS* is divided into three successive phases: consultant, teacher, and maintenance. The consultant phase begins with a daily 20-minute session with the student, called the Green-Red Card Game. Initially, the consultant, in close proximity to the target student, monitors his or her classroom behavior using a red and green card. During this time, there are random moments when the coach will check if the card is displaying green or red. If the card is on green the student earns a point. To meet criterion, the student must earn a minimum of 80% of the possible points for the session. Those who meet criterion earn a prearranged classroom reward, such as playing a game with the whole class. The student will also earn a special reward activity with his or her parents at home. The parents are given daily feedback regarding their student's progress and are encouraged to provide home activities, such as reading a book or playing a game, as a reward for days the student earned a reward at school. As the game progresses, the session length becomes longer and the interval in which points and praise can be earned is gradually extended from 30 seconds to 10 minutes. Additionally, in later stages of the program, the target student must work in blocks of multiple days to earn a reward. Thus, the program becomes more demanding as the student progresses through it, and the student must sustain acceptable performance for progressively longer periods of time in order to be successful.

The "teacher phase" (Program Days 6–20) is operated by the classroom teacher in whose room the program is initially implemented. The teacher assumes control of the program's operation on Program Day 6 but with close supervision and support provided by the behavioral coach. The consultant provides monitoring and technical assistance on an as-needed basis for the teacher throughout the remainder of the teacher phase. Teacher phase implementation tasks include (a) operating the program daily, (b) awarding praise and points according to program guidelines and contingent on student performance, (c) supervising delivery of group activity and school rewards, and (d) communicating with parents on a regular basis regarding the target student's performance. The teacher works closely with the behavioral coach, student, parents, and peers throughout the total implementation period.

The "maintenance phase" lasts from Program Days 21 through 30, after which the school intervention is terminated. In this final phase, the target student is rewarded primarily with praise and expressions of approval or recognition from the teacher at school and the parents at home. An attempt is made during this phase to reduce the student's dependence on the program by substituting adult praise for points, reducing the amount of daily feedback given, and making occasional rewards available contingent on exemplary performance. In the majority of the cases, target students who successfully complete the teacher phase of the program are able to sustain their improved behavior in this phase despite these program changes.

Home Module. The home module (HomeBase) consists of a series of six lessons designed to enable parents and caregivers to build student competencies and skills in six areas that affect school adjustment and performance: (a) communication and sharing in school, (b) cooperation, (c) limit setting, (d) problem solving, (e) friendship making, and (f) development of confidence. HomeBase contains lessons, instructional guidelines, and parent-child games and activities for teaching these skills. HomeBase requires six weeks for implementation and begins after the target student has completed Program Day 10 of the *First Step to Success* program.

The *First Step to Success* behavioral coach visits the student's home weekly and conducts the HomeBase lessons in that setting. Following each session, materials are left with the parents that facilitate daily review and practice of each skill with the target student. The HomeBase lessons require approximately one hour each. Parents are encouraged to work with their child 10 to 15 minutes daily and to focus on practicing the HomeBase skills being taught.

In addition to these standard protocol interventions, a number of other interventions have been documented to be effective for small groups of students. Examples include individual schedules to increase daily structure, contingencies across groups of students, and closer supervision (Horner, Sugai, & Anderson, 2010).

Also, monitoring of the progress of all students receiving the secondary-level interventions is conducted. Progress monitoring is frequent to identify whether the intervention is having its desired effect (behavior goals being met) and to allow for an adjustment if students are not meeting behavioral goals. Progress monitoring can be achieved efficiently for secondary-level interventions using variations of teacher rating scales that reflect students' academic and behavior goals (the schoolwide expectations). A sample scale used within a behavior report card is presented in Figure 12.5. Additionally, samples of these scales for behavior can be accessed at the Florida PBS (*http://flpbs.fmhi.usf.edu/*) or Intervention Central (*http://www.interventioncentral.org/*) websites. Most commonly, rating scales require a teacher (or another adult) to record opinions about a student's behavior during a specific time period, such as a 50-minute class or subject period (e.g., language arts or math). When filling out the rating scale, the teacher provides brief, specific verbal feedback to the student about why he or she earned that rating.

Figure 12.5	Sample Behavior Report Card

Behavior Report Card

Name: _____ Date: _____

Intervention Program: _____

Points Possible: _____

Points Received: _____

% of Points: _____

Goal Achieved?   Y   N

Rating Scale: 3 = Good day   2 = Mixed day   1 = Will try harder tomorrow

GOALS:

Teacher Comments:

_____

_____

Parent Signature(s) and Comments: _____

_____

SOURCE: Adapted from D. A. Crone, R. H. Horner, L. S. Hawken, *Responding to Problem Behavior in Schools The Behavior Education Program 2e*. Copyright © 2010 by Guilford Press.

Tertiary (Tier 3)

Tertiary-level interventions are designed for students who have not responded or are unlikely to respond to the primary-level program or to secondary-level interventions. Students receiving tertiary services in most cases continue to participate in the universal (tier 1) interventions to the maximum extent possible. Within RTI, tertiary-level interventions can be both standard protocol or problem solving based to meet the multiple and unique needs of each student. Regardless of the type, tertiary-level interventions require significant time, resources, and expertise to guide development and implementation. For example, Marchand-Martella et al. (2007) described the use of 110 minutes of daily reading instruction in the special education resource room as the tier 3 intervention. More intensive instruction using *Reading Mastery Plus* was implemented; a problem-solving approach was added wherein one-on-one instruction, focused work on sounds, sound amplifiers, laser pointers, and motivational systems were used. Within-program assessments were conducted on a frequent basis. Twenty-eight students in Grades K through 3 received this intensive intervention.

Tertiary interventions within SWPBIS are individualized and generally based on an FBA (Horner et al., 2010). (See Chapters 3–6 for individualized behavior management approaches.) The FBA focuses on identifying factors in the environment that are affecting a student's behavior. Results of the FBA are integrated with other academic and social information to build a comprehensive tertiary-level behavior support plan. The support plan typically consists of multiple components including strategies to influence the larger social context around a student, prevent the occurrence of problem behavior, teach new skills, ensure that appropriate behavior is reinforced, and minimize the likelihood that problem behavior is reinforced (Horner et al., 2010). As with secondary interventions, tertiary ones require frequent progress monitoring to ensure a student is making adequate progress and that the intervention is being implemented as designed. At this level, more intensive progress monitoring techniques are typically applied. The teacher rating scales used for secondary-level interventions can still play an important role in this process. However, they may be adjusted to provide more detailed information. For example, time periods within the rating scale may be reduced to create a more precise measure of how the student's behavior improves or worsens over time. When students repeatedly show poor response to intervention, it may be necessary to gather data on specific instances of behavior using direct observation or to conduct a more comprehensive FBA.

VIGNETTE REVISITED   Investigating the Impact of an Effective RTI and SWPBIS Approach

Mr. Gonzalez is pleased to find that RTI and SWPBIS share the same elements. These elements include universal screening; data-based problem-solving processes; a continuum of evidence-based interventions at the primary, secondary, and tertiary levels; and progress monitoring. The fact that RTI and SWPBIS share the same elements. These elements include universal screening; data-based problem-solving processes; a continuum of evidence-based interventions at the primary, secondary, and tertiary levels; and progress share these common elements will make it easier for staff to take on these two initiatives.

Mr. Gonzalez is also pleased to discover that both RTI and SWPBIS focus on prevention—of learning problems and behavior difficulties, respectively. Over the years, he has been frustrated because students fail before receiving an intervention. He believes waiting for students to fail before introducing an intervention reduces the success and outcomes of students.

Mr. Gonzalez decides it was important for the school staff to consider carefully the underlying concepts of standard protocol and problem solving. Although these two approaches are clearly compatible with one another, the school staff must reflect thoroughly on their implications for the RTI and SWPBIS approach the school has adopted. Other concepts of importance to staff are the differences between response and resistance to interventions, response and responsiveness to interventions, and instruction and intervention. Although, on the surface, the distinctions in these concepts may not be evident, they have implications for the type of RTI and SWPBIS approach staff will develop. Mr. Gonzalez believes it is important for staff members to understand these concepts as they move forward with developing and implementing Elliot's RTI and SWPBIS approach.

Summary

Both RTI and SWPBIS programs rely on comprehensive multitiered prevention and early intervention approaches guided by a problem-solving approach. RTI intervention models originated from the behavioral and public health fields. In the behavioral health field, the RTI intervention levels are correlated directly with the levels of risk experienced by students (i.e., students are assigned directly to the intervention level based on their degree of risk). These models are sometimes referred to as risk-matching models. In the public health field, the RTI intervention levels are directed at students based on their response to each level of intervention attempted. These models are sometimes referred to as response to intervention models. Regardless of the approach taken by schools, RTI models are proactive and preventive in nature. Additionally, a number of research strands and educational practices have served to shape current conceptualizations of multitiered models used in schools. These conceptualizations include prereferral interventions and teacher assistance teams, behavioral problem solving, diagnostic and prescriptive teaching, curriculum-based measurement, precision teaching, effective teacher research, direct instruction, and applied behavior analysis.

In addition to differences in behavioral and public health RTI models, there are differences in the basic analytical approach used by schools: problem solving or standard protocol. The fundamental difference between problem-solving and standard protocol approaches involves both the level of individualization and the depth of problem analysis that occurs prior to the selection, design, and implementation of an intervention. Thus, both problem-solving and standard protocol approaches fit within a problem-solving framework. A problem-solving intervention model is a more flexible process with an emphasis on individualized interventions that are derived from an in-depth analysis of both skill deficits and instructional and environmental conditions. In contrast, a standard protocol intervention model relies on minimal analysis of the skill deficit to identify the most appropriate standard and empirically supported instructional approach, such as direct instruction of phonics skills.

RTI has six general defining features that are applicable across academic areas and social behavior. These include the use of (a) screening measures for early identification of students at risk for school failure; (b) scientifically based interventions; (c) a tiered continuum of interventions (e.g., primary, secondary, tertiary) that increase in intensity (e.g., frequency, duration, individualization, specialized supports); (d) a problem-solving protocol for assessment and instructional decision making; (e) explicit data-based decision rules and graphing for assessing student progress and making instructional and intervention adjustments; and (f) treatment integrity measures to ensure high-quality implementation of interventions.

RTI intervention models are designed to achieve the following outcomes in relationship to the primary (universal), secondary (selected), and tertiary (indicated) interventions. Primary interventions are presented to all and are expected to prevent the development of academic difficulties and problem behavior in a majority of students in the school and to sustain the reductions in academic achievement difficulties and problem behavior achieved by the secondary and tertiary interventions. Secondary interventions are designed to prevent the onset of significant academic difficulties and problem behavior by students at risk of school failure through the application of interventions early enough to make intervention efforts effective. Tertiary interventions are expected to decrease the severity and duration of significant academic difficulties and problem behavior of students experiencing or at high risk of school failure.

Key Terms

curriculum-based measurement (CBM)   369

externalizing behaviors   380

internalizing behaviors   380

multiple-gating procedure   380

precision teaching   369

progress monitoring   375

resistance to intervention   373

response to instruction   373

response to intervention (RTI)   366

responsiveness to intervention   373

standard protocol   372

universal screening   374

Discussion Questions

1. What are the main similarities and differences between three-tier interventions in the behavioral and public health fields?

2. How has education policy influenced the development of RTI?

3. What effects are the primary-, secondary-, and tertiary-level interventions expected to have on student outcomes?

4. Explain the difference between the problem-solving and standard protocol approaches.

5. What is the difference between response to intervention and resistance to intervention?

6. What is the difference between response to intervention and responsiveness to intervention?

7. What is the difference between instruction and intervention?

8. Describe the key elements of RTI intervention models.

9. What are the common elements or links between RTI and SWPBIS?

10. Are RTI and SWPBIS compatible with one another? Explain.

Glossary

A-B design: Single-case design that combines the "A" condition or baseline/pre-intervention measurements with a "B" condition to determine the effectiveness of an intervention.

A-B-A design: (See Withdrawal design).

A-B-A-B design: Single-case design that combines the "A" condition or baseline/pre-intervention measurements with a "B" condition or intervention to determine the effectiveness of the intervention; the "B" condition is followed by a second "A" condition and ends with a return to the intervention ("B" condition).

A-B-C analysis: Observation of a student during normal activities when a specific behavior is most likely to happen.

Abolishing operation: Environmental event that decreases the reinforcing value of something.

Academic functional assessment: Assessment conducted to help determine the function or purpose of a student's behavior as it relates to his or her academic performance.

Academic learning time: Amount of time students spend engaged in learning activities and being successful.

Academic support system: Integration of evidence-based academic skill support practices and interventions in three key skill areas (i.e., beginning reading, language, and mathematics) at the secondary and tertiary levels of intervention.

Acquisition stage: First stage of learning; it is the entry point when learning a skill.

Adaptation stage: Students learn to categorize, make decisions, see relationships/analogies, analyze, estimate, compare/contrast, show flexibility, and identify items that are irrelevant.

Allocated time: Amount of time a teacher or school delegates for content/subject area.

Alterable variable: Things that affect student achievement that we can change, such as teaching skills, the quantity of teacher-to-student interactions, and the use of instructional time.

Alternating treatments design: Single-case design having as its main purpose making comparisons between or among two or more conditions or interventions such as baseline and interventions or multiple interventions.

Antecedent: Something that occurs just before a behavior.

Antecedent prompt and fade: Providing a more intrusive prompt on initial instructional trials and then removing the prompt in a systematic manner.

Antecedent prompt and test: Prompting students during instruction and then providing them with practice or test trials after removing all prompts.

Antiseptic bounding: Quiet reflective period in which everyone disengages from a student.

Antisocial behavior: Behavior that violates socially prescribed norms or patterns of behavior.

Applied behavior analysis (ABA): Behavioral model based on the understanding that the environment causes many of our behaviors to occur; the study of how the environment affects our behavior and how changing these environmental events will lead to behavior change.

Appropriate error corrections: (See Error correction procedures).

Appropriate instructions: Statements that state the command succinctly without phrasing it as a question; specify a desired motoric or verbal response; use a neutral or positive/pleasant tone of voice; and have a time delay of 5 seconds between commands, as opposed to rapidly repeating the command several times.

Arbitrary consequences: Consequences that are not aligned with the offense.

Available time: The amount of time available for instruction.

Aversive: Anything that results in an escape or avoidance response.

Avoidance conditioning: Negative reinforcement procedure in which an aversive is prevented from occurring only when the student acts a certain way.

Avoidance response: Response that allows for the removal or delay of something aversive.

Backward chaining: Teaching the final step in the chain until it is mastered, then teaching the next to the last step together with the final step, and so on.

Baseline: The "A" condition in single-case designs; the level at which the participant performs a behavior without the intervention; the repeated measurement of a behavior under natural conditions.

Behavior: Act that can be clearly defined and observed.

Behavior-based time-out: Removing the source of reinforcement until the student is calm and ready to rejoin the group.

Behavior intervention plan (BIP): (See Behavior support plan).

Behavior support plan: Written document describing the environmental changes that will need to take place to bring about changes in a wanted or an unwanted behavior.

Behavior support team: Collaborative team comprised of teachers, administrators, and support staff who possess the knowledge and competencies necessary to address complex student problems by analyzing and designing interventions and supports to improve student outcomes.

Behavioral contract: Contract that specifies what both the teacher and the student must do; involves three main components: the task, the reward, and the task record.

Behavioral debriefing: Self-evaluation of the student's behavior.

Behavioral deficiency: Behavior that does not occur enough.

Behavioral excess: Behavior that occurs too often.

Behavioral model: Position that assumes human behavior is determined by a person's interaction with his or her environment, which includes the physical setting and the social surroundings; this position is a firmly grounded scientific approach.

Behavioral momentum: Desired behaviors are more likely to occur if preceded by reinforcement for other behaviors; used to increase the likelihood of compliance.

Behavioral objectives: Specific statements about student performance typically including information about the conditions under which a student will perform the behavior, the behavior (in observable terms), and criteria under which the student will display the behavior.

Behavioral trapping: Involves the maintenance of a behavior by normally occurring reinforcers.

Benchmarks for Advanced Tiers (BAT): Self-assessment with 56 items organized into 10 sub-scales developed by Anderson et al. (2009) to measure the implementation status of secondary- and tertiary-level behavior support systems.

Big ideas: Underlying concepts or skills that allow students to apply or generalize what they learn.

Chain stopping: Breaking a chain of responses by intervening at one of the earlier links.

Chaining: Putting individual behaviors together to form a more complex behavior.

Changing-criterion design: Single-case design that looks like an A-B design but includes "phase" lines (i.e., changes within the intervention condition); a criterion is established within each phase to reduce or increase some dependent variable in a stepwise manner.

Character education: Focused work on teaching students respect, being fair and trustworthy, caring for others, being responsible, and being better citizens.

Checklist: Indirect assessment by caregivers, such as parents, or teachers who check off possible antecedents and consequences the students may be exposed to when specific behaviors occur.

Chemical restraint: Using medication to control behavior or to restrict movement.

Classroom organizational system: Instructional settings in which teachers supervise and teach groups of students.

Classroom structure: Seating arrangements, rules, and routines present in the classroom.

Cognitive theory: Position that internal mental processes can cause external behavior to occur. Internal processes transform environmental stimuli; this transformation determines the behavior the individual will emit. Therefore, internal mental events can be considered independent variables.

Condition: Description of the context under which the target behavior is measured.

Conditional threat: Threat that warns that a violent act will happen unless a demand or set of demands is met.

Conditioned aversive: (See Secondary aversive).

Conditioned positive reinforcer: (See Secondary positive reinforcer).

Consequence: Something that occurs just after a behavior.

Conspicuous strategy: Explicit teaching strategy that ensures student mastery of skills.

Constant time delay: Providing a set amount of time between two prompts on subsequent learning trials.

Contextual stimulus: (See Setting event).

Contingency contract: (See Behavioral contract).

Contingent exertion: Exercise; refers to having a student do some physically exerting behavior as punishment for an unwanted behavior.

Continuous reinforcement schedule: Reinforcement for each behavior a student displays.

Contrived reinforcers: Reinforcers that are not typically used in a particular setting, such as paying a student for good grades.

Correspondence training: Teaching students how to report on what they have done or will do accurately.

Criterion: Minimum level required for acceptable performance.

Curriculum-based measurement (CBM): Standardized method teachers use to assess how students are progressing in basic academic areas such as math, reading, writing, and spelling.

Curriculum pacing: Rate at which students progress through the curricula or program used in the classroom.

Dead man's test: Term that refers to a problematic definition of behavior and to the reinforcement of a lack of behavior on the part of an individual: "if a dead man can do it, it's not behavior."

Deductive criminal profiling: Interpreting forensic evidence from a crime or crime scene after it has occurred to reconstruct behavior patterns and deduce offender characteristics, demographics, emotions, and motivations.

Dependent group management: Providing consequences to the group based on the behavior of a selected group member or a small number of members of a larger group.

Dependent variable: Behavior that is changed when the independent variable is manipulated.

Deprivation: Increase in the reinforcing value of something due to a lack of it.

Descriptive analyses: Direct assessments or observations of the unwanted and wanted behaviors under naturalistic conditions.

Differential reinforcement: Involves reinforcing a behavior in the presence of something, while not reinforcing in the presence of something else.

Differential reinforcement of alternative behavior (DRA): Involves reinforcing a more appropriate form of an unwanted behavior.

Differential reinforcement of incompatible behavior (DRI): Involves reinforcing a behavior that is topographically incompatible or opposite with the behavior targeted for reduction.

Differential reinforcement of low-rate behavior (DRL): Method used to reduce but not totally eliminate a behavior.

Differential reinforcement of other behavior (DRO): Time-based reinforcement schedule in which reinforcement is provided if unwanted behavior has not occurred within an established time period; also called differential reinforcement of zero rates of behavior and omission training.

Differential reinforcement of zero rates of behavior (DRO): (See Differential reinforcement of other behavior).

Differentiated instruction: Adjusting instruction to meet the unique needs of students.

Direct instruction: Showing students how to act and then giving them opportunities to practice the skills they learned; differs from Direct Instruction, which is a published series of programs.

Direct Instruction: Comprehensive system of instruction that focuses on active student involvement, mastery of skills, empirically validated curricula, and teacher-directed activities.

Direct threat: Threat that identifies a specific act against a specific target that is delivered in a straightforward, clear, and explicit manner.

Discipline: Methods to prevent or respond to behavior problems so they do not occur in the future; training to act in accordance with rules, as well as instruction and exercises designed to train proper conduct or action; behavior in accord with rules of conduct; a set or system of rules and regulations.

Discriminative stimulus (S^D): Signal indicating a response in its presence was reinforced in the past and will likely result in a reinforcer in the future.

Dual stimulus function: Each link serves as an S^D for the next link and as a conditioned reinforcer for the previous link.

Duration recording: Measurement of the time a response or behavior lasts.

Effect size: Quantification of the difference between the experimental and control/comparison groups in experimental studies; provides a measure of intervention strength, a summary when visual judgments do not agree, and a method for comparing relative intervention success across single-case studies.

Engaged time: Amount of time students are on task or actively engaged in learning activities.

Error correction procedures: Providing an effective model, a lead, a test, and a delayed test.

Escape conditioning: Negative reinforcement procedure in which an ongoing aversive is removed only if the student behaves appropriately.

Establishing operation: Environment event that increases the value of something as a reinforcer.

Event recording: Tallying occurrences to establish a numerical dimension of a behavior.

Evidence-based research: Research that involves the application of rigorous, systematic, and objective procedures to obtain reliable and valid knowledge relevant to educational activities and programs.

Exclusionary time-out: Temporary removal of the source of reinforcement contingent on an unwanted behavior by removing the student from the group or environment.

External validity: Asks this question: "What is the generalizability of these techniques?"

Externalizing behaviors: Behaviors directed outwardly by the student toward the external social environment.

Extinction: Permanent removal of the source of reinforcement for a behavior.

Extinction burst: Rapid increase in the frequency, duration, or intensity of an unwanted behavior during the extinction process.

Extrinsic reward: Something given to reward a student such as praise, tokens, stickers, or candy.

Fact-based threat assessment: Approach to evaluate the likelihood that students will actually carry out a threat; used to make an informed judgment on how credible and serious the threat is.

Fair-pair rule: Teaching a wanted behavior to take the place of an unwanted behavior.

Family dynamics: Patterns of behaviors, relationships, thinking, beliefs, traditions, and family crises that make up the way a family exists together.

First-time corrects: Counting the number of tasks in which students provide responses and the number of times students respond correctly and then dividing the correct responses by the total responses, multiplying by 100 to get a percentage.

Fixed-interval DRO: Reinforcing a student if he or she refrains from the unwanted behavior for the entire interval.

Fixed-interval schedule of reinforcement: Reinforcement of the first response after a set time has elapsed.

Fixed-momentary DRO: Reinforcing a student at the end of a fixed time period for each interval.

Fixed-ratio one (FR-1): (See Continuous reinforcement schedule).

Fixed-ratio schedule of reinforcement: Reinforcement of a certain number of responses; the last response in a series of responses is reinforced.

Flexible skill grouping: Grouping students according to skill; however, students can move into other groups depending on their skill performance.

Forward chaining: Teaching the first step in a chain of behaviors until it is mastered, then teaching the first and second steps together until they are mastered, and so on.

Four-term contingency: Addition of a setting event prior to the antecedent, behavior, and consequence in a three-term contingency.

Frequency recording: (See Event recording).

Functional analysis: Quantitative direct observation of behavior under preselected and controlled conditions.

Functional Analysis Screening Tool (FAST): 18-item rating scale in which a "yes" or "no" is used to determine if an item statement accurately describes the student's unwanted behavior; developed by Iwata and DeLeon (1996).

Functional behavior assessment (FBA): Assessment that is used to determine the environmental functions of wanted and unwanted behaviors.

Functional relationship: Interaction between behavior and consequences.

Funding capacity: Fiscal resources available to implement interventions.

Generalization stage: Occurs when students use their newly learned skills in novel situations.

Generalized reinforcer: Reinforcer paired with several other reinforcers (both primary and secondary); not dependent on the same reinforcer used for conditioning.

Goal: Broad statement of what is to be accomplished by the end of an academic term; also termed a long-term objective.

Goal setting: Establishment of performance criteria and the identification and use of solutions to meet an established goal.

Graduated guidance: Similar to the most-to-least prompting procedure except it involves more of a fluid movement from the highest level of prompt to the lowest level.

Grandma's rule: (See Premack principle).

Group alerting: Making sure students are paying attention and then providing them with specific instruction on what they are supposed to do at any one time.

Group-oriented management approaches: Providing consequences based on the behavior of one member of a group, a small number of students within the group, or all members of the group.

Guided practice: Teacher actively participates in the learning with the students.

Guided rehearsal: (See Guided practice).

High-level threat: Threat whose contents suggest students are likely to carry it out.

High-probability response sequence: (See Behavioral momentum).

Human capacity: Staff and volunteers who are currently available or could be available to implement the interventions.

Incidental teaching: (See Training loosely).

Independent group management: Having the same response requirements for each student while providing individual consequences based on the behavior of each student.

Independent practice: Students complete work on their own after an 80% success rate is achieved on guided practice; examples are cooperative learning and homework.

Independent variable: Something under teacher control that is being manipulated in order to change a behavior.

Indirect assessment: Involves gaining information from other sources rather than a first-hand analysis of the environmental events.

Indirect threat: Threat that is vague, unclear, and ambiguous; the plan is expressed tentatively.

Individual organizational system: Specific supports for students who are at risk of or are experiencing learning and behavioral difficulties.

Inductive criminal profiling: Looking for patterns in the present data to induce possible outcomes; strategy used to predict behavior and intervene before potential offenders commit a crime.

Informal procedure: Procedure that does not require explicit behavior management plans.

Instructional momentum: The movement of students quickly and successfully through the curriculum.

Interdependent group management: Treating a group of students as a single individual; setting the same response requirements for all group members; delivering consequences based on the performance of all members of the group.

Intermittent reinforcement schedule: Reinforcement given on a periodic basis following student behaviors; consists of fixed-interval, variable-interval, fixed-ratio, and variable-ratio reinforcement.

Internal validity: Addresses this question: "Did the independent variable make the difference or was the change due to something else?"

Internalizing behaviors: Behaviors directed inwardly and representing problems with self.

Interobserver agreement: Percentage of agreement between two or more persons concurrently observing a behavior.

Interresponse time (IRT): The time period between responses.

Interspersed requests: (See Behavioral momentum).

Interval recording: Provides an estimate of the percentage of intervals in which a behavior occurred; involves dividing observational periods into units of time.

Intervention: Specific set of procedures or practices and associated materials developed to prevent or remediate learning and behavior difficulties.

Intervention condition: The period when the behavior support plan is in effect.

Interview assessment: Method used to determine the source of reinforcement for a behavior by asking people in the student's life what they think the likely function of the challenging behavior is.

Intrinsic reward: Some rewarding thing that occurs inside the individual, such as pride, interest, and self-esteem.

Intrusiveness: Involves the extent to which behavioral interventions infringe on a person's bodily or personal rights.

Judicious review: Sequence and schedule of opportunities for students to apply and develop fluency with newly acquired skills.

Latency recording: Involves recording the time from a specified event to the start of the targeted behavior or the completion of the response.

Law of Effect: States that, when a behavior is reinforced, the behavior is more likely to occur in the future, and, when a behavior is not reinforced, it will extinguish.

Leadership organizational system: System in which the school's role is key in developing a leadership team that implements a continual strategic planning process to achieve a safe and disciplined school environment maximizing student learning.

Least-to-most prompting: Increasing assistance when a student does not perform a behavior.

Lesson pacing: Pace at which teachers conduct individual or daily lessons.

Level I procedure: Least restrictive approach aimed at reducing unwanted behavior; systematically planned and implemented.

Level II procedure: Second least restrictive approach aimed at reducing unwanted behavior; involves the removal of the source of reinforcement.

Level III procedure: More restrictive and aversive approach that involves the contingent removal of something reinforcing.

Level IV procedure: Approach with the highest level of restrictiveness; involves the use of something aversive.

Limited-responding DRL: Reinforcement is presented if a certain number of behaviors or fewer is emitted.

Logical consequences: Consequences that are connected in some manner with the behavior.

Low-level threat: Threat whose contents suggest students are unlikely to carry it out.

Maintenance: The endurance of a behavior after the intervention has been removed.

Maintenance stage: Periodic practice and review of the skill to ensure that students maintain skill mastery over time.

Mastery: Performing skills at high, successful levels.

Mechanical restraint: Using a device or object to limit bodily movement.

Mediated scaffolding: Adjustments to the level of instruction provided students as they move through material enabling them to bridge the gap between current skill level and the goal of instruction.

Medium-level threat: Threat whose contents suggest students could carry it out but that does not appear entirely realistic.

Minimal intervention: (See Training loosely).

Modeling: Showing students how to do the skill.

Moment of transfer: Point at which the prompt to which you want the student to respond gains stimulus control.

Momentary DRO: Observing the student at the end of a stated time period to see if the misbehavior is occurring.

Momentary time sampling: Procedure to record behavior only if it is occurring at the end of a specified time interval.

Momentum: Movement through lessons, including beginning lessons immediately after the start of class.

Most-to-least prompting: Progressively decreasing assistance to a student in a progressive fashion and creating a prompt hierarchy.

Motivating operations: Environmental variables that change the reinforcing value of something.

Motivation (violence): Reason behind the threat.

Motivation Assessment Scale (MAS): 16-item rating scale developed by Durand and Crimmins (1987); requires a specific description of the challenging behaviors and a description of the settings in which they occur.

Multiple-baseline design: Single-case design that involves a series of staggered A-B designs; includes the placement of individual graphs on top of each other; can be used across participants, behaviors, or settings.

Multiple-baseline design across behaviors: Single-case design involving a series of staggered A-B designs that requires at least two separate behaviors, which are independent of one another.

Multiple-baseline design across settings: Single-case design involving a series of staggered A-B designs that requires behavior measurement in two or more settings.

Multiple-baseline design across students: Single-case design involving a series of staggered A-B designs that requires two or more students.

Multiple-gating procedure: Series of assessments designed to screen out, in a systematic fashion, students with or at risk of learning or behavior problems.

Multiple-probe design: Single-case design that is essentially a multiple-baseline design in which the measurements are not conducted on a frequent basis; overcomes the problem of using repeated measurements by probing (assessing) the behavior every so often; probes are also used in assessing generalization and maintenance of intervention effects.

Natural consequences: Consequences that normally occur without any teacher intervention.

Natural reinforcers: Reinforcers that are typically used in a certain environment, such as providing grades for good performance in school.

Naturalistic teaching: (See Training loosely).

Negative practice: Requires the repetition of the unwanted behavior to punish or to satiate students with that behavior.

Negative punishment: Removal of something reinforcing contingent on a behavior that results in a decrease in the future likelihood of the behavior.

Negative reinforcement: Removal of something aversive contingent on the occurrence of a behavior that results in an increase in the future likelihood of the behavior.

Negative scanning: Trying to find students misbehaving.

Negative trap: Provision of punishment techniques in such a manner that the negative interactions escalate.

Nonalterable variable: Something that affects student achievement that we cannot change, such as ethnicity, socioeconomic status, gender, and home background.

Nonclassroom organizational system: Organizational structure at particular times or in particular places where supervision is emphasized in a school setting outside of the classroom, such as hallways, cafeteria, playground, and bus.

Nonexclusionary time-out: Temporary removal of the source of reinforcement contingent on an unwanted behavior without removing the student from the group or environment.

Nonintensive teaching: (See Training loosely).

Objective: (See Behavioral objectives).

Observation form: Descriptive analysis that structures the observation into a checklist format with operational definitions of each of the target behaviors.

Observer drift: Occurs when observers change the way they employ the definition of behavior over the course of a study.

Observer expectations: Expectations of the observers that can influence what is observed.

Omission training: (See Differential reinforcement of other behavior).

Operational definition (for a program): Specific elements of the intervention can be observed and counted.

Outcome evaluation: Assessment of whether or not interventions are effective and meet the established goals.

Overcorrection: Aversive procedures aimed at decreasing unwanted behaviors by requiring the student to engage in a behavior that is related to correcting the damage caused by the unwanted behavior.

Overlapping: Teachers control or have an influence over several activities that overlap.

Partial-interval recording: Procedure used to record a behavior if it occurs at any point within a specified time interval.

Pause and punch: Vocal variation in timing and then in tone, loudness, or pitch that provides additional information to students, such as the emphasis of a particular word.

Performance contingent: Providing external reinforcers if students have met a predetermined performance criterion.

Permanent product recording: Involves the teacher observing the enduring product or outcome of a student's behavior (e.g., worksheet completion, written spelling words).

Personality: Pattern of traits or behaviors that characterize individual students.

Physical capacity: Setting selected in which the interventions will occur.

Physical restraint: Restricting the movement of a person's body.

Positive practice overcorrection: Having students repeatedly engage in an alternative appropriate behavior instead of an inappropriate one.

Positive punishment: Something added to the environment contingent on the occurrence of a behavior that results in a decrease in the likelihood of that behavior over time.

Positive reinforcement: Something added to the environment contingent on the occurrence of a behavior that results in an increase in the future likelihood of the behavior.

Positive scanning: Watching for positive behaviors to occur.

Postreinforcement pause: Delay that occurs after reinforcement on a fixed-ratio schedule.

Praise around technique: Students surrounding a misbehaving student are praised for appropriate behavior.

Precision teaching: Standardized methods with which to evaluate the effectiveness of instruction and curriculum in a formative fashion.

Precorrection: Active teacher supervision and effective instruction during which students are taught expectations, rules, and routines to prevent a misbehavior from occurring.

Preferred activity time (PAT): Procedure that involves allowing students access to those things students enjoy but are an extension of the academic content.

Premack principle: Getting a less preferred behavior to occur by reinforcing it with a more

preferred one; indicates a high-probability behavior can reinforce a low-probability behavior; also called Grandma's rule.

Pretask requests: (See Behavioral momentum).

Preventive strategies: (See Informal procedure).

Primary aversive: Something that is not learned that results in an escape or avoidance response (e.g., electric shock, nauseating smells).

Primary level: Instructional and behavioral focus is on a schoolwide basis so that students do not become at risk for learning and behavior difficulties.

Primary positive reinforcer: Something that is a reinforcer without being learned; also called an unconditioned reinforcer (e.g., food, water, warmth).

Primed background knowledge: Connection of previously acquired knowledge to the skills about to be taught.

Principle of least dangerous assumption: Suggests the strategy selected should produce the least amount of harm if the procedure is ineffective.

Problem Behavior Questionnaire: 15-item rating scale that measures the frequency with which an event is likely to be seen; developed by Lewis, Scott, and Sugai (1994).

Problem solving: Process of reaching a successful outcome or solving a problem; can be taught to students as a self-management procedure.

Process evaluations: Assessment of fidelity of implementation (i.e., extent to which the intervention is delivered as intended).

Proficiency stage: Follows acquisition; once students have acquired a skill, they must be able to perform the skill at a fluent or automatic level.

Program: Grouping of interventions designed to prevent or remediate learning and behavior difficulties.

Program common stimuli: Instruction or support occurs under conditions that are broadly available in different classrooms and other environments within the school.

Progress monitoring: Ongoing use of formative assessment procedures to determine the extent to which students are benefiting from classroom instruction and to monitor the effectiveness of the core curriculum and instruction program as well as of secondary- and tertiary-level interventions.

Progressive time delay: Time delay between two prompts is gradually increased on subsequent learning trials.

Prompted practice: (See Guided practice).

Proximity control: Decreasing unwanted behaviors by positioning the teacher somewhere next to the student.

Punishment: As a consequence for behavior, the presentation or removal of something that reduces the future likelihood of that behavior.

Rating scale: Indirect assessment completed by parents or teachers that provides a level of likelihood that an antecedent or consequence would occur before or after the target behavior.

Reactivity: Differences in interobserver agreement that result from observers being aware that their observations will be checked.

Redirection: Informal method in which students are prompted to do something that interferes with the unwanted behavior.

Regression discontinuity designs: Designs in which participants are assigned to the intervention and the comparison conditions based on a cutoff score on a pre-intervention measure that typically assesses need or merit.

Reinforcement: Presentation or removal of something that increases the future likelihood of a behavior as a consequence for that behavior.

Reliability: Consistency of results over time.

Reprimands: Strong negative verbal statements.

Response cost: Involves the permanent removal of some portion of a reinforcer.

Response deprivation hypothesis: Any behavior that is reduced below its baseline level can function as a reinforcer.

Response generalization: Behavior being more likely to occur in the presence of something as a result of another behavior having been reinforced and strengthened in its presence.

Response-induced aggression: Aggression toward a person providing aversives or toward others associated with this person.

Response to intervention (RTI): Initiative aimed at providing a high-quality continuum of instruction and interventions matched to student need and at monitoring progress frequently to make decisions about changes in what students need to be successful.

Restitutional overcorrection: Involves having the student return the environment to a better state than the one in which it was before.

Restraint: Limiting or restricting an individual from behaving in some way.

Restrictiveness: Involves the extent to which an individual has limited access to basic human freedoms.

Review: Having students perform skills over time so the skills are not forgotten.

Reward: Something given to a student that does not necessarily result in the increased future likelihood of the behavior.

Ripple effect: Tendency for primary-aged students to react to a teacher's actions when those actions are aimed at other students.

Routines: Sets of actions students take to reach specific outcomes in the most efficient manner.

Rule-governed behavior: A behavior controlled by verbal or written rules.

Rules: Statements that contain one or more of the three terms in the three-term contingency (i.e., antecedent, behavior, consequence).

S-delta (S$^\Delta$): Indicates a behavior in its presence will not be reinforced.

Satiation: Decrease in the reinforcer effectiveness of a stimulus due to receiving that stimulus.

Scatter plot: Descriptive analysis that enables the observer to monitor target behaviors over an extended period of time.

Schedules of reinforcement: Points at which reinforcers are delivered for the purpose of increasing or maintaining behavior.

School dynamics: Patterns of behaviors, relationships, thinking, beliefs, and traditions that make up the school culture.

School-wide Evaluation Tool (SET): Assessment developed by Sugai, Lewis-Palmer, Todd, and Horner (2001) with 28 items organized into seven subscales to assess and evaluate the critical features of the primary level of SWPBIS.

Schoolwide organizational system: Organizational structure involving all students and staff in all settings within a school.

Schoolwide positive behavior intervention and support program (SWPBIS): Application of positive behavioral interventions and supports to achieve socially important behavior change across all of the school environments.

Seatwork variety and challenge: When teachers make seatwork interesting to students.

Seclusionary time-out: Temporary removal of a student from the group to an isolated area.

Secondary aversive: Things that are learned that result in an escape or avoidance response; things that are not aversive from the time we are born (e.g., grades, reprimands).

Secondary level: Instructional and behavioral focus is on providing academic and behavior support to students at risk for learning and behavior difficulties.

Secondary positive reinforcer: Something that has acquired a reinforcing function through pairing with a previously established reinforcer; those reinforcers that are learned (also called conditioned reinforcers), including praise, money, grades, and reprimands.

Self-charting: Self-management procedure; students graph their own behavior.

Self-evaluation: Self-management procedure; students measure their own behavior against some specified standard.

Self-instruction: Self-management procedure; students are taught to "talk to themselves" or engage in covert verbal responses.

Self-management: Variety of methods used by students to manage their own behavior.

Self-monitoring: Self-management procedure; students observe and record their own behavior without the use of a prompt.

Self-recording: Self-management procedure; students observe and record their own behavior using a prompt.

Self-reinforcement/punishment: Self-management procedure; students provide consequences for their own behavior.

Sequential modification of the training situation: Involves successfully implementing the management program in one setting and then changing the management system in another setting to match that of the first setting.

Setting event: Antecedent occurring in the environment that sets the occasion for certain behaviors; also, part of a four-term contingency.

Setting/situation generalization: (See Stimulus generalization).

Shaping: Reinforcement of successive approximations of the behavior; progressing step by step toward a terminal objective.

Signposts: Behaviors that indicate students are planning a targeted act of violence.

Single-case design: Experiment in which the participants serve as their own control group; intent is to establish a relationship between the dependent and independent variables.

Situational inducement: Involves manipulating contexts that already have a history of control over the behavior.

Smoothness: Being able to conduct a lesson without undue interference or changes that disrupt the students.

Social dynamics: Patterns of behaviors, relationships, thinking, beliefs, and traditions that make up the culture of the larger community in which students live and go to school.

Spaced-responding DRL: Reinforcing a behavior if a certain amount of time (interresponse time) has elapsed between responses.

Specific praise: Precise statements of praise in a neutral or positive/pleasant tone of voice that reflect a positive response to a specific desired behavior.

Spontaneous recovery: Return of a behavior at various times after that behavior seems to be eliminated.

Standard protocol: Any set of activities designed to evaluate the effects of instruction or intervention on student achievement.

Stimulus control: Situation in which a behavior is changed by providing or removing an antecedent stimulus.

Stimulus generalization: A student using new and appropriate behaviors in contexts other than where they have been taught.

Strategic integration: Integration of concepts, content, and skills that are mutually facilitative of each other or arranged so that instruction communicates generalizations to new areas removed from the original area of instruction.

Strategy: General conceptual approach or framework for preventing or remediating learning and behavior difficulties.

Student accountability: Keeping students involved in the lesson.

Success contingent: Providing external reinforcers, with additional reinforcers along the way, if students have met predetermined performance criteria.

Sustainability: An intervention is durable and likely to continue over a period of time and has the resources to support it.

Task analysis: Breakdown of a task into several links or steps.

Task contingent: Providing reinforcement to students for simply engaging in a task for some period of time without requirements on quality of performance.

Teaching functions: Classroom experiences that move students from lack of skill mastery to mastery.

Technical capacity: Administrative and specialized support necessary to implement interventions.

Tertiary level: Instructional and behavioral focus is on students who display a life course of persistent learning and behavior difficulties.

Think Time®: Empirically validated disciplinary response used by classroom teachers and playground/lunchroom supervisors that includes three interventions common to schools: an effective request for appropriate behavior, antiseptic bounding, and behavioral debriefing.

Threat: Spoken, written, or symbolic expression of intent to do harm or act out violently against someone or something.

Three-term contingency: Made up of the antecedent, behavior, and the consequence; used to explain behavior.

Tier 1: (See Primary level).

Tier 2: (See Secondary level).

Tier 3: (See Tertiary level).

Time-based time-out: Removing the source of reinforcement for a set amount of time.

Time delay: Initially presenting at the same time a prompt to which you ultimately want the students to respond, such as a list of homework assignments written on the board, and another prompt, such as a verbal directive for students to write assignments in their agendas, and then delaying presentation of the second cue.

Time-out: Temporary removal of the source of reinforcement contingent on an unwanted behavior; considered a negative punisher.

Token economy system: System in which, contingent on some behavior, tokens are provided that can be turned in for backup reinforcers; tokens serve as secondary reinforcers.

Total task chaining: (See Whole task chaining).

Train sufficient response exemplar: Involves teaching students several appropriate responses to a given situation.

Train sufficient stimulus exemplars: Using multiple examples of the targeted skills during teaching.

Training loosely: Involves varying the situation under which the behavior support plan is introduced.

Trait: Psychological characteristic of a person, including disposition to discriminate between or among different situations similarly and to respond to them consistently despite changing conditions.

Unconditioned aversive: (See Primary aversive).

Unconditioned positive reinforcer: (See Primary positive reinforcer).

Unison oral responding: All students respond together and receive feedback from the teacher.

Universal screening: Assessment procedures that are characterized by the administration of quick, low-cost, repeatable evaluations of critical academic skills and that are used to assess all students.

Valence and challenge arousal: Stimulating a positive reaction to a lesson by showing enthusiasm and using a variety of activities when teaching students.

Variable-interval DRO: Reinforcing a student if he or she refrains from the unwanted behavior for an average amount of time.

Variable-interval schedule of reinforcement: Reinforcement of the first response after an average amount of time has elapsed.

Variable-momentary DRO: Reinforcing a student if there is a lack of unwanted behavior at the end of varying interval lengths.

Variable-ratio schedule of reinforcement: Reinforcement after an average number of responses.

Vary the acceptable responses during training: Require different responses during training.

Veiled threat: Threat that strongly implies but does not explicitly threaten violence.

Visual analysis: Prominent technique for judging the magnitude of the intervention effects from single-case studies by assessing all conditions within the design.

Wait time: Gives students the opportunity to think about the answer before they actually say it.

Whole-interval DRO: Observing a student's behavior consistently over a time period.

Whole-interval recording: Procedure used to record behaviors only if they occur throughout the entire specified time interval.

Whole task chaining: Teaching the chain of behaviors at once.

Withdrawal design: Also called A-B-A design; a single-case design that combines the "A" condition or baseline/pre-intervention measurements with a "B" condition or intervention to determine the effectiveness of the intervention; the "B" condition is followed by a second "A" condition.

Withitness: Act of teachers being aware of what is going on in the classroom.

References

Adams, G. L., & Engelmann, S. (1996). *Research on Direct Instruction: 25 years beyond DISTAR.* Seattle, WA: Educational Achievement Systems.

Agran, M., & Martella, R. C. (1991). Teaching self-instructional skills to persons with mental retardation: A descriptive and experimental analysis. In M. Hersen, R. M. Eisler, & P. M. Miller (Eds.), *Progress in behavior modification* (Vol. 27, pp. 36–55). Newbury Park, CA: SAGE.

Alberto, P. A., & Troutman, A. C. (2009). *Applied behavior analysis for teachers* (7th ed.). Upper Saddle River, NJ: Pearson.

American Academy of Pediatrics. (2003). Out-of-school suspension and expulsion. *Pediatrics, 112,* 1206–1209.

American Psychological Association, Commission on Violence and Youth. (1993). *Violence and youth: Psychology's response* (Vol. 1). New York, NY: Author.

Anderson, C. M., Childs, K. E., Kincaid, D., Horner, R. H., George, H., Todd, A.W., Sampson, N., & Spaulding, S. A. (2009). *Benchmarks for Advanced Tiers (BAT)* [Unpublished instrument]. University of Oregon & University of South Florida.

Anderson, C. M., & Spaulding, S. A. (2007). Using positive behavior support to design effective classrooms. *Beyond Behavior, 16,* 27–31.

Arlin, M. (1979). Teacher transitions can disrupt time flow in classrooms. *American Educational Research Journal, 16,* 42–56.

Armbruster, B. B., Lehr, F., & Osborn, J. (2006). *Put reading first: The research building blocks for teaching children to read—Kindergarten through Grade 3* (3rd ed.). Jessup, MD: National Institute for Literacy.

Association for Behavior Analysis International. (1989). *Statement on the right to effective behavioral treatment.* Retrieved from http://www.abainternational.org/ABA/statements/treatment.asp

Association for Behavior Analysis International. (1990). *Statement of students' right to effective education.* Retrieved from http://www.abainternational.org/ABA/statements/education.asp

Association for Behavior Analysis International. (2010). *Statement on restraint and seclusion.* Retrieved from http://www.abainternational.org/ABA/statements/RestraintSeclusion.asp

Axelrod, S. (1987a). Doing it without arrows [Review of the book *Alternative to punishment: Solving behavior problems with non-aversive strategies*]. *The Behavior Analyst, 10,* 243–251.

Axelrod, S. (1987b). Functional and structural analyses of behavior: Approaches leading to reduced use of punishment procedures. *Research in Developmental Disabilities, 8,* 165–178.

Ayllon, T., & Azrin, N. (1968). *The token economy: A motivational system for therapy and rehabilitation.* New York, NY: Appleton-Century-Crofts.

Baer, D. M., & Wolf, M. M. (1970). The entry into natural communities of reinforcement. In R. Ulrich, T. Stachnik, & J. Mabry (Eds.), *Control of human behavior* (Vol. 2, pp. 319–324). Glenview, IL: Scott Foresman.

Barlow, D. H., Nock, M. K., & Hersen, M. (2009). *Single case experimental designs: Strategies for studying behavior change* (3rd ed.). Boston, MA: Allyn & Bacon.

Barrett, B. H., Beck, R., Binder, C., Cook, D. A., Engelmann, S., Greer, R. D., Kyrklund, S. J., Johnson, K. R., Maloney, M., McCorkle, N., Vargas, J. S., & Watkins, C. L. (1991). The right to effective education. *The Behavior Analyst, 14,* 79–82.

Barrish, H. H., Saunders, M., & Wolf, M. M. (1969). Good Behavior Game: Effects of individual contingencies for group contingencies on disruptive behavior in a classroom. *Journal of Applied Behavior Analysis, 2,* 119–124.

Battistich, V., Schaps, E., Watson, M., & Solomon, D. (1996). Prevention effects of the Child Development Project: Early findings from an ongoing multisite demonstration trial. *Journal of Adolescent Research, 11,* 12–35.

Battistich, V., Schaps, E., Watson, M., Solomon, D., & Lewis, C. (2000). Effects of the Child Development Project on students' drug use and other problem behaviors. *The Journal of Primary Prevention, 21,* 75–99.

Beets, M. W., Flay, B. R., Vuchinich, S., Acock, A. C., Li, K. K., & Allred, C. (2008). School climate and teachers' beliefs and attitudes associated with implementation of the Positive Action Program: A diffusion of innovations model. *Prevention Science, 9,* 264–275.

Bellini, S., Peters, J. K., Benner, L., & Hopf, A. (2007). A meta-analysis of school-based social skills interventions for children with autism spectrum disorders. *Remedial and Special Education, 28,* 153–162.

Benner, G. J., Nelson, J. R., Stage, S. A., & Ralston, N. C. (2011). The influence of fidelity of implementation on the reading outcomes of middle school students experiencing reading difficulties. *Remedial and Special Education, 32,* 79–88.

Blood, E., & Neel, R. S. (2007). From FBA to implementation: A look at what is actually being delivered. *Education and Treatment of Children, 30,* 67–80.

Bloom, B. S. (1980). The new direction in educational research: Alterable variables. *Phi Delta Kappan, 61,* 382–385.

Borg, W. R. (1977). Changing teacher and pupil performance with protocols. *Journal of Experimental Education, 45,* 9–18.

Borg, W. R., Langer, P., & Wilson, J. (1975). Teacher classroom management skills and pupil behavior. *Journal of Experimental Education, 44,* 52–58.

Bradley, R., Danielson, L., & Hallahan, D. P. (2002). *Identification of learning disabilities: Research to practice.* Mahwah, NJ: Lawrence Erlbaum.

Brooks, K., Schiraldi, V., & Ziedenberg, J. (2000). *School house hype: Two years later.* Washington, DC: Justice Policy Institute.

Brown-Chidsey, R., & Steege, M. W. (2005). *Response to intervention: Principles and strategies for effective practice.* New York, NY: Guilford Press.

Browning-Wright, D., Saren, D., & Mayer, G. R. (2003). *The Behavior Support Plan—Quality Evaluation Guide.* Retrieved from http://www.pent.ca.gov

Bruns, E. J., Moore, E., Stephan, S. H., Pruitt, D., & Weist, M. D. (2005). The impact of school mental health services on out-of-school suspension rates. *Journal of Youth and Adolescence, 34,* 23–30.

Burns, M. K., & Ysseldyke, J. E. (2009). Reported prevalence of evidence-based instructional practices in special education. *The Journal of Special Education, 43,* 3–11.

Campbell, C. R., & Stremel-Campbell, K. (1982). Programming "loose training" as a strategy to facilitate language generalization. *Journal of Applied Behavior Analysis, 15,* 295–301.

Canter, L., & Canter, M. (1992). *Assertive discipline: Positive behavior management for today's classroom* (2nd ed.). Santa Monica, CA: Canter and Associates.

Capps, R., Fix, M., Ost, J., Reardon-Anderson, J., & Passel, J. S. (2004). *The health and well being of young children of immigrants.* Washington, DC: The Urban Institute.

Carnine, D., Silbert, J., Kame'enui, E., & Tarver, S. (2010). *Direct instruction reading* (5th ed.). Upper Saddle River, NJ: Merrill/Prentice Hall.

Carr, E. G., Horner, R. H., Turnbull, A. P., Marquis, J. G., Magito McLaughlin, D., McAtee, M. L., Smith, C. E., Anderson, R. K., Ruef, M. B., & Doolabh, A. (1999). *Positive behavior support for people with developmental disabilities: Research synthesis* (American Association on Mental Retardation Monograph Series). Washington, DC: American Association on Mental Retardation.

Catania, A. C. (1998). *Learning* (4th ed.). Englewood Cliffs, NJ: Prentice Hall.

Chance, P. (1992). The rewards of learning. *Phi Delta Kappan, 73,* 200–207.

Chandler, L. K., & Dahlquist, C. M. (2010). *Functional assessment: Strategies to prevent and remediate challenging behavior in school settings* (3rd ed.). Upper Saddle River, NJ: Pearson.

Character Education Partnership. (2010). *Defining and understanding character education.* Retrieved from http://www.character.org/definingand understandingce

Charles, C. M. (1996). *Building classroom discipline* (5th ed.). White Plains, NY: Longman.

Christ, T. J., Burns, M. K., & Ysseldyke, J. E. (2005). Conceptual confusion within response-to-intervention vernacular: Clarifying meaningful differences. *NASP Communiqué, 34,* 34–37.

Christenson, L., Thurlow, M. L., Sinclair, M. F., Lehr, C. M., Kaibel, A. L., Reschly, A. L., Mavis, A., & Phol, A. (2008). *Check & Connect: A comprehensive student engagement intervention manual.* Minneapolis: University of Minnesota.

Cipani, E. (2008). *Classroom management for all teachers: Plans for evidence-based practice* (3rd ed.). Upper Saddle River, NJ: Pearson.

Clarizio, H. F. (1986). *Toward positive classroom discipline* (3rd ed.). New York, NY: Wiley.

Clonin, S. M., McDougal, J. L., Clark, K., & Davison, S. (2007). Use of office discipline referrals in school-wide decision making: A practical example. *Psychology in the Schools, 44,* 19–27.

Coalition for Evidence-Based Policy. (2003). *Identifying and implementing educational practices supported by rigorous evidence: A user friendly guide.* Washington, DC: National Center for Education Evaluation and Regional Assistance, Institute of Education Sciences. Retrieved from http://www.ed.gov/rschstat/research/pubs/rigorousevid/index.html

Cohen, J. (1988). *Statistical power analysis for the behavioral sciences* (2nd ed.). Hillsdale, NJ: Lawrence Erlbaum.

Cohen, L. G., & Spenciner, L. J. (2011). *Assessment of children and youth with special needs* (4th ed.). Upper Saddle River, NJ: Merrill.

Colvin, G., Sugai, G., & Patching, B. (1993). Precorrection: An instructional approach for managing predictable problem behaviors. *Intervention in School and Clinic, 28,* 143–150.

Committee for Children. (1997). *Second Step: A violence prevention curriculum* (2nd ed.). Seattle, WA: Author.

Cook, C. R., Mayer, G. R., Browning-Wright, D., Kraemer, B., Wallace, M. D., Dart, E., Collins, T., & Restori, A. (2010). Exploring the link among behavior intervention plans, treatment integrity, and student outcomes under natural educational conditions. *The Journal of Special Education.* Advance online publication. doi: 10.1177/0022466910369941

Cooper, H. (1989). Synthesis of research on homework. *Educational Leadership, 47*(3), 85–91.

Cooper, J. O., Heron, T. E., & Heward, W. L. (2007). *Applied behavior analysis* (2nd ed.). Upper Saddle River, NJ: Pearson.

Council for Children with Behavioral Disorders. (2009a). CCBD's position summary on the use of physical restraint procedures in school settings. *Behavioral Disorders, 34,* 223–234.

Council for Children with Behavioral Disorders. (2009b). CCBD's position summary on the use of seclusion in school settings. *Behavioral Disorders, 34,* 235–243.

Couvillon, M. A., Bullock, L. M., & Gable, R. A. (2009). Tracking behavior assessment methodology and support strategies: A national survey of how schools utilize functional behavioral assessments and behavior intervention plans. *Emotional and Behavioral Difficulties, 14,* 215–228.

Crone, D. A., Horner, R. H., & Hawkin, L. S. (2010). *Responding to problem behavior in schools.* New York, NY: Guilford Press.

Dalton, T., Martella, R. C., & Marchand-Martella, N. E. (1999). The effects of a self-management program in reducing off-task behavior of middle school students with disabilities. *Journal of Behavioral Education, 9,* 157–176.

Deci, E. L., Koestner, R., & Ryan, R. M. (1999). A meta-analytic review of experiments examining the effects of extrinsic rewards on intrinsic motivation. *Psychological Bulletin, 125,* 627–668.

Deci, E. L., & Ryan, R. M. (1985). *Intrinsic motivation and self-determination in human behavior.* New York, NY: Plenum Press.

Deitz, S. M., & Repp, A. C. (1973). Decreasing classroom misbehavior through the use of DRL schedules of reinforcement. *Journal of Applied Behavior Analysis, 6,* 457–463.

Deno, S. L. (1985). Curriculum-based measurement: The emerging alternative. *Exceptional Children, 52,* 219–232.

Deno, S. L. (2002). Problem solving as "best practice." In A. Thomas & J. Grimes (Eds.), *Best practices in school psychology–IV* (pp. 37–55). Bethesda, MD: National Association of School Psychologists.

Donohue, E., Schiraldi, V., & Ziedenberg, J. (1998). *School house hype: School shootings and the real risks kids face in America.* Washington, DC: Justice Policy Institute.

Dorsey, M. E., Iwata, B. A., Ong, P., & McSween, T. E. (1980). Treatment of self-injurious behavior using a water mist: Initial response suppression and generalization. *Journal of Applied Behavior Analysis, 13,* 343–353.

Doyle, W. (1986). Classroom organization and management. In M. C. Wittrock (Ed.), *Handbook of research on teaching* (pp. 392–431). New York, NY: Collier Macmillan.

Dreikurs, R. (1968). *Psychology in the classroom: A manual for teachers* (2nd ed.). New York, NY: Harper and Row.

Dreikurs, R., Cassel, P., & Ferguson, E. D. (2004). *Discipline without tears: How to reduce conflict and establish cooperation in the classroom.* Mississauga, ON, Canada: Wiley.

Dunlap, G., dePerczel, M., Clarke, S., Wilson, D., Wright, S., White, R., & Gomez, A. (1994). Choice making to promote adaptive behavior for students with emotional and behavioral challenges. *Journal of Applied Behavior Analysis, 27,* 505–518.

Dunlap, G., Iovannone, R., Wilson, K. J., Kincaid, D. K., & Strain, P. (2010). Prevent-teach-reinforce: A standardized model of school-based behavioral intervention. *Journal of Positive Behavior Interventions, 12,* 9–22.

Dupper, D. R., Theriot, M. T., & Craun, S. W. (2009). Reducing out-of-school suspensions: Practice guidelines for school social workers. *Children & Schools, 31,* 6–14.

Durand, V. M., & Crimmins, D. B. (1987). Assessment and treatment of psychotic speech in an autistic child. *Journal of Autism and Developmental Disabilities, 17*(1), 17–28.

Dwyer, K., Osher, D., & Warger, C. (1998). *Early warning, timely response: A guide to safe schools.* Washington, DC: U.S. Department of Education.

Dynarski, M., Clarke, L., Cobb, B., Finn, J., Rumberger, R., & Smink, J. (2008). *Dropout prevention: A practice guide* (NCEE 2008-4025). Washington, DC: National Center for Education Evaluation and Regional Assistance, Institute of Education Sciences, U.S. Department of Education. Retrieved from http://ies.ed.gov/ncee/wwc

D'Zurilla, T. J., & Goldfried, M. R. (1971). Problem solving and behavior modification. *Journal of Abnormal Psychology, 78,* 107–126.

Eber, L., & Nelson, C. M. (1997). School-based wraparound planning: Integrating services for students with emotional and behavioral needs. *American Journal of Orthopsychiatry, 67,* 385–395.

Engelmann, S. (2007). Student-program alignment and teaching to mastery. *Journal of Direct Instruction, 7,* 45–66.

Epstein, M., Atkins, M., Cullinan, D., Kutash, K., & Weaver, R. (2008). *Reducing behavior problems in the elementary school classroom: A practice guide* (NCEE No. 2008-012). Washington, DC: National Center for Education Evaluation and Regional Assistance, Institute of Education Sciences, U.S. Department of Education. Retrieved from http://ies.ed.gov/ncee/wwwc/publications/practiceguides

Etscheidt, S. K. (2006). Behavioral intervention plans: Pedagogical and legal analysis of issues. *Behavioral Disorders, 31,* 223–243.

Fay, J. (1981). *Love and logic solution: Three types of parents.* Golden, CO: Cline/Fay Love and Logic Institute.

Ferster, C. B., & Skinner, B. F. (1957). *Schedules of reinforcement.* New York, NY: Appleton.

Fey, G., Nelson, J. R., & Roberts, M. L. (2000). There are plenty of ambiguity and legal ramifications to be considered if educators plan to identify students who seem inclined to commit violent acts. *The School Administrator, 57,* 10–12.

Flay, B. R., & Allred, C. G. (2003). Long-term effects of the *Positive Action* program. *American Journal of Health Behavior, 27*(Suppl. 1), S6–S21.

Flay, B. R., Allred, C. G., & Ordway, N. (2001). Effects of the *Positive Action* program on achievement and discipline: Two matched-control comparisons. *Prevention Science, 2,* 71–89.

Flay, B. R., Biglan, A., Boruch, R. F., Castro, F. G., Gottfredson, D., Kellam, S., Mościcki, E. K., Schinke, S., Valentine, J. C., & Ji, P. (2005). Standards of evidence: Criteria for efficacy, effectiveness and dissemination. *Prevention Science, 6,* 151–175.

Fletcher, J. M., Coulter, W. A., Reschly, D. J., & Vaughn, S. (2004). Alternative approaches to the definition and identification of learning disabilities: Some questions and answers. *Annals of Dyslexia, 54*(2), 304–331.

Flick, G. L. (2011). *Understanding and managing emotional and behavioral disorders in the classroom.* Boston, MA: Pearson.

Florida's Positive Behavior Support Project. (2002). Retrieved from http://flpbs.fmhi.usf.edu/

Foorman, B. R., & Moats, L. C. (2004). Conditions for sustaining research-based practices in early reading instruction. *Remedial and Special Education, 25,* 51–60.

Foxx, R. M., & Bechtel, D. R. (1983). Overcorrection: A review and analysis. In S. Axelrod & J. Apsche (Eds.), *The effects of punishment on human behavior* (pp. 133–220). New York, NY: Academic Press.

Foxx, R. M., Martella, R. C., & Marchand-Martella, N. E. (1989). The acquisition, maintenance, and generalization of problem-solving skills by closed head-injured adults. *Behavior Therapy, 20,* 61–76.

Foxx, R. M., & Shapiro, S. T. (1978). The timeout ribbon: A nonexclusionary timeout procedure. *Journal of Applied Behavior Analysis, 11,* 125–136.

Fuchs, D., Fuchs, L. S., & Stecker, P. M. (2010). The "blurring" of special education in a new continuum of general education placements and services. *Exceptional Children, 76,* 301–323.

Fuchs, D., Mock, D., Morgan, P. L., & Young, C. L. (2003). Responsiveness-to-intervention: Definitions, evidence, and implications for the learning disabilities construct. *Learning Disabilities Research and Practice, 18,* 157–172.

Fuchs, L. S., & Fuchs, D. (2007). A model for implementing responsiveness to intervention. *Teaching Exceptional Children, 39*(5), 14–20.

Gable, R. A., Hester, P. H., Rock, M. L., & Hughes, K. G. (2009). Back to basics: Rules, praise, ignoring, and reprimands revisited. *Intervention in School and Clinic, 44,* 195–205.

Gargiulo, R. M., & Metcalf, D. (2010). *Teaching in today's inclusive classrooms: A universal design for learning approach.* Belmont, CA: Wadsworth.

Gettinger, M., & Seibert, J. K. (2002). Best practices in increasing academic learning time. *Best Practices in School Psychology, 4,* 1–15.

Gibbs, N. (1999, May 3). The monsters next door. *Time,* 35–37.

Ginott, H. G. (1971). *Teacher and child.* New York, NY: Macmillan.

Glasser, W. (1965). *Schools without failure.* New York, NY: Harper and Row.

Goetz, E. M., & Baer, D. M. (1973). Social control of form diversity and the emergence of new forms in children's blockbuilding. *Journal of Applied Behavior Analysis, 6,* 209–217.

Gordon, R. (1983). An operational classification of disease prevention. *Public Health Reports, 98,* 107–109.

Greenberg, M. T., Kusche, C., & Mihalic, S. F. (1998). *Blueprints for violence prevention, Book 10: Promoting Alternative Thinking Strategies (PATHS).* Boulder, CO: Center for the Study and Prevention of Violence.

Gresham, F. M. (1989). Assessment of treatment integrity in school consultation and prereferral intervention. *School Psychology Review, 18,* 37–50.

Gresham, F. M. (2001, August). *Responsiveness to intervention: An alternative approach to the identification of learning disabilities.* Paper presented at the Learning Disabilities Summit, Washington, DC.

Gresham, F. M. (2004). Current status and future directions of school-based behavioral interventions. *School Psychology Review, 33,* 326–343.

Gresham, F. M. (2005). Response to intervention: An alternative means of identifying students as emotionally disturbed. *Education and Treatment of Children, 28,* 328–344.

Gresham, F. M., Cook, C. R., Crews, S. E., & Kern, L. (2004). Social skills training for children and youth with emotional and behavioral disorders: Validity considerations and future directions. *Behavioral Disorders, 30,* 32–46.

Gresham, F. M., & Elliott, S. (1990). *The Social Skills Rating System (SSRS).* Circle Pines, MN: American Guidance System.

Gresham, F. M., Sugai, G., & Horner, R. H. (2001). Interpreting outcomes of social skills training for students with high-incidence disabilities. *Exceptional Children, 67,* 331–334.

Grossman, H. (1995). *Classroom behavior management in a diverse society* (2nd ed.). Mountain View, CA: Mayfield.

Harniss, M., Hollenbeck, K., & Dickson, S. (2004). Content areas. In N. E. Marchand-Martella, T. A. Slocum, & R. C. Martella (Eds.), *Introduction of Direct Instruction* (pp. 246–279). Boston, MA: Allyn & Bacon.

Hart, B., & Risley, T. R. (1995). *Meaningful differences in the everyday experience of young American children.* Baltimore, MD: Paul H. Brookes.

Hattie, J., & Timperley, H. (2007). The power of feedback. *Review of Educational Research, 77,* 81–112.

Hawkins, R. P., & Dobes, R. W. (1977). Behavioral definitions in applied behavior analysis: Explicit or implicit? In B. C. Etzel, I. M. Leblanc, & D. M. Baer (Eds.), *New directions in behavioral research:*

Theory, methods, and applications (pp. 167–188). Hillsdale, NJ: Lawrence Erlbaum.

Hawkins, R. P., & Dotson, V. A. (1975). Reliability scores that delude: An Alice in Wonderland trip through the misleading characteristics of interobserver agreement scores in interval recording. In E. Ramp & G. Semb (Eds.), *Behavior analysis: Areas of research and application* (pp. 359–376). Englewood Cliffs, NJ: Prentice-Hall.

Haydon, T., & Scott, T. M. (2008). Using common sense in common settings: Active supervision and precorrection in the morning gym. *Intervention in School and Clinic, 43,* 283–290.

Henggeler, S. W., Schoenwald, S. K., Borduin, C. M., Rowland, M. D., & Cunningham, P. B. (1998). *Multisystemic treatment of antisocial behavior in children and adolescents.* New York, NY: Guilford Press.

Heward, W. L. (2009). *Exceptional children: An introduction to special education* (9th ed.). Upper Saddle River, NJ: Pearson.

Hofmeister, A., & Lubke, M. (1990). *Research into practice: Implementing effective teaching strategies.* Boston, MA: Allyn & Bacon.

Hops, H., & Walker, H. M. (1988). *CLASS: Contingencies for Learning Academic and Social Skills.* Seattle, WA: Educational Achievement Systems.

Horner, R. H., Carr, E. G., Halle, J., McGee, G., Odom, S., & Wolery, M. (2005). The use of single-subject research to identify evidence-based practice in special education. *Exceptional Children, 71,* 165–179.

Horner, R. H., Sugai, G., & Anderson, C. M. (2010). Examining the evidence base for school-wide positive behavior support. *Focus on Exceptional Children, 42,* 1–24.

Horner, R. H., Sugai, G., Todd, A. W., & Lewis-Palmer, T. (2005). Schoolwide positive behavior support. In L. M. Bambara & L. Kern (Eds.). *Individualized supports for students with problem behaviors* (pp. 359–390). New York, NY: Guilford Press.

Horner, R. H., Todd, A. W., Lewis-Palmer, T., Irvin, L. K., Sugai, G., & Boland, J. B. (2004). The *School-wide Evaluation Tool (SET):* A research instrument for assessing school-wide positive behavior support. *Journal of Positive Behavior Interventions, 6,* 3–12.

Individuals with Disabilities Education Improvement Act of 2004 (IDEA). (2004). Pub. L. No. 108-446, 118 Stat. 2647.

Iwata, B. A., & DeLeon, I. G. (1996). *The functional analysis screening tool.* Gainesville, FL: The Florida Center on Self-Injury.

Iwata, B. A., Vollmer, T. R., & Zarcone, J. R. (1990). The experimental (functional) analysis of behavior disorders: Methodology, applications, and limitations. In A. C. Repp & N. N. Singh (Eds.), *Perspectives on the use of nonaversive and aversive interventions for persons with developmental disabilities* (pp. 301–330). Sycamore, IL: Sycamore.

Ji, P., Segawa, E., Burns, J., Campbell, R. T., Allred, C. G., & Flay, B. R. (2005). A measurement model of student character as described by the *Positive Action* program. *Journal of Research in Character Education, 3,* 109–120.

Jones, F. H. (1987). *Positive classroom discipline.* New York, NY: McGraw-Hill.

Kauffman, J. M., Pullen, P. L., Mostert, M. P., & Trent, S. C. (2011). *Managing classroom behavior: A reflective case-based approach* (5th ed.). Boston, MA: Pearson.

Kaufman, J. S., Jaser, S. S., Vaughan, E. L., Reynolds, J. S., Di Donato, J., Bernard, S. N., & Hernandez-Brereton, M. (2010). Patterns in office referral data by grade, race/ethnicity, and gender. *Journal of Positive Behavior Interventions, 12,* 44–54.

Kazdin, A. E. (2001). *Behavior modification in applied settings* (6th ed.). Belmont, CA: Wadsworth.

Kennedy, C. H. (2005). *Single-case designs for educational research.* Boston, MA: Allyn & Bacon.

Kerr, M. M., & Nelson, C. M. (2010). *Strategies for managing behavior problems in the classroom* (6th ed.). Boston, MA: Pearson.

Killu, K. (2008). Developing effective behavior intervention plans: Suggestions for school personnel. *Intervention in School and Clinic, 43,* 140–149.

Knitzer, J., Steinberg, Z., & Fleish, B. (1990). *At the school-house door: An examination of programs and policies for children with behavioral and emotional problems.* New York, NY: Bank Street College of Education.

Kohler, F. W., & Greenwood, C. R. (1986). Toward technology or generalization: The identification of natural contingencies of reinforcement. *The Behavior Analyst, 9,* 19–26.

Kohn, A. (1993a). *Punishment by rewards: The trouble with gold stars, incentive plans, A's, praise, and other bribes.* New York, NY: Houghton Mifflin.

Kohn, A. (1993b). Rewards versus learning: A response to Paul Chance. *Phi Delta Kappan, 74,* 783–786.

Kounin, J. (1970). *Discipline and group management in classrooms.* New York, NY: Holt, Rinehart and Winston.

Kounin, J. S., Friesen, W., & Norton, A. E. (1966). Managing emotionally disturbed children in regular classrooms. *Journal of Educational Psychology, 57,* 1–13.

Kounin, J. S., & Gump, P. V. (1958). The ripple effect in discipline. *The Elementary School Journal, 59,* 158–162.

Kounin, J. S., & Gump, P. V. (1974). Signal systems of lesson settings and the task-related behavior of preschool children. *Journal of Educational Psychology, 66,* 554–562.

Kounin, J. S., & Obradovic, S. (1968). Managing emotionally disturbed children in regular classrooms: A replication and extension. *The Journal of Special Education, 2,* 129–135.

Landrum, T. J., Tankersley, M., & Kauffman, J. M. (2003). What is special about special education for students with emotional or behavioral disorders? *The Journal of Special Education, 37,* 148–156.

Lane, K. L., Wehby, J. H., Robertson, E. J., & Rogers, L. A. (2007). How do different types of high school students respond to schoolwide positive behavior support programs? Characteristics and responsiveness of teacher-identified students. *Journal of Emotional and Behavioral Disorders, 15,* 3–20.

Latham, G. I. (1992). *Managing the classroom environment to facilitate effective instruction.* Logan, UT: P&T Ink.

Lawrence, D. H. (2004). The effects of reality therapy group counseling on the self-determination of persons with developmental disabilities. *International Journal of Reality Therapy, 23,* 9–15.

Lewis, R. B., & Doorlag, D. H. (2011). *Teaching students with special needs in general education classrooms* (8th ed.). Boston, MA: Pearson.

Lewis, T. J., Colvin, G., & Sugai, G. (2000). The effects of pre-correction and active supervision on the recess behavior of elementary students. *Education and Treatment of Children, 23,* 109–121.

Lewis, T. J., Scott, T., & Sugai, G. (1994). The problem behavior questionnaire: A teacher-based instrument to develop functional hypotheses of problem behavior in general education classrooms. *Dianostique, 19*(2/3), 103–115.

Lignugaris/Kraft, B., Marchand-Martella, N. E., & Martella, R. C. (2001). Strategies for writing better goals and short-term objectives or benchmarks. *Teaching Exceptional Children, 34,* 52–58.

Lloyd, K. E. (2002). A review of correspondence training: Suggestions for a revival. *The Behavior Analyst, 25,* 57–73.

Luiselli, J. K. (2006). *Antecedent assessment and intervention: Supporting children and adults with developmental disabilities in community settings.* Baltimore, MD: Paul H. Brookes.

Lynch, A., Theodore, L. A., Bray, M. A., & Kehle, T. J. (2009). A comparison of group-oriented contingencies and randomized reinforcers to improve homework completion and accuracy for students with disabilities. *School Psychology Review, 38,* 307–324.

Maag, J. W. (2006). Social skills training for students with emotional and behavioral disorders: A review of reviews. *Behavioral Disorders, 32,* 5–17.

Mace, F. C., & Belfiore, P. (1990). Behavioral momentum in the treatment of escape-motivated stereotypy. *Journal of Applied Behavior Analysis, 23,* 507–514.

Mace, F. C., Hock, M. L., Lalli, J. S., West, B. J., Belfiore, P., Pinter, E., & Brown, D. K. (1998). Behavioral momentum in the treatment of noncompliance. *Journal of Applied Behavior Analysis, 21,* 123–141.

Mager, R. (1962). *Preparing instructional objectives.* Palo Alto, CA: Fearon.

Malmgren, K. W., Trezek, B. J., & Paul, P. V. (2005). Models of classroom management as applied to the secondary classroom. *Clearing House: A Journal of Educational Strategies, Issues, and Ideas, 79,* 36–39.

Malott, R. W., & Trojan Suarez, E. A. (2008). *Principles of behavior* (6th ed.). Upper Saddle River, NJ: Pearson.

Marandola, P., & Imber, S. C. (1979). Glasser's classroom meeting: A humanistic approach to behavior change with preadolescent inner-city learning disabled children. *Journal of Learning Disabilities, 12,* 30–34.

Marchand-Martella, N. E., Blakely, M., & Schaefer, E. (2004). Aspects of schoolwide implementations. In N. E. Marchand-Martella, T. A. Slocum, & R. C. Martella (Eds.), *Introduction of Direct Instruction* (pp. 304–334). Boston, MA: Allyn & Bacon.

Marchand-Martella, N. E., & Martella, R. C. (2009). Explicit instruction. In W. L. Heward (Ed.), *Exceptional children: An introduction to special education* (9th ed., pp. 196–198). Upper Saddle River, NJ: Merrill.

Marchand-Martella, N. E., & Martella, R. C. (2010a). *Read to Achieve: Comprehending content-area text.* Columbus, OH: Science Research Associates/McGraw-Hill.

Marchand-Martella, N. E., & Martella, R. C. (2010b). *Read to Achieve: Comprehending narrative text.* Columbus, OH: Science Research Associates/McGraw-Hill.

Marchand-Martella, N. E., Ruby, S., & Martella, R. C. (2007, May). A three-tier strategic model of intensifying reading instruction. *TEACHING Exceptional Children Plus.* Retrieved from http://escholarship.bc.edu/cgi/preview.cgi?article=1313&context=education/tecplus

Marchand-Martella, N. E., Slocum, T. A., & Martella, R. C. (Eds.). (2004). *Introduction to Direct Instruction.* Boston, MA: Allyn & Bacon.

Martella, A. M. (2009). A high school student's perspective on homework. *ASCD Express, 4.* Retrieved from http://www.ascd.org/ascd_express/vol4/426_newvoices.aspx

Martella, R. C. (1994). The place of the self in self-instruction. *Behaviorology, 2,* 55–61.

Martella, R. C., Agran, M., & Marchand-Martella, N. E. (1992). Problem solving to prevent accidents in supported employment. *Journal of Applied Behavior Analysis, 25,* 637–645.

Martella, R. C., Leonard, I. J., Marchand-Martella, N. E., & Agran, M. (1993). Self-monitoring negative statements. *Journal of Behavioral Education, 3,* 77–86.

Martella, R. C., Marchand-Martella, N. E., & Agran, M. (1993). Using a problem-solving strategy to teach adaptability skills to individuals with mental retardation. *Journal of Rehabilitation, 59,* 55–60.

Martella, R. C., Marchand-Martella, N. E., & Cleanthous, C. (2001). *ADHD: A comprehensive approach.* Dubuque, IA: Kendall/Hunt.

Martella, R. C., Marchand-Martella, N. E., Macfarlane, C. A., & Young, K. R. (1993). Improving the classroom behavior of a student with severe disabilities via paraprofessional training. *British Columbia Journal of Special Education, 17,* 33–44.

Martella, R. C., Marchand-Martella, N. E., Miller, T. L., Young, K. R., & Macfarlane, C. A. (1995). Teaching instructional aides and peer tutors to decrease problem behaviors in the classroom. *Teaching Exceptional Children, 27,* 53–56.

Martella, R. C., Marchand-Martella, N. E., Woods, B., Thompson, S., Crockett, C., Northrup, E., Benner, G. J., & Ralston, N. C. (in press). Positive behavior support: Analysis of consistency between office discipline referrals and teacher recordings of disruptive classroom behaviors. *Journal of Behavior Assessment and Intervention in Children.*

Martella, R. C., Nelson, J. R., & Marchand-Martella, N. E. (1999). *Research methods: Learning to become a critical research consumer.* Boston, MA: Allyn & Bacon.

Martin, G., & Pear, J. (2007). *Behavior modification: What it is and how to do it* (8th ed.). Upper Saddle River, NJ: Prentice Hall.

Matson, J. (2007). *Handbook of assessment in persons with intellectual disability.* Amsterdam, The Netherlands: Elsevier.

Matyas, T. A., & Greenwood, K. M. (1990). Visual analysis of single-case time series: Effects of variability, serial dependence, and magnitude of intervention effects. *Journal of Applied Behavior Analysis, 23,* 341–351.

McGraw, K. O., & Wong, S. P. (1992). A common language effect-size statistic. *Psychological Bulletin, 111,* 361–365.

McKinney, S. E., Campbell-Whately, G. D., & Kea, C. D. (2005). Managing student behavior in urban classrooms: The role of teacher ABC assessments. *Clearing House: A Journal of Educational Strategies, Issues, and Ideas, 79,* 16–20.

McLoughlin, J. A., & Lewis, R. B. (2008). *Assessing students with special needs* (7th ed.). Upper Saddle River, NJ: Merrill.

McPartland, J. M., & McDill, E. L. (1977). *Violence in schools.* Lexington, MA: D. C. Heath.

Meese, R. L. (2001). *Teaching learners with mild disabilities: Integrating research and practice* (2nd ed.). Belmont, CA: Wadsworth/Thomson Learning.

Meichenbaum, G., & Goodman, J. (1971). Training impulsive children to talk to themselves: A means of developing self-control. *Journal of Abnormal Psychology, 77,* 115–126.

Michael, J. L. (1993). *Concepts and principles of behavior analysis.* Kalamazoo, MI: Society for the Advancement of Behavior Analysis.

Michael, J. L. (2004). *Concepts and principles of behavior analysis* (Rev. ed.). Kalamazoo, MI: Society for the Advancement of Behavior Analysis.

Miltenberger, R. G. (2007). *Behavior modification: Principles and procedures* (4th ed.). Belmont, CA: Wadsworth/Thomson.

Moffitt, T. (1994). Adolescence-limited and life-course persistent antisocial behavior: A developmental taxonomy. *Psychological Review, 100,* 674–701.

Mrazek, P. G., & Haggerty, R. J. (1994). *Reducing risks for mental disorders: Frontiers for preventive intervention research.* Washington, DC: National Academy Press.

Munoz, M. A., & Vanderhaar, J. E. (2006). Literacy-embedded character education in a large urban district: Effects of the Child Development Project on elementary school students and teachers. *Journal of Research in Character Education, 4,* 47–64.

National Association of State Directors of Special Education. (2006, May). *Myths about response to intervention (RtI) implementation.* Retrieved from http://www.nasdse.org/Portals/0/Documents/Download Publications/Myths about RtI.pdf

National Center for Education Statistics. (2009a). *Indicators of school crime and safety.* Washington, DC: U.S. Department of Education, Institute of Education Sciences, National Center for Education Statistics. Retrieved from http://nces.ed.gov/programs/crimeindicators/

National Center for Education Statistics. (2009b). *The Nation's Report Card: Reading 2009* (NCES 2010-458). Washington, DC: Institute of Education Sciences, U.S. Department of Education.

National School Safety Center. (1999). *Checklist of characteristics of youth who have caused school-associated violent deaths.* Retrieved from http://www.schoolsafety.us/media-resources/checklist-of-characteristics-of-youth-who-have-caused-school-associated-violent-deaths

National School Safety Center. (2010). *School associated violent deaths.* Retrieved from http://www.schoolsafety.us/media-resources/school-associated-violent-deaths

NCLB. (2001). Pub. L. No. 107-110, 115 Stat. 1425 (2001).

Nelson, J. R. (1996a). *Designing predictable and supportive school environments.* Spokane, WA: Cyprus Group.

Nelson, J. R. (1996b). Designing schools to meet the needs of students who exhibit disruptive behavior. *Journal of Emotional and Behavioral Disorders, 4,* 147–161.

Nelson, J. R., Benner, G. J., Reid, R. C., & Epstein, M. H. (2002). Convergent validity of office discipline referrals with the CBCL-TRF. *Journal of Emotional and Behavioral Disorders, 10,* 181–188.

Nelson, J. R., Duppong-Hurley, K., Synhorst, L., Epstein, M. H., & Stage, S. (2009). The child outcomes of a three tier behavior model. *Exceptional Children, 76,* 7–30.

Nelson, J. R., Gutierrez-Ohrman, C., Roberts, M. L., & Smith, D. J. (2000, April). *Preventing behavioral earthquakes: A validated antecedent manipulation strategy for minor problem behaviors.* Paper presented at the 2000 National Association of School Psychologists Conference, New Orleans, LA.

Nelson, J. R., Martella, R. C., & Garland, B. (1998). The effects of teaching school expectations and establishing consistent consequences on formal office disciplinary actions. *Journal of Emotional and Behavioral Disorders, 6,* 153–161.

Nelson, J. R., Martella, R. C., & Marchand-Martella, N. E. (2002). Maximizing student learning: The effects of a comprehensive school-based program for preventing disruptive behaviors. *Journal of Emotional and Behavioral Disorders, 10,* 136–148.

Nelson, J. R., & Roberts, M. L. (2000). Ongoing reciprocal teacher-student interactions involving disruptive behaviors in general education classrooms. *Journal of Emotional and Behavioral Disorders, 8,* 27–38.

Nelson, J. R., Roberts, M. L., & Smith, D. J. (1998). *Conducting functional behavioral assessments in school settings: A practical guide.* Denver, CO: Sopris West.

Nicholls, D., & Houghton, S. (1995). The effect of Canter's assertive discipline program on teacher and student behavior. *British Journal of Educational Psychology, 65,* 197–210.

Office of Special Education Programs. (2005). *Alignment with the No Child Left Behind Act.* Washington, DC: U.S. Department of Education, Office of Special Education Programs. Retrieved from http://www.ed.gov/about/offices/list/osers/index.html

Oliver, R., & Skinner, C. H. (2002). Applying behavior momentum theory to increase compliance: Why Mrs. H. revved up the elementary students with the Hokey-Pokey. *Journal of Applied School Psychology, 19,* 75–94.

Olson, J. L., & Platt, J. M. (2000). *Teaching children and adolescents with special needs* (3rd ed.). Upper Saddle River, NJ: Merrill.

O'Neill, R. E., Horner, R. H., Albin, R. W., Sprague, J., Storey, K., & Newton, J. S. (1997). *Functional assessment and program development for problem behavior: A practical handbook.* Pacific Grove, CA: Brooks/Cole.

O'Neill, R. E., McDonnell, J. J., Billingsley, F. F., & Jenson, W. R. (2011). *Single case research designs in educational and community settings.* Boston, MA: Pearson.

O'Reilly, M., Rispoli, M., Davis, T., Machalicek, W., Lang, R., Sigafoos, J., Kang, S., Lancioni, G., Green, V., & Didden, R. (2010). Functional analysis of challenging behavior in children with autism spectrum disorders: A summary of 10 cases. *Research in Autism Spectrum Disorders, 4,* 1–10.

O'Shaughnessy, T. E., Lane, K. L., Gresham, F. M., & Beebe-Frankenberger, M. E. (2003). Children placed at risk for learning and behavioral difficulties: Implementing a school-wide system of early identification and intervention. *Remedial & Special Education, 24,* 27–35.

Paine, S. C., Radicchi, J., Rosellini, L. C., Deutchman, L., & Darch, C. B. (1983). *Structuring your classroom for academic success.* Champaign, IL: Research Press.

Parker, R. I., & Brossart, D. F. (2006). Phase contrasts for multiple-phase single case intervention designs. *School Psychology Quarterly, 21,* 124–136.

Parker, R. I., & Hagan-Burke, S. (2007). Useful effect size interpretations for single case research. *Behavior Therapy, 38,* 95–105.

Parker, R. I., Hagan-Burke, S., & Vannest, K. (2007). Percentage of non-overlapping data (PAND): An alternative to PND. *The Journal of Special Education, 40*(4), 194–204.

Parker, R. I., Vannest, K. J., & Brown, L. (2009). The improvement rate difference for single-case research. *Exceptional Children, 75,* 135–150.

Patterson, G. R. (1982a). *Coercive family process: A social learning approach.* Eugene, OR: Castalia.

Patterson, G. R. (1982b). Performance models for antisocial boys. *American Psychologist, 41,* 432–444.

Payne, L. D., Marks, L. J., & Bogan, B. L. (2007). Using curriculum-based assessment to address the academic and behavioral deficits of students with emotional and behavioral disorders. *Beyond Behavior, 16,* 3–6.

Premack, D. (1959). Toward empirical behavioral laws: I. Positive reinforcement. *Psychological Review, 66,* 219–233.

Raffaele Mendez, L. M., & Knoff, H. M. (2003). Who gets suspended from school and why: A demographic analysis of schools and disciplinary infractions in a large school district. *Education and Treatment of Children, 26,* 30–51.

Reid, J. (1993). Prevention of conduct disorder before and after school entry: Relating interventions to developmental findings. *Development and Psychopathology, 5*(1/2), 243–262.

Risley, T. R., & Hart, B. (1968). Developing correspondence between the non-verbal and verbal behavior of preschool children. *Journal of Applied Behavior Analysis, 1,* 267–281.

Rolider, A., & Van Houten, R. (1993). The interpersonal treatment model: Teaching appropriate social inhibitions through the development of personal stimulus control by the systematic introduction of antecedent stimuli. In R. Van Houten & S. Axelrod (Eds.), *Behavior analysis and treatment.* New York, NY: Plenum.

Rosenshine, B., & Stevens, R. (1986). Teaching functions. In M. C. Wittrock (Ed.), *AERA handbook of research on teaching* (3rd ed., pp. 376–391). New York, NY: Macmillan.

Rosenthal, R., Rosnow, R., & Rubin, D. (2000). *Contrasts and effect sizes in behavioral research: A correlational approach.* Cambridge, UK: Cambridge University Press.

Sabornie, E. J., & DeBettencourt, L. U. (2009). *Teaching students with mild and high-incidence disabilities at the secondary level* (3rd ed.). Upper Saddle River, NJ: Merrill.

Salend, S. J. (2011). *Creating inclusive classrooms: Effective and reflective practices* (7th ed.). Boston, MA: Pearson.

Salvia, J., Ysseldyke, J., & Bolt, S. (2010). *Assessment in special and inclusive education* (11th ed.). Belmont, CA: Wadsworth.

Sandomierski, T., Kincaid, D., & Algozzine, B. (2010). *Response to intervention and positive behavior support: Brothers from different mothers or sisters from different misters?* Tampa, FL: Florida Technical Assistance Center on Positive Behavioral Interventions & Supports. Retrieved from http://www.flpbs.fmhi.usf.edu

Scheirer, M. A., & Kraut, R. E. (1979). Increasing educational achievement via self concept change. *Review of Educational Research, 49*(1), 131–150.

Scott, T. M., Anderson, C. M., & Spaulding, S. A. (2008). Strategies for developing and carrying out functional assessment and behavior intervention planning. *Preventing School Failure, 52,* 39–49.

Scott, T. M., Nelson, C. M., & Liaupsin, C. J. (2001). Effective instruction: The forgotten component in preventing school violence. *Education and Treatment of Children, 24,* 309–322.

Seligman, M. P. (1995). *The optimistic child: A proven program to safeguard children against depression and build lifelong resilience.* Boston, MA: Houghton Mifflin.

Severson, H. H., Walker, H. M., Hope-Doolittle, J., Kratochwill, T. R., & Gresham, F. M. (2007). Proactive, early screening to detect behaviorally at-risk students: Issues, approaches, emerging innovations, and professional practices. *Journal of School Psychology, 45,* 193–223.

Sherman, L. W., Gottfredson, D. C., MacKenzie, D. L., Eck, J., Reuter, P., & Bushway, S. D. (1998). *Preventing crime: What works, what doesn't, what's promising.* Washington, DC: National Institute of Justice.

Sidman, M. (1989). *Coercion and its fallout.* Boston, MA: Authors Cooperative.

Sigafoos, J., Arthur, M., & O'Reilly, M. (2003). *Challenging behavior and developmental disability.* London: Whurr Publishers.

Simonsen, B., Shaw, S. F., Faggella-Luby, M., Sugai, G., Coyne, M. D., Rhein, B., Madaus, J. W., & Alfano, M. (2010). A schoolwide model for service delivery: Redefining special educators as interventionists. *Remedial and Special Education, 31,* 17–23.

Sinclair, M. F., Christenson, S. L., & Thurlow, M. L. (2005). Promoting school completion of urban secondary youth with emotional or behavioral disabilities. *Exceptional Children, 71,* 465–482.

Singer, G. H., Singer, J. S., & Homer, R. H. (1987). Using pretask requests to increase the probability of compliance for students with severe disabilities. *Journal of the Association for Persons With Severe Disabilities, 12,* 287–291.

Skiba, R. J., & Rausch, M. K. (2006). Zero tolerance, suspension, and expulsion: Questions of equity and effectiveness. In C. M. Evertson & C. S. Weinstein (Eds.), *Handbook of classroom management: Research, practice, and contemporary issues* (pp. 1063–1089). Mahwah, NJ: Lawrence Erlbaum.

Skinner, B. F. (1953). *Science and human behavior.* New York, NY: Free Press.

Skinner, B. F. (1969). *Contingencies of reinforcement: A theoretical analysis.* New York, NY: Appleton-Century-Crofts.

Slavin, R. E. (2009). *Educational psychology: Theory and practice* (9th ed.). Upper Saddle River, NJ: Pearson.

Smith, D. D., & Tyler, N. C. (2010). *Introduction to special education: Making a difference* (7th ed.). Upper Saddle River, NJ: Merrill.

Solomon, D., Battistich, V., Watson, M., Schaps, E., & Lewis, C. (2000). A six-district study of educational change: Direct and mediated effects of the child development project. *Social Psychology of Education, 4,* 3–51.

Sprick, R. (1981). *The solution book: A guide to classroom discipline.* Chicago, IL: Science Research Associates.

Sprick, R. (2009). Doing discipline differently. *Principal Leadership, 9*(5), 19–22.

Stein, M., Kinder, D. B., Sibert, J., & Carnine, D. (2006). *Designing effective mathematics instruction: A direct instruction approach* (4th ed.). Upper Saddle River, NJ: Pearson Merrill Prentice Hall.

Stevens, L. J., & Price, M. (1992). Meeting the challenge of educating children at risk. *Kappen, 74*(1), 18–23.

Stewart, R., Benner, G., Martella, R. C., & Marchand-Martella, N. E. (2007). Three-tier models of reading and behavior: A research review. *Journal of Positive Behavior Interventions, 9,* 239–253.

Stewart, R. M., Martella, R. C., Marchand-Martella, N. E., & Benner, G. J. (2005). Three-tier models of reading and behavior. *Journal of Early and Intensive Behavior Intervention, 2,* 115–124.

Stokes, T. F., & Baer, D. M. (1977). An implicit technology of generalization. *Journal of Applied Behavior Analysis, 10,* 349–367.

Stokes, T. F., & Osnes, P. G. (1989). An operant pursuit of generalization. *Behavior Therapy, 20,* 337–355.

Strahan, D. B., Cope, M. H., Hundley, S., & Faircloth, C. V. (2005). Positive discipline with students who need it most: Lessons learned in an alternative approach. *Clearing House: A Journal of Educational Strategies, Issues, and Ideas, 79,* 25–30.

Sugai, G. (2007). Promoting behavioral competence in schools: A commentary on exemplary practices. *Psychology in the Schools, 44,* 113–118.

Sugai, G., & Horner, R. H. (2009). Responsiveness-to-intervention and school-wide positive behavior supports: Integration of multi-tiered system approaches. *Exceptionality, 17,* 223–237.

Sugai, G., Lewis-Palmer, T., Todd, A. W., & Horner, R. H. (2001). *School-wide evaluation tool.* Eugene: University of Oregon.

Sulzer-Azaroff, B., & Mayer, G. R. (1991). *Behavior analysis for lasting change.* Fort Worth, TX: Holt, Rinehart and Winston.

Swinson, J., & Cording, M. (2002). Assertive discipline in a school for pupils with emotional and behavioural difficulties. *British Journal of Special Education, 29,* 72–75.

Taylor, I., & O'Reilly, M. F. (1997). Toward a functional analysis of private verbal self-regulation. *Journal of Applied Behavior Analysis, 30,* 43–58.

Thorndike, E. L. (1905). *The elements of psychology.* New York, NY: Seiler.

Tilly, W. D., III, Reschly, D. J., & Grimes, J. (1999). Disability determination in problem solving systems: Conceptual foundations and critical components. In D. J. Reschly, W. D. Tilly III, & J. P. Grimes (Eds.), *Special education in transition: Functional assessment and noncategorical programming* (pp. 221–251). Longman, CO: Sopris West.

Timberlake, W., & Allison, J. (1974). Response deprivation: An empirical approach to instrumental performance. *Psychological Review, 81,* 146–164.

Tomlinson, C. A., & McTighe, J. (2006). *Integrating differentiated instruction + understanding by design.* Alexandria, VA: ASCD.

Touchette, P. E., MacDonald, R. E., & Langer, S. N. (1985). A scatter plot for identifying stimulus control of problem behavior. *Journal of Applied Behavior Analysis, 18,* 343–351.

Trussell, R. P. (2008). Classroom universals to prevent problem behaviors. *Intervention in School and Clinic, 43,* 179–185.

Turnbull, A., Turnbull, R., & Wehmeyer, M. L. (2010). *Exceptional lives: Special education in today's schools* (6th ed.). Upper Saddle River, NJ: Merrill.

U.S. Department of Education. (1998). *Early warning, timely response: A guide to safe schools.* Washington, DC: Author.

Van Houten, R., Axelrod, S., Bailey, J. S., Favell, J. E., Foxx, R. M., Iwata, B. A., & Lovaas, O. I. (1988). The right to effective behavioral treatment. *Journal of Applied Behavior Analysis, 21,* 381–384.

Vaughn, B. J., & Horner, R. H. (1997). Identifying instructional tasks that occasion problem behaviors and assessing the effects of student versus teacher choice among these tasks. *Journal of Applied Behavior Analysis, 30,* 299–312.

Vaughn, S., Linan-Thompson, S., & Hickman, P. (2003). Response to instruction as a means of identifying students with reading/learning disabilities. *Exceptional Children, 69,* 391–409.

Vaughn, S., Wanzek, J., Woodruff, A. L., & Linan-Thompson, S. (2007). Prevention and early identification of students with reading disabilities. In D. Haager, J. Klingner, & S. Vaughn (Eds.), *Evidence-based reading practices for response to intervention* (pp. 11–27). Baltimore, MD: Brookes.

Vincent, C. G., Cartledge, G., May, S., & Tobin, T. J. (2009, October). Do elementary schools that document reductions in overall office discipline referrals document reductions across all student races and ethnicities? *PBIS Evaluation Brief, 5.* Retrieved from www.pbis.org

Vossekuil, B., Reddy, M., Fein, R., Borum, R., & Modzeleski, W. (2000). *USSS Safe School Initiative: An interim report on prevention of targeted violence in schools.* Washington, DC: U.S. Secret Service.

Walker, H. M. (1997). *The acting-out child: Coping with classroom disruption* (2nd ed.). Longmont, CO: Sopris West.

Walker, H. M. (2000). *Current issues in the field of emotional and behavioral disorders.* Paper presented at the Annual Research Seminar Series. University of Nebraska, Lincoln.

Walker, H. M., & Buckley, N. K. (1972). Programming generalization and maintenance of treatment effects across time and across settings. *Journal of Applied Behavior Analysis, 5,* 209–224.

Walker, H. M., Colvin, G., & Ramsey, E. (1995). *Antisocial behavior in school: Strategies and best practices.* Pacific Grove, CA: Brooks/Cole.

Walker, H. M., Homer, R. H., Sugai, G., Bullis, M., Sprague, J. R., Bricker, D., & Kaufman, M. (1996).

Integrated approaches to preventing antisocial behavior patterns among school-age children and youth. *Journal of Emotional and Behavioral Disorders, 4,* 194–209.

Walker, H. M., Seeley, J. R., Small, J., Severson, H. H., Graham, B. A., Feil, E. G., Serna, L., Golly, A. M., & Forness, S. R. (2009). A randomized controlled trial of the *First Step to Success* early intervention: Demonstration of program efficacy outcomes within a diverse urban school district. *Journal of Emotional and Behavioral Disorders, 17,* 197–212.

Walker, H. M., & Severson, H. H. (1992). *Systematic Screening for Behavior Disorders (SSBD): User's guide and administration manual.* Longmont, CO: Sopris West.

Walker, H. M., Stiller, B., Golly, A., Kavanagh, K., Severson, H. H., & Feil, E. (1997). First Step to Success: *Helping young children overcome antisocial behavior.* Longmont, CO: Sopris West.

Watkins, C. L., & Slocum, T. A. (2004). The components of Direct Instruction. In N. E. Marchand-Martella, T. A. Slocum, & R. C. Martella (Eds.), *Introduction of Direct Instruction* (pp. 28–65). Boston, MA: Allyn & Bacon.

Watson, M., Battistich, V., & Solomon, D. (1997). Enhancing students' social and ethical development in schools: An intervention program and its effects. *International Journal of Educational Research, 27,* 571–586.

Westling, D. L. (2010). Teachers and challenging behavior: Knowledge, views, and practices. *Remedial and Special Education, 31,* 48–63.

What Works Clearinghouse. (2007a). *Character education: Topic report.* Washington, DC: Institute of Education Sciences, U.S. Department of Education.

What Works Clearinghouse. (2007b). *Character education: WWC intervention report—Caring School Community.* Washington, DC: Institute of Education Sciences, U.S. Department of Education.

What Works Clearinghouse. (2007c). *Character education: WWC intervention report—Positive Action.* Washington, DC: Institute of Education Sciences, U.S. Department of Education.

What Works Clearinghouse. (2008). *Procedures and standards handbook.* Washington, DC: Institute of Education Sciences, U.S. Department of Education.

White, O. R., & Haring, N. G. (1980). *Exceptional teaching* (2nd ed.). Columbus, OH: Merrill.

Wilkins, K., Caldarella, P., Crook-Lyon, R. E., & Young, K. R. (2010). The civil behavior of students: A survey of school professionals. *Education, 130,* 540–555.

Witt, J., & Beck, R. (1999). *One minute academic functional assessments and interventions: "Can't" do it . . . or "won't" do it?* Longmont, CO: Sopris West.

Witt, J., LaFleur, L., Naquin, G., & Gilbertson, D. (1999). *Teaching effective classroom routines.* Longmont, CO: Sopris West.

Wolery, M., Bailey, D. B., & Sugai, G. M. (1988). *Effective teaching: Principles and procedures of applied behavior analysis with exceptional students.* Boston, MA: Allyn & Bacon.

Wood, S., Hodges, C., & Aljunied, M. (1996). The effectiveness of assertive discipline training: Look before you leap off this wagon. *Educational Psychology in Practice, 12,* 175–181.

Zabel, M. (1986). Timeout use with behaviorally disordered students. *Behavioral Disorders, 11,* 15–20.

Zirkel, P. A. (2009). What does the law say? *Teaching Exceptional Children, 41*(5), 73–75.

Zirpoli, T. J. (2008). *Behavior management: Applications for teachers* (5th ed.). Upper Saddle River, NJ: Pearson.

Index

About the Authors

Ronald C. Martella, Ph.D., is a professor of special education at Eastern Washington University, teaching classes in behavior management and research methodology. He has more than 25 years of experience working with at-risk populations. He provides technical assistance to numerous states and districts on positive behavior support (PBS)/behavior management for students with or without disabilities. Dr. Martella has more than 130 professional publications including a six-level supplemental reading program (*Lesson Connections*) for *Reading Mastery Signature Edition* and a two-level adolescent literacy program (*Read to Achieve*). Finally, for the State of Washington, he served on the statewide PBS Leadership Team and as a PBS coach for several schools throughout eastern Washington and serves as a consultant for the Washington State Striving Readers Grant, which features the adolescent literacy program he co-wrote.

J. Ron Nelson, Ph.D., is a professor at the University of Nebraska–Lincoln. Dr. Nelson has more than 20 years experience in the field of special education as a teacher, technical assistance provider, and professor. He has a national reputation as an effective researcher and received the 2000 Distinguished Initial Career Research Award, awarded by the Council for Exceptional Children. Dr. Nelson's research career includes over 22 million dollars in external funding and the publication of more than 150 articles, book chapters, and books that focus on serving children at risk of school failure and research issues. He has developed a number of behavior and literacy interventions that have been recognized by the U.S. Department of Education (e.g., the registered behavioral strategy Think Time®, *Stepping Stones to Literacy, Early Vocabulary Connections*, and the *Multiple Meaning Vocabulary Program*).

Nancy E. Marchand-Martella, Ph.D., is a professor of special education at Eastern Washington University. She has more than 25 years of experience working with at-risk populations. For the State of Washington, she serves as a consultant for the Washington Improvement and Implementation Network and the Washington State Striving Readers Grant, which features an adolescent literacy program she co-wrote. She has also served as a Reading First panel member for selecting core, supplemental, and intervention programs for students in Grades K through 12. Dr. Marchand-Martella has more than 140 professional publications including a two-level vocabulary program (*Multiple Meaning Vocabulary*), a six-level supplemental reading program (*Lesson*

Connections) for *Reading Mastery Signature Edition,* and a two-level adolescent literacy program focused on comprehending content-area and narrative text (*Read to Achieve*).

Mark O'Reilly, Ph.D., BCBC-D, is Mollie Villeret Davis Professor of Learning Disabilities at the University of Texas at Austin. His research and teaching primarily focus on the education and behavioral support of children with autism spectrum disorders. He is also interested in the development and evaluation of assistive technology for use with individuals with profound multiple disabilities. He has coauthored more than 200 peer-reviewed articles and book chapters in these areas. His research has been funded through grants from the European Union and the Institute for Educational Sciences. He is a former associate editor of the *Journal of Applied Behavior Analysis* and was vice president of the Society for the Experimental Analysis of Behavior.